D0983257

# Archaeology
## and the
# Galilean Jesus

# Archaeology and the Galilean Jesus

## A Re-examination of the Evidence

Jonathan L. Reed

TRINITY PRESS INTERNATIONAL
Harrisburg, Pennsylvania

Trinity Press International
P.O. Box 1321, Harrisburg, PA 17105

*Trinity Press International is a division of the Morehouse Group.*

*Cover art:* Overview of Sepphoris, photographed by Jonathan Reed. Courtesy of the Sepphoris Regional Project.

*Cover design:* Thomas Castanzo

*Library of Congress Cataloging-in-Publication Data*
Reed, Jonathan L.
  Archaeology and the Galilean Jesus: a re-examination of the evidence / Jonathan L. Reed.
    p. cm.
  Includes bibliographical references and index.
  ISBN 1-56338-324-1 (pbk. : alk. paper)
    1. Jesus Christ—Historicity. 2. Galilee (Israel)—Social life and customs. 3. Excavations (Archaelogy)—Israel—Galilee. I. Title.

BT303.2 .R44 2000
225.9'3—dc21                                          00-030280

Printed in the United States of America

00  01  02  03  04  05    10  9  8  7  6  5  4  3  2  1

*To Eric and Carol Meyers*

# Table of Contents

# List of Illustrations

# List of Tables

# List of Abbreviations

AASOR   Annual of the American Schools of Oriental Research
ABD     *Anchor Bible Dictionary*
AJP     *American Journal of Philology*
AJSR    *American Jewish Society Review*
ANRW    *Aufstieg und Niedergang der Römischen Welt*
ASNU    Acta seminarii neotestamentici upsaliensis
ASOR    American Schools of Oriental Research
BA      *Biblical Archaeologist*
BAGD    W. Bauer, W. F. Arndt, F. W. Gingrich, and F. W. Danker,
        *Greek-English Lexicon of the New Testament*
BAR     *Biblical Archaeology Review*
BARIS   British Archaeological Reports International Series
BASOR   *Bulletin of the American Schools of Oriental Research*
BBET    Beiträge zur biblischen Exegese und Theologie
BETL    Bibliotheca ephemeridum theologicarum lovaniensium
BHT     Beiträge zur historischen Theologie
Bib     *Biblica*
BK      *Bibel und Kirche*
BN      *Biblische Notizen*
BZ NF   *Biblische Zeitschrift* Neue Folge
CBQ     Catholic Biblical Quarterly
CII     *Corpus inscriptionum iudaicarum*
CIL     *Corpus inscriptionum latinarum*
CQ      *Classical Quarterly*
CRBS    *Current Research in Biblical Studies*
CSEL    Corpus scriptorum ecclesiasticuorum latinorum
EI      *Eretz Israel*
ESI     *Excavations and Surveys in Israel*
ET      *Evangelische Theologie*
FB      Forschung zur Bible
FRLANT  Forschungen zur Religion und Literatur des Alten und
        Neuen Testaments
HTR     *Harvard Theological Review*
IDBS    *Interpreter's Dictionary of the Bible Supplementary Volume*
IEJ     *Israel Exploration Journal*
INJ     *Israel Numismatic Journal*
JBL     *Journal of Biblical Literature*
JJS     *Journal of Jewish Studies*
JPOS    *Journal of the Palestinian Oriental Society*
JQR     *Jewish Quarterly Review*

| | |
|---|---|
| JR | *Journal of Religion* |
| JRS | *Journal of Roman Studies* |
| JSJ | *Journal for the Study of Judaism in the Persian, Hellenistic and Roman Period* |
| JSNTSS | Journal of the Study of the New Testament—Supplementary Series |
| JSOT | *Journal of the Study of the Old Testament* |
| JSOTSS | Journal of the Study of the Old Testament—Supplementary Series |
| JSP | *Journal for the Study of the Pseudepigrapha* |
| JThS | *Journal of Theological Studies* |
| LA | *Liber Annus* |
| MB | *Monde du Bible* |
| MDOG | Mitteilungen der deutschen Orient-Gesellschaft |
| NEAEHL | *New Encyclopedia of Archaeological Excavations in the Holy Land* |
| Neot | *Neotestamentica* |
| NovT | *Novum Testamentum* |
| NTAbh NF | Neutestamentliche Abhandelungen Neue Folge |
| NTS | *New Testament Studies* |
| NTTS | New Testament Tools and Studies |
| OEANE | *Oxford Encyclopedia of Archaeology in the Near East* |
| PEQ | *Palestine Exploration Quarterly* |
| PWSup | Pauly-Wissova, *Real-encyclopädie der classischen Altertumswissenschaft* Supplementary Volume |
| RB | *Revue biblique* |
| RHPR | *Revue d'histoire et de philosophie religieuses* |
| SBLDS | Society of Biblical Literature Dissertation Series |
| SBLSP | *Society of Biblical Literature Seminar Papers* |
| SBT | Studies in Biblical Theology |
| SNTSMS | Society for New Testament Studies Monography Series |
| ST | *Studia theologica* |
| TDNT | *Theological Dictionary of the New Testament* |
| TSAJ | Texte und Studien zum Antiken Judentum |
| USQR | *Union Seminary Quarterly Review* |
| WMANT | Wissenschaftliche Monographien zum Alten und Neuen Testament |
| WUNT | Wissenschaftliche Untersuchungen zum Neuen Testament |
| ZDPV | *Zeitschrift des deutschen Palästina Vereins* |
| ZNW | *Zeitschrift für die neutestamentliche Wissenschaft* |
| ZTK | *Zeitschrift für Theologie und Kirche* |

# Preface

Many studies in historical Jesus research focus on careful and detailed analyses of Gospel stratigraphy. Very few, however, are attuned to careful and detailed analysis of the stratigraphy of Galilean archaeological sites. This collection is designed to help fill this void by examining some of the implications for historical Jesus research that the archaeology of Galilee has raised.

This book neither collects archaeological artifacts that Jesus might have come into contact with, nor illustrates places he visited according to the Gospels. It is not a catalogue, handbook, or dictionary containing descriptions or drawings of archaeological items. Nor is its goal the integration of some of the material culture into a sketch of Galilee at the time of Jesus drawn from the literary sources, nor are some artifacts here offered as a visual aid. Instead, these studies put the archaeological evidence front and center by synthesizing the available material, and then interpreting the material culture of first-century Galilee in such a way as to suggest some implications for Jesus and the Gospels.

Competing field excavation techniques, excavators' varied interests, and the disparity of artifacts published (or not published) by archaeologists undermine the compilation of absolute or at times even meaningful statistical or quantified archaeological studies. Often, therefore, the interpretation of first-century Galilean life offered here is based on anecdotal evidence and only with faint patterns apparent in the material culture. An awareness of sociological models, cross-cultural analogies, and texts from antiquity have been combined in a more or less eclectic manner to marshal the archaeological evidence. An element of intuition, however, acquired in over a decade of fieldwork at Capernaum and Sepphoris, discussions with field archaeologists and visits to their sites, and the reading of a vast number of diverse archaeological reports and studies, has certainly guided these studies more than any theory or method. On the surface these studies are foremost about the archaeology of Galilee. They then leap directly to the implications for historical Jesus research and early Christian literature, without articulating the guiding theories of religion or sociology. These are intentionally in the background, but for those interested in such issues, the models are plain.

Seán Freyne provided the impetus for this volume by suggesting that I assemble several of my essays published in less accessible volumes, as well as papers delivered at scholarly meetings. In the process of collecting these, some changes of mind, new ideas, and recent developments necessitated at times extensive changes and significant additions. At its completion, only three chapters overlap at all with earlier publications. Each chapter stands independently, but each chapter and the collection as a whole have the same strategy: interpreting the archaeology is primary, to which the implications for Jesus research react. Part one has two chapters that deal with significant demographic issues relating to ethnicity, religion and socio-economics. Each also raises some implications for our understanding of Christian origins. Part two has two chapters that provide a thick archaeological description of two sites of importance to the historical Jesus, Sepphoris and Capernaum; each chapter in turn makes a contribution to our understanding of his life and teachings. Part three has two chapters that are more exegetical, one on the sayings source Q as a whole and the other on a single passage therein, but each localizes these texts in a Galilean context as generated from the archaeological data.

Chapter two is a substantial revision and elaboration of "Galileans, 'Israelite Village Communities,' and the Sayings Gospel Q," published in *Galilee: Confluence of Cultures* (Duke Judaic Studies Series 1; ed. E. Meyers; Winona Lake, Indiana: Eisenbrauns, 1999) 87–108. Chapter six is based on "The Social Map of Q," published in *Conflict and Invention: Literary, Rhetorical, and Social Studies on the Sayings Gospel Q* (ed. J. Kloppenborg; Philadelphia: Trinity Press International, 1995) 17–36. Chapter seven is a revision of "The Sign of Jonah and Other Epic Traditions in Q," published in *Rethinking Christian Origins: Festschrift for Burton Mack* (eds. E. Castelli and H. Taussig; Philadelphia: Trinity Press International, 1996) 130–43.

The spelling of place names is somewhat eclectic, though in general I have followed those of the *New Encyclopedia of Archaeological Excavations in the Holy Land*. For places known from the New Testament I have kept their familiar spellings, and for major sites during the Hellenistic and Roman Periods I have tended to use their spellings derived from Greek.

This work owes much to others. First of all, I am grateful to my wife Annette and my children Natania and Levi, who alternately put up with living with me on an excavation or being left at home while I participated in the excavations. I thank also Henry Carrigan for encouraging the project, and the editors at Trinity Press International are to be thanked for cleaning up my manuscript. The University of La Verne provided several Summer Travel Fellowships (thanks to John Gingrich), a writing grant (thanks to Bill Cook), funds for a proofreader (thanks to Al Lalane), an artist (thanks to Keith Lord), and a scanner (thanks to Kevin Holland), as well as a sabbatical leave in the fall of 1999 to complete this manuscript. I thank also the many archaeologists who provided tours of their sites, notably Moti Aviam, Vasilios Tzaferis, John Wilson, Rami Arav, James F. Strange, Dennis Groh, and Doug Edwards. To the faculty and staff of the excavations at Sepphoris, with whom many hours in the field and in the camp were spent discussing a variety of issues, I owe the greatest intellectual debt: Melissa Aubin, Alysia Fischer, Bill Grantham, Byron McCane, Mark Chancey, J. P. Dessel, Ken Hoglund, Milton Moreland, Stuart S. Miller, Adam Porter, Greg Smith, and Jürgen Zangenberg.

I am most grateful, however, to Eric and Carol Meyers, to whom this book is dedicated. At a scholarly level, this is in appreciation for putting Galilean archeology on the map of New Testament scholarship and for fostering an interdisciplinary dialogue, but more so at a personal level for their graciousness in inviting me to join their staff at Sepphoris in 1988 and for their warm and personal tutelage ever since.

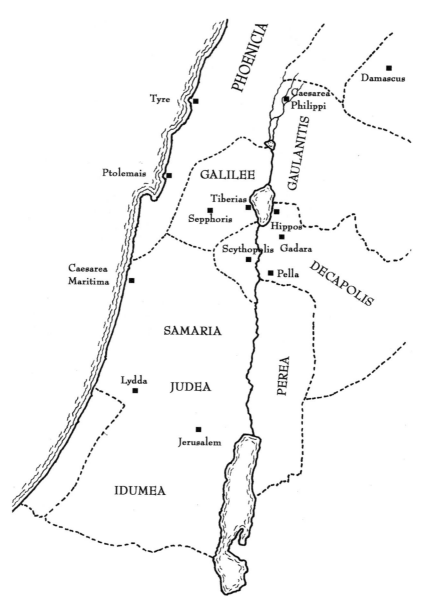

*Figure 1.1 Political Map of Palestine*

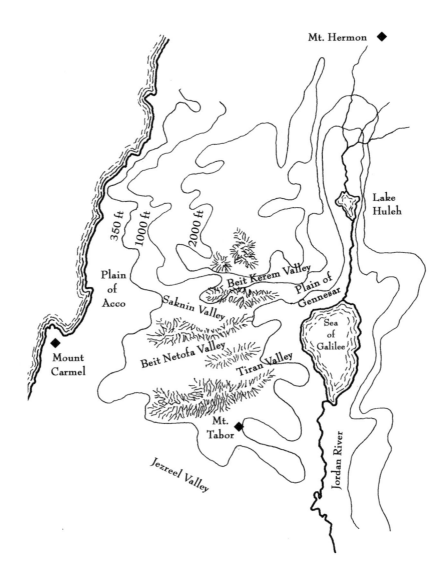

*Figure 1.2 Topographical Map of Galilee*

# CHAPTER 1

# Galilean Archaeology and the Historical Jesus

For the most part, biblical scholarship has been the domain of literary studies and text-centered. The text of the Bible was the primary object of study, and exegesis the chief goal. This near myopic focus on words, perhaps a remnant of Christian and particularly Protestant theology, rendered archaeology biblical studies' "handmaiden," whose role was to assist exegesis or discover new written materials.[1] The discovery of new documents, inscriptions, or papyri earned archaeology some respect, and New Testament scholars heralded the Dead Sea Scrolls, the Pilate inscription from Caesarea Maritima, and the Oxyrhynchus Papyri as important discoveries that provided new documents, literary parallels, and philological insights. The unearthing of nonverbal art and iconography by archaeologists, particularly depictions of the biblical narrative like that found in the Dura Europas synagogue, were likewise deemed significant, though interpreting nonverbal material and symbols apart from literary texts was suspect, reckoned akin to a Rorschach test.[2] Preoccupied with exegesis, scholars had misgivings about nonwritten sources.

---

1. In some sense, revelation through the word within an ecclesiastical context was replaced by interpretation of the New Testament within the academy, Jonathan Z. Smith, *Drudgery Divine* (Chicago: University of Chicago Press, 1990) 55. However, a similar privileging of texts as a source has dominated classical studies, see David Small, "Introduction," in *Methods in the Mediterranean: Historical and Archaeological Views on Texts and Archaeology* (ed. David Small; Leiden: E. J. Brill, 1995) 1–10; and S. L. Dyson, "Classical Archaeology," in *Classics: A Discipline and Profession in Crisis* (eds. Phyllis Culham and Lowell Edmunds (Lanham, Maryland: University Press of America, 1989) 211–13.

2. One should note the general deprecation by scholars of Erwin R. Goodenough's monumental multi-volume study, *Jewish Symbols in the Greco-Roman*

Nevertheless, a voyeuristic attitude toward the material culture could be detected: New Testament scholars stole occasional glances at an archaeological discovery here or an artifact there, but made only feeble attempts to interact with archaeologists or integrate their findings as a whole. An occasional spectacular find by archaeologists served as a refreshing illustration to an otherwise text-driven enterprise, such as the first-century "Jesus" boat found protruding from the mud in the Sea of Galilee that tantalized exegetes with its capacity of twelve,[3] or the discovery of a theater at Sepphoris leading to speculation that Jesus' use of *hypocrite*—Greek for "stage actor"—was rooted in visits to the theater.[4] Short of a visual aid or direct link to Jesus, however, New Testament scholars could make little of archaeology as a whole.[5] Select discoveries or artifacts from the material culture were appropriated in an *ad hoc* manner to buttress specific claims, and if the artifacts supported their arguments or interpretations, New Testament scholars attached surprisingly forceful rhetorical values to them as *facta bruta*.[6] Archaeological evidence, however, just because it is tangible and composed of substance, is neither objective nor a historical reality at face value. Individual artifacts need to be interpreted as part of broader patterns in the

*Period* (New York: Pantheon, 1953–68). See the insightful comments by Jonathan Z. Smith, *Imagining Religion: From Babylon to Jonestown* (Chicago: University of Chicago Press, 1982) 32–33.

3. See the fine excavation report by Shelly Wachsmann et al, "The Excavations of an Ancient boat in the Sea of Galilee," *'Atiqot* (English Series 19; Jerusalem: Israel Antiquities Authority, 1990); and more popularly, S. Wachsmann, "The Galilee Boat: 2,000-Year-Old Hull Recovered Intact," *BAR* 14.5 (Sept./Oct. 1988) 18–33.

4. On the discovery of the theater at Sepphoris, see Leroy Waterman, *Preliminary Report of the University of Michigan Excavations at Sepphoris, Palestine in 1931* (Ann Arbor: University of Michigan Press, 1937); on the implications for Jesus, see Benedict Schwank, "Das Theater von Sepphoris und die Jugendjahre Jesu," *Erbe und Auftrag* 52 (1976) 199–206; and Richard Batey, "Jesus and the Theater," *NTS* 30 (1984) 563–74; see also pp. 107–108.

5. Exceptional in Germany were the topographical and ethnographic studies by Gustaf Dalman and Joachim Jeremias in the early twentieth century; Dalman, *Orte und Wege Jesu* (BFCT 2.1; Gütersloh: Bertelsmann, 1919) and *Arbeit und Sitte in Palästina* (Gütersloh: Bertelsmann, 1928–42); and Jeremias, *Jerusalem zur Zeit Jesu: Eine kulturgeschichtliche Untersuchung zur neutestamentlichen Zeitgeschichte* (2 vols.; Göttingen: Vandenhock & Ruprecht, 1923–37). Exceptional in North American scholarship was the work of Chester C. McCown, which was almost entirely ignored, *The Ladder of Progress in Palestine: A Story of Archaeological Adventure* (New York: Harper & Brothers, 1943).

6. Christian Frevel, "Dies ist der Ort, von dem geschrieben steht . . .," *BN* 47 (1989) 40; Roland deVaux, "On Right and Wrong Uses of Archaeology," in *Near Eastern Archaeology in the Twentieth Century: Festschrift for Nelson Glueck* (ed. James Sanders; New York: Doubleday) 69–70; and Ian Hodder, *The Archaeological Process: An Introduction* (Oxford: Blackwell, 1999) 30–79.

material culture. Artifacts cannot be excised from their stratigraphic or regional contexts and injected into a reconstruction of ancient life within a framework established from the literary sources. Like the interpretation of written sources, which has its own hermeneutic and is based on philology, so too archaeology has its own hermeneutic and is based on typology, the basic method with which archaeologists infer patterns from a series of micro-observations and make an interpretation of ancient life.[7]

There is a growing need in New Testament scholarship to take account of the archaeological data as a whole by listening to the interpretations archaeologists have to offer and to integrate the archaeological findings in a more sophisticated manner. The task is not simply to become aware of more artifacts; rather it is to examine the patterns of evidence in the material culture that impinge on the study of Christian origins. The studies collected in this book focus on one field of New Testament studies, namely historical Jesus research, and are restricted to one geographical area, Galilee. These studies first summarize some of the key patterns in the material culture of Galilee unearthed by archaeologists, and only then raise implications for historical Jesus research. Each of the studies examines an element of the archaeology of Galilee or characterizes a feature of Galilean life during the first century C.E., and then sketches its relevance for historical Jesus research and Christian origins or, alternatively, places a New Testament text into a reconstruction of Galilee generated from the archaeological record.

## The Rising Interest in Galilee

The resurgence of historical Jesus research within New Testament studies has coincided with an intense interest in Galilee among historians of late antiquity, and both have been invigorated by the proliferation of archaeological excavations and surveys in Galilee. Although rabbinic scholars have held an interest in Galilee as the crucible of normative Judaism for the better part of the century,[8] the contemporary trend across all historical

---

7. On the importance of typology, and the similar use of typology in writing and ceramics, see the important article by Frank M. Cross, "Alphabets and Pots: Reflections on Typological Method in the Dating of Human Artifacts," *MAARAV* 3 (1982) 121–36.

8. See, for example, the work of Adolf Büchler, including '*Am Ha-'Arez Ha-Galili* (trans. I. Eldad; Jerusalem: Mosad ha-Rav Kuk, 1964); and *The Political and Social Leaders of the Jewish Community of Sepphoris in the Second and Third Centuries* (Oxford: Oxford University Press, 1909); and Samuel Klein, *Galiläa vor der Makkabäerzeit bis 67* (Vienna: Menorah, 1928). The regional approach to Galilee was pioneered by Eric Meyers, "Galilean Regionalism as a Factor in Historical Reconstruction," *BASOR* 220/221 (1975/76) 93–101; and "The Cultural Setting of

disciplines toward regional studies has roused curiosity about the contours of Galilee's character among New Testament scholars as well. Today, the dialogue over Galilee is more interdisciplinary than ever before and is debated by those intent on describing Galilee as the setting for the historical Jesus, as well as those interested in it as the setting for early Judaism.[9] The escalating archaeological excavations have unearthed considerable portions of the Galilee's material culture, and archaeologists are now frequent participants in the debate over Galilean life and the Galileans in late antiquity. Although New Testament scholars' curiosity in Galilean studies and archaeology has been piqued by interaction with other disciplines and the publicizing of archaeological finds, internal pressures arising from a re-conceptualization of the discipline have also made the need to integrate Galilean archaeology with studies on Christian origins more urgent.

Historical Jesus Research and Galilee

Among the many contemporary competing approaches to the study of the New Testament, one dominant trend has been a move away from the text and exegesis of the New Testament onto the social history of the communities behind these texts, as well as an attempt to look through the pages of the Gospels for traces of the historical Jesus. This contrasts with the nineteenth-century liberal quest for the historical Jesus, which sought to discover the most reliable documents that chronicled Jesus' itinerary and recorded his teaching. Source-criticism was the leading method with the goal of determining, in a stratigraphic manner, the earliest and hence most reliable texts that preserved the chronology of Jesus' ministry and his individual psyche. As the earliest Gospel, Mark was seen to preserve better than the other synoptics or John the itinerary of Jesus' ministry, and the Sayings Source Q was simply a cipher for Jesus' teaching verbatim preserved.[10] Together, these two

Galilee: The Case of Regionalism and Early Judaism," *ANRW* 2.19.1 (eds. Wolfgang Haas and Hildegard Temporini; Berlin: Walter de Gruyter, 1979) 686–701. See earlier, Yohanan Aharoni, "Survey in Galilee: Israelite Settlements and Their Pottery," *EI* 4 (1956) 56–64 [Hebrew].

9. Notable are the two Galilee conferences and their volumes, *The Galilee in Late Antiquity* (ed. Lee Levine; New York: The Jewish Theological Seminary of America, 1992); and *Galilee Through the Centuries* (ed. Eric Meyers; Duke Judaic Studies Series 1; Winona Lake, Indiana: Eisenbrauns, 1999); see also papers collected in *Archaeology and the Galilee: Texts and Contexts in the Graeco-Roman and Byzantine Periods* (eds. Douglas Edwards and C. Thomas McCollough; South Florida Studies in the History of Judaism 143; Atlanta: Scholars Press, 1997).

10. E.g., Heinrich Julius Holzmann, *Die Synoptischen Evangelien: Ihr Ursprung und geschichtlicher Charakter* (Leipzig: Wilhelm Engelmann, 1863); and Adolf von Harnack, *Sprüche und Reden Jesu. Beiträge zur Einleitung in das Neue Testament II* (Leipzig: J. C. Hinrichs, 1907).

earliest Gospel sources both provided the basis for a psychological profile of Jesus, especially with regard to his motivation and messianic consciousness, and preserved his ethics. The identification of the earliest texts, read at face value, was the operative mode of the initial quest for the historical Jesus. Albert Schweizer's bold exposé of these early Jesus descriptions as scholarly projections of nineteenth-century ethical and human ideals, and his own assessment that Jesus was an apocalyptic prophet from another time and place inaccessible to moderns, led to the demise of historical Jesus research. Around the same time, William Wrede's work on the messianic secret in Mark pointed out the tendentiousness of the Markan plot, and Karl Ludwig Schmidt's synoptic analysis of pre-Markan units and their assemblage into Mark's chronological framework undermined any notion that a curriculum vitae of Jesus' ministry could be attained.[11] Shortly thereafter, Rudolf Bultmann's form-critical program created an even more hostile climate for historical Jesus by shifting attention from Jesus to the proclamation of the early Church in its various oral and literary forms.[12] The gulf between Jesus and the kerygma could not be bridged, and Bultmann rejected as impossible a psychological profile of Jesus, more importantly stressing the theological illegitimacy of the quest as avoiding the demand for an existential decision. His existentialist hermeneutic concentrated on individuals' (ancient and modern) response to the Christ event, and hence the theologies of Paul and John became the main focus.[13]

The preoccupation with the kerygma elevated form- and redaction-criticism as the essential tools of New Testament scholarship and refocused the discipline onto the New Testament and its texts. Philological projects aimed at the vocabulary of the New Testament and theological tendencies of early Christian literature were in vogue, and a protective hedge was set around Jesus that guarded against projections like those of the first quest.[14] The chasm between the early Christian proclamation of the Christ event, primarily in a Hellenistic context, and Jesus' ministry and teaching, within a Jewish Palestinian context, was not to be bridged, and interest in the literary

---

11. Karl Ludwig Schmidt, *Der Rahmen der Geschichte Jesu: Literarkritische Untersuchungen zur ältesten Jesus-Überlieferung* (Berlin: Trowitsch & Sohn, 1919); William Wrede, *Das Messiasgeheimnis in den Evangelien* (Göttingen: Vandenhock & Ruprecht, 1901).

12. See especially, Rudolf Bultmann, *Die Geschichte der synoptischen Tradition* (2nd ed.; FRLANT 29; Göttingen: Vandenhock & Ruprecht, 1931).

13. See notably, Rudolf Bultmann, *Theologie des Neuen Testaments* (Tübingen: J. C. B. Mohr (Paul Siebeck), 1948–53). The most insightful analysis of the situation is offered by James M. Robinson, *A New Quest of the Historical Jesus and Other Essays* (Philadelphia: Fortress, 1983).

14. Notably the *Theologisches Wörterbuch zum Neuen Testament* (eds. Gerhart Kittel and Gerhart Friedrich; Stuttgart: W. Kohlhammer, 1933–79).

manifestations of the kerygma was cultivated at the expense of an understanding of the world of Jesus and Galilee.

During this climate in the first half of the century, attempts to characterize the background of Jesus' life and teaching were doomed. More conservative circles generated some interest in the realia of Jesus' world, such as Gustaf Dalman's reports on Palestinian archaeology and topography, or Joachim Jeremias's archaeological and ethnographic studies.[15] But these were dismissed as reactionary and seen as motivated by pious attempts to revive the quest along previous lines. Other ulterior motives in pre-war Germany showed an interest in Galilee and the history of the Galileans as a means to distance Jesus from Judaism. Whether more sophisticated and subtle in characterizing the history of Galilee,[16] or more overtly and crudely propagandistic of Nazi racial theories, these attempts were disgraced in the war's aftermath. New Testament scholarship at this time concentrated on theological issues, and the dominant methods of form- and redaction-criticism refocused attention on literary and philological concerns.

The very tools of form- and redaction-criticism, however, proved the starting point of the subsequent wave of historical Jesus research after World War II, with Bultmann's students leading the way. The gap between the kerygma and Jesus' own teaching was bridged by stressing that, in spite of adaptation and redaction, residual bits of authentic material were discernible in the sayings of Jesus as preserved by the Gospels, and that only certain deeds of Jesus could account for particular features in the Gospels.[17] This "second quest" held no hope of reconstructing a chronology of Jesus' life, like the first quest, but did offer some general characterizations of his activities; nor did it attempt to compile a record of his teachings, but did propose some of its distinctive traits. In some sense, this renewed quest for the historical Jesus was analogous to particle physics, in which the various effects of an event are apparent, so that something about the cause, itself invisible, can nevertheless be said.[18] Unlike source criticism of the nineteenth

---

15. E.g., Dalman, *Orte und Wege Jesu; Arbeit und Sitte in Palästina*; and Jeremias, *Jerusalem zur Zeit Jesu*. Similarly Shirley-Jackson Case, "Jesus and Sepphoris," *JBL* 45 (1926) 14–22.

16. Walter Bauer, "Jesus der Galiläer," reprinted from the 1927 original in *Aufsätze und kleine Schriften* (ed. Georg Strecker; Tübingen: J. C. B. Mohr (Paul Siebeck), 1967) 91–108; and Walter Grundmann's *Jesus der Galiläer und das Judentum* (Leipzig: Wigand, 1940).

17. The new quest was launched by Ernst Käseman's lecture to Bultmann's students in 1953 on the sayings material, published as "Das Problem des historischen Jesu," *ZTK* 51 (1954) 125–53; and carried out systematically with regard to both the sayings and the deeds of Jesus by Günther Bornkamm, *Jesus von Nazareth* (Stuttgart: Kohlhammer, 1956).

18. This analogy is borrowed from Morton Smith, *Jesus the Magician* (New York: Harper & Row, 1978) 6.

century that eliminated the later layers to locate the earliest documents, the renewed quest analyzed the stratigraphy of the fragments within the various forms and the redaction of these forms into coherent wholes, analyzing the trajectories across which early Christian teachings traveled.[19] Thus, the life and teachings of Jesus cannot be seen directly, but, in Morton Smith's words, "by tracing these trajectories back to their common origin, and by calculating the force necessary to make the[m] move as they did, we can locate and describe the invisible cause."[20] Although New Testament scholars sought to locate this unseen Jesus through a careful analysis of early Christian texts, little attention was paid to his precise geographical or social location.[21] Jesus was mapped out on the religious matrix of antiquity—notably with Gnosticism and caricatures of Pharisaism as a foil, and within a simplistic dichotomy between Hellenism and Judaism—but the quest for the historical Jesus was first and foremost a literary enterprise, focusing on early Christian texts or contemporaneous religious texts.

The revival of Jesus research witnessed by the past decades, the so-called "third quest" or "third wave," has at its core a fundamentally different approach, one in which the New Testament texts are no longer the exclusive focus. Not only have the canonical boundaries eroded, so that now the Gospel of Thomas or the *Didache* are readily examined, but the approach to early Christian texts is to reconstruct the social history and community formation of early Christianity, rather than a study of the texts as an end in itself. In terms of particle physics, the object of study is not only the effect, written in texts, but the very context or crucible from which the cause emanated, and within which this cause must be understood. With a focus on social history and social location, the social, economic, cultural, and religious matrix within which early Christian groups emerged is more intensively examined.[22] And the methods are no longer exclusively from literary and historical studies, but borrow from the social sciences, cross-cultural anthropology, or theories of religion, and focus increasingly on the particularities of the region at hand, and in the case of Jesus, Galilee.[23]

---

19. See the important methodological essays and case studies by James M. Robinson and Helmut Koester, *Trajectories Through Early Christianity* (Philadelphia: Fortress, 1971).

20. Smith, *Jesus the Magician*, 6.

21. Somewhat exceptional was Ethelbert Stauffer, who sought to ground the renewed quest in a better understanding of first-century Palestine based especially on the works of Dalman and Jeremias, as well as the recently discovered Dead Sea Scrolls, *Jesus: Gestalt und Geschichte* (München: Francke, 1957).

22. See, e.g., Paul Hoffmann, *Studien zur Theologie der Logienquelle* (NTAbh NF 8; Münster: Aschendorf, 1972); Gerd Theissen, "Wanderradikalismus. Literatursoziologische Aspekte der Überlieferung von Worten Jesu im Urchristentum," *ZTK* 70 (1973) 245–71; and Wayne Meeks, *The First Urban Christians: The Social World of the Apostle Paul* (New Haven: Yale University Press, 1983).

Historical Jesus research today must be bifocal. This includes both a critical and informed reading of the early Christian texts and their reading within a plausible reconstruction of their background. Historical Jesus research cannot turn back the clock and neglect the mistakes of the previous quests, and cannot avoid careful form- and redaction-criticism nor evade the basic stratigraphic problems within the Gospels. It must remain critical and neither try to write a biography of Jesus' life, nor be content with compiling lists of the authentic teachings of Jesus. Instead, historical Jesus research must focus on an interpretation of Jesus within his environment, and go about reconstructing that environment as critically and as knowingly as possible while it goes about examining the literature.[24]

## The Debate over Galilee and Literary Evidence

The importance of the nature and character of Galilee as the location of Jesus' life and teachings is recognized across the board in the contemporary debate over the historical Jesus. Scholars dig down through the literary and theological strata, strip off later accretions with varying degrees of radicalism or conservatism, and then interpret their bundle of authentic sayings and plausible deeds against a concrete background. While the previous generations described the background with facile divisions between Palestine and the broader Mediterranean, Judaism and Hellenism, or urban and rural, the current debate focuses primarily on Galilee and acknowledges a more complex reality of the blend of cultures and rural-urban relations. Since descriptions of the realities in Galilee to a large extent determine the interpretation of Jesus' teachings and his life, it is not surprising that the renewed quest has witnessed variously shaded Galilees to make the competing descriptions of the historical Jesus more credible. The ethos of first-century Galilee has been positioned along a series of axes: in terms of ethnicity, it has been described as Jewish, "Israelite," or even syncretistic and Gentile; in terms of cultural traditions and religion, Galilee has been portrayed as either conservatively Jewish or Hellenistic; in terms of economics, either

---

23. See e.g., Bruce Malina, *The New Testament World: Insights from Cultural Anthropology* (rev. ed.; Louisville: Westminster John Knox, 1993); Richard Rohrbaugh, ed., *The Social Sciences and New Testament Interpretation* (Peabody, Massachusetts: Hendrickson, 1996). The most explicit connection between cross-cultural anthropology and historical Jesus research is found in John Dominic Crossan, *The Historical Jesus: The Life of a Mediterranean Jewish Peasant* (San Francisco: HarperSanFrancisco, 1988).

24. Placing Gospel units within their particular context has been pioneered by Gerd Theissen, who has examined the *Lokalkolorit* of various passages, see *The Gospels in Context: Social and Political History in the Synoptic Tradition* (Minneapolis: Fortress Press, 1991).

impoverished or prosperous; in terms of its political climate, it has been portrayed as either zealously nationalistic or shrewdly acquiescent.[25] How Galilee is shaded has a profound impact on how Jesus' life and teachings are interpreted. In terms of ethnicity, whether the first-century Galileans were descendants of Judean settlers under the Maccabean expansion, the remnant of Israelites from the Northern Kingdom now subject to Jerusalem's control, or a syncretistic blend including recently circumcised Itureans absorbed into the Herodian kingdom, has a critical effect on how Jesus the Galilean's actions in Jerusalem are portrayed. In terms of culture, whether Galilee was Hellenized—that is to say Greek-speaking and conversant in the art, architecture, and thought of the broader Greco-Roman world—or essentially Semitic—that is to say Aramaic-speaking, aniconic, provincial in its architecture, and steeped in rabbinic teachings—makes a difference in the way scholars view the preservation of his sayings by his disciples and their interpretation. In terms of economics, whether Herod Antipas's building programs at Sepphoris and Tiberias fueled the economy, generated wealth among its inhabitants, and provided employment across the board, or strained the productive capabilities of Galilee, broadened the gulf between the classes, and made the relative depravity of the Galilean peasantry more apparent, makes for different interpretations of Jesus' activities. The character of Galilee has generated so much debate among scholars that Seán Freyne recently quipped humorously that "the quest for the

---

25. Opting for an essentially Jewish Galilee, see E. P. Sanders, *The Historical Figure of Jesus* (London: Allen Lane, 1983) and Paula Fredrickson, *Jesus of Nazareth, King of the Jews: a Jewish life and the Emergence of Christianity* (New York: Knopf, 1999). As "Israelite," see Richard Horsley, *Galilee: History, Politics, People* (Valley Forge, Pennsylvania: Trinity Press International, 1995); and *Archaeology, History and Society in Galilee: The Social Context of Jesus and the Rabbis* (Valley Forge, Pennsylvania: Trinity Press International, 1996). For a syncretistic population, see Burton Mack, *The Lost Gospel: The Book of Q and Christian Origins* (San Francisco: HarperSanFrancisco, 1993). As untouched by Hellenism, see Seán Freyne, *Galilee from Alexander the Great to Hadrian, 323 B.C.E. to 135 C.E.* (Wilmington: Michael Glazier, 1980). For the Galilee as heavily Hellenized (making the Cynic hypothesis likely), see F. Gerald Downing, *Christ and the Cynics* (JSOT Manuals 4; Sheffield: JSOT, 1988); *Cynics and Christian Origins* (Edinburgh: T & T Clark, 1992). An impoverished Palestine and Galilee is argued by Luise Schottroff and Wolfgang Stegemann, *Jesus von Nazareth—Hoffnung der Armen* (Stuttgart: Kohlhammer, 1978); for a more prosperous Galilee, see Howard Clark Kee, "Early Christianity in the Galilee: Reassessing the Evidence from the Gospels," in *The Galilee in Late Antiquity*, 3–22. The classic description of Galilee as a hotbed of revolutionaries is S. F. G. Brandon, *Jesus and the Zealots* (Manchester: University Press, 1967); a more sophisticated and sociologically informed perspective is found in Richard Horsley and John S. Hanson, *Bandits, Prophets, and Messiahs: Popular Movements at the Time of Jesus* (New York: Winston [A Seabury Book], 1985).

historical Jesus is rapidly in danger of becoming the quest for the historical Galilee."[26]

The key issue, of course, is not only the various reconstructions, but the methods and evidences used to reconstruct Galilee. Most of the reconstructions of Galilee's character rely almost exclusively on collages pieced together from citations and allusions in literary texts, such as the Gospels themselves, Josephus, and the rabbinic corpus. Literary evidence, however, offers only limited information for Galilee, is beset with historical problems, and often has religious interests or biases that are misleading about the character of Galilee.[27]

The Gospels themselves present little useful information about Galilee that helps set the context for understanding Jesus and his ministry. More than sixty references to Galilee or places in Galilee in the Gospels, and the description of Jesus (Matt 26:69) and his followers (Mark 14:70) as Galileans, certify that Jesus' ministry is to be located in Galilee and that he was a Galilean.[28] Yet these texts provide virtually no descriptive information about Galilee, and some statements are misleading. For example, Matthew's use of the biblical epitaph "Galilee of the Gentiles" (4:15) as part of his quotation of Isaiah 9:1–2 foreshadows the theme of the mission to the Gentiles; it cannot, however, in any way be taken to imply that Galilee was heavily populated with Gentiles, as several scholars have implied.[29] Although the Gospels certainly contain material that was first spoken in Galilee, and some forms might even have been penned there, the Gospels as we have them were composed outside Galilee, making it difficult to discern the former from the latter.[30] Those sayings spoken by Jesus in Galilee, perhaps even modified or augmented by his followers in Galilee, were integrated into Gospel narratives by authors living far from Galilee, who perhaps lacked any first-hand knowledge of Galilee. They were not interested in the movement's social history

26. Freyne, "The Geography, Politics, and Economics in Galilee and the Quest for the Historical Jesus," in *Studying the Historical Jesus: Evaluations of the State of Current Research* (eds. Bruce Chilton and Craig Evans; NTTS 19 (Leiden: E. J. Brill, 1994) 76.

27. Moses Finley, *Ancient History: Evidence and Models* (London: Chatto & Windus, 1985).

28. Seán Freyne, *Galilee, Jesus, and the Gospels: Literary Approaches and Historical Investigation* (Philadelphia: Fortress, 1988).

29. See the astute comments by Mark A. Chancey, "The Myth of a Gentile Galilee: The Population of Galilee and New Testament Studies" (Ph.D. dissertation, Duke University, 1999) 255–59.

30. Although there have been suggestions that Matthew could plausibly be located in Galilee, see J. Andrew Overman, *Matthew's Gospel and Formative Judaism: The Social World of the Matthean Community* (Minneapolis: Fortress, 1990) 158–9; and Anthony Saldarini, "The Gospel of Matthew and Jewish Christian Conflict in the Galilee," *The Galilee in Late Antiquity*, 23–38.

and did not use descriptive language for Jesus' Galilean setting, but were theologically motivated to shape their communities and employed religious rhetoric flowing from a mythological world view.

The writings of Josephus provide a wealth of information about Jewish history and Galilee in particular, though none of it is without interpretive problems. A military leader in Galilee during the first Jewish revolt, he had first-hand knowledge of Galilee and experiences with Galileans, but writing under royal subvention the *Jewish War*, the *Antiquities of the Jews*, and finally his *Life*, he focused on extolling the virtues of the Flavians, authenticating the Jewish religion, and defending his career. When these overlaps are synoptically compared, Josephus is seen, as Shaye J. D. Cohen put it, to "invent, exaggerate, over-emphasize, distort, suppress, or, occasionally, tell the truth. Often we cannot determine where one practice ends and another begins."[31] Josephus has considerable merit as a historian of his day, but like all ancient historians, his perspectives were mostly upper-class and male, his interests were mostly military-political, and his particular agenda was pro-Roman early in his career, more pro-Jewish later, and throughout, self-serving.

The rabbinic literature anecdotally supplies information about Jewish daily life in antiquity, but its late date renders it problematic for first-century Galilee. Certainly, the Mishnah contains judgments of first-century rabbis, but these were codified in the second century C.E., and combined with third- and fourth-century C.E. commentaries in the Talmud. The opinions and pronouncements attributed to first-century sages such as Hillel or Shammai may be subject to later accretions. Opinions attributed to later rabbis or cited without any attribution might in fact originate in the first century. These chronological problems caution against accepting the rabbinic literature at face value for the first century, as does the kind of literature it was. Although the rabbis were respected and viewed as authoritative, rabbinic pronouncements were neither a law book nor a constitution that governed daily life per se. They were an intellectual enterprise that speculated on, discussed, and debated living the ideal life from the rabbis' perspective, which lacked civic and legal backing under Roman rule. The rabbinic corpus contains many descriptive examples or anecdotes about daily life, but they were not legally prescriptive for first-century Jewish life, nor are they clear about when they are especially descriptive of a particular (likely upper-) class practice.[32]

---

31. Shaye J. D. Cohen, *Josephus in Galilee and Rome: His Vita and Development as a Historian* (Leiden: E. J. Brill, 1979) 181.

32. See most radically, Jacob Neusner, *Rabbinic Traditions about the Pharisees Before 70*, vols. 1–3 (Leiden: E. J. Brill, 1971). Earlier treatments tended to fuse the literary and archaeological worlds, see Samuel Krauss, *Talumudische Archäologie*, 3 vols. (Leipzig: G. Fock, 1910–12); others dealt with the literature at face value but created a world as described by the rabbis Ayre Ben-David. *Talmudische Ökonomie*, vol. 1 (Hildesheim: G. Olms, 1974).

Ironically, the rabbinic literature is most helpful in those areas that are incidental to its point and that its authors care the least about. But the vast corpus and the many technical issues require a specialization that lies beyond this author's capabilities so that, though occasionally citations from the rabbinic literature appear in the subsequent essays, a systematic discussion of the material lies beyond the scope of this book.

The literary evidence that either comments directly on Galilee, or indirectly informs us about its being written there, can only be used to reconstruct Galilee after having undergone a critical evaluation and careful interpretation. However, even thereafter, we must keep in mind that such a collage of literary sources will be biased. Writing in antiquity was an upper-class phenomenon; the masses neither read nor wrote. Aristocratic male interests dominate the historical literature; its pages are filled with politics, great speeches by leading men, and heroic battles, and when the masses are mentioned, it is mostly because they caused political unrest. To say anything about the common people or daily life from the Greco-Roman historians, especially in a place as remote as Galilee was from the center of political power, is highly problematic. Likewise, the documents left behind for religious communities were written by upper-class males, since scribal training alone implied some degree of wealth, and was typically limited to males. Furthermore, such authors either assumed or did not care about many things that everyone took for granted, and without which the literature cannot be interpreted. These texts leave remarkable gaps in information and present a mythological veneer or religious interpretation to events and daily life that obscure such structural or economic forces in which social historians are interested. Thus, a literary framework of Galilean life in antiquity is fashioned with the lenses of the literary elite or those with particular religious concerns. Such a collage is, of course, more sophisticated or substantive if it is held together with a sociological or cross-cultural anthropological framework, but these are likewise disputed and must still interact with the available evidence.

## The Emergence of Galilean Archaeology

Given some of the limitations and the gaps in the literary evidence, it is not surprising that the growing archaeological evidence has been drawn upon to fill out the sketch of first-century Galilee. The growing interest in the social history of early Christianity, and the desire to place Jesus in a well-articulated Galilee, has coincided with an expansion of the volume of archaeological excavations in and around Galilee. New Testament scholars paid a disproportionate amount of attention to the archaeology of Jerusalem— the location of the tomb in the Holy Sepulcher, the site of Golgotha, or the position of the Temple-because so little had been done in Galilee. A generation ago Chester C. McCown could title a chapter in his archaeological handbook "Neglected Galilee," and lament its lack of archaeological activity. What had been excavated of the Roman-Byzantine Periods represented, on the one hand, Christian holy sites under custodial care, or, on the other hand, sites of importance to Jewish religion excavated by fledgling Israeli archaeology, such as the Jewish necropolis at Beth She'arim on the very edge of Galilee and the late synagogue at Hammath Tiberias.[33] Very few of the excavations at holy sites commemorating stories found in the Gospels, however, unearthed significant finds from the Early Roman Period, with the notable exception of Nazareth, Jesus' hometown, and Capernaum, the site most frequently associated with his ministry.[34] Most of the sites were churches or monasteries from the Byzantine period, such as Tabgha, a shrine over the alleged site of the multiplication of loaves and fishes, or Kursi, a monastery commemorating the swine miracle.[35]

Thanks in large part to the pioneering efforts of Eric Meyers and James F. Strange, many Roman-Byzantine sites in Galilee lie exposed. Beginning in the seventies, they directed excavations at a series of villages and synagogues in Upper Galilee, and in the process invigorated the archaeology of the Roman-Byzantine Period, drew attention to daily life in Galilee at more remote sites, and expanded the focus that previously was on Christian holy sites and monumental architecture.[36] Subsequently, as Israeli archaeology

---

33. Benjamin Mazar, "The Excavations at Beth She'arim," *IEJ* 4 (1954) 88–107; *IEJ* 5 (1955) 205–39; *IEJ* 7 (1957) 73–92, 239–55; and *IEJ* 9 (1959) 205–220. Baruch Lifshitz, "Die Entdeckung einer alten Synagoge bei Tiberias," *ZDPV* 78 (1962) 180–84; and Moshe Dothan, *Hammath Tiberias: Early Synagogues and the Hellenistic and Roman Remains* (Jerusalem: Israel Exploration Society, 1983).

34. For Nazareth, see Bellarmino Bagatti, *Excavations in Nazareth. Volume I: From the Beginning till the XII Century* (Jerusalem: Franciscan Printing Press, 1969). For Capernaum, see Virgilio Corbo, *Cafarnao 1: Gli edifici della città* (Studium Biblicum Franciscanum 19; Jerusalem: Franciscan Printing Press, 1975); Stanislao Loffreda, *Cafarnao II: La ceramica* (Studium Biblicum Franciscanum 19; Jerusalem: Franciscan Printing Press, 1974); Augusto Spijkerman, *Cafarnao III: Catalogo della monete della città* (Studium Biblicum Franciscanum 19; Jerusalem: Franciscan Printing Press, 1975); and Emmanuel Testa, *Cafarnao IV: I graffiti della casa di S. Pietro* (Studium Biblicum Franciscanum 19; Jerusalem: Franciscan Printing Press, 1972). For Magdala, see Virgilio Corbo, "Scavi archeologici a Magdala (1971–1973)," *LA* 24 (1974) 5–37; "La città romana di Magdala, Rapporto preliminare dopo la quara campagna del 1975," *Studia Hierosolymitana* 1 (1976) 355–78; and "Piazza e villa urbana a Magdala," *LA* 28 (1978) 232–40.

35. For an overview, see Jack Finegan, *The Archaeology of the New Testament: The Life of Jesus and the Beginning of the Early Church* (rev. ed.; Princeton: Princeton University Press, 1992).

36. Eric Meyers, et al., "The Meiron Excavation Project: Archaeological Survey in Galilee and Golan, 1976," *BASOR* 230 (1978) 1–24; *Ancient Synagogue*

Figure 1.3 Major Excavations in and near Galilee

came into full bloom, other excavations and surveys in and around Galilee have taken place. In particular, interest in Jewish history and a fascination with Jewish resistance to Rome have motivated excavation at the sites of Yodefat and Gamla, two walled sites that were destroyed by the Roman Legions in 67 C.E.[37] Studies on the distribution patterns in Galilee of pottery

---

at Khirbet Shemaʿ, Upper Galilee, Israel 1970–1972 (AASOR 42; Durham, North Carolina: ASOR, 1976); Excavations at Ancient Meiron, Upper Galilee, Israel 1971–72, 1974–75, 1977 (Cambridge, Massachusetts: American Schools of Oriental Research, 1981); "Preliminary Report on the 1980 Excavations at en-Nabratein, Israel," BASOR 244 (1981) 1–26; "Second Preliminary Report on the 1980 Excavations at en-Nabratein, Israel," BASOR 246 (1982) 35–54; and Excavations at the Ancient Synagogue of Gush Ḥalav. Meiron Excavation Project Volume V (Winona Lake, Indiana: Eisenbrauns, 1990).

37. S. Gutman, "Gamla," NEAEHL 2.463–64; Danny Syon, "Gamla: Portrait of a Rebellion," BAR 18 (Jan.–Feb., 1992): 23–24; and David Adan-Bayewitz and Mordechai Aviam, "Iotapata, Josephus, and the Siege of 67: Preliminary Report on the 1992–94 Seasons," JRS 10 (1997) 131–165.

produced at the village of Kefar Hananya, and excavations of the pottery kilns themselves, have likewise contributed to our knowledge of markets and movement of goods.[38] The region's urban sites have also been excavated over the past decades. Sepphoris, the former capital of Galilee, has been simultaneously excavated by as many as four different teams since the 1980s, and excavations at Tiberias on the Sea of Galilee have been conducted in and around its modern urban sprawl.[39] Other urban centers outside of Galilee have been uncovered by archaeological excavations, such as Caesarea Maritima, the harbor built by Herod the Great, and two cities build or rebuilt by Herod's son: Banias/Caesarea Philippi near the source of the Jordan river, and Bethsaida/Julias where the Jordan enters the Sea of Galilee.[40] Scythopolis/Beth-Shean on the southern border of Galilee, the largest ancient city in northern Palestine, has been subject to one of the largest excavations in Israel.[41] And to the north of Galilee around the Huleh Valley, the Syro-phoenician village of Tel Anafa was excavated, and the spade has just been put to the city of Kedesh and a Roman style temple at Umm Reit.[42] To these excavations one can add several surveys of Upper and Lower Galilee, numerous salvage excavations conducted in advance of modern construction projects, and the availability of new archaeological encyclopedias and the convening of congresses on Galilee, all of which combine to give the available archaeological evidence a critical mass.[43]

---

38. David Adan-Bayewitz and Isadore Pearlman, "The Local Trade of Sepphoris in the Roman Period," *IEJ* 40 (1990) 153–172; and David Adan-Bayewitz, *Common Pottery in Roman Galilee: A Study of Local Trade* (Ramat-Gan, Israel: Bar-Ilan University Press, 1993).

39. See the articles and bibliography in Rebecca Nagy et al., eds., *Sepphoris in Galilee: Crosscurrents of Culture* (Raleigh, North Carolina: North Carolina Museum of Art, 1996); and Yizhar Hirshfeld, "Tiberias: Preview of Coming Attractions," *BAR* 17.2 (March/April 1991) 44–55.

40. Kenneth Holum, *King Herod's Dream: Caesarea by the Sea* (New York: Norton, 1988); John Wilson and Vasilios Tzaferis, "Banias Dig Reveals King's Palace," *BAR* 24.1 (Jan–Feb 1998) 54–61; and Rami Arav and Richard Freund, *Bethsaida: A City by the Northern Shore of the Sea of Galilee* (Bethsaida Excavations Project I; Kirkesville, Missouri: Thomas Jefferson University Press, 1995).

41. Gideon Foerster and Yoram Tsafrir, "Bet Shean Project," in *ESI* 1987/1988 vol. 6 (Jerusalem: The Israel Antiquities Authority, 1988) 10–43.

42. Sharon Herbert, *Tel Anafa I. Final Report on Ten Years of Excavation at a Hellenistic and Roman Settlement in Northern Israel* (JRA Sup. Ser. 10.1; Ann Arbor, Michigan: The Kelsey Museum of Archaeology); Kedesh is currently being excavated by Sharon Herbert and Andrea Berlin, and Umm Reit by J. Andrew Overman.

43. A more cautious view on the availability of Early Roman materials is still suggested by Dennis Groh, who nevertheless stresses that a diachronic approach offers optimism for reconstructing first-century Galilee, see "The Clash Between Literary and Archaeological Models of Provincial Palestine," in *Archaeology and the Galilee: Texts and Contexts in the Graeco-Roman and Byzantine Periods* (eds. Douglas Edwards and C. Thomas McCollough; South Florida Studies in the History of Judaism 143; Atlanta: Scholars Press, 1997) 31–33.

## Integrating Archaeological and Literary Evidence

The interest among New Testament scholars in the contribution of archaeology to the social history of early Christianity and the Galilee of Jesus has coincided with the dramatic rise in archaeological activity. Not surprisingly, there have been attempts at integrating Galilean archaeology and historical Jesus research. The initiative for this dialogue originated to a considerable extent from the archaeological side. In the early eighties, Meyers and Strange co-authored *Archaeology, the Rabbis and Early Christianity*, which presented a survey of the pertinent archaeological issues relating to Galilee, and considered some of the implications for historical Jesus research.[44] More recently, each has also made independent statements on how an archaeologically defined Galilee impinges on the historical Jesus.[45] From the literary side, the work of Seán Freyne has increasingly incorporated in a more and more sophisticated manner the archaeological data and dialogue with archaeologists into his reconstruction of Galilee.[46] More recently, Richard Horsley has also taken up a dialogue with archaeologists, and in sketching the contours of Galilee's history and society, has made heavy use of archaeological evidence and literary evidence in socio-economic modeling.[47]

The problem of integrating the book and the spade is vexing, however, since texts and archaeology represent different kinds of evidence about different aspects of past life and require different interpretive strategies. In many ways, integrating the literary and archaeological evidence to reconstruct social history is analogous to a crossword puzzle in that the clues are given in two distinct lists in the form of two sets of independent questions, whose respective answers nevertheless interlock to produce a single representation. Ideally, crossword puzzles are completed by simultaneously

---

44. Most prominently for historical Jesus research, the languages and the structure of the synagogue were discussed, Eric Meyers and James F. Strange, *Archaeology, the Rabbis and Early Christianity* (Nashville: Abingdon, 1981).

45. James F. Strange, "Some Implications of Archaeology for New Testament Studies," in *What Has Archaeology to Do With Faith?* (eds. James Charlesworth and Walter Weaver; Valley Forge, Pennsylvania: Trinity Press International, 1992) 23–59; "The Sayings of Jesus and Archaeology," in *Hillel and Jesus: Comparative Studies of Two Major Religious Leaders* (ed. James Charlesworth; Minneapolis: Fortress, 1998) 291–305; and "First Century Galilee from Archaeology and from Texts," in *Archaeology and the Galilee*, 39–48.

46. See especially "Jesus and the Urban Culture of Galilee," in *Texts and Contexts: Biblical Texts and Their Textual and Situational Contexts* (eds. Tord Fornberg and David Hellholm; Oslo: Scandinavian University Press, 1995) 596–622.

47. Richard Horsley, *Galilee: History, Politics, People* (Valley Forge, Pennsylvania: Trinity Press International, 1995); and *Archaeology, History and Society in Galilee: The Social Context of Jesus and the Rabbis* (Valley Forge, Pennsylvania: Trinity Press International, 1996).

working the horizontal rows and vertical columns, using the former to fill in lacunae, partially spell out answers, or correct inconsistencies in the latter, and vice versa.[48] But a simultaneous approach involves some thorny problems in the case of the historical Jesus and the Galilee. For one, unspoken theological assumptions and long-held interpretations of the early Christian literature have writ their letters in ink in some rows, while in others runs the rut left by the continued erasures and rewritings of heated exegetical disputes. In the process, answers to many textual clues are tenaciously clung to, in spite of unintelligible letters and garbled sounds in the corresponding rows.

With primary training in philology, literary studies, and theology, New Testament scholars have traditionally, and perhaps naturally, relegated archaeology to an ancillary role. The traditional role of "biblical archaeology" within biblical studies especially among theological faculties was to confirm the biblical record. In terms of the crossword puzzle analogy, certain vertical columns of the archaeological record were checked to confirm the horizontal rows of the biblical record or its interpretation, such as the date of the conquest, the extent of the Solomonic building projects, or the Assyrian withdrawal from Jerusalem. This approach is rooted in the beginnings of archaeology as a discipline, which aimed at historical truth arrived at in a scientific way in opposition to myth and folklore.[49] Not surprisingly, biblical archaeology was preoccupied with distinguishing the narratives of the sacred scriptures as history from myth.[50] In fact, the legacy of William F. Albright and his students was to situate the biblical narratives in history in order to certify the interaction between God and humans as "real" historical events as opposed to mythology.[51] This preoccupation determined the development of fieldwork and methods of digging a site, in which digging stratigraphically, with a preoccupation with sequential layering, was designed to verify the biblical chronology. Biblical sites were excavated with the purpose of correlating their destruction to the biblical accounts, and ceramic typology

---

48. In a manner similar to what Strange has called a dialogical approach, "Some Implications of Archaeology," 23–31; similar to that advocated by Ian Hodder, *The Archaeological Process: An Introduction* (Oxford: Blackwell, 1999).

49. Such as the popular excavations of Schleiermann at Troy that sought to root the Iliad in a historical event, Ian Hodder, *The Archaeological Process*, 1.

50. Evident in the 1870 foundational document of the Palestine Exploration Society, in which . . . "whatever goes to verify the Bible history as real, in time, place and circumstances, is a refutation of unbelief." Cited in Roland de Vaux, "On Right and Wrong Uses of Archaeology," in *Near Eastern Archaeology in the Twentieth Century: Festschrift for Nelson Glueck* (ed. James Sanders; New York: 1970), 67.

51. Still seen in many Bible handbooks, which tend to pick and choose among the excavations and finds those that lend historical credence to the biblical record, without mentioning others, James C. Moyers and Victor H. Matthews, "The Use and Abuse of Archaeology in Current Bible Handbooks," *BA* 48 (1985) 149–159.

focused almost exclusively on chronological concerns arising from establishing sequence and chronology.

Since New Testament scholars were interested in few archaeologically
datable events—Jesus and his followers left behind no building projects nor
inscriptions, nor did any event in the New Testament create a destruction
layer—there was little interest in what this kind of archaeology had to offer.
"New Testament archaeology," therefore, was dwarfed in its development
compared to "Old Testament" archaeology and the finds relating to ancient
Israel. A more subtle misuse of archaeology as proving the Bible was occasionally committed by New Testament scholars, namely displaying artifacts
or sites as visual aids or illustrations. More benign than the claims of the
Albright school or more conservative biblical archaeologists about the history of Israel, illustrations from the archaeological record served as latent
proof that the stories of the New Testament were to be understood as having occurred in history, were historical, and "true." Thus, the Pilate inscription found at Caesarea Maritima in 1962, which commemorated his
dedication of a public building honoring the Emperor Tiberias, is displayed
as a contemporary witness to this prominent New Testament figure.[52]

How, then, does the archaeological and literary evidence relate? In terms
of the crossword puzzle analogy, we must be aware first and foremost that a
different set of questions is asked of the archaeological evidence. Often asked
of the archaeological evidence are questions of locating this or that place
where a certain event in the Gospels is said to have occurred, or finding evidence of early Christians.[53] The locating of a particular site, and the dating of
a particular structure, to correlate it directly with the life of Jesus, however,
minimizes the contribution that archaeology has to offer. Likewise, the concern to locate a particular set of Christian evidence in the first centuries fails
to focus on understanding Jesus and his earliest followers within Judaism.

Archaeology's chief contribution to the study of historical Jesus research
lies in its ability to reconstruct his social world. The traditional focus of biblical archaeology on diachronic issues and chronology has been shifting over

---

52. See, e.g., Rami Arav and John J. Rousseau, *Jesus and His World: An Archaeological
and Cultural Dictionary* (Minneapolis: Fortress, 1995) 225–27. Exceptional in this
regard is the fine study on stone vessels by Roland Deines, which does not simply
display them as visual aids, but examines what they tell us about first century
Judaism, *Jüdische Steingefäße und pharisäische Frömmigkeit. Ein archäologisch-
historischer Beitrag zum Verständnis von Joh 2,6 und der jüdischen Reinheitshalacha
zur Zeit Jesu* (WUNT ser. 2, vol. 52; Tübingen: J. C. B. Mohr [Paul Siebeck], 1993).

53. Note the considerable interest in the location of Saint Peter's house. There
has been considerable speculation on the presence of Jewish Christians in the first
centuries C.E. in Palestine based on symbols and graffiti, see e.g., Frédéric Manns,
*Essais sur le judéo-christianisme* (Jerusalem: Franciscan Printing, 1977); these have
been criticized by Joan Taylor, *Christians and the Holy Places: The Myth of Jewish-
Christian Origins* (Oxford: Clarendon, 1993).

the past years to include more of a synchronic approach, that is to say, to look at various sites and society as a whole at a particular time period. Archaeology is no longer simply a tool to assess chronology and confirm dates, or a tool to tract down a site or structure; rather, it provides a more general picture of the material culture of any given historical period. The archaeological record helps to assess demographic issues, such as the ethnicity and religion of a region based on settlement patterns and socialized sets of behavior, or the socio-economic forces of a region based on site size, population distribution, and agricultural practices. The archaeological record also furnishes a thicker description of sites in terms of ethnicity, religion, social class, and economics; and sites can be compared within and outside any given region.

This provides social historians with a fundamentally different set of evidence than what the literary texts offer. Literary texts are intentional witnesses from antiquity, whose authors want to tell a story, make a plea, or regulate life. The archaeological evidence presents both intentional and unintentional witnesses from antiquity. On the one hand, public structures were designed to communicate a message: of Rome's grandeur, of the city founder's prestige and wealth, or of its leading citizen's munificence. The cities' overall grid patterns, its enclosing walls, and its vistas were also designed to communicate a sense of order and to highlight the social hierarchy. Their effect on wider classes as a whole can be judged in terms of expense, though their effect on the minds of the people is more difficult to judge (from the archaeological record), an effect that might be more readily examined in the written evidence. On the other hand, archaeologists for the most part uncover many unintentional witnesses to life in antiquity in the form of artifacts that make up "the paraphernalia of everyday life": sherds from pots and pans, hidden coins, discarded kitchen scrap—all afford a glimpse behind closed doors of antiquity.[54] Archaeology has the advantage of uncovering the interrelated aspects of public and private spheres of antiquity. The public sphere was open and visible to all, controlled by the elites and their political decisions; and the private sphere, though of course influenced by the elites, was determined by individuals, though within the socio-economic confines. Aspects of the public realm, which archaeologists can examine, include settlement patterns, site size, trade routes, and topography, as well as the various sites' public architecture, the types of structures that were built, how they were arranged, and what materials were used in their constructions. Understanding aspects of this public space raises the question of how Jesus would have experienced the amalgamation of structures in the villages, towns, and cities of Galilee that he visited; what impression the cities gave as opposed to villages; and what impact these differences

---

54. Meyers and Strange, *Archaeology, the Rabbis and Early Christianity*, 28.

had on social relations. In the private sphere, archaeology can compare the differing sizes of domestic houses; the expense of materials used in their construction; and can pry inside and compare their kitchens, utensils, and how the people cooked and what they ate. How many luxury items could have been afforded in which houses and at which sites, how did these distinguish one's socio-economic status, and what was used to distinguish one's religion or religious fervor? Artifacts provide both unintentional witnesses to such features of life and intentional witnesses left behind by those who sought to distinguish themselves and impress others. Together they can paint a picture of much in everyday life in antiquity that is neglected in the literature, ironically because these eyewitnesses ignored the commonplace, visual aspects of everyday life, and assumed this knowledge on the part of the reader.

Again using the crossword puzzle analogy, the approach of the studies collected in this book is not to use Galilean archaeology as the down columns against which the answers in the across rows of Gospel studies can be checked. Instead, they naively start the puzzle afresh, begin with questions generated from Galilean archaeology, and favor the archaeological data unabashedly. In each chapter, only after an archaeological profile has been examined will the implications for the Gospel and historical Jesus research be sketched.

The crossword puzzle analogy raises two serious problems, however. First, only a limited number of clues exist, either from the material culture or the literary texts. Not all Galilean sites have been excavated, nor has each excavated site been uncovered entirely. Many lack any clear evidence for the first century, and certainly many of the excavators have not yet, or have inadequately, published their finds. The clues are simply limited, and the temptation must be resisted to broaden the chronological parameters too far beyond the first century C.E., that is to say, to use artifacts from the Middle or Late Roman Periods anachronistically for the Early Roman Period. Nor should one assume that any archaeological evidence outside Galilee, such as from Judea, is applicable to its material culture.[55]

The incompleteness of the archaeological evidence for Galilee points out the inferential nature of the enterprise of reconstructing its social history and makes the second problem more pressing, namely the template being used for the crossword puzzle. The assumptions about ancient life and social models influence how the limited evidence is interpreted and shape the process of reconstructing Galilee at the time of Jesus. Heavy-handed approaches to such sociological modeling by scholars run the risk of

---

55. Concise methodological considerations for regional archaeology are spelled out by Ruth Vale, "Literary Sources in Archaeological Description: The Case of Galilee, Galilees and Galileans," *JSJ* 18 (1987) 209–226.

| Iron II | 1000 - 733/32 B.C.E. |
|---|---|
| Iron III | 733/32 - 586 B.C.E. |
| Persian | 586 - 332 B.C.E. |
| Early Hellenistic | 332 - 167 B.C.E. |
| Late Hellenistic | 167 - 63 B.C.E. |
| Early Roman | 63 B.C.E. - 135 C.E. |
| Middle Roman | 135 - 250 C.E. |
| Late Roman | 250 - 363 C.E. |

*Table 1.1 Chronological Periods*

squeezing each and every bit of evidence into models; those who reject models, of course, are simply using unarticulated models.[56] This collection of essays leans heavily toward the latter horn of the dilemma. Rather than, at the outset, articulating the theories and the models, the sociology and anthropology, or the economic and the religious theory that influence the presentation of the evidence, each chapter simply elevates a synthesis of the archaeological evidence relating to a particular topic. The models and assumptions, though unarticulated, will be clear to those interested.

## Outline and Coherence of the Studies

Each of these studies stands on its own, though a certain sequential coherence exists in the division into three parts. Part one focuses on the archaeology of some basic demographic issues in Galilee, the ethnicity and religion of the inhabitants in the first century (chapter two), and the socio-economic forces brought about by its urbanization (chapter three). Using surveys and excavations at particular sites in Galilee, as well as some key components of their material culture, particularly stone vessels, *miqwaoth*, and burial practices, chapter two argues that the inhabitants of Galilee were descendants of the Judeans who resettled in Galilee under the Hasmoneans. Focusing on

---

56. Hanson and Oakman, *Palestine in the Time of Jesus*, 3–17.

shifts in population distribution and the extent of urban construction projects, chapter three argues that the primary impact of Herod Antipas's building of Sepphoris and Tiberias was a socio-economic strain on the population, and to a lesser extent cultural or religious. Each chapter concludes with some observations on the relevance for historical Jesus research.

Part two presents the archaeology of two Galilean sites, the former capital Sepphoris (chapter four) and Capernaum on the northern shore of the Sea of Galilee (chapter five). Chapter four shows how Sepphoris was a city inhabited primarily by Jews, onto which Antipas had grafted a Greco-Roman architectural veneer without offending Jewish sensibilities. Most of the characteristic Greco-Roman finds at Sepphoris date to a later period, showing that Antipas began an architectural trajectory toward Hellenization or Romanization, which came into full bloom at a much later date. Thus, the question of Sepphoris and Jesus, who was raised only 5 kilometers away in Nazareth, has focused too much on the misleading dichotomies between Hellenism and Judaism, urban and rural. Chapter five summarizes the archaeological evidence for Capernaum, and rather than focusing on the authenticity of Saint Peter's house and the date of the synagogue, as is typical, examines Capernaum in light of its domestic architecture and regional context. As Capernaum was a large fishing and agricultural village at the lower end of the socio-economic scale, the site's location on the Sea of Galilee, in close proximity to Philipp's territory and regions populated by Gentiles, but far from Antipas's centers of power, shaped considerable portions of the Gospel traditions.

Part three shifts the methodological sequence. While previous chapters moved from Galilean archaeology to historical Jesus research, those in part three begin with texts and situate them in the Galilee, as reconstructed by archaeology. Chapter six attempts to locate the Sayings Gospel Q and its community in Galilee, and shows how the situations in Galilee, as articulated from the archaeological record, work themselves out in the text. Chapter seven illustrates how an awareness of the specific Galilean context helps illuminate interpretation and guide exegesis. By noting some of the regional Galilean history underlying the Sign of Jonah passage (Q 11:29–32), notably Jonah's connections to Gath-Heper in Galilee, this chapter concludes with many other seemingly northern epic references in Q that are suitable to a Galilean setting.

## PART ONE

CHAPTER 2

# The Identity of the Galileans: Ethnic and Religious Considerations[*]

## Scholarly Alternatives for the Galileans' Identity

Discovering the identity of the Galileans in the first century underlies any study of the historical Jesus and reconstruction of Christian origins. While an earlier generation debated the issue under the shadow of Nazi racial theories and scurrilous attempts at an Aryan Jesus, the recent discussion's impetus is the recognition of diversity in early Judaism and the role of regionalism as a factor in historical reconstruction.[1] The present study is indebted to both of these recognitions and is much less concerned with the Galileans' racial identity in genetic or biological terms, but focuses rather on the Galileans' ethnic identity in terms of their socialized patterns of behavior, including religious aspects embedded in this behavior.[2] Ethnic groups

---

[*] This chapter is a substantial revision and elaboration of my earlier "Galileans, 'Israelite Village Communities,' and the Sayings Gospel Q," in *Galilee: Confluence of Cultures* (ed. Eric Meyers; Winona Lake, Indiana: Eisenbrauns, 1999) 87–108.

1. The most offensive attempt to remove Jesus' Jewishness was Walter Grundmann's *Jesus der Galiläer und das Judentum* (Leipzig: Wigand, 1940). On the history of scholarship in general, see Hans-Dieter Betz, "Wellhausen's Dictum 'Jesus was not a Christian, but a Jew' in Light of Present Scholarship," *ST* 45 (1991) 83–100. The regional approach to Galilee was pioneered by Eric Meyers, "Galilean Regionalism as a Factor in Historical Reconstruction," *BASOR* 220/221 (1975–76) 93–101; and "The Cultural Setting of Galilee: The Case of Regionalism and Early Judaism," *ANRW* 2.19.1 (1979) 686–702.

2. See R. Cohen, "Ethnicity: Problem and Focus in Anthropology," *Annual Review of Anthropology* 7 (1978) 379–403; and the articles in Stephen Shennan, *Archaeological Approaches to Cultural Identity* (London: Unwin Hyman, 1989).

are typically conscious of descent, and the post-exilic laws concerning inter-marriage heightened this sense in Judaism. Ethnicity, however, is not simply a matter of genetics, but a concept that reflects the symbols and behaviors with which a group defines itself and distinguishes itself from others. The previous debate over the Galileans' identity has, for the most part, revolved primarily around descent, by focusing on the significance of the Hasmonean annexation of Galilee at the end of the second century B.C.E. and the racial identity of its prior inhabitants. Whether or not the Hasmoneans were enthusiastically received or bitterly resented turns on whether its inhabitants are construed as Gentile, Jewish, or "Israelite," a question that has been dis-puted by scholars for some time. Rather than focusing diachronically and exclusively on descent, this study will also attend to synchronic aspects of the Galilean question and will examine the artifacts and behaviors with which Galileans defined themselves and distinguished themselves after the Hasmonean conquest. The importance of this issue for New Testament studies cannot be underestimated, since its answer determines how Galilee-Jerusalem relations are envisioned at the time of Jesus, the significance of Jesus' visit to the Temple, and ultimately, his death.

Of the various approaches to the Galileans' identity, one has been to argue that Galilee was essentially Jewish in the first century, either because it was already inhabited by Jews prior to the Hasmonean annexation, or because they colonized and populated it with Judeans.[3] Either way, the implications for the historical Jesus are clear: Galileans were Jews and, as such, one of their most powerful and persuasive religious symbols was the Temple in Jerusalem. Along with whatever socio-political functions the Temple apparatus held in Jerusalem's relationship with Galilee, Galileans viewed Jerusalem and the Temple as a sort of axis mundi, and pilgrimage was not uncommon.[4] Criticism of the institution was certainly possible, as the earlier Israelite prophets demonstrated, but this was because of a sense of social exploitation or perceived failures of the system, and not the cen-trality of Jerusalem.[5]

---

3. The first sustained argument for a Jewish population in Galilee was made by Samuel Klein, *Galilaea vor der Makkabäerzeit* (Palästina-Studien 4; Berlin: Menorah, 1928). See more recently Seán Freyne, *Galilee from Alexander to Hadrian: A Study of Second Temple Judaism* (Wilmington, Delaware: Michael Glazier, 1980) 43–44; and "Bandits in Galilee: A Contribution to the Study of Social Conditions in First-Century Palestine," in *The Social World of Formative Christianity and Judaism* (ed. J. Neusner et al.; Philadelphia: Fortress, 1988) 50–68.

4. Joachim Jeremias, *Jerusalem zur Zeit Jesu. Eine kulturgeschichtliche Untersuchung zur neutestamentlichen Zeitgeschichte* (3rd ed.; Göttingen: Vandenhoeck & Ruprecht, 1969) 66–98; and Freyne, *Galilee*, 259–304 and "Galilee-Jerusalem Relations according to Josephus' *Life*," *NTS* 33 (1987) 600–609.

5. Seán Freyne, *Galilee, Jesus and the Gospels: Literary Approaches and Historical Investigations* (Philadelphia: Fortress, 1988) 178–190, 224–239.

Alternatively, pre-Hasmonean Galilee has been construed as essentially Gentile. At the turn of this century, Emil Schürer argued for a primarily Iturean population in Galilee, which converted to Judaism under Hasmonean coercion in the late second century B.C.E.[6] His influence is explicit in such works as Walter Bauer's "Jesus der Galiläer," and seems to be implicit in several recent studies that accentuate a more cosmopolitan and syncretistic Galilee.[7] This position implies a fundamental hostility between Galilee and Jerusalem, in which the former's inhabitants would ignore, resent, or mock the latter's claims of centrality. In this view, Jesus' critique of the Temple would represent the fundamental division between Galilee and Jerusalem, as Bauer explains: "Der Tempel ist ihm in seinen letzten Tagen Kampfplatz, nicht Stätte der Anbetung." ("For him, the Temple is in his last days a place of conflict, not a place of worship.")[8]

Albrecht Alt pioneered a third hypothesis a generation ago that assumed that a good portion of the Northern Kingdom's population survived the Assyrian conquest and deportations of the late eighth century B.C.E. in Galilee, and cultivated its own traditions over the centuries there.[9] Richard Horsley has recently given a socio-economic spin to this position, noting "that during second-temple times most inhabitants of Galilee were descendants of the northern Israelite peasantry."[10] This thesis implies that Jesus and his first Galilean followers stood in the northern prophetic tradition calling for the revitalization of Israelite village communities and a return to covenantal principles as a means of redressing social, political, and economic injustices. Their antagonism toward Jerusalem, articulated in Q 11:49–51 and 13:34–35, stems from the pervasive Galilean hostility toward outside rule, and from their role as inheritors of the ancient northern prophetic critique of Jerusalem.

The diversity of scholarly opinion on the Galileans' identity in the first century is due in large part to the meager evidence in the literature, which

---

6. *The History of the Jewish People in the Time of Jesus Christ, I–III* (rev. and ed. by Geza Vermes et al.; Edinburgh: Clark, 1973–87) 1.142; 216–218; 561–73.

7. Walter Bauer, "Jesus der Galiläer," reprinted in *Aufsätze und Kleine Schriften* (ed. Georg Strecker; Tübingen: J. C. B. Mohr [Paul Siebeck], 1967) 91–108; more recently, see Burton Mack, *The Lost Gospel: The Book of Q and Christian Origins* (San Francisco: HarperSanFrancisco, 1993) 51–68.

8. Bauer, "Jesus der Galiläer," 102–3.

9. "Zur Geschichte der Grenze zwischen Judäa und Samaria" and "Galiläische Probleme," reprinted in *Kleine Schriften zur Geschichte des Volkes Israel II* (München: C. H. Beck'sche, 1959) 346–362, 363–435; see also Francis Loftus, "The Anti-Roman Revolts of the Jews and the Galileans," *JQR* 68 (1977) 78–98.

10. Horsley, *Galilee: History, Politics, People* (Valley Forge, Pennsylvania: Trinity Press International, 1995) 40 (italics mine); and *Archaeology, History and Society in Galilee: The Social Context of Jesus and the Rabbis* (Valley Forge, Pennsylvania: Trinity Press International, 1996).

includes only scattered hints in or inferences from the scant textual evidence of the Hasmonean annexation, and the problems of using literature written well after the events they describe as evidence for the Galileans' identity. Each of the few relevant texts relating to the Hasmonean annexation is dubious. The Maccabean books project the ideals of Davidic kingship, deuteronomistic theology, and biblical phraseology onto the Hasmonean expansion, which cannot be assumed as a model for the situation in Galilee.[11] Josephus's account that Aristobolus permitted Itureans to remain (in Galilee?) only if they circumcised themselves and obeyed Jewish laws is cited from Strabo, who in turn relies on Timagenes (*Ant.* 13.318–19).[12] Those texts that describe the "Galileans" in the first century offer little help in characterizing Galilean ethnicity. Josephus uses the term "Galileans" so inconsistently and ambiguously that no single explanation of its meaning has won scholarly consensus. Numerous scholars hold that it refers to a particular group during the revolt without any geographic connotations, though likely "the Galileans" in Josephus's *Life* refer primarily to his militant supporters from Galilee, while in his *War* they refer primarily to the inhabitants of Galilee in general.[13]

Early Christian traditions arising in a Galilean setting assume the identity of the Galileans as self-evident and do not comment on their religious or ethnic identity. When the Gospels, which probably all were written outside of Galilee, compose these traditions into a coherent whole, they foist literary or theological schemes onto the traditions that mention "Galilee" and "the Galileans." Regardless of whether Mark's division between Galilee and Jerusalem represents two traditions within early Christianity, or the likelihood that it is a literary device, clues for the Galileans' identity can hardly be teased out of his Gospel. Much the same can be said of the other synoptic Gospels, and certainly Luke's geographical scheme heavily redacted the tradition, which belies any attempts to uncover Galilean identity. The role of "the Galileans" in John is much like the problem of his use of "the Jews," on occasion archetypal and theological, at other times reflective of memories in the tradition. Distinguishing the two is troublesome.

The late or uncertain date of the rabbinic texts renders them especially problematic for describing the Galileans in Second Temple times. Facile attempts to interpret the *'Amei-Ha-aretz* as Galileans fail to take into consideration

---

11. Seth Schwartz, "Israel and the Nations Roundabout: 1 Maccabees and the Hasmonean Expansion," *JJS* 41 (1991) 16–38; and Horsley, *Galilee*, 40.

12. A. K. M. Adam, "According to whose Law?: Aristobolus, Galilee and the *nomoi ton Ioudaion*," *JSP* 1996 (14) 15–21.

13. Freyne, "The Galileans in the Light of Josephus' *Vita*," *NTS* 26 (1980) 397–413. Solomon Zeitlin argued that "Galileans" has no geographic connotation whatsoever, "Who were the Galileans? New Light on Josephus' Activities in Galilee," *JQR* (64 (1974) 189–203); similarly Francis Loftus, "A Note on σύνταγμα τῶν Γαλιλαίων B.J. iv 558," *JQR* 65 (1974) 182–83.

the complex socio-economic aspects apparent in the use of this term and its development over time. The derogatory term was applied to some Jews in Galilee because they did not adhere to what the rabbis deemed normative purity concerns (e.g., *b. Hag.* 24b), and, as time went on, for their alleged ignorance of Torah (*b. Erub.* 53a/b; *b. Meg.* 24b). That this pejorative accurately reflects the populace of all Galilee, however, is doubtful. More likely, it functioned socio-economically as part of the condescending attitude of some wealthier urban rabbis toward Jewish rural peasants.[14] What is implausible, however, is that the term is synonymous with Galileans.

Because of the problems with the literary evidence, the present study on the Galileans' identity in the first century focuses primarily on the archaeological evidence, which is often neglected. The literary sources are not ignored, but are addressed only tangentially, and after an analysis of the archaeological data. This study will look at the Galileans' ethnic identity by considering what the archaeological record tells about their descent, in terms of the settlement patterns leading up to the Early Roman Period, and about their socialized patterns of behavior and use of artifacts, with which Galileans distinguished themselves from other groups in the first century C.E. The scope expands beyond the Hasmonean annexation to the *longue duree* of Galilean history, from the Iron Age through the Roman Periods, in order to assess diachronic aspects relating to settlement patterns and the first-century Galileans' origins. It also focuses synchronically on the material culture of the Galileans of the Early Roman Period in terms of their identity markers.

The first part of this study surveys the settlement patterns of Galilean sites from the Iron Age through the Roman Period, which reveal an almost complete abandonment of the region at the close of the Iron Age, essentially ruling out any direct continuity between the northern Israelites and the first-century Galileans. The second part describes the sudden rise in the number of sites in a sparsely populated Galilee beginning in the Late Hellenistic Period, as well as the increase in overall material culture recovered by archaeologists beginning at this time. Since Early Roman Period Galilee and Judea share indicators of Jewish religious identity in their material cultures, this increase can be linked to a Judean colonization of a scarcely inhabited

---

14. For a complete analysis summary of the issues, see Aharon Oppenheimer, *The 'Am Ha-Aretz: A Study in the Social History of the Jewish People in the Hellenistic-Roman Period* (Leiden: E. J. Brill, 1977). See also Lee Levine, *The Rabbinic Class of Roman Palestine in Late Antiquity* (New York: Jewish Theological Seminary of America, 1989); Shaye J. D. Cohen, "The Place of the Rabbi in Jewish Society of the Second Century," in *The Galilee in Late Antiquity* (ed. Lee Levine; New York: Jewish Theological Seminary of America, 1992) 157–73; and the keen insights by Gildas Hamel, *Poverty and Charity in Roman Palestine, First Three Centuries C.E.*, (Near Eastern Studies 23; Berkeley: University of California, 1990) 202–206.

Galilee.[15] Stone vessels, stepped pools, burial practices, and a diet without pork make up the archaeological profile of sites in both Judea and Galilee. Even if the material culture cannot reveal the Galileans' religious attitudes, such as loyalty to Jerusalem or devotion to the Temple, this shared profile points to a common heritage and means to distinguish them as a group over against others. The third part of this study briefly reads several key literary texts alongside the archaeological record, which likewise attest to an extensive Judean colonization of a scarcely inhabited Galilee beginning in the first century B.C.E. Finally, some implications for historical Jesus research and specifically the sayings tradition will be sketched at the conclusion of this chapter. *In nuce*, the ties between Galilee and Jerusalem must be taken into consideration in any discussion on the historical Jesus: 1) implements relating to purity were common to both Galilee and Judea; 2) Jesus' actions in the Temple represented some "in house" dynamics; and 3) the "northern" prophetic aspects in the tradition do not imply genealogical continuity with the northern Israelites, but rather illustrate the imaginative creativity of early Christianity in fashioning their own communal identity.

## Archaeology and Galilean Settlement Patterns

The Assyrian Conquest and Northern Israelite Survivors

The debate over the identity of the first-century Galileans has its point of departure with the Assyrian advances into Palestine in the late eighth century B.C.E. Any alleged continuity between Galileans at the time of Jesus and the northern Israelites of the Iron Age depends on a sufficient number of the latter surviving in Galilee the campaigns of the Assyrian king Tiglath-pileser III in 733–32 B.C.E. The meager textual evidence consists of 2 Kings 15 and a few Assyrian texts. The former offers only that Tiglath-pileser III conquered Hazor, as well as "Gilead and Galilee and the whole land of Naphthali," and that he led "the population into exile in Assyria" (2 Kings 15:29). The fragmentary Assyrian texts offer only the complete names of Hannathon and Merom, and four numbers of exiles from Galilee (625, 650, 656, and 13,520).[16] These texts leave unanswered precisely which cities were

---

15. See the cautious remarks on ethnicity by Eric Meyers, "Identifying Religious and Ethnic Groups through Archaeology," in *Biblical Archaeology Today, 1990* (eds. Avraham Biran and Joseph Aviram; Jerusalem: Israel Exploration Society, 1990) 738–45; see also William Dever, "The Impact of the New Archaeology," in *Benchmarks in Time and Culture. An Introduction to Palestinian Archaeology. Dedicated to Joseph A. Callaway* (eds. Joel Drinkard et al.; Atlanta: Scholars Press, 1988) 337–352.

16. Hayim Tadmor, *The Inscriptions of Tiglath-Pileser III King of Assyria: Critical Edition, with Introductions, Translations, and Commentary* (Fontes ad res Judaicas

destroyed, the location of those that are mentioned, and the extent of the deportations.

The past decades' archaeological surveys and excavations in Galilee, however, permit a more comprehensive analysis of the actual situation on the ground. Most significant is Zvi Gal's survey of the Lower Galilee, which, when coupled with the results of stratigraphic excavations in Upper and Lower Galilee, paint a picture of a totally devastated and depopulated Galilee in the wake of the Assyrian campaigns of 733/732 B.C.E.[17] The systematic collection of surface sherds in Gal's and others' archaeological field surveys provide a provisional picture of the entire region, which the results of each stratigraphic excavation to date have confirmed. Gal's surface survey of the Lower Galilee found no occupational evidence from the seventh and sixth centuries B.C.E. at any of the more than eighty sites inspected, that is to say, after Tiglath-pileser III's expedition. Conceding any reservations concerning the reliability of surveys, the lack of seventh-century surface sherds at any given site can perhaps be attributed to the surveyor's vagaries or the site's preservation history. But their lack at each and every site in such a large sample defies coincidence.

Two corollary aspects of Gal's survey verify a depopulated Galilee after the Assyrian invasion. First, while single-period sites existed from the twelfth through eighth centuries and subsequently in the fifth century, none have been found from the seventh or sixth centuries. If the Lower Galilee had been occupied after the Assyrian conquest, then one would expect considerable instability among its resettled sites, with some having been occupied briefly until settlement patterns stabilized. But not a single such short-lived site has been found. Second, the absence in Lower Galilee of any Assyrian style pottery or local imitations thereof starkly contrasts with their presence in Samaria and along the coast, areas that were populated in the seventh and sixth centuries.[18] Like Lower Galilee, surveys show that the Assyrians did not spare Upper Galilee, in spite of its less accessible terrain. Surface sherds from

spectantes; Jerusalem: Israel Academy of Sciences and Humanities, 1994); Bustenay Oded, "The Inscriptions of Tiglath-pileser III: Review Article," *IEJ* 47 (1997) 104–108; and Nadav Na'aman, "Population Changes in Palestine following Assyrian Deportations," *Tel Aviv* 20 (1993) 104–106. Bustenay Oded has stressed the reliability of the figures in the Assyrian bureaucratic lists, and has noted how they include all classes, *Mass Deportation in the Neo-Assyrian Empire* (Wiesbaden: Reichert, 1979) 6–16.

17. *The Lower Galilee during the Iron Age* (ASOR Dissertation Series 8; Winona Lake, Indiana: Eisenbrauns, 1992); and "The Lower Galilee in the Iron Age II: Analysis of Survey Material and its Historical Interpretation," *Tel Aviv* 15–16 (1988–1989) 56–64.

18. A point that also confirms Gal's ceramic chronology upon which a deserted Galilee is based, *The Lower Galilee during the Iron Age*, 82.

after 732 B.C.E. can be confirmed at only one site surveyed by the Meiron Excavation Project in the late seventies, Gush Ḥalav.[19] A more recent survey of the Upper Galilee by Mordechai Aviam reports limited evidence for the Persian Period in Upper Galilee and a significant resettlement only in the Hellenistic period.[20]

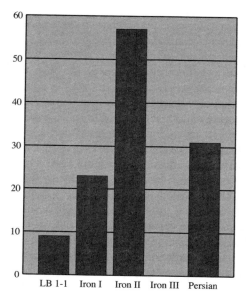

*Table 2.1 Sites per Period in Lower Galilee*

The stratigraphic excavations in Galilee confirm its abandonment in the seventh and sixth centuries. Conflagration layers at the end of the eight century B.C.E. cover many sites in and around the Galilee, a phenomenon attributed to the Assyrian conquest. The major urban sites south of Galilee—Megiddo and Beth-Shean—were radically reduced in size. An Assyrian style administrative building along with modest domestic

---

19. The Meiron Project uses the designation "Iron 2" for the period 1000–586 B.C.E., and lists sherds from this period at three sites, Beer Sheba, Yodefat, and Gush Ḥalav, Eric Meyers et al., "The Meiron Excavation Project: Archaeological Survey in Galilee and Golan, 1976," *BASOR* 230 (1978) 1–24. However, not all sites contain sherds from what Gal calls Iron III, that is to say 733–586 B.C.E. The current excavations at Yodefat report no seventh or sixth centuries B.C.E. evidence from their stratigraphic excavations. David Adan-Bayewitz and Mordechai Aviam, "Iotapata, Josephus, and the Siege of 67: Preliminary Report on the 1992–94 Seasons," *JRS* 10 (1997) 131–165. Beer Sheba is very likely not from the seventh or sixth century, which has only been confirmed in stratigraphic excavations at Gush Ḥalav, which is exceptional in Galilee.

20. Mordechai Aviam, "Galilee," *NEAEHL* 2.453.

dwellings was rebuilt at Megiddo, and smaller sites were resettled toward the coastal plain near Megiddo (e.g., Tel Qashish, Tel Qiri, and Tel Jokneam), but these lie well outside of Galilee.[21] Tel Chinnereth, on the northern shore of the Sea of Galilee at the eastern extremity of Galilee, and Hazor, in the Huleh Valley, also were destroyed at the end of the eight century B.C.E. Possible Assyrian administrative buildings were then built, but without any evidence of a surrounding population.[22] In the Galilean heartland, however, every single excavated site, including Tel Qarnei-Hittin and Gath-Hepher in eastern Lower Galilee, Tel Mador abutting the Acco Plain, and Tel Harashim in Upper Galilee, was destroyed or abandoned at the end of the eighth century. Other Iron Age sites that have been excavated in Galilee, such as the villages of Tel el-Wawiyat, Sasa, and Tel 'Ein-Zippori along the Beth Netofah Valley, as well as the Phoenician fortress at Horvat Rosh Zayit, were already abandoned in earlier periods.[23] Nor have excavators of the many Roman-Byzantine sites in Galilee published evidence, whether pottery, small finds, or architectural structures, that could be dated to the two centuries following the Assyrian campaigns, though pottery from the Bronze and Iron I Ages has often been found. This list includes the excavations at Beth She'arim, Capernaum, Chorazin, Hammath Tiberias, Horvat Arbel, Yodefat, Khirbet Shema', Meiron, Nabratein, Nazareth, and Tiberias. Only Gush Halav's few sherds, from fill in a Late Roman tomb, and one or two isolated structures near Hazor and on Tel Chinnereth, exist as evidence for the period in question. This should not obscure the fact, however, that the labor of all the excavations and surveys in Galilee to date has produced literally only a handful of possible seventh- and sixth-century sherds.[24]

---

21. Amihai Mazar, "Beth-Shean," *OEANE* 1.308; David Ussishkin, "Megiddo," *OEANE* 3.467–68; and Larry Herr, "The Iron Age II Period: Emerging Nations," *BA* 60 (1997) 167–168.

22. At Tel Chinnereth, it is difficult to determine the date of the structure; it could be Babylonian or Persian as well, Volkmar Fritz, *Kinneret, Ergebnisse der Ausgrabungen auf dem Tell el-'Oreme am See Gennesaret 1982–1985* (Wiesbaden: Otto Harrassowitz, 1990) 18; and Amnon Ben-Tor, "Hazor," OEANE 3.4–5.

23. Gal, *Lower Galilee during the Iron Age*, 36–47; Beth Zakkai, "Tell el-Wawiyat," *NEAEHL* 4.1500–1501; Carol Meyers, "Sepphoris and Lower Galilee: Earliest Times through the Persian Period," in *Sepphoris in Galilee* (Winona Lake, Indiana: Eisenbrauns, 1996) 15–19; J. P. Dessel, "Tel 'Ein Zippori," *OEANE* 2.227–28; Gal, "Horvat Rosh Zayit," *NEAHL* 4.1289–90; for Tel Harashim and Sasa, see Gal, "Galilee," *NEAEHL* 2.451.

24. At Gush Halav, the excavators are clear that not much evidence, and no structures, have been found for the end of the Iron Age (*Gush Halav*, 124). A surface survey of Shikhin has found a few pottery sherds that could be either eighth or possibly seventh century; the survey found virtually no sherds from the Iron Age 2C/3 when compared to the later Hellenistic and Roman periods, and the one sherd in question (drawn as fig. 18, 178) is parallel to seventh-century levels at Tanaach, but is also present there in eighth-century assemblages, James F. Strange et al., "Excavations at Sepphoris. The Location and Identification of Shikhin, Part II," *IEJ* 45 (1995) 171–187.

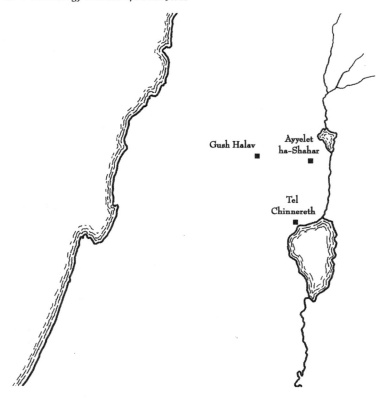

*Figure 2.1 Possible Iron III Sites in Galilee*

There was simply an insufficient amount of material culture in Galilee following the campaigns of Tiglath-pileser III for serious consideration of any cultural continuity between the Iron Age and subsequent periods. The Galilean ceramic traditions show no continuity between the pre-732 B.C.E. and later periods, whose forms and types are derived from elsewhere and closely parallel those of Judea in the Hellenistic and Roman Periods. There are no villages, no hamlets, no farmsteads, nothing at all indicative of a population that could harvest the Galilean valleys for the Assyrian stores, much less sustain cultural and religious traditions through the centuries.

After Tiglath-pileser's campaign, Assyria established the provincial capital at Megiddo to the southwest of Galilee, which was rebuilt and repopulated. Only on the fringes of Galilee have modest military or administrative outposts been found near Hazor at Ayelet ha-Shahar and at Tel Chinnereth. Both are without any significant domestic areas and were abandoned after Babylon broke Assyrian domination. Neither continued through the Persian

Period into the Late Hellenistic or Early Roman Period.[25] After the Assyrian campaigns one perhaps can imagine the presence of some way stations north of the lake along a road, with a branch crossing through Galilee at Gush Ḥalav's, but there is no archaeological evidence for an indigenous population in the centuries after 733/2 B.C.E.

| | Iron I | Iron II | Iron III | Pers. | Hell I | Hell II | ER | MR-LR |
|---|---|---|---|---|---|---|---|---|
| Sasa | ● | | | | | | ? | ? |
| Tell el-Wawiyat | ● | | | | | | | |
| Tel 'Ein-Zippori | ● | ● | | | | | | |
| Tel Qarne-Hittin | | ● | | | | | | |
| Tel Mador | | ● | | | | | | |
| H. Rosh Zayit | | ● | | | | | | |
| Tel Chinnereth | ● | ● | ● | ? | ? | | | |
| Ayelet ha- Shahar | | | ? | ? | | | | |
| Tel Harashim | ● | ● | | ? | ? | | | |
| Hazor | ● | ● | | ? | ? | | | |
| Bethsaida | ● | ● | | ? | ? | | | |
| Gush Ḥalav | ● | ● | ● | ● | ● | ● | ● | ● |
| Capernaum | ● | | | ? | | ● | ● | ● |
| Nazareth | ● | ? | | | | ? | ● | ● |
| Sepphoris | | ? | | | ● | ● | ● | ● |
| Tel Anafa | | | | ? | ● | ● | ● | |
| Gamla | | | | | | ● | ● | |
| Yodefat | | | | | | ● | ● | |
| Khirbet Shema' | | | | | | ● | ? | ● |
| Hammath Tiberias | | | | | | ● | ● | ● |
| Meiron | | | | | | ● | ● | ● |
| Qatzrin | | ? | | | | ● | ● | ● |
| Ḥorvat Arbel | | | | | | ● | ● | ● |
| Nabratein | | | | | | | ● | ● |
| Beth She'arim | | | | | | | ● | ● |
| Chorazin | | | | | | | ● | ● |
| Tiberias | | | | | | | ● | ● |

*Table 2.2 Strata from Excavated Sites in Galilee*

A totally depopulated Galilee is in no way at odds with Assyrian imperial policies. The Assyrian documentary evidence on mass deportation reveals policy variation from region to region and over time, and deportation was never restricted to a single class. Very often the lower classes, including peasants and manual laborers, were deported from peripheral regions to Assyria

---

25. Ruth Amiran and Immanuel Dunayevski, "The Assyrian Open Court Building and Its Palestinian Derivates," *BASOR* 149 (1958) 25–32; Volkmar Fritz, "Die Paläste während der assyrischen, babylonischen und persischern Vorherrschaft in Palästina," *MDOG* 111 (1979) 63–74; and Ronny Reich, "The Persian Building at Ayyelet ha-Shahar: The Assyrian Palace of Hazor?" *IEJ* 25 (1975) 233–37.

proper or other provinces for agricultural labor.[26] The Assyrians had an intense interest in southern Palestine, which served as a military base facing Egypt, the western terminus for spice trade, and a center for olive oil industries, as the excavations at Tel Miqne (Ekron) have brought to light.[27] The Assyrians also patronized the Phoenician maritime trade along the coast, so that Megiddo was oriented primarily toward the south and the coast, while Galilee, which did not figure in the Assyrians' resettlement plans, was neglected and deserted.[28] Assyrian geopolitics make sense out of the stratigraphic excavations' post-732 vacuum, which corroborate Gal's conclusion that Lower Galilee was deserted, a conclusion that can be extended to the entire Galilee. To summarize the situation with Gal's words:

> The events of 732/732 B.C.E. provide a tragic landmark in the history of Israelite settlement in Galilee, particularly Lower Galilee. This was an extremely violent and almost total destruction. Whatever had not been destroyed by the wars was removed or laid waste by the exiles, and the region was not occupied during the seventh and sixth centuries B.C.E.[29]

The Iturean Hypothesis and the Galileans' Alleged Gentile Origins

The absence of Galilean settlements for over a century after the conquest of Tiglath-pileser III rules out the hypothesis of an Israelite village culture spanning the Iron Age to Roman Periods. The position of Alt and its revival by Horsley must be abandoned. The two remaining hypotheses, that of a Gentile population, likely Iturean, converted by the Hasmoneans,

---

26. Oded, *Mass Deportation*, 22 and 91. Horsley incorrectly assumes, without any evidence for Galilee, that the situation there was analogous to that in Samaria, where in fact only the upper classes were deported, *Galilee*, 25–29; and *Archaeology, History, and Society in Galilee*, 21–24. Since the number and classes of deportees varied within each region and between regions, the Samaritans and the Galileans do not have analogous histories.

27. Seymour Gitin, "Tel Miqne-Ekron: A Type Site for the Inner Coastal Plain in the Iron II Period," in *Recent Excavations in Israel: Studies in Iron Age Archaeology* (AASOR 49; eds. Seymour Gitin and William Dever; Winona Lake, Indiana: Eisenbrauns, 1989) 59–79.

28. Eliezer Oren, "Ethnicity and Regional Archaeology: The Western Negev under Assyrian Rule," *Biblical Archaeology Today, 1990*, 102–105; Nadav Na'aman, "The Brook of Egypt and Assyrian Policy on the Border of Egypt," *Tel Aviv* 6 (1979) 68–90; and "Population Changes," 104–106.

29. Gal, *Lower Galilee during the Iron Age*, 108. Gal notes also that the legible numbers in the fragmentary Assyrian texts (the largest being 13,520) would have represented a substantial portion of the Galilean population, *Lower Galilee during the Iron Age*, 109. The paucity of Assyrian administrative documents dealing with Galilee confirms its insignificance and indirectly suggests its desertion.

or alternatively a Jewish population settling Galilee from Judea, remain to be evaluated in light of the archaeological data. Archaeological surveys and excavations show that, after lying uninhabited following the Assyrian conquest, Galilee began to be settled during the Persian and Early Hellenistic Periods, albeit only sparsely. Persian administrative and economic interests concentrated along the coast and along the fertile Jezreel Valley. Surface surveys show how several small rural settlements arose during the Persian Period in the Jezreel Valley, and the Zeno Papyri and Ḥefẓi Bah Inscription attest to some small settlements of peasant farmers, perhaps working royal estates in the larger valleys during the Early Hellenistic Period.[30]

Only a modest pattern of settlement can be detected in Galilee during the Persian and Late Hellenistic Period, with several very small sites clustered in the valleys, perhaps centrally administered out of Sepphoris. The Galilee's Persian Period sites are almost all less than a single hectare and are mostly scattered around the fertile Beth Netofah Valley.[31] Since few architectural remains have been uncovered, the material culture is difficult to describe. Their concentration, especially along the Naḥal Zippori, points to an agricultural basis, and since thatch and mud houses simply leave fewer traces than ashlar constructions with sturdy foundations would have, one assumes a rural, peasant existence. Lacking metal workers, stone cutters, or mints, these hamlets left virtually no small finds nor coins. Since these villages had no ability to trade, imported items are almost entirely lacking at these Galilean sites. In contrast, at coastal sites during this period, fine imported Greek pottery, particularly luxury wares, perfumed oil flasks and wine-related vessels begin to appear in quantity at some fortified ports, including Dor, Acco, and Shiqmona, which protected Persian mercantile interests.[32] Although neither architectural structures nor Greek imported pottery from the Persian Period have been recovered at Sepphoris, two finds, a drinking

---

30. Nehemia Zori, "An Archaeological Survey in the Beth-Shean Valley," *The Beth-Shean Valley: The Seventeenth Archaeological Convention* (Jerusalem: Israel Exploration Society, 1962) 135–198 [Hebrew]; *The Land of Issachar: An Archaeological Survey* (Jerusalem: Israel Exploration Society, 1977) [Hebrew]; and Martin Hengel, *Judaism and Hellenism: Studies in their Encounter in Palestine during the Early Hellenistic Period* (Philadelphia: Fortress, 1974) 39–47.

31. Gal, *Lower Galilee during the Iron Age*, 12–35. On the Persian Period in general, see Ephraim Stern, *The Material Culture of the Land of the Bible in the Persian Period 538–332 B.C.* (Warminster: Aris and Philips, 1982; and "Between Persia and Greece: Trade, Administration and Warfare in the Persian and Hellenistic Periods," in *The Archaeology of Society in the Holy Land* (ed. Thomas Levy; London: Leicester University Press, 1995) 432–45; see also Andrea Berlin, "Between Large Forces: Palestine in the Hellenistic Period," *BA* 60 (1997) 3–4.

32. Jane Waldbaum, "Greeks in the East or Greeks and the East? Problems in the Definition and Recognition of Presence," *BASOR* 305 (1997) 1–18.

rhyton and a multilingual inscription, suggest the presence of provincial elites and an administrative center.[33] The ornately decorated terra cotta drinking cup, its base shaped like a griffin, a symbol of the Achmemic ruling house of Persia, was modeled after gold and silver rhytons found in the Persian Empire in the fourth century B.C.E., which were popular among the upper classes. The inscription preserves the royal name Artaxerxes in Achaemenid, Babylonian, Elamite, and Egyptian scripts, attesting to administrative connections between Sepphoris and the broader Persian Empire. However, no architectural remains survive from the Persian Period at Sepphoris, though some sherds from this period have been found at the very top of the acropolis. One cannot imagine that the few thinly scattered finds represent an urban site, but the rhyton and the inscription hint that Sepphoris served as an outpost overlooking the fertile Beth Netofah valley and its traffic lanes, similar to what was at Megiddo or Beth-Yerach in the Jezreel Valley. None of these can be categorized as urban centers, however, which did not exist in Galilee under Persian administration. The scattered sherds from cooking pots or storage jars at sites indicate that Galilee was resettled during the Persian period; but other than their peasant character, little more can be said.

This general picture continues into the Early Hellenistic Period in Galilee, though several coastal sites, including Galilee's nearest port, Ptolemais, were being refounded as *poleis*. Elsewhere on Galilee's periphery *poleis* were founded, notably the short-lived Philoteria, and several Decapolis cities such as Scythopolis, Hippos, and Gadara. At larger urban sites such as Dor, Ptolemais, Samaria, and Scythopolis, there is an increase in the number of fine ceramic wares being imported from the Aegean, and in addition to other luxury items, there is considerable evidence for the importation of Rhodian and Kindian wines.[34] Nothing of the sort has been found in Galilee, and the archaeological evidence indicates that it remained demographically stagnant.[35] The Ḥefẓi Bah Inscription and the Zeno Papyri indicate that the emerging economic development in Palestine under the Ptolemies was making its presence felt around Galilee, especially on the coast, along the Jordan Valley, at Scythopolis, and in the Transjordan. The Ḥefẓi Bah inscription gives some indication of the diminutive agricultural

33. Rebecca Nagy et al., *Sepphoris in Galilee: Crosscurrents of Culture* (Raleigh, North Carolina: North Carolina Museum of Art, 1996) 162–63, 166–67.

34. Berlin, "Between Large Forces," 48. The pattern of Rhodian stamped handles described by Hengel, along the coast and in major inland cities, has in essence been confirmed after over two decades of additional excavations, *Judaism and Hellenism II*, 35 note 342.

35. F. L. Koucky has pointed to a climatic cycle that would have left the Persian and Late Hellenistic Periods in drought-like conditions, "The Regional Environment," in *The Roman Frontier in Central Jordan I* (BAR International Series 340[i]; ed. Thomas Parker; London: BAR, 1987) 11–40.

enterprise, when its author complains that billeting by small contingents of traveling administrators upset the profits that the ruler took from his villages.[36] The Zeno Papyri, which preserve a Ptolemaic official's notes from a visit to Palestine, show that considerable portions of land around Galilee were used as royal estates, or were "the king's land," and point to not insignificant amounts of grain, olive oil, and even wine being shipped back from the Transjordan to Egypt. Numerous scholars have assumed that Zeno's circuit led him through Galilee when he visited vineyards at a Beth Anath belonging to a district official named Apollonius, and have concluded that the Galilee was included in the thriving economy in Ptolemaic Palestine. However, the location of Beth Anath is uncertain and one only presumes it was in Galilee on the basis of some reconstructions of Zeno's itinerary. According to the surviving papyri, he disembarked at Straton's Tower, continued through Jerusalem to Jericho and into the Transjordan, where he inspected the Tobiad palace at Birtha ('Iraq el-Emir), then Philadelphia before returning to the port of Ptolemais. On the way from Philadelphia he stops to pick up provisions at three unknown sites named Lakasoi, Noei, Eitoui, then at Beth Anath, and finally at Kedesh (P. Cairo Zen. 59004). The latter site is well known, lying just beyond the border of Upper Galilee in the agricultural hinterland of the Phoenician coastal cities, which traditionally also included the Huleh Valley. Beth Anath was thus on the way from Kedesh to Ptolemais, right along the border of Upper Galilee, though its precise whereabouts are unknown.[37]

Settlement patterns at the time provide some significant data that has not been brought to bear on the question of Beth Anath's location. The entire swath of land from the Jordan River tributaries, the Huleh Valley, the lands just north of Upper Galilee, including Kedesh, and all the way to the Coastal Plain, shared a common pottery in the Hellenistic Period known as "spatter painted ware." Andrea Berlin has shown that this ware is Phoenician in origin and that the types are indicative of a distinctive culinary preference.[38] Evidence exists that this land was directly farmed for the king as royal land, and Zeno may have traveled back to Ptolemais taking the older

---

36. In lines 13 and 14, Yohanan H. Landau, "A Greek Inscription Found Near Hefzibah," *IEJ* 16 (1966) 54–70; and Berlin, "Between Large Forces," 14.

37. Hengel tends to include Galilee based on Beth Anath in the Ptolemaic activities elsewhere that he analyzes, *Judaism and Hellenism*, 39–47. On the location of Beth Anath, see G. Harper, "A Study in the Commercial Relations between Egypt and Syria in the Third Century before Christ," *AJP* 49 (1928) 1–35; Victor Tcherikower, "Palestine under the Ptolemies (A Contribution to the Study of the Zenon Papyri)," *Mizraim* 4–5 (1937) 9–90; and Félix-Marie Abel, "La liste géographique du papyrus 71 du Zénon," *RB* 32 (1923) 409–15. Albrecht Alt suggests it is *el-Eb'ene* in the *Sahl Battof*, "Hellenistische Städte und Domänen," in *Kleine Schriften*, 2:395.

38. "From Monarchy to Markets: The Phoenicians in Hellenistic Palestine," *BASOR* 306 (1997) 75–88.

(Assyrian) route from the Huleh Valley and the springs at Banias, to Kedesh, north of Gush Halav, and on to the coast. Zeno's visit to the viticultural village of Beth Anath, if located in Phoenician territory, would mean he did not travel through Galilee. In either case, the village was a settlement of agricultural workers and administrators who were tenants on the king's land, somewhere north of Upper Galilee, perhaps even in Upper Galilee, but there is no evidence elsewhere to suggest that Galilee participated fully in the Ptolemaic economic activities. Prior to Seleucid control, the area around Philoteria and Scythopolis, according to the Hefzi Bah inscription, was surrounded by small peasant villages whose villagers harvested large tracts of land for the crown. If similar settlements existed throughout Galilee as well, we do not know of them. In Upper Galilee several small sites began to be inhabited, but we lack any concrete evidence tying them to the Ptolemaic administration.[39]

As in the Persian Period, the ethnicity of the people inside Galilee in the Early Hellenistic Period is difficult to determine, since their material remains consist of only locally made utilitarian pottery. Whoever they were, they were poor and acquired little from the outside world by way of trade, in contrast to Galilee's urban neighbors along the coast and at some inland cities. They may, however, have been active in producing such produce as grain, olives, or even wine for the Ptolemaic rulers.

But is there any evidence to suggest that the few inhabitants of Galilee were Itureans? After the power vacuum left by the collapse of the Seleucid Empire in the second century B.C.E., considerable shifts in settlement patterns throughout the Levant occurred, including the northward expansion of the Hasmoneans and the southward movement of the Itureans. The Itureans originated in southern Lebanon and expanded toward the Hermon and northern Golan. There, archaeological evidence for the southward movement of the Itureans is clearly traceable through their distinct material culture in the Late Hellenistic Period.

Itorean settlements and architectural remains are characteristic of a pastoral group: the settlements are mostly small, unwalled farmsteads or nucleated farmsteads with simple single-room buildings made of field stones with enclosures for livestock. At the larger sites, temples in the tradition of Canaanite open-air *masseboth* were found. The pottery is a distinct brownish-pink, heavily tempered ware, somewhat clumsily made, which the excavators call "Golan" or "Iturean-ware."[40] Such settlement types and their

---

39. Aviam, "Galilee," *NEAEHL* 2.453.

40. Shimon Dar, "The History of the Hermon Settlements," *PEQ* 120 (1988) 26–44; for a typical site, see M. Hartel, "'Khirbet Zemel' 1985–6," *IEJ* 37 (1987) 270–2. For later epigraphic confirmation of the identification of these sites as pagan and Iturean, see Shimon Dar and Nikos Kokkinos, "The Greek Inscriptions from Senaim on Mount Hermon," *PEQ* 124 (1992) 9–25.

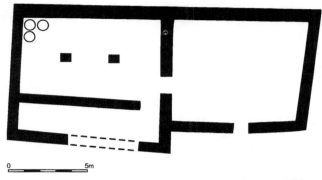

*Figure 2.2 Iturean Farmstead (Hartel 1987)*

pottery point to a semi-nomadic pastoral culture at its infancy in sedeta-rization. They have been found across the Hermon Range and the Lebanon Range, and even reaching the northern Golan, but they do not reach even Upper Galilee, nor the Golan proper, and no such sites nor even their pottery have been found in Lower Galilee. Hence Schürer's hypothesis that the Galileans were converted Itureans should be abandoned.[41]

### The Settlement of Galilee in the Late Hellenistic Period

Previous scholarship on the Galileans' identity in the first century has concentrated on the inhabitants in Galilee prior to the Hasmonean annexation at the end of the second century B.C.E. However, since the number of sites and the overall material culture is so meager prior to the late second and early first century B.C.E., who the few inhabitants of Galilee had been is less important than the fact that Hasmonean rule coincided with an increase in sites and population growth. During the Late Hellenistic Period, after the Hasmonean dynasty was established in Judea, many new sites began to be settled across Galilee and some also in the Golan that have a material culture paralleling Judea's. The Meiron Excavation Project reports a jump from zero to ten sites at this time out of a sample of twenty, and a more recent and comprehensive survey in Upper Galilee puts the number at thirty-nine

---

41. Dar, "The History of the Hermon Settlements," 26–44. On the instability of the Itureans and their southern expansion in the Early Hellenistic Period as reflected in the literary sources, see Willi Schottroff, "Die Ituräer," *ZDPV* 98 (1982) 125–52. Berlin states the case against Josephus (and Schürer) strongly: "There is, in fact, no evidence that this area [south of Hermon and northern Golan] ever came under Hasmonean political or economic control. Nor is there evidence for Iturean settlement in Galilee itself. These discrepancies suggest that Josephus misrepresented the conquests of Aristobolus," "Between Large Forces," 37.

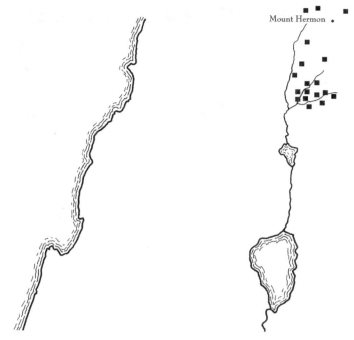

*Figure 2.3 Iturean Settlements (Hartel 1987)*

sites.[42] The vast majority of stratigraphically excavated sites from the Roman-Byzantine Period contain their earliest recoverable strata, that is to say the earliest architecture and first significant pottery assemblage, from the Late Hellenistic Period or first century B.C.E. This is the case at Capernaum, Hammath Tiberias, Horvat Arbel, Yodefat, Khirbet Shema', Meiron, Nazareth, and Sepphoris, and in the Golan at Qatzrin and Gamla.[43] One of the earliest traceable architectural structures at Sepphoris is a large military

---

42. Eric Meyers, et al., "The Meiron Excavation Project: Archaeological Survey in Galilee and Golan, 1976," *BASOR* 230 (1978) 7–8; Mordechai Aviam, "Galilee: The Hellenistic to Byzantine Periods," *NEAEHL* 2.453.

43. Meyers et al., *Excavations at Ancient Meiron, Upper Galilee, Israel 1971–72, 1974–75, 1977* (Cambridge, Massachusetts: American Schools of Oriental Research, 1981) 155; idem, *Ancient Synagogue Excavations at Khirbet Shema', Upper Galilee, Israel 1970–1972* (AASOR 42; Durham, North Carolina: ASOR, 1976) 2, 257; Moshe Dothan, *Hammath Tiberias: Early Synagogues and the Hellenistic and Roman Remains* (Jerusalem: Israel Exploration Society, 1983) 10; Z. Ilan, "Horvat Arbel," *ESI* 7–8 (1988–89) 8–9; and James F. Strange, "Nazareth," *ABD* 4.1051; idem, "Nazareth," *OEANE* 4.113–14. At a few sites, handfuls of earlier, fourth- or third-century sherds have also been found, but at insufficient levels for the excavators to label them as a stratum.

complex on the acropolis full of Jannaean coins, suggesting that the Hasmoneans fortified the site. The population of Galilee continued to increase through the Early Roman Period, and several stratigraphically excavated sites reveal initial settlement around the turn of the millennium or in the first century C.E. This is the case at Beth She'arim, Nabratein, Chorazin, and, of course, Herod Antipas's Tiberias.[44] Pottery counts from Sepphoris, as recorded by the University of South Florida excavation, most clearly illustrate the dramatic rise in material culture in the Late Hellenistic and Early Roman Periods. Virtually no sherds were collected from the Persian and Early Hellenistic Periods, but around 100 sherds were collected from the Late Hellenistic Period, and nearly 3,000 from the Early Roman Period, a pattern that is replicated at most sites in the Galilee.[45]

The numismatic profile of excavated sites in Galilee mirrors the increase in ceramics. Beginning in the early first century B.C.E., the number of coins proliferates, with an overwhelming Hasmonean, particularly Jannaean,

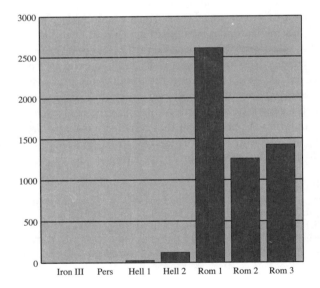

*Table 2.3 Pottery Counts at Sepphoris,*
*USF Excavations (Strange 1995)*

---

44. Yizhar Hirshfeld, "Tiberias," *NEAEHL* 4.1464–73; Meyers et al., "Preliminary Report on the 1980 Excavations at en-Nabratein, Israel," *BASOR* 244 (1981) 1–26; "Second Preliminary Report on the 1980 Excavations at en-Nabratein, Israel," *BASOR* 246 (1982) 35–54; and Zeev Yeivin, "Chorazin," *NEAEHL* 1.301–304.

45. James F. Strange et al., "Excavations at Sepphoris: The Location and Identification of Shikhin. Part II," *IEJ* 45 (1995) 180.

component.[46] The emergence of Hasmonean coinage at sites throughout Galilee points to its economic and political orientation toward Judea, a point especially apparent when Tyrian coinage is taken into account. The latter was dominant in the numismatic profile of Galilee throughout the Hellenistic and Roman Periods, as it was for the entire Levant, while Hasmonean coins were limited to sites around Judea, Galilee, and the Golan. Crucial is the consideration that Tyrian coins represented the larger denominations, didrachmas and tetradrachmas, while Hasmonean coinage was for the smallest denominations, the prutach. Thus the Tyrian coins were reserved for the realm of trade as well as the Temple economy, which required only an annual payment on the part of the populace, as well as hoarding by the wealthier. The Hasmonean prutachs, however, were used for bread or a grain dole, indicating that the Hasmonean coinage played a large role in the everyday lives of the masses.[47] This indicates that Galilee's population growth at this time was connected to Hasmonean policies.

A corollary to the Hasmonean settlement of Galilee is the destruction or abandonment of gentile sites between Judea and Galilee, and on Galilee's periphery. Hasmonean influence clearly spread out from Judea around the time of the Maccabean King Jannaeus in the first century B.C.E. His coins show up in excavated strata at previously gentile sites on the coast and central hill country.[48] Around this time, the thriving Idumean city of Marisa is in part destroyed and then abandoned, and more ominously, in spite of added fortifications, Gezer was destroyed and resettled by Jews who dug stepped pools into the houses that they resettled.[49] Hebrew-Greek bilingual boundary markers were erected around Gezer to delineate the area around the city as Jewish.[50] Conflagration layers dating to this period point to the

---

46. See, e.g., Meyers et al., *Ancient Synagogue Excavations at Khirbet Shema'*, 147–152; and *Excavations at Meiron*, 155.

47. Richard Hanson, *Tyrian Influence in the Upper Galilee* (Cambridge: ASOR, 1980); Dan Barag, "Tyrian Currency in Galilee," *INJ* 67 (1982–3) 7–13; and Joyce Raynor and Yaakov Meshorer, *The Coins of Ancient Meiron* (Winona Lake, Indiana: Eisenbrauns, 1988).

48. See Berlin, "Between Large Forces," 37–43. Such coins reflect either Judean colonization, or more likely an attempt to bring these people into the Hasmonean economic sphere. The former is argued by Shimon Applebaum, *Judea in Hellenistic and Roman Times: Historical and Archaeological Essays* (Leiden: E. J. Brill, 1989) 21, the latter by Aryen Kasher, *Jews and Hellenistic Cities in Eretz-Israel* (TSAJ 21; Tübingen: J. C. B. Mohr [Paul Siebeck], 1990) 142.

49. Amos Kloner, "Mareshah (Marisa)," *NEAEHL* 3:953; and Ronny Reich, "Archaeological Evidence of the Jewish Population at Hasmonean Gezer," *IEJ* 31 (1981) 48–52.

50. Ronny Reich, "The 'Boundary of Gezer' Inscriptions Again," *IEJ* 40 (1990) 43–46.

end of settlement at Shiqmona, Ashdod, Yavneh-Yam, and Strato's Tower on the coast, and Shechem and Mount Gerizim in Samaria.[51] Closer to Galilee, the city of Philoteria was abandoned after the Ptolemaic Period, not to be inhabited again until a Roman fort was built atop the ruins in the second century C.E. The Phoenician site of Tel Anafa was likewise deserted in the Late Hellenistic Period.[52] A small pagan shrine built in Syro-Egyptian style at Mount Mizpe Yammim on the border between Upper Galilee and the Tyrian plain was also abandoned in the late second century B.C.E.[53] It is fitting to interpret this archaeological evidence as a result of the instability caused by the Seleucid's waning control throughout the Levant, which is when the Hasmoneans expanded their rule northward and settled Galilee. The increase of sites in Galilee during the Late Hellenistic Period and the introduction of Hasmonean coinage there testify to the economic and political connections between Galilee and Jerusalem.

## Archaeology of Private Space in First Century Galilee

The Archaeological Indicators of Jewish Identity

The settlement history and the numismatic profile suggest that the Galileans were descendants of Judeans, a point that their socialized patterns of behavior left in the material culture indicate. The question of cultural influences, particularly the extent to which Palestine was Hellenized, is often discussed in archaeological terms by looking at a site's public architecture, the languages on public inscriptions, or civic decorative elements. But these tend to be more informative of the rulers' predilections than the populace's preferences, and are less significant for determining a region's ethnicity. The absence of pagan cultic sites or shrines in Galilee from the Late Hellenistic Period should not be ignored; it shows that the Hasmoneans did not tolerate public displays of paganism, and even under the Herodians none have been present, seemingly indicating their sensitivity to the general populace.[54]

---

51. Joseph Elgavish, *Archaeological Excavations at Shiqmona. Report Number 2. The Level of the Hellenistic Period—Stratum H* (Haifa: Museum of Art, 1974); Lee Levine, "The Hasmonean Conquest of Strato's Tower," *IEJ* 24 (1974) 62–69; and Berlin, "Between Large Forces," 31.

52. R. Hestrin, "Beth-Yerach," *NEAEHL* 1:255–259; on the identification of Philoteria with Beth-Yerach, see Douglas Edwards, "Beth-Yerach," *ABD* 1:699–700; Sharon Herbert, *Tel Anafa I. Final Report on Ten Years of Excavation at a Hellenistic and Roman Settlement in Northern Israel* (JRA Supplemental Series 10.1; Ann Arbor, Michigan: Kelsey Museum of Archaeology, 1994).

53. Rafael Frankel, "Har Mitspe Yamim 1988–9," *ESI* 9 (1989–90) 100–102.

54. This is more telling than the absence of pre-70 synagogues, which at this time might have met in public squares or private houses, Sidney Hoenig, "The

But all public architecture was built either by the local rulers or built with their permission, so that the population's socialized pattern of behavior is not easily determined by monumental architecture, nor even the overtly religious symbols or iconography on them, which are notoriously difficult to interpret. The Galileans' ethnic identity in the first century can best be determined by examining the material culture inside domestic or private space, since it indicates the populace's behavior and selection of artifacts. Patterns of artifacts inside of the indigenous population's houses, in realms of life that they determined within their economic abilities, provide the clearest data on ethnicity. How groups define themselves over against other groups is most clearly visible in private space.

The archaeological artifacts found in Galilean domestic space are remarkably similar to those of Judea. In particular, they share four indicators of Jewish religious identity: 1) the chalk vessels, 2) stepped plastered pools, 3) secondary burial with ossuaries in loculi tombs, and 4) bone profiles that lack pork. The first two items are particularly helpful because they are typically identified by field archaeologists and published.

Hand- or lathe-made chalk or soft limestone vessels, often referred to as stone vessels or Herodian stoneware, are easily identified in excavation. Literary evidence ties them to a concern for ritual purity, where, according to the Mishnah, vessels made of stone are deemed impervious to ritual impurity (e.g. *Kelim* 10:1). All types of stone vessels, such as bowls, basins, cups, or craters, that have been discovered were designed to hold liquids, or were lids for ceramic vessels, a possible means of avoiding contamination according to *Kelim* 2:1. They have been tied to priestly households and related to the Temple, pharisaic circles, and the washing of hands or, more broadly, are attributed to common Judaism; but regardless of their owners' intentions, they are ubiquitous in Jerusalem and Judea, Galilee and Golan. Frequently found in strata up to the first century C.E., they fade out of use in the early second century.[55]

Ancient City-Square: Forerunner of the Synagogue," *ANRW* 2.19.1 (1979) 448–76. This is not to imply that public architecture is unimportant for understanding first-century Galilee, especially socio-economic and political aspects, a topic to be discussed in the next chapter.

55. Yizhak Magen, *The Stone Vessel Industry in Jerusalem in the Days of the Second Temple* (Tel Aviv: Society for the Protection of Nature, 1988) [Hebrew]; "Jerusalem as a Center of the Stone Vessel Industry during the Second Temple Period," in *Ancient Jerusalem Revealed* (ed. Hillel Geva; Jerusalem: Israel Exploration Society, 1994) 244–256; Jane C. Cahill, "The Chalk Assemblages of the Persian/Hellenistic and Early Roman Periods," in *Excavations at the City of David 1978–1985 Directed by Yigal Shiloh III: Stratigraphical, Environmental, and Other Reports* (eds. Alon de Groot and Donald Ariel; Qedem 33; Jerusalem: Hebrew University Press, 1992) 190–274; and Roland Deines, *Jüdische Steingefäße und pharisäische Frömmigkeit. Ein archäologisch-historischer Beitrag zum Verständnis von Joh 2,6 und der jüdischen Reinheitshalacha zur Zeit Jesu* (WUNT ser. 2, vol. 56; Tübingen: J. C. B. Mohr [Paul Siebeck], 1993).

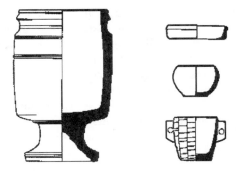

Figure 2.4 Stone Vessel Fragments (adapted from Magen 1988)

Figure 2.5 Stone Vessel, Jerusalem, Herodian period, 1st century B.C.E.–1st century C.E.
(© The Israel Museum, Jerusalem. Used by permission.)

Plastered stepped pools, most of which can be identified as Jewish ritual baths or *miqwaoth*, are another indicator of Jewish identity.[56] To date, well over 300 stepped immersion pools have been excavated in Palestine. They are most frequent in Judea, Galilee, and Golan, but relatively sparse along the

---

56. Ronny Reich, "Miqwaot (Jewish Ritual Baths) in the Second Temple Period and the Period of the Mishnah and Talmud," Ph.D. diss. (Hebrew University of Jerusalem, 1990) [Hebrew with English Abstract]; "The Hot Bath-House (*balneum*), the *Miqweh*, and the Jewish Community in the Second Temple Period," *JJS* 39

coast and virtually absent in Samaria.[57] Smaller ones are mostly located in larger and urban private houses, and larger pools are found near olive presses or in synagogues. Archaeologically speaking, *miqwaoth* are water installations from the Second Temple period, which are "cut or built into the ground, into which rainwater, spring waters, or runoff could be led, which had a staircase offering convenient access into the water, and which could be plastered to prevent leakage."[58] Like stone vessels, the rabbinic literature ties them to a concern for ritual purity. An entire tractate of the Mishnah, *Miqwa'ot*, is devoted to the details of how and when one should enter oneself, or immerse objects in a *miqweh*, or bathe in a natural body of water, in order to achieve ritual purification. Although many of the plastered pools excavated do not meet the rather strict standards set forth by the rabbis— some may not have an accompanying *otzar* or storage cistern, and others might not hold the required amount of water—there is no reason to dismiss the mass of stepped pools as not being indicative of Jewish inhabitants. Certainly the question as to whether these pools reflect a concern for ritual purity as expressed in the rabbinic literature is open to debate, as is the role of the Pharisees as advocates of such a practice. The Essenes' obsession with purity, and their many documents that criticize the practices of others, make it clear that while other Jewish groups were "doing it wrong," there is no doubt that they were "doing it."[59] The various Jewish groups share an underlying assumption about the importance and function of immersion and purity, though its exact interpretation and basic ritual prescriptions are in dispute. Reich's compilation and survey of the evidence convincingly shows that these installations are uniquely Jewish and are the artifactual

(1988) 102–107; "The Great Mikveh Debate," *BAR* 19 (1993) 52–53; and "Ritual Baths," *OEANE* 4.430–31. A convenient summary of the archaeology of *miqwaoth* and the textual evidence is found in E. P. Sanders, *Judaism: Practice and Belief 63 B.C.E.–66 C.E.* (Philadelphia: Trinity Press International, 1992) 222–229.

57. Yizhak Magen's suggestion that he possibly has found another, Samaritan *miqweh* does not seriously challenge Reich's conclusions, "The Ritual Baths (*Miqva'ot*) at Qedumim and the Observance of Ritual Purity Among the Samaritans," in *Early Christianity in Context: Monuments and Documents* (eds. Frédéric Manns and Eugenio Alliata; Jerusalem: Franciscan Printing Press, 1993) 181–192.

58. Reich, "Miqvaot (Jewish Ritual Baths) in the Second Temple Period," Ph.D. diss. (Hebrew University of Jerusalem, 1990) English Abstract, 5.

59. See Joseph M. Baumgarten, "The Purification Rituals in DJD 7," in *The Dead Sea Scrolls: Forty Years of Research* (eds. Devorah Dimant and Uriel Rappaport; Leiden/Jerusalem: E. J. Brill/Magnes/Yad Izhak Ben-Zvi, 1992) 199–209; "The Pharisaic-Sadducean Controversies about Purity and the Qumran Texts," *JJS* 31 (1980) 157–70; and Hannah Harrington, *The Impurity Systems of Qumran and the Rabbis* (SBLDS 143; Atlanta: Scholars Press, 1993).

correspondence to the Jewish ablutions prevalent in the literature of antiquity.[60] This is perhaps nowhere better illustrated than in the Late Hellenistic strata at Gezer, where, after the takeover and re-population of the site by the Maccabees, stepped pools were added to houses.[61]

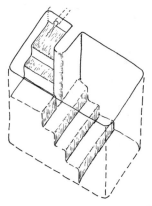

*Figure 2.6 Typical* Miqweh *(J. Rosenberg)*

The two additional indicators of Jewish religious identity used in this study, burial practices and dietary habits, are unfortunately less consistently excavated, recorded, or published. However, wherever they have been examined in Galilee, they confirm the basic parallels in material culture with Judea. Since burial practices are one of the most stable and enduring traditions in groups and are tied to religious beliefs, the parallels between Judean and Galilean burial are certainly significant. At the higher levels of socioeconomics, secondary burial using soft limestone ossuaries was common.

Placing ossuaries inside so-called *kokhim* or loculi, horizontally shafted underground family tombs, was a distinctly Jewish phenomenon at the end of the Second Temple Period. Although elements of burial practices from the broader Hellenistic and Semitic world were adopted, Jews combined these into secondary burial in *kokhim* with ossuaries "in such a way that they created burial customs and rites that are uniquely Jewish."[62]

60. On the connection between the (non-rabbinic) literature and the archaeological finds, see Benjamin Wright III, "Jewish Ritual Baths—Interpreting the Digs and the Texts: Some Issues in the Social History of Second Temple Judaism," in *The Archaeology of Israel: Constructing the Past, Interpreting the Present* (eds. Neil A. Silberman and David Small; JSOTSS 237; Sheffield: Sheffield Academic Press, 1997) 190–214.

61. Reich, "Archaeological Evidence of the Jewish Population at Hasmonean Gezer," *IEJ* 31 (1981) 48–52.

62. Rachel Hachlili and Ann Killebrew, "Jewish Funerary Customs during the Second Temple Period, in the Light of the Excavations at the Jericho Necropolis,"

*Figure 2.7 Ossuary of Joseph Bar Caiaphas, Jerusalem, 1st century C.E.
(© The Israel Museum, Jerusalem. Used by permission.)*

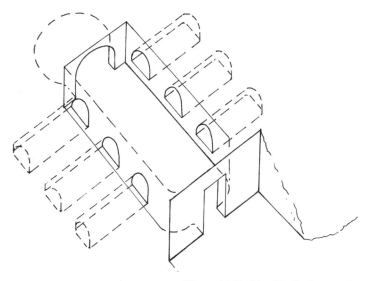

*Figure 2.8* Kochim *Tombs (J. Rosenberg)*

*PEQ* 115 (1983) 129; see also the valuable summaries by Byron McCane, "Ossuaries," *OEANE* 4.187–88; and "Burial Techniques," *OEANE* 1.386–7. Recent examples near Jerusalem are reported by Amos Kloner, "A Tomb with Inscribed Ossuaries in East Talpiyot, Jerusalem," *'Atiqot* 29 (1996) 15–22; and Samuel Wolff, "A Second Temple Period Tomb on the Shu'afat Ridge, North Jerusalem," *'Atiqot* 29 (1996) 23–28.

Bone profiles without pork confirm a Jewish presence especially in combination with the other indicators. By the Late Hellenistic Period, pig avoidance was a clear Jewish boundary marker, prominently featured in both Jewish and gentile literary sources of the time, and apparent in the archaeological record where zooarchaeological data is analyzed.[63] Together, this fourfold cluster offers a reliable indicator of Jewish religious identity, which is the well-established pattern in Jerusalem and Judea of the period.[64]

Jewish Indicators in Galilee

Although the number of sites with abundant first-century evidence is limited, the existing finds consistently mirror those of Judea, and are remarkably homogeneous with regard to these four religious indicators. At Sepphoris, the earliest recoverable stratum in the western domestic quarters from about 100 B.C.E. to 70 C.E. includes more than one hundred stone vessel fragments and more than twenty *miqwaoth*. Significant for the identification of the Sepphorean and other stepped pools as Jewish *miqwaoth* is a single house at Sepphoris. Occupied from the first through fourth centuries, its first-century strata includes many stone vessels (mostly in the kitchen), four stepped plastered pools, two of which may be later additions, an absence of pork in the zooarchaeological profile, and (though slightly later) an oil lamp decorated with a menorah. The other domestic units at Sepphoris, though at times less well preserved in the first century, contain stone vessels, *miqwaoth*, but no pork. Outside the city, typical Second Temple Jewish tombs have also been found in a necropolis. Though current antiquities laws forbid their excavation, they are *kochim*-style burial, and fragments of ossuaries have been noted around the area.[65] At Tiberias, where the modern city precludes widespread excavation, work in mostly public

---

63. Brian Hesse and Paula Wapnish, "Can Pig Remains Be Used for Ethnic Diagnosis in the Ancient Near East?" in *The Archaeology of Israel: Constructing the Past, Interpreting the Present*, 238–270.

64. See, e.g. Nahman Avigad, *Archaeological Discoveries in the Jewish Quarter of Jerusalem. Second Temple Period* (Jerusalem: The Israel Museum, 1976); *Discovering Jerusalem* (Nashville: Thomas Nelson, 1983); and the appropriate articles in *Ancient Jerusalem Revealed* (ed. Hillel Geva; Jerusalem: Israel Exploration Society, 1994).

65. I am currently preparing the stone vessels of the western domestic quarters at Sepphoris for publication. The *miqwaoth* are reported in Eric Meyers, "Roman Sepphoris in the Light of New Archaeological Evidence and Research," in *The Galilee in Late Antiquity*, 332; on the tombs in the Sepphorean hillsides, see Zeev Weiss, "Hellenistic and Roman Sepphoris: The Archaeological Evidence," *Sepphoris in Galilee*, 35; Bill Grantham, the zooarchaeologist of the Sepphoris Regional Project, reports a shift in diet (including pork) after the 363 C.E. earthquake, with virtually no pork in any of the first century domestic units.

structures has nevertheless uncovered stone vessel fragments and a *miqweh*, as well as ossuaries in tombs. The scant Early Roman evidence under the synagogue at Hammath Tiberias also contains stone vessel fragments.[66] At less urban sites with considerable first-century evidence, the same pattern is repeated. At Yodefat, which was destroyed in the first Jewish war with Rome, about two hundred stone vessels have been found, as well as two *miqwaoth* in the domestic quarters. The excavators have concluded, on the basis of numismatic and ceramic evidence, the material culture as a whole, and literary evidence, that the site was first inhabited as part of the Hasmonean expansion with a continued Jewish occupation until its fall in 67 C.E.[67] The publications of the limited Franciscan excavations at Nazareth cite four stone vessels and a *miqweh*, and the tombs outside the ancient village are *kokhim* style, with many ossuary fragments strewn about.[68] At Reina, a few kilometers from Nazareth and Sepphoris, a stone vessel manufacturing site has also been found at a calcite outcropping; based on matches found in first-century contexts at Sepphoris, it certainly dates to the first century B.C.E. or C.E.[69] In Capernaum's Late Hellenistic and Early Roman loci, around 150 stone vessel fragments have been uncovered. Stone vessel fragments are present in each of the domestic units on the Franciscan side, including those under the synagogue and St. Peter's house, attesting to their widespread distribution.[70] Little exists by way of tombs, other than the small Middle or Late Roman mausoleum with a few sarcophagi just to the north of the site. Strikingly absent at Capernaum are *miqwaoth*, which can be attributed to the fact that the lake provided an alternative for acceptable bathing. At Gamla, which has its foundations in the late second or early first century, many stone vessels as well as two or possibly three *miqwaoth* have been found, one connected with the synagogue, one with an olive press, and one in a house.[71]

---

66. Yizhar Hirshfeld, Tiberias, "*NEAEHL* 4.1468; F. Vitto, "Tiberias: The Roman Tomb," *NEAEHL* 4.1473; Dothan, *Hammath Tiberias*, 63, Fig. 4, S; and Deines, *Jüdische Steingefäße*, 147.

67. Bayewitz and Aviam, "Iotapata, Josephus, and the Siege of 67," 161–165.

68. Bellarmino Bagatti reports stone vessels, a seven-stepped *miqweh* filled in under a later mosaic, and *kokhim*-type tombs with ossuary fragments strewn about, but no bone profile is reported, *Excavations in Nazareth, Volume I: From the Beginning till the XII Century* (Jerusalem: Franciscan Printing Press, 196), 237–24, 318. Strange suggests a second-century date for the *miqweh*, *ABD* 4.1051.

69. Zvi Gal, "A Stone-Vessel Manufacturing Site in the Lower Galilee," '*Atiqot* 20 (1991) 25*–26* [Hebrew], English Summary 179–180.

70. The author wishes to thank Father Stanislao Loffreda for his generosity in permitting an examination of all the site's stone vessels. A study on these is in progress. The absence of *miqwaoth* at Capernaum is notable and worthy of further study, especially since socio-economic factors might also be involved. The excavators report no bone profile.

71. S. Gutman, "Gamla," *NEAEHL* 2.463; S. Gutman and D. Wagner, "Gamla— 1984/1985/1986," *ESI* 5 (1986) 41.

At several sites where first-century remains are less well preserved, *miqwaoth*, stone vessels, and tombs have been uncovered. The finds of stone vessels are particularly significant. Since they went out of use in the late first century, their fragmentary presence in Middle or Late Roman Period fill indicates their use at the site in earlier periods. In addition to the above-mentioned sites, stone vessels have been found in various strata from the Galilean sites of Bethlehem, Gush Ḥalav, Ibelin, Kefar Ḥananya, Kafr Kanna, Khirbet Shemaʿ, Meiron, Migdal Ha-Emeq, and Nabratein.[72] *Miqwaoth* have been discovered at Chorazin, Beit Yinam, Beth-Sheʿarim, Har Arbel (?), Khirbet Shemaʿ, and Sasa.[73] First-century *kokhim*-type tombs with ossuaries were excavated on a large scale, under earlier antiquities laws, at the famous necropolis of Beth-Sheʿarim, and also at the smaller sites of Kafr Kanna, Ḥuqqoq, Reina, and Nazareth.[74] Insofar as these many excavations contain representative samples of private life in first-century Galilee, they each fit a distinct pattern of behavior: stone vessels and *miqwaoth* show some kind of Jewish purity concerns, the tombs reflect Jewish views of the afterlife, and the avoidance of pork conforms to Jewish dietary laws.

Non-Jewish Sites on Galilee's Perimeter

The basic homogeneity of Galilean sites, which parallels that of Judea with regard to these four religious indicators, contrasts with gentile sites of the Late Hellenistic and Early Roman Period. At the sites outside of Galilee and the Golan, stone vessels, *miqwaoth*, Jewish burials, and pork-avoidance are not present in the archaeological profile of private space.[75]

---

72. For stone vessels, see *Khribet Shemaʿ* Plate 8.8, no. 18 (?); *Meiron*, Plate 9.22, no 15; David Adan-Bayewitz, "Kfar Ḥananya," *ESI* 7–8 (1988–89) 108; and Yizhak Magen, *"Purity Broke out in Israel:" Stone Vessels in the Late Second Temple Period* (Catalogue No. 9, The Reuben and Edith Hecht Museum; Haifa: University of Haifa, 1994) 24–25.

73. *Miqwaoth* are listed with varying degrees of probability in Ronny Reich, "Miqvaoth (Jewish Ritual Immersion Baths) in Eretz-Israel."

74. On typically Jewish burial sites, see Benjamin Mazar, *Beth Sheʿarim. Report on the Excavations during 1936–1940 I–III* (2nd edition; Jerusalem: Israel Exploration Authority, 1957) [Hebrew with English summary]; A. Berman, "Kfr Kanna," *ESI* 7–8 (1988–89) 107–108; B. Ravani and P. P. Kahane, "Rock-cut Tombs at Huqoq," *ʿAtiqot* 3 (1961) 121–147, N. Najjar, "Kafr Reina," *ESI* 18 (1988) 28 [English], 41 [Hebrew]; Z. Yavor, "Nazareth," *ESI* 18 (1988) 32 [English], 48 [Hebrew].

75. Stone vessels do appear in a few sites in Transjordan, at Mount Nebo, ʿAin ez-Zara, and at Machaerus, each of which could be connected to Jews in light of Herod Antipas's control of Peraea, see J. Saller, "Hellenistic to Arabic Remains at Nebo, Jordan," *LA* 17 (1967) 41–43; Crista Clamer, "'Ain ez-Zara Excavations 1986," *Annual of the Department of Antiquities of Jordan* 33 (1989) 219; and Cahill, "Chalk Vessel Assemblages," 231.

Furthermore, Galilee and Judea's ceramic traditions and the extent of imported wares also substantiate their distinct character of domestic space over against other regions in Palestine. Eastern sigillata A (ESA), a red-slipped fine ware produced and transported by Phoenician merchants, was distributed throughout the southeastern Mediterranean, including the coast of Palestine in the Hellenistic and Roman Periods. These fine ware dining and drinking vessels show up in excavations all along the coast from Idumea to the Phoenician cities of Tyre and Sidon, inland around the major urban sites in the Jezreel Valley and Scythopolis, in the major Transjordanian sites, and in the Huleh Valley. However, as Berlin points out, "the most interesting aspect of this distribution was not, however, its breadth, but its gaps . . . ESA is absent in Judea and Galilee."[76] At the very least, this attests to a Hasmonean monopoly on oil and wine trade in such vessels, or, since the ware continued to almost the turn of the millennium, shared culinary preferences among the people of Galilee and Judea. Berlin has also traced the distribution of another Late Hellenistic Period ceramic assemblage, called "Phoenician semi-fine ware." This well-levigated and pale buff ware, restricted to five basic forms, is prevalent along the Phoenician market routes from the coast along the Acco Plain toward the Huleh Valley, and south along the coast, but entirely absent in Galilee and Judea.[77] This ware is predominant at Tel Anafa north of Upper Galilee, a site where no stone vessels and no *kokhim*-style tombs have been unearthed, and where instead of *miqwaoth*, a private house's ornate bathing complex, in a room with stucco and mosaics, was found.[78] The ware is also scattered on the surface at Kedesh in the Tyrian Plain, where the remains of a pagan temple still stand to this day, and where a mausoleum with sarcophagi bears witness to different burial patterns than was typical among Jews.[79]

## Summary of the Archaeological Evidence

To summarize the archaeological evidence on the Galileans' identity: The overall settlement history of Galilee shows a substantial gap after the Assyrian conquest in the eight century B.C.E., with an inkling of repopulation beginning in the Persian Period. Substantial settlement and population growth in Galilee begins with Hasmonean rule of Galilee in the first centuries B.C.E. and continues through the first century C.E. Key aspects of the Galilean material culture of this period match that of Judea: stone vessels,

---

76. "Between Large Forces," 25–26.
77. Berlin, "From Monarchy to Markets," 75–88.
78. Herbert, *Tel Anafa* I, 62–64.
79. A. Ovadiah, M. Fisher, and I. Roll, "Kedesh," *NEAEHL* 3:857.

*miqwaoth* in houses but no pork wherever bone profiles are published, and secondary burial with ossuaries in *kokhim*. This essentially rules out the possibility that Galileans were descendants of either Israelites or Itureans. Because of the evidence within domestic space, Hasmonean rule in Galilee should not be construed as a political-economic or administrative veneer over an indigenous Galilean population; wherever archaeologists have excavated, Jewish religious indicators permeate Galilean domestic space in the Early Roman Period. It is difficult to determine whether the few previous inhabitants, and their number was small regardless of who they were, readily adopted Judaism and flourished as they adopted it, or whether Judeans colonized the Galilee and overwhelmed the few prior inhabitants, who may have been earlier Jewish settlers. In either case, and the latter is more likely, the crucial point is that Galilee's population, which grew drastically in the Late Hellenistic/Early Roman Period, adhered to or adopted patterns of behavior in private space that is also found in Jerusalem and Judea, so that in terms of ethnicity, the Galileans should be considered Jewish.

Integrating the Literary Sources

It is worth pointing out that none of the key literary texts undermines the conclusion from the archaeological evidence of a sparsely populated Galilee prior to the Hasmonean period, nor do any seriously challenge the idea of a shared Galilean-Judean material culture with regard to a common Jewish religious heritage.[80] A few passages merit consideration. First, noticeable population growth in Judea in the third and second centuries B.C.E. is apparent in 1 Maccabees, where both Jonathan and Simeon are said to have sent troops to Demetrius I and II because they could not be fed (e.g. 10:25–45, 13:40). Demographic pressure in the south set the stage for immigration to Galilee.[81] Polybus reports that Antiochus III captured Philoteria and Scythopolis, then defeated the Ptolemaic army on Mount Tabor, but lists no other encounters in Galilee, presumably because there were no other significant settlements or fortifications there (*Hist.* 5.62). In fact, a fortification atop Mount Tabor has been excavated from this time period, but without any domestic area or village.[82] The key to Schürer's argument for a non-Jewish

---

80. See E. P. Sanders' notion of a "common Judaism," *Judaism: Practice and Belief 63 B.C.E.–66 C.E.* (Philadelphia: Trinity Press International, 1992).

81. Bezalel Bar-Kochva has convincingly argued for a demographic cycle under the Maccabees in which population pressure in Judea fostered the enlistment of young landless males, who were then resettled in conquered territories, "Manpower, Economics, and Internal Strife in the Hasmonean State," in *Armées et fiscalité dans le monde antique* (Paris: Editions du centre national de la recherche scientifique, 1977) 167–194.

82. Mordechai Aviam, "Mount Tabor," *OEANE* 5.152.

Galilee, 1 Macc 5:14-5, is the report that Simeon evacuated all the Jews of Galilee and Arbatta to Jerusalem, a feat possible only if they were few in number. Even if the text is reliable, it only indicates how few Jews were in Galilee prior to the Hasmonean annexation. Certainly their small number does not imply a large number of Gentiles, as Schürer inferred.[83] Josephus describes how Hyrcanus's defeat of Scythopolis left Galilee open for resettlement, implying that no other defensible gentile sites were present in Galilee, or that it was thinly populated (*Ant.* 13.28; *War* 1.64). Josephus's description of Ptolemy Lathyrus's attack on Sepphoris suggests that the Sabbath was observed in Galilee already at the beginning of the first century B.C.E. (*Ant.* 13.337–338). The archaeological evidence also calls into question interpretations of Josephus that place the conversion of the Itureans in Galilee (*Ant.* 13.319). The text itself never specifies Galilee as the locale, and since no archaeological evidence exists for Itureans in Galilee, its reliability even outside of Galilee is questionable. The alleged Iturean conversion is simply not a significant factor in assessing the ethnicity of the Galileans.[84]

More generally, Josephus's ambiguous use of Galileans contrasts with his unequivocal description of Idumeans, Itureans, and Samarians as non- or half-Jews.[85] He and the Jerusalem Council assume that a priest from the Temple would have status among Galileans, and he writes that Galileans regularly visited the Temple ("as was their custom," *War* 2.237 and *Ant.* 20.123). Of course, Josephus's writings tell us more about Jerusalemite expectations than Galilean loyalty, but the important point is that Galileans had an acceptable pedigree in Josephus's opinion, unlike Judea's neighbors.[86] In the rabbinic texts, although there were Galilean variations in a few details such as the calendar or measurements, their basic *halakhic* principles did not differ substantially from the Judeans.[87] In light of the archaeological evidence, one would suspect that the acrimonious rhetoric against the '*Amei Ha-aretz* by the rabbis was not directed at Galileans in general nor a distinct Galilean religious character, but rather suggests differences due to social status.[88]

---

83. Schürer, *History* 1.142, 216–218. Freyne suggests, based on the textual uncertainty and location of "Arbella," that the Jews were removed only from Galilee's western fringe, *Galilee*, 37.

84. Josephus's report of the enslavement of 10,000 inhabitants (*Ant.* 13.337) cannot be taken to indicate a substantial population in the Galilee; he elsewhere uses the term loosely.

85. See Aryen Kasher, *Jews, Idumeans, and Ancient Arabs* (TSAJ 19; Tübingen: J. C. B. Mohr [Paul Siebeck], 1988).

86. Freyne, "Galilee-Jewish Relations," 600–607.

87. Lawrence Schiffman, "Was there a Galilean Halakhah?" in *The Galilee in Late Antiquity*, 143–156.

88. Lee Levine, *Rabbinic Class of Roman Palestine* (New York: Jewish Theological Seminary of America, 1989); and Oppenheimer, *The 'Am Ha-Aretz*.

For these reasons the term Jews is thoroughly appropriate for the inhabitants of Galilee in the first century, as is the characterization of the Galilee as Jewish. In fact, the term's geographical root (Ἰουδαῖοι) accurately grasps the Galileans' religious roots in Judea.[89] In terms of ethnicity, they shared the same socialized patterns of behavior, and they were conscious of a mutual descent in Judea, dating back to the Maccabean revolt, the occupation of the *Diadochoi*, the rebuilding of the Temple, Babylonian exile, and beyond. To speak of Galilean Judaism or Galilean Jews is to add an important qualifier, a point Meyers's important work on Galilean regionalism stressed, but to juxtapose Galileans with Judeans as different, and to stress their geographical differences at the expense of their common ethnicity, skews their common heritage and obscures their historical connections. Galilean Jews had a different social, economic, and political matrix than Jews living in Judea or the Diaspora, and even among themselves held diverse attitudes, practices, and goals—among them those preserved in the Jesus tradition—but they all were Jewish.[90]

## Some Implications for the Jesus Tradition

The archaeological analysis does not, of course, solve the question of what kind of Judaism existed in first-century Galilee. The interpretation or significance given by various people to their stone vessels or *miqwaoth* cannot be determined by the artifacts alone, and certainly regional variations existed between Judea and Galilee, as well as within Galilee. Yet, the Galilean settlement patterns and the Galilee's shared religious indicators with Judea have considerable implications for Christian origins. The early Jesus traditions point to a Jewish religious milieu—appeal is made to the Hebrew scriptures, questions of faithful Torah observance are raised, Jewish heroes are mentioned, and Gentiles are used to shame "this generation"—a point so

---

89. Certainly the term is used in Diaspora texts to designate someone from Judea, and the author does not suggest that the primary connotation is geographical; see A. Thomas Kraabel, "The Roman Diaspora: Six Questionable Assumptions," *JJS* 33 (1982) 445–64. Evidence for the term in Diaspora inscriptions includes those who were not born Jewish and who converted, which I do not suggest applies to the case of Galileans either, see Ross Kraemer, "On the Meaning of the Term 'Jew' in Greco-Roman Inscriptions," *HTR* 82 (1989) 35–53.

90. See further the work of Shaye J. D. Cohen, who discusses the use of the designation Jew in terms of people who follow Jewish customs, including circumcision, and embrace monotheism, "Crossing the Boundary and Becoming a Jew," *HTR* 82 (1989) 26; "Religion, Ethnicity, and Hellenism in the Emergence of Jewish Identity in Maccabean Palestine," in *Religion and Religious Practice in the Seleucid Kingdom* (eds. Per Bilde et al.; Aarhus: Aarhus University Press, 1990) 204–223.

self-evident it needs no further elaboration.[91] Yet, the survey of the archaeological data in Galilee raises three particular issues of some concern in historical Jesus research: Galileans and purity, Galileans and the Temple, and
"Israelite" or northern traditions in Galilee, the implications of which will be
briefly sketched.

## Purity and Jesus in Galilee

Purity in Second Temple Judaism is a complex issue in and of itself; add the
role of the Pharisees as advocates for purity in Galilee in the first century, as
well as Jesus' attitude toward the matter eliciting various Jewish responses,
and no answer can easily be proffered.[92] Without suggesting that the archaeological evidence described above solves these problems, much less the
broader question of Jesus and the Torah or *halakha*, it does provide some
important considerations that are at the basis of a discussion of Jesus and
Jewish purity concerns. The implements related to purity were commonplace in first-century Galilean homes and distinguished Jews from non-Jews.
Stone vessels are ubiquitous in households of Galilee and Judea in the first
century. Likewise, *miqwaoth* have been uncovered in most Early Roman
strata of Galilean sites, some around industrial installations or synagogues,
or, more frequently, in private houses. Wherever found, burial traditions are
in chalk stone ossuaries in *kokhim*-style tombs outside cities, clearly the
result of a world view that accepts corpse impurity as fundamental.
Wherever analyzed, the bone profile is without pig. A point to be underscored is that the sites most closely associated with the Jesus tradition,
Capernaum and Nazareth, share the same pattern in religious indicators as
Galilee's two urban sites, Sepphoris and Tiberias.

In spite of being pervasive in the material culture, these archaeological
items play a minimal role in the earliest traditions in the Gospels. The controversy between Jesus and the Pharisees in Mark 7:1–23, in its caricature of

---

91. For specifically the Sayings Gospel Q, see Wendy Cotter, "Prestige, Protection
and Promise: A Proposal for the Apologetics of Q2," in *The Gospel Behind the
Gospels* (ed. R. Piper; Leiden: E. J. Brill, 1995) 117–138, esp. 124–25; and Dale
Allison, *The Jesus Tradition in Q* (Harrisburg, Pennsylvania: Trinity Press
International, 1997) 49–54, 192–204.

92. See, for example, the debate over the role of the Pharisees, Martin Hengel
and Roland Deines, "E. P. Sanders' "Common Judaism," Jesus, and the Pharisees,"
*JThS* NS 46 (1995) 1–70, published in an expanded German version as "E. P.
Sanders' "Common Judaism, Jesus und die Pharisäer," in Martin Hengel, *Judaica et
Hellenistica. Kleine Schriften I* (Tübingen: J. C. B. Mohr [Paul Siebeck], 1996)
392–479. E. P. Sanders, *Jewish Law from Jesus to the Mishnah. Five Studies*
(Philadelphia: Trinity Press International, 1990); and *Judaism: Practice and Belief.*

Jewish and Pharisaic practices, does not even mention stone vessels ("and there are many other traditions that they observe, the washing of cups, pots, and bronze kettles," Mark 7:4). At the heart of this pericope is the division between outward uncleanness and inward cleanness, a point present in earlier traditions as well. General purity concerns at meals and the use of clean cups are specifically mentioned in Q 11:39–40, but the alleged superficiality of the Pharisees is criticized without undermining the practice per se.[93] Likewise, Q does not comment on *miqwaoth* or ritual washings, except to say that John's baptism should be accompanied by internal purity and should promote "fruits worthy of repentance" (Q 3:8). The practice of bathing in *miqwaoth*, however, is not censured. The use of stone vessels is likewise not censured. It can be assumed that both were commonplace and somewhat of a moot point by Jesus and the earliest followers. Much the same can be said of burial practices and avoidance of pork. The former is not a topic in Q, though secondary burial was an assumed practice.[94] The latter's omission is of note insofar as Jesus' laxity in selecting his dining company is defended, but not his diet, which apparently was not under scrutiny by the Q community's critics.

However this question is solved, one should not envision a basic dichotomy between Jewish *halakha* and Galilean lack of concern for purity. Jesus never articulated the fundamental issue of purity, and not until the inclusion of Gentiles did the early Christian community begin the complex and painful process of articulating an acceptable position. Jesus' critique of an alleged lack of internal integrity accompanying the purity practices of some of his contemporaries became a renunciation of Jewish purity concerns well over a generation after the critique was first offered.[95]

## The Temple and Jesus in Jerusalem

Jesus' actions in the Temple and his teachings therein cannot be re-interpreted based on the archaeological evidence for the first-century Galileans. This debate will continue. Two points, however, should be made. First, some pilgrimage from Galilee to Jerusalem is to be expected in light of the Galileans' Judean origins. The roughly one-week trip by foot from Galilee was certainly made by priests and pious Jews, however defined. Josephus's

---

93. Much the same applies for tithing, Q 11:42–43, and can be said of the Sabbath issue in general (e.g., Mark 2:23–3:5).

94. Byron McCane, "Let the Dead Bury Their Own Dead: Secondary Burial and Mt. 8:21–22," *HTR* 83 (1990) 31–43.

95. See the helpful discussion in Hengel and Deines, "E. P. Sanders' "Common Judaism', Jesus und die Pharisäer," 398–407.

estimate of 3,000,000 people at Passover in Jerusalem in 64 C.E. (*War* 2.280) is a fanciful exaggeration, but since the bulk of the Galilean population were descendants of Judean families, it is possible that more than priests and the very pious went; indeed, several Galileans would still have had family in Judea. Given that Galilee's population rose after the Hasmonean annexation, many Galileans at the time of Jesus likely had great-grandparents or grandparents, and some perhaps even parents, who were born in Judea, so that contacts still existed between families and clans. Pilgrimage need not only be seen in terms of Galilean loyalty to Jerusalem, the Temple, and the cult. Pilgrimage was more than a religious phenomenon, it was also a social event. In addition to the more solemn aspects of Passover, pilgrims sang, drank, and spent money in Jerusalem.[96] And it may also have renewed kinship ties; it is not unreasonable to assume that many Galileans stayed with kin in Jerusalem.

The second point to be made, based on the shared archaeological indicators of ethnicity between Judea and Jerusalem, is that when Galileans did visit Jerusalem, they would have felt at home in these houses. They would have recognized stepped pools in public spaces or private houses and known their use and purpose, even if different interpretations abounded. They would have been familiar with stone vessels at the table, perhaps even used for the Passover meal. They would have expected a shared diet without pork. And, significantly, people from Galilee would have been familiar with the burial customs of Jerusalem, a point of some note with regard to the preparation of Jesus' tomb in the Gospels. These elements would have indicated to the Galilean visitors that they were not in a foreign or some "others'" place, but were within their group.

## "Israelite" or Northern Prophetic Traditions in Early Christianity

Finally, the frequency of what can be described as northern or Israelite traditions, in particular their prophetic imagery, is notable. This is most apparent in the Sayings Gospel Q. Prophetic forms, themes, and allusions permeate the Sayings Gospel, many with possible northern associations. The term "Israel" is used in Q 7:9 and notably in Q 22:30, where Jesus' followers are promised ultimately to judge the twelve tribes of Israel, glancing nostalgically back to pre-monarchic times, when no specific tribe or locale had primacy.[97] Likewise in John the Baptist's speech, religious identity is described in patriarchal terms of being "children of Abraham," a pre-monarchic concept

---

96. E.g., Deut 14:26; Josephus, *Ant.* 4.203; and Philo, *Spec. Laws* 1.70. For a good discussion on the realia of pilgrimage and the Passover, see Sanders, *Judaism: Practice and Belief*, 125–131.

97. Horsley, "Social Conflict in the Synoptic Sayings Source Q," *Conflict and Invention*, 38–39.

(Q 3:9). The term 'Ιουδαῖοι/"Jews," which is ambiguous with regard to Judean origins, never appears in Q. In fact, Zion or its theology is also avoided. In Q 11:29–31 Jesus is compared to Jonah, a northern prophet who is said to have originated in the Galilean village of Gath-Hepher, and who was likely venerated as a local hero in first-century Galilee.[98] Allusions to the northern prophets Elijah and Elisha also appear in Q as in Mark. Q 7:22–23, though quoting Isaiah, has close narrative parallels in the Elijah and Elisha cycles, with the raising of the dead and the cleansing of a leper (1 Kings 17:17–24; 2 Kings 4:18–37; and 2 Kings 5). Likewise, Q 7:21 quotes in part Mal 3:1, which yearns for a future *Elias redivivus.* Jesus' call to discipleship in Q 9:57–62 echoes Elijah's call to his followers, and if Luke 9:61–62 is in Q, we have a near verbatim quote of 1 Kings 19:19–21.[99] While prophets rank high on Q's scale of values, kings and priests, remarkably David and Moses, are absent in Q. Both had become localized in Jerusalem as the center for political and religious rule; the Davidic king would return to rule in Jerusalem, and the priests officiated in the Temple in Jerusalem. The prophet, however, was not localized; in fact, prophets served as moral and social critics of kings and priests, as well as their centralization in Jerusalem in particular, a recurrent theme especially among northern prophets and prophets outside Jerusalem. In a similar vein, Q criticizes the localization of the divine in Jerusalem; the Temple is described as deserted (Q 13:34–35), and the Temple's blood-stained past serves as a reminder of its current proprietors' moral impurity (Q 11:49–51). The prophet was an understandable choice for a religious community in a Galilean setting. The prophetic role model did not succumb to the Jerusalemite cultic hegemony and provided a traditional avenue for criticizing Jerusalem's religious and political structures in a way that justified rejection. As the adoption of the deuteronomistic theology makes clear, the Q community thought of themselves as prophets in such a way that they justified past and anticipated future rejection (Q 6:23; 11:47–51; and 13:34–35; somewhat also 7:33–35; 9:58; and 11:31–32).[100]

---

98. Jonathan L. Reed, "The Sign of Jonah (Q 11:29–31) and Other Epic References in Q," in *Reimagining Christian Origins: A Colloquium Honoring Burton L. Mack* (eds. Elizabeth Castelli and Hal Taussig; Valley Forge, Pennsylvania: Trinity Press International, 1996) 130–143.

99. A possible allusion to 2 Kings 4:29 is in the prohibition against greeting anyone on the road (Q 10:4b); on Q's allusions to Elijah, see Mikagu Sato, *Q und Prophetie. Studien zur Gattungs- und Traditionsgeschichte der Quelle Q* (WUNT ser. 2, vol. 29; Tübingen: J. C. B. Mohr [Paul Siebeck] 1988) 144–45; 376–77, 385, 400; on John as Elijah redivivus in early Jewish and Christian literature, see Robert Webb, *John the Baptizer and Prophet: A Socio-Historical Study* (JSNTSS 62; Sheffield: Sheffield Academic Press, 1991) 250–54.

100. On the development of deuteronomistic theology, see Odil Hannes Steck, *Israel und das gewaltsame Geschick der Propheten* (WMANT 23: Neukirchen-Vluyn: Neukirchener Verlag, 1967). For various interpretations of its use in Q, see Paul

These prophetic elements in Q with a particular "northern" spin do not, however, based on the archaeological analysis above, represent a revival of indigenous northern Israelite traditions by their later genealogical heirs in Galilee. Rather, they represent one particular Galilean community's carefully crafted epic imagination to locate themselves on their social map. They pictured themselves in the role of prophets proclaiming new rules for social intercourse, family structures, and personal relationships, and criticized, somewhat like the ancient northern prophets, aspects of Jerusalem's economic and political structures. Their yearning for the "good old times," the cancellation of debts, and lending without returning (or borrowing without repaying!) echoes much of what we have in the prophets.[101] This tradition was preserved through the destruction of Jerusalem and the Babylonian exile, transmitted and nurtured by scribes during the return and restoration in the South, and mediated by scribal circles into Galilee in the Late Hellenistic Period.

The early Christian tradition was crafted from the many possibilities of the Hebrew Bible at their disposal. It is not surprising that a Galilean group would gravitate at times toward prophetic passages from a northern perspective, since they shared with the northern prophets a common geographical and spiritual distance from the center of Jerusalem and shared the concomitant economic and political implications. The earliest Christians linked themselves with the northern prophets, but we should not confuse this shared imagination with genealogy. In that sense, how they imagined themselves was not who they were.

One final thought. The Galileans' historical roots were Judean. The religious indicators show that Galileans and Judeans had much in common in their daily religious practices. The rabbis could interpret these common concerns and interests more readily after the destruction of the Temple, which had likely been an earlier source of friction between Galilee and Jerusalem. The rabbis' codification of how to negotiate everyday life in the fields, farms, villages, and cities of Galilee was not an alien framework superimposed from outside and above onto Galileans, but was an idealized

---

Hoffmann, *Studien zur Theologie der Logienquelle* (NTAbh NF 8; Münster: Verlag Aschendorff, 1972) 158–90; Dieter Lührmann, *Die Redaktion der Logienquelle* (WMANT 33; Neukirchen-Vluyn: Neukirchener Verlag, 1969); and Arland Jacobson, "The Literary Unity of Q," *JBL* 101 (1982) 365–89.

101. William Arnal, "Gendered Couplets in Q and Legal Formulations: From Rhetoric to Social History," *JBL* 116 (1997) 75–94. See the provocative essay by Rainer Kessler on how studies on the Israelite prophets have in fact served as critiques of contemporary economic policies, "Frühkapitalismus, Rentenkapitalismus, Tributarismus, antike Klassengesllschaft. Theorien zur Gesellschaft des alten Israels," *ET* 54 (1994) 413–427.

codification of principles and intellectual reflection on items and activities that had already been present in Galilean daily life. On the other hand, the Jesus movement, especially as reflected in the Sayings Gospel Q, could not as easily represent the Galileans in general. As several sayings in Q illustrate, the earliest followers felt most alienated from "this generation" (Q 7:31; 11:29, 31, 32, 51), a more holistic term for Israel or Jews. And three villages—Chorazin, Bethsaida, and Capernaum—receive the most vehement condemnation because they rejected Jesus' signs (Q 10:13–15). Although the Pharisees and scribes had close historical connections with Jerusalem and are perceived as a threat in Q (3:7–9, 11:39–51), this threat was not perceived as problematic to most Jews in Galilee. It appears that the earliest Christians in Galilee marginalized themselves, and were never a major concern to Judaism as a whole in Galilee until after Constantine, when Christian political power came from outside to the Holy Land.[102]

---

102. See the helpful comments in Stuart S. Miller, "The *Minim* of Sepphoris Reconsidered," *HTR* 86 (1993) 377–402.

# CHAPTER 3

# Population Numbers in Galilee: Urbanization and Economics

## Galilean Urbanization and Hellenization

For some time, historical Jesus research has been plagued by the simplistic categories of Judaism and Hellenism. The history of religions school in particular has bequeathed to the discipline the heuristic division between the "Palestinian primitive community" (read Jewish Christianity) and the "Hellenistic community" (read gentile Christianity).[1] Unable to exorcise the demons of the past, the current discussion of Galilee as the setting for Jesus is still subject to the kindred debate over Hellenism or Judaism. Their relationship and history are complicated, and their terminological use in scholarly literature so muddled, that Martin Hengel prudently advises that "the term 'Hellenistic' as currently used no longer serves to make any meaningful differentiation in terms of the history of religions within the history of early Christianity."[2]

Very few of the recent studies on the historical Jesus advocate an either-or approach to Judaism and Hellenism, and most, when carefully read, understand the historical complexity and terminological ambiguity when discussing early Christian texts. Nevertheless, a clear division exists among reconstructions of the historical Jesus, which tend to fall along the earlier demarcation: Jesus was either, on the one hand, analogous to a Jewish prophet or a rabbi, or, on the other hand, akin to a Hellenized Jewish sage or

---

1. A concise survey of the history of scholarship can be found in Martin Hengel, *The 'Hellenization' of Judaea in the First Century after Christ* (Philadelphia: Trinity Press International, 1989) 1–6.

2. Hengel, *The 'Hellenization' of Judaea*, 53.

even a Cynic.[3] Studies on the Gospels likewise reflect this tension: some look to the Old Testament, consult Strack-Billerbeck, and reconstruct an Aramaic Vorlage to exegete passages; others look to the broader Mediterranean thought world, Hellenistic paidea, and the Homeric epic for understanding. In studies on the sayings source Q, divisions exist between those who advocate a primary ecstatic and prophetic layer, which is accompanied by a later wisdom tradition; and those who advocate an early sapiential layer, which is later apocalypticized.[4] This disagreement is even more pronounced when

*Figure 3.1 Cities in the Late Hellenistic and Roman Periods*

---

3. Some examples suffice: for Jesus as prophet, see E. P. Sanders, *The Historical Figure of Jesus* (London: Penguin, 1993); and in the role of the rabbi, see Geza Vermes, *The Religion of Jesus the Jew* (Minneapolis: Fortress, 1993). As a charismatic sage, see Marcus Borg, *Jesus: A New Vision* (San Francisco: HarperSanFrancisco, 1991); and as a Cynic, see G. Downing, *Cynics and Christian Origins* (Edinburgh: T. & T. Clark, 1992).

4. Mikagu Sato, *Q und Prophetie. Studien zur Gattungs- und Traditiongeschichte der Quelle Q* (WUNT ser. 2, vol. 29; Tübingen: J. C. B. Mohr [Paul Siebeck], 1988); and alternatively, John Kloppenborg, *The Formation of Q: Trajectories in Ancient Wisdom Collections* (Studies in Antiquity and Christianity; Philadelphia: Fortress,

the ethos of Galilee as the milieu of Jesus' life and ministry is discussed. The role of its two urban centers, Sepphoris and Tiberias, is often placed under the simplistic rubric of Hellenism over against Judaism, and Jesus' possible presence there; or their influences upon him serves as a kind of litmus test to determine a scholar's position.

Contributing to this dichotomy was Seán Freyne's magisterial study on Galilean history, *Galilee from Alexander the Great to Hadrian*, which analyzed the two phases of urbanization around and in Galilee in terms of Hellenistic influences.[5] Freyne noted how in the first phase, several Hellenistic cities were built on Galilee's periphery in the second and first centuries B.C.E., and then in the second phase, Herod Antipas built the, in his opinion Hellenistic, cities of Sepphoris and Tiberias inside Galilee around the beginning of the common era. At the time Freyne noted how the Hellenistic flavor emanating from these cities did not penetrate into the rest of rural Galilee. While he has since articulated these cities' impact on Galilee in a more nuanced manner, interrelating political, socio-economic, and religious aspects, many scholars have reacted against his initial presentation to characterize the whole Galilee as a highly urbanized and hence Hellenized area within the Mediterranean world.[6] This has been motivated in part by attempts to accentuate the parallels between Jesus and Greco-Roman Cynicism, with some even suggesting a genealogical relationship between Cynics and Jesus, wherein Sepphoris and Tiberias are characterized as cosmopolitan urban centers through which peripatetic Cynics wandered.[7] A simplistic use of population numbers has

---

1987; 2nd edition Trinity Press International, 2000). Earlier Sigfried Schulz divided pericopes in Q between those from the Palestinian and Hellenistic communities, *Q: Die Spruchquelle der Evangelistien* (Zürich: Theologischer Verlag, 1972).

5. Seán Freyne, *Galilee from Alexander the Great to Hadrian 323 B.C.E. to 125 C.E.: A Study of Second Temple Judaism* (Notre Dame: Notre Dame University Press, 1980).

6. Seán Freyne, "Jesus and the Urban Culture of Galilee," in *Texts and Contexts: Biblical Texts and Their Textual and Situational Contexts. Essays in Honor of Lars Hartman* (eds. T. Fornberg and D. Hellholm; Oslo: Scandinavian University Press, 1995) 597–622. Freyne's study, as well as numerous conversations with Seán Freyne, has contributed considerably to my understanding of Galilee. For a more urbanized Galilee, see Howard Clark Kee, "Early Christianity in the Galilee: Reassessing the Evidence from the Gospels" in *The Galilee in Late Antiquity* (ed. L. Levine; New York: The Jewish Theological Seminary of America, 1992) 3–22; and J. Andrew Overman, "Who Were the First Urban Christians?" *SBLSP* 1988 (ed. D. Lull; Atlanta: Scholars Press, 1988) 160–168.

7. Most prominently F. Gerald Downing, "The Social Contexts of Jesus the Teacher: Construction or Reconstruction," *NTS* 33 (1987) 449; *Christ and the Cynics* (JSOT Manuals 4; Sheffield: JSOT, 1988) x; and *Cynics and Christian Origins* (Edinburgh: T. & T. Clark, 1992). See further, Burton Mack, *The Lost Gospel: The Book of Q and Christian Origins* (San Francisco: HarperSanFrancisco, 1993) 51–68. C. M. Tuckett has ruled out any genealogical relationship between Jesus and Cynics, "A Cynic Q?" *Biblica* 10 (1989) 349–376; and the thesis in general has been criticized by Hans-Dieter Betz, "Jesus and the Cynics: Survey and Analysis of a Hypothesis," *JR* 74 (1994) 453–475.

accompanied this scheme. High numbers are equated with urbanization, and urbanization in turn correlates with Hellenization. Even Capernaum, Jesus' base of operations, according to the Gospels, has been deemed an urban center in this scheme. The estimates of its population provide a barometer of the climate among New Testament scholars. In spite of the dearth of evidence in the Gospels, the lack of epigraphic sources, the dubious numbers given by Josephus, and the complexity involved in estimating an ancient locale's population, scholars have wagered guesses of Capernaum's population in the first century that are increasingly higher. Traditionally described as a small fishing village with fewer than 1,000 inhabitants, it has since been endowed with a much larger population of between 12,000 and 15,000, and even estimates as high as 25,000 have been entertained to stress the cosmopolitan and urbane milieu of Jesus' ministry.[8] Such inflated estimates are then commonly accepted by others and are cited without evidence or argument to accentuate Galilee's urbane or Hellenized character in the first century.[9]

Although this study focuses on population numbers, it does not assume that higher populations necessarily imply a greater degree of Hellenization. By focusing on demographic aspects relating to Herod Antipas's urbanization of Galilee, specifically the rebuilding of Sepphoris and the building of Tiberias, the primary concern is the socio-economic strains that affected the culture and religion of Galilee.[10] It is clear that most of the inhabitants of Galilee, including the cities of Sepphoris and Tiberias, were Jews.[11] Although Sepphoris and Tiberias had Hellenistic leanings and influenced Galilee in cultural ways, these cities and their impact should not be treated solely in terms of Hellenistic culture.[12] For the moment, this study focuses on aspects of urbanization culled from the archaeological record that are primarily

---

8. Lower estimates can be found in Stanislao Loffreda, *A Visit to Capernaum* (Jerusalem: Franciscan Press, 1972) 20; and Bellarmino Bagatti, "Capharnaum," *MB* 27 (1983) 9. An increase in Capernaum's population estimate began with James F. Strange, "Capernaum," *IDBSup* 140; this was increased drastically to the frequently cited number 12,000–15,000 given by Eric Meyers and James F. Strange, *Archaeology, the Rabbis, and Early Christianity* (Nashville: Abingdon, 1981) 58. A figure as high as 25,000 was offered by Howard Clark Kee, "The Import of Archaeological Investigations in Galilee for Scholarly Reassessment of the Gospels" (paper presented at the annual meeting of the Society of Biblical Literature [SBL] in Anaheim, Calif., November 20, 1989).

9. E.g., Overman, "Who Were the First Urban Christians?" 162; Anthony J. Saldarini, "The Gospel of Matthew and Jewish-Christian Conflict in the Galilee," in *The Galilee in Late Antiquity*, 27 n. 9; and Arland Jacobson, "Divided Families and Christian Origins," in *The Gospel Behind the Gospels: Current Studies on Q* (ed. Ronald Piper; Leiden: E. J. Brill, 1995) 379.

10. See pages 170–196.

11. See pages 23–61.

12. See pages 100–138.

demographic in nature; first and foremost, the archaeological evidence apropos Sepphoris and Tiberias's population size, and their relationship to socio-economic conditions in Galilee. It needs to be stressed, however, that high population numbers are not a cipher for Hellenism.

## Urbanization and the Consumer City

The size of an urban site's population provides an important gauge of its impact on the surrounding region. Rome and her client kings' rule in the Mediterranean world urbanized regions, which realigned their socio-economic patterns, and did not simply sprinkle it with cities. Urbanization introduced a power relationship onto a region in which categorically larger settlements centered agriculture, trade, and manufacturing onto themselves, wherein the ruling and social elites lived, who constructed and maintained civic buildings primarily through rents and taxes from the countryside.[13] The significance of any ancient city to its citizens and rural dependents was rooted in power relations—political rule, economic control, and social status. As the writings of Josephus tell us, Herod Antipas's ruling apparatus at the time of Jesus was located in these urban sites, first in Sepphoris, which he rebuilt after 4 B.C.E., and then in Tiberias, which he founded in 18 C.E. Based on Josephus as well as from what we know of Roman rule elsewhere, the social elites in these cities exerted economic control over Galilee. The present concern is not to detail the literary sources' comments on the Galileans' perception of Sepphoris and Tiberias in terms of political power; like most literature from antiquity, they simply assume tense urban-rural relations.[14] Nor is the concern to understand literary or epigraphic terminology for these settlements (such as their status as πόλεις or the meaning of αὐτορατής, *Ant.* 18.27). Such inquiries dead end in linguistic minutiae and contribute little to social history. Instead, the purpose of this study is to explore traces left in the archaeological record by Sepphoris and Tiberias and their impact on Galilee. Attempts have been made to "read" semiotically how a site's architecture communicates issues of power, or even how cities themselves made visual power statements in a region.[15] The intent here, however,

---

13. See the valuable essays edited by John Rich and Andrew Wallace-Hadrill, *City and Country in the Ancient World* (Leichester-Nottingham Studies in Ancient Society 2; London: Routledge, 1991); and Zeev Safrai, *The Economy of Roman Palestine* (London and New York: Routledge, 1994).

14. Ramsey McMullen, *Roman Social Relations: 50 B.C. to A.D. 284* (New Haven: Yale University Press, 1974).

15. James F. Strange and John Stambaugh have offered "semiotic" readings of how sites communicate power relationships, a somewhat speculative enterprise, "Some Implications of Archaeology for New Testament Studies," in *What Has*

is to pursue a somewhat less speculative approach and to ask questions that the archaeological record is more readily suited to address. By looking at the population sizes of Sepphoris and Tiberias, the level of their consumption, primarily agricultural, will be examined, and then the extent of their public buildings and the economic strain their construction placed on the surrounding countryside will be gauged.

This approach to urbanization and the city in antiquity does, in many ways, reflect Moses Finley's model of the ancient city as a "consumer city," a notion adapted from Max Weber's distinction between the ancient and medieval city.[16] Fundamental to this understanding of the city are the primacy of agriculture in the ancient economy and the prohibitive cost of overland trade. Because of the expense involved in transporting bulky items including grain, cities strove toward self-sufficiency, especially for their basic food needs, a principle that villages, hamlets, and peasant families on the land pursued as well.[17] To ensure their self-sufficiency, cities encouraged or forced the fusion of smaller plots of diverse produce together into larger tracts of a single crop that created economies of scale. For the most part, peasants and their families sought to produce what they consumed and hoped to pass on the required taxes in kind from their surplus, without cutting into their sustenance. Rome tended to rule—more precisely extract taxes—through cities, and it orchestrated local elites such as the Herodians as funnels for taxes, who exchanged agricultural goods into currency and passed it on to Rome.[18] As they taxed, cities also monetized the local

---

*Archaeology to Do with Faith?* (eds. James H. Charlesworth and Walter Weaver; Philadelphia: Trinity Press International, 1992) 31–41; and John Stambaugh, *The Ancient Roman City* (Baltimore: John Hopkins University Press, 1988).

16. Moses Finley, "The Ancient City: From Fustel de Coulanges to Max Weber and Beyond," *Comparative Studies in Society and History* 19 (1977) 305–327; and *The Ancient Economy* (Berkeley: The University of California Press, 1973) 123–149. See also Peter Garnsey and Richard Saller, *The Roman Empire: Economy, Society and Culture* (Berkeley: The University of California Press, 1987) 26–40. See Donald Engels, *Roman Corinth: An Alternative Model for the Classical City* (Chicago: The University of Chicago, 1990); and the scathing review by Richard Saller in *Classical Philology* 86 (1991) 351–358. See originally, Max Weber, *The City* (trans. and ed. by Don Martindale and Gertrud Neuwirth; Glenco, Illinois: Free Press, 1958).

17. This description is *in nuce* that set forth by Moses Finley, *The Ancient Economy*; and found earlier in Arnold H. M. Jones, *The Roman Economy* (Totowa, New Jersey: Rowman and Littlefield, 1974). These have effectively criticized and replaced the earlier "modernized" economic model advocated by Michael Rostovtzeff, which assumed a high degree of manufacturing, monetization, and international trade, *The Social and Economic History of the Roman Empire I–II* (2nd rev. ed. by P. M. Fisher; Oxford: Clarendon, 1957).

18. Mireille Corbier, "City, Territory and Taxation," in *City and Country in the Ancient World*, 211–239.

economies.[19] On the one hand, the local elites passed on coinage to Rome, and, on the other hand, paid for the services of the ruling apparatus, purchased locally made manufactured goods, and acquired smaller luxury items from afar with cash.[20] Most significantly, however, local rulers and the social elites paid for the construction of civic building projects in the cities. The urbanization of a region, whether under direct or indirect Roman rule, also commercialized traditional agrarian societies; that is to say, rural peasants moved from sustaining themselves and passing on the surplus to passing on higher quantities of produce in exchange for cash with which to pay taxes, a process that rendered self-sufficiency less feasible.[21] Commercialization pushed peasants working their family-owned plots into debt, then tenancy, then some off the land to return seasonally as day laborers, or into lives as artisans, beggars, or bandits.[22]

Since cities' populations fed off the countryside's agricultural supply, and since the ruling elites built civic architecture with taxes and rents collected from the countryside, the strain placed on the surrounding area can be approximated from the size of the city and the extent of its building projects. For Galilee, the impact of Herod Antipas's urbanization on the entire region can be gauged by the population sizes of Sepphoris and Tiberias and by the extent of their civic building projects. The archaeological evidence for Galilean urbanization thus defined incorporates the sites' population size, the presence and quality of public buildings, and the available arable land.

---

19. Keith Hopkins, "Economic Growth in Towns in Classical Antiquity," in *Towns and Societies: Essays in Economic History and Historical Sociology* (eds. Philip Abrams and E. A. Wigley; Cambridge: University Press, 1978) 35–77; and "Taxes and Trade in the Roman Empire," *JRS* 70 (1980) 101–25.

20. See esp. John Patterson, "Settlement, City and Elite in Samnium and Lycia," in *City and Country in the Ancient World*, 147–168.

21. For a more positive view of Galilee than that offered here, see Douglas Edwards, "First Century Urban/Rural Relations in Lower Galilee: Exploring the Archaeological and Literary Evidence," in *SBLSP 1988*, 183–199; "The Socio-Economic and Cultural Ethos of Lower Galilee in the First Century: Implications for the Nascent Jesus Movement," in *The Galilee in Late Antiquity*, 53–73; and David Adan Bayewitz and Isadore Perlman "The Local Trade of Sepphoris in the Roman Period," *IEJ* 40 (1990) 153–172.

22. John Kautsky, *The Politics of Aristocratic Empires* (Chapel Hill, North Carolina: University of North Carolina Press, 1982); Gerhard Lenski, *Power and Privilege* (New York: McGraw Hill, 1966); this process has been traced in Palestine under the Herodians by David Fiensy's important work, *The Social History of Palestine in the Herodian Period. The Land is Mine* (Studies in the Bible and Early Christianity 20; Lewiston: Edwin Mellen, 1991). John Dominic Crossan has suggested the implications of the commercialization of Galilee for our understanding of the Jesus movement, *The Birth of Christianity*, 157–159, 215–235; without referring to Kautsky or his terminology, Freyne has noted the same phenomenon in Galilee, "Jesus and the Urban Culture of Galilee," 604–610.

The focus of this study is not restricted, however, to the archaeology of Sepphoris and Tiberias: their size and construction projects will also be compared to those of other sites, both inside and outside Galilee. The extent of agricultural produce that they needed for consumption, and the potential of the surrounding Galilean countryside, helps assess the strain upon local farming patterns and practices.

In emphasizing demographics, population numbers, and urban architecture, practical concerns coalesce with theoretical issues: Sepphoris and Tiberias can be measured, and even if only partially excavated, their populations over historical periods can be estimated. In like manner, remains of Sepphoris and Tiberias's public architecture can be examined and described both in their quality and quantity. The magnitude of these two factors, population size and urban architecture, determines their impact on the surrounding regions, primarily in terms of agricultural production and land ownership patterns, and also in terms of local manufacturing and international trade.

## Determining Population Numbers from Antiquity

The estimates of Sepphoris and Tiberias's populations in the first century depends on a reliable method. Scholars have estimated the populations of ancient sites using literary sources, epigraphic data, topographical constraints, and the size of public buildings. Each of these methods is problematic, and none can be applied with confidence to any Galilean site, including Sepphoris and Tiberias. The ancient literary texts grossly exaggerate population numbers, for which David Hume chastised their authors as early as 1742: "With regard to remote times, the numbers of people assigned are often ridiculous, and lose all credit and authority."[23] Frequently ancient authors simply invoked multiples of the term μυριάς to describe large quantities of people, without having exactly 10,000 people per myriad in mind.[24] Josephus's figures, the only ones for first-century Galilee, follow this pattern and lack credibility. His general comments on Galilee, that its

---

23. "Essay XI: Of the Populousness of Ancient Nations," in *Essays, Moral, Political, and Literary* (ed. Eugene Miller; Indianapolis: Liberty Classics, 1985) 422. Hume criticized notions of a superior golden age in antiquity in which the alleged grandeur of Rome (whose population was estimated at over 14,000,000 by Montesquieu!) was contrasted to the decadence of the present.

24. μυριάς is defined as both the literal number 10,000 and "of a very large number, not exactly defined," *BAGD* 529. On the unreliable use of this term and numbers in general in Josephus, see Anthony Byatt, "Josephus and Population Numbers in First Century Palestine," *PEQ* 105 (1973) 51; and Magen Broshi, "The Population of Western Palestine in the Roman-Byzantine Period," *BASOR* 236 (1980) 6.

inhabitants "have always been numerous," and that "the towns are thickly distributed," deserve a fair hearing (*War* 3.42–43[author's translation]). But his specific numbers are fanciful exaggerations. If one takes his statements literally, that even "the smallest villages contains more than 150,000 inhabitants" (read fifteen *myriads*, *War* 3.43), and multiplies it by the number of villages he says are in Galilee (204, *Life* 234), then the Galilee would have an absurdly high population of 3,000,000![25] Josephus's motive is self-aggrandizement and presenting himself, his army, and his nation as a worthy foe for Vespasian, his Legions, and Rome.[26] In addition to the untrustworthy figures in ancient literary texts, the various Greek and Latin terms for urban sites in no way correlate with population size. Population size was never a criterion for a polis. In fact, Aristotle was not at all impressed by the enormity of Babylon's population; its size was for him symptomatic of unchecked barbarism rather than civilization. His concern was the ideal polis, which in his opinion would have to limit its population (*Politics* 1265a). The bewildering variety of Greek and Latin words used for urban sites has more to do with administrative privileges, tax distinctions, or philosophical ideals, and cannot be used to gauge a site's population.[27] Nor do the various terms for settlements in the rabbinic literature correlate with site size. The terms *kefar* ("village"), '*yr* ("town"), and *kerach* ("polis") give some indication of their relative size, but the terms are inconsistently applied to individual sites, and are based primarily on certain rabbinic concerns, such as the preponderance of Gentiles at a site (*kerach*), or whether they were walled ('*yr* vs. *kefar*), but not their population size.[28]

Population numbers in epigraphic sources tend to be more reliable than those found in ancient literature. However, inscriptions from antiquity show little interest in the total population of cities or territories, nor do they distinguish the population of a city from its territory. The well-known census inscription of P. Sulpicius Quirinius dated to 6–7 C.E. illustrates this. It cites

---

25. Byatt has noted this and other problems in Josephus's numbers. One of his examples: if the smallest village is said to have at least 15,000 inhabitants, then how can the largest village, Japha, have 17,130 inhabitants (*Life* 235), only 2,130 more? See his "Josephus and Population Numbers," 52.

26. Shaye J. D. Cohen, *Josephus in Galilee and Rome: His* Vita *and Development as a Historian* (Leiden: E. J. Brill, 1979) 201.

27. Moses Finley, "The Ancient City," 305. After surveying and examining the number, size, and function of *poleis* in the Greco-Roman world, Norman Pounds concluded that most *poleis* were, in terms of population, surprisingly small. The average was just under 4,000 inhabitants, but the lower end went below 1,000, "The Urbanization of the Classical World," *Annals of the Association of American Geographers* 59 (1969) 143, 153.

28. Valuable discussions of these terms use in the rabbinic literature can be found in Ayre Ben-David, *Talmudische Ökonomie* I (Hildersheim: Georg Olms, 1974), 48–52; and Safrai, *The Economy of Roman Palestine*, 17–19.

Syrian Apameia as having 117,000 free inhabitants (*CIL* 3 Sup. 6687); it did not include slaves, nor, it is likely, children, nor certainly the destitute and outcasts. Thus Paul Harvey, in discussing the epigraphic evidence for population numbers, wryly recalls Brecht's dictum and applies it to census inscriptions in antiquity: *Die im Dunkeln sieht man nicht* ("Those in darkness are unseen").[29] Furthermore, the figure of 117,000 combined the inhabitants of the urban core of Apameia with the inhabitants of its surrounding villages and territory, because like other censuses in antiquity it sought to establish tax rates of administrative districts extracted through the city and including the surrounding countryside and villages.[30] Thus, the few surviving census reports, and none survive for Galilee, are of little value in determining the population of a single site. City and town populations have been deduced from other kinds of epigraphic evidence, such as those preserving the financial details of private gifts to citizens.[31] For example, an inscription from Siagu in Tunisia honors a patron who distributed 1,000 *denarii* at the annual athletic games "at the rate of one *sestertius* per head." The prescribed *sportula* rate of one *sesterce*, a quarter of a *denarius*, accounts for 4,000 recipients. Since only citizens, males above the age of eighteen, were targeted as recipients, 4,000 can be multiplied by a factor of 3.5, the typical ratio of males over eighteen to the remaining population in demographically similar cultures, to estimate Siagu's population at 14,000 (3.5 x 4,000). Unfortunately, no such epigraphic evidence exists for any Galilean site.

Scholars have inferred cities' populations from the seating capacity of public buildings, including theaters or synagogues. But issues of civic pride, wealth, and even rivalry determine these structures' size more than demographic requirements.[32] While Thysdrus in Roman Africa boasted an amphitheater seating 60,000, the third largest in the Roman world, it was nowhere near the third largest city of the Empire, nor even North Africa.[33]

---

29. Paul Harvey, "Calculo de la poblacion de la antigua Roma: Datos, modelos y metodos," *Semana de Estudios Romanos VI* (Instituto de Historia, Universidad Catolica de Valparaiso, 1991) 177.

30. Harvey, "Calculo de la poblacion," 177–179.

31. Richard Duncan-Jones, "City Population in Roman Africa," *JRS* 53 (1963), 85–90; "Human Numbers in Towns and Town-Organizations of the Roman Empire: The Evidence of Gifts," *Historia* 13 (1964) 199–208; and *The Economy of the Roman Empire* (2nd ed.; Cambridge: Cambridge University Press, 1982), 259–287.

32. Richard Duncan-Jones, *The Economy of the Roman Empire*, 262.

33. R. M. Haywood, "Roman Africa," in *An Economic Survey of Ancient Rome* IV (ed. Tenney Frank; Baltimore: The Johns Hopkins Press, 1938) 112. Furthermore, some theaters functioned as regional sites. The theater at Pompeii had a seating capacity of 12,000, and Nero closed it for ten years because of rioting between the citizens of Pompeii and of Nuceria Alfaterna, a city over 10 kilometers to the east, clear evidence that the theater was designed for visitors as well (Tacitus, *Annales*, xiv.17).

Likewise, the seating capacity of Galilean public buildings does not help determine the population of their sites. The 4,000-seat theater at Sepphoris, for example, is only slightly smaller than the theaters at Scythopolis or Caesarea Maritima, the two largest cities in Roman Palestine.[34] Similar disparities are apparent in Palestinian synagogues, where structure size does not correlate with town size. The synagogues at smaller sites such as Gamla (320 m²), Meiron (375 m²), and Beth She'arim (420 m²) were relatively large, and the fifth-century C.E. synagogue at Capernaum is one of the largest excavated to date, with a main hall enclosing 450 m². In contrast, the main halls of synagogues at some of Palestine's largest cities are remarkably small; that at Scythopolis is 240 m² and that of Caesarea Maritima is only 162 m².[35] Factors such as the number of synagogues per settlement, whether the site was home to a rabbinic school as at Meiron, or whether it was a pilgrimage site, as Beth She'arim, are more important in determining synagogue size than the number of the site's inhabitants. In short, seating capacity of public buildings cannot be correlated with population size.

Topographical methods have also been used to gauge the population of ancient sites: limits to population size can be placed on sites using agronomic calculations of its surrounding area's maximum yields or its available water supply. Unfortunately, assessing the potential water supply is of little help in estimating Tiberias and Sepphoris's population, since the former has an unlimited water source in the Sea of Galilee, and the latter was near the springs at 'Ein Zippori, and Roman aqueduct technology delivered water from several springs to the East of Sepphoris through an underground system.[36] Even though not nearly as vast as the Jezreel Valley or Shefelah, the fertile valleys of Lower Galilee had considerable agricultural potential, as did the Gennesaur Plain along the Sea of Galilee, which Josephus praises since there is "not a plant which its fertile soil refuses, and its cultivators grow them all" (*War* 3.516). An upper parameter on a region's population can be set using data on the annual per capita consumption of grain in antiquity, crop yields, and seed required for planting when combined with factors like

---

34. A similar picture emerges from the comparative data on theaters' seating capacity in the Roman East, Arthur Segal, *Theaters in Roman Palestine and Provincia Arabia* (Leiden: E. J. Brill, 1995).

35. Only two synagogues found in Israel have larger main halls: Beth Yera'h (760 m²) and Gaza (780 m²); for comparative architectural data, see Marilyn Chiat, *Handbook of Synagogue Architecture* (Brown Judaic Studies 29; Chico, California: Scholars Press, 1982).

36. The main construction of the underground aqueduct dates to the second century C.E.; however, there is evidence for some type of water system dating to either the first century B.C.E. or C.E., see Tsvika Tzuk, "The Aqueducts of Sepphoris," in *Sepphoris in Galilee: Crosscurrents of Culture* (eds. Rebecca Nagy et al.; Winona Lake, Indiana: Eisenbrauns, 1996) 45–49.

the biennial fallow and tax rates. But this does not help in determining the size of individual sites. However, once a site's population has been estimated, such figures give some indication of the amount of agricultural produce a site demanded, a point of some importance to be considered below for Sepphoris and Tiberias.

The most reliable method to estimate the number of residents at an ancient site is by measuring the extent of its ancient ruins and assessing the density of its living quarters, that is to say, by multiplying the number of hectares of a site by an approximate number of people per hectare. Ethnographers and archaeologists have rather extensively researched the correlation between population size and settlement area.[37] Computation of population densities in antiquity rest on the assumption that the human numbers correspond to the material remains, rendering a precise count unrealistic, but not the basic parameters.[38] A series of ethnoarchaeological analogies, where site size and populations are known with relative certainty, help determine the populations of other sites. For example, census data is available for European cities of the Middle Ages where the walls' circumference is known; records on inhabitants and village size exist for pre-modern Palestinian villages under British mandate; and census data have been collected from modern walled and unwalled rural villages in Mesopotamia.[39]

These ethnoarchaeological parallels show that there is no single standard coefficient for population density, given that settlement types differed over time and across regions, and that family demographics varied among cultures. But they reveal a series of predictors based on the type of site with which reasonable estimates can be made. For example, as a rule, walled cities have considerably higher population densities than do unwalled

---

37. The basic correlation between population size and settlement area has been demonstrated in a variety of studies: William Sumner, "Estimating Population by Analogy: An Example," in *Ethnoarchaeology: Implications of Ethnography for Archaeology* (ed. Carol Kramer; New York: Columbia University Press, 1979) 168; David W. Read, "Towards a formal theory of population size and area of habitation," Current *Anthropology* 19 (1978) 312–317; and Fekri Hassan, *Demographic Archaeology* (New York: Academic Press, 1981). I have examined the applicability of various methods to Capernaum in "The Population of Capernaum," *Occasional Papers of the Institute for Antiquity and Christianity* 24 (Claremont, 1992) 4–9.

38. See the cautious remarks in Andrew Wallace-Hadrill, *Houses and Society in Pompeii and Herculaneum* (Princeton: Princeton University Press, 1994) 91–117.

39. See the classic study by Josiah C. Russell, *Late Ancient and Medieval Population* (Transactions of the American Philosophical Society N.S. 48.3; Philadelphia: American Philosophical Society, 1958); for data on Palestine, see Chester C. McCown, "The Density of Population in Ancient Palestine," *JBL* 66 (1947) 425–436; and for Mesopotamia, see Robert McC. Adams, *Heartland of Cities: Surveys of Ancient Settlement and Land Use on the Central Floodplain of the Euphrates* (Chicago: The University of Chicago Press, 1981).

cities, particularly those from periods of relative political instability. Walled cities in the Aegean during the Bronze Age, as well as walled cities in Palestine during the Iron Age, provided housing and security for the surrounding areas' populations, driving the population densities to over 300 persons per hectare.[40] In contrast, unwalled villages, whether from Mesopotamia, Palestine, or Mesoamerica, have population densities well below 200.[41] Other important considerations are architectural styles, open areas at a site, and kinship patterns. Whether multiple-storied houses were a technological possibility or a cultural desideratum and how much open public space was expected must be considered. The average household size and whether single households dwelt in each housing unit are also important factors.

| Site | Density per Ha. |
|---|---|
| Roman Ostia | 360 - 435 |
| Bronze Age Aegean Walled City | ca. 300 |
| Iron Age Palestinian Walled City | ca. 300 |
| Mediaeval Walled Cities | ca. 250 |
| Roman Pompeii | 125 - 190 |
| Unwalled Mesopotamian Village | 100 - 150 |
| Unwalled 19th Cent. Palestinian Village | 100 - 150 |

*Table 3.1 Comparative Population Densities*

The two key variables that need to be scrutinized at Sepphoris and Tiberias are the extent of their ruins and the densities of their populace. The most helpful analogies for assessing their population densities are the excavated cities of Ostia and Pompeii in Italy. Both sites have been almost entirely excavated, and their states of preservation permit population estimates of some credibility. Both are contemporaneous with Sepphoris and Tiberias, were likewise walled cities, and share similar construction techniques. Both

---

40. For the former, see Colin Renfrew, *The Emergence of Civilization* (London: Methuen, 1972) 251. For Palestine, see Yigal Shiloh, "The Population of Iron Age Palestine in the Light of a Sample Analysis of Urban Plans, Areas, and Population Density," *BASOR* 239 (1980), 25–35; Shiloh's very high estimate of around 500 is effectively criticized by Magen Broshi and Ram Gophna, "The Settlements and Population of Palestine During the Early Bronze Age II–III," *BASOR* 253 (1984) 51 note 4. The most recent statement on ancient Palestine has been made by Jeffrey Zorn, "Estimating the Population Size of Ancient Settlements: Methods, Problems, Solutions, and a Case Study," *BASOR* 295 (1994) 31–48.

41. Adams, *Heartland of Cities*, 350; and Sumner, "Estimating Population by Analogy," 165–166.

also belong to the broader Mediterranean world with comparable household sizes and kinship patterns. These two sites provide reliable coefficients for inhabitants per hectare, to which those of the Galilean cities can be compared. Ostia was one of the most densely populated cities in the Roman Empire. Hemmed in by the Tiber and a swamp, the new-style Neronian apartment buildings or insulae provided space vertically for people attracted to the city's harbor facilities. The insulae in Ostia were on average three stories high, and some had more than four stories.[42] An examination of Ostia's city plan, insula by insula, and room by room, and assuming an average household size of four to nine persons as determined from literary sources and funerary inscriptions, sets the city's population inside the walls at between 25,000 and 30,000.[43] Since the entire area enclosed by Ostia's walls was just shy of 70 hectares, Ostia had a population density of between 360 and 435 persons per hectare.

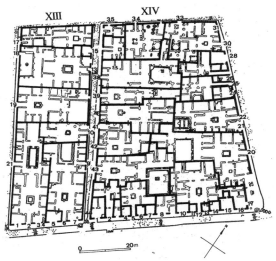

Figure 3.2 Insula at Pompeii

42. Meiggs, *Roman Ostia*, 240ff, 533; and Gustav Hermansen, *Ostia: Aspects of Roman City Life* (Edmonton: The University of Alberta Press, 1981) 51 note 27.

43. James E. Packer, *The Insulae of Imperial Ostia* (Memoirs of the American Academy in Rome 31; Rome: American Academy in Rome, 1971) 70. This estimate should be increased slightly to 30,000 for two reasons: Packer assumes that the unexcavated third of Ostia contains the same proportion of living quarters to public buildings—temples, baths, streets, storage magazines, and a forum. But likely the excavators tended to concentrate on and migrate toward public structures. Thus, the unexcavated areas probably have a higher ratio of private residences to public spaces. Second, Packer is overly conservative in assigning only one person to each *cubicum*, and a family of four to each shop, even to large shops with mezzanine floors and back rooms.

Pompeii, a much more typical Italian city, grew in semi-regular geometric patterns into an irregular oval shape. In contrast to Ostia, Nero's new-style architecture of multi-storied apartments made little headway in Pompeii, where houses were mostly single- or double-storied. There was only a modest vertical growth at Pompeii, where occasionally staircases and upper rooms were added to houses; more often, larger villas were split into multi-family dwellings. As a rule, single households inhabited each domestic unit with a mean of just under 200 m², though they varied considerably in size, from 25 m² to 2,500 m². The common household range per house was between four and nine members, but households of two or three members, with larger extended families and servants, resulting in twelve to sixteen members, were also encountered.[44] The city walls enclosed an area of 64 hectares, of which as much as one-third were open spaces for gardens or plazas, considerably more than at Ostia.[45] Recent estimates based on dwelling space suggest a population of between 8,000 and 12,000 for Pompeii.[46] A population of this size within Pompeii's walls (64 hectares) renders a population density of 125–190 persons per hectare, considerably lower than Ostia's.

Before comparing Sepphoris and Tiberias's population density with those established for Pompeii and Ostia, the second factor, the extent of their area, merits some initial comments. In determining settlement size, one must take into consideration the growth of a community over time. Cities were not static, but dynamic and changing, and the entire area covered by ruins may not have been occupied at any given period. In the case of Galilee, it is important to remember that urbanization intensified under direct Roman rule after the Bar Kochba Revolt in the second century C.E., and most cities reached their apex in the Late Roman and Byzantine Periods; especially Christian sites underwent population growth after Constantine.[47] Therefore, instead of just measuring the circumference of Sepphoris and Tiberias, one must clarify as best one can, with the results of stratigraphic excavations and probes across the site, the extent of the cities at the time of Herod Antipas. Although the particular interest in this study is the growth of these cities

---

44. Wallace-Hadrill, *Houses and Society in Pompeii and Herculaneam*, 91–117, and 187–216.

45. M. Grant, *Cities of Vesuvius: Pompeii and Herculaneum* (New York: Penguin, 1971) 53.

46. Hans Escheman, *Die städtebauliche Entwicklung des antiken Pompeji* (Römische Abteilungen, siebzehntes Ergänzungsheft; Heidelberg: F. H. Kerle, 1970) 60–61.

47. A point stressed by Arnold H. M. Jones, "The Urbanization of Palestine," *JRS* 21 (1931) 78–85; and more fully articulated by Michael Avi-Yonah, *The Holy Land from the Persian to the Arab Conquests: An Historical Geography* (Grand Rapids, Michigan: Baker, 1977).

from the Late Hellenistic to the Early Roman Period, the likelihood of expansion during the later Roman Periods and under Byzantine Rule is taken into consideration.

## Sepphoris and Tiberias as Consumer Cities

Calculating Sepphoris and Tiberias's population size in the first century with this method does not have absolute figures with an intrinsic value as its goal. Instead, the purpose is to set reasonable parameters of their populations that move beyond impressionistic quantification, and in particular, to gain some sense of their demographic impact on Galilee as a whole. The numbers at these urban sites provide some indication of the strain placed on the surrounding Galilean countryside to feed their inhabitants and, when coupled with the level of expenditures on public buildings at Sepphoris and Tiberias, the added strain placed on the countryside in terms of rents and taxes can be appraised.

The Extent of Sepphoris in the First Century

Sepphoris was continuously occupied until 1947, and the ruins from all periods at the site, ancient to modern, encompass an area of well under 100 hectares. Since the first-century occupation did not likely spread across this entire area, the results of excavations and probes across these remains must be scrutinized to approximate the extent of the first-century city. Extensive excavations on the acropolis and along the large terrace to the east and probes running eastward toward the aqueduct reveal the modest size of the Hellenistic Period's settlement and the city's dramatic growth in the Early Roman Period. Across all excavated areas, there is a virtual absence of architecture and a general lack of ceramic evidence from the Early and Late Hellenistic Periods. One of the few traceable Hellenistic Period structures is a double-walled military complex, either a fortress or barracks, at the top of the acropolis. Along with a few catapult *ballistae* stones and an arrowhead, the numerous Janneaen coins on its foundation indicate it served as a Maccabean stronghold during the first century B.C.E.[48] The fortress was likely surrounded by residential quarters stacked up rather tightly along the slope of the acropolis, but only a small area of about 2–3 hectares at the very top of the acropolis could have been settled in the first century B.C.E.[49] Late

---

48. Eric Meyers, "Sepphoris on the Eve of the Great Revolt (67–68 C.E.): Archaeology and Josephus," in *Galilee through the Centuries* (ed. E. Meyers; Winona Lake, Indiana: Eisenbrauns, 1999) 109–122.

49. Zeer Weiss and Ehud Netzer, "Hellenistic and Roman Sepphoris: The Archaeological Evidence," *Sepphoris in Galilee*, 29–30.

Hellenistic Sepphoris was a Hasmonean military and administrative settlement with a modest population of fewer than 1,000, most of whom were probably soldiers, officials, and their families.

During the Early Roman Period, the city expanded rapidly and drastically. Traces of Early Roman architecture, as well as pottery and numismatic finds, are present in most loci excavated by the current teams across the various areas of the site. All over the acropolis and the western domestic quarters, in the lower market area toward the aqueduct, and in scattered probes, an area covering at least 30 hectares, remains from the first century C.E. have been found.

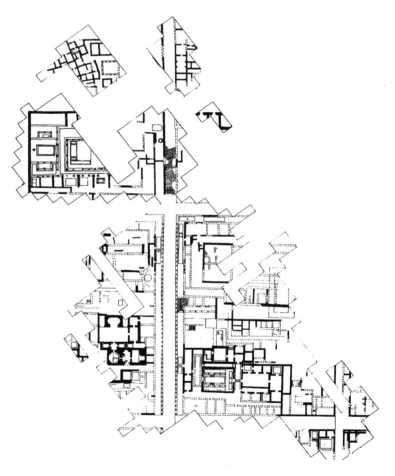

*Figure 3.3 The Lower Market at Sepphoris, Excavated by Hebrew University and University of South Florida (Nagy et al., 1996)*

Future excavations could unearth more Early Roman remains in as yet unexcavated areas, but the first-century site was at least 30 hectares. Like other sites in the Levant, Sepphoris continued to grow through the Middle and Late Roman Periods, when the city reached its zenith before the earthquake of 363 C.E., which devastated Northern Palestine. Estimates of the extent of the site over the entire Roman-Byzantine Periods lie around 60 hectares at the lower end, and in a more recent estimate by James F. Strange is placed at around 100 hectares at the higher end.[50] In the latter survey using subsurface interface radar, Strange traced a 50-hectare area likely enclosed by a city wall, with another possible 50 hectares outside the city walls. Whether this entire area was occupied during the first century remains uncertain; some of the ruins likely represent occupation from the later Byzantine or Arab city whose center may have shifted after the 363-C.E. earthquake. The first-century city was between 30 hectares, the area where Early Roman evidence was actually found, and an absolute maximum of 100 hectares, the total area of the ruins from all periods. Presumably the size of the first-century city would be close to the area Strange suggests lies within the walls, that is to say, an area of around 50 hectares, but reasonable parameters for first-century Sepphoris would more generally be between 40 and 60 hectares.

## The Population Density of Ancient Sepphoris

The current excavations provide considerable information on Sepphoris's population density, as numerous houses have been excavated on the western slope of the acropolis. A complete first-century house that has been excavated measures ca. 150 m², and others initially constructed in the Early Roman Period measure between 100 and 250 m², the common range of houses at Pompeii. Each of the houses excavated in the domestic quarters could have supported a second story, since walls were built atop solid boulder foundations sunk into the ground, and the first courses were constructed with limestone ashlars in header-stretcher technique measuring 60 to 70 cm in width. A vaulted building in the market area on the eastern side of the hill may have supported three stories, but that would be exceptional.[51]

Apartment style multi-storied insulae, as at Ostia, have not been found at Sepphoris, nor anywhere in Palestine for that matter; so that one can

---

50. For the former, see Magen Broshi, "The Population of Western Palestine," 4–5; for the latter the author is grateful to James F. Strange for sharing the plans of the USF Excavations at Sepphoris. Strange's estimates are based in large part on the 1984 and 1985 surveys reported in "Six Campaigns at Sepphoris," in *The Galilee in Late Antiquity*, 343; and Richard Batey, "Subsurface Interface Radar at Sepphoris, 1985," *Journal of Field Archaeology* 14 (1987) 1–8.

51. Strange, "Six Campaigns at Sepphoris," 349–350.

assume its population density to be more like Pompeii's, where single house-holds dwelt in each architectural unit, a longtime tradition of houses in Palestine.[52] Given the similarity of house size, a reasonable density coefficient for Sepphoris would be around 150 persons per hectare, accounting for about the same amount of open spaces, much of which was for gardens and plazas at Pompeii. One suspects that Sepphoris would have also had vacant lots set aside for future public buildings. Sepphoris could have been more crowded, and a desire to stay within the city's walls could have driven up the population density, especially in later periods, but lacking apartment style buildings, it could not have been near Ostia's density. Sepphoris's first-century population would then be at the very least 6,000 (40 x 150), and at the very most 15,000 inhabitants (60 x 250). Given these two extremes, a working population estimate for the first century would be 8,000–12,000 inhabitants.[53]

The Extent and Population Density of Ancient Tiberias

Determining the parameters of Tiberias's first-century population is more difficult, since the site was occupied continuously and today is a thriving city, making wide-scale excavation impossible. The excavations have been limited to a small area along the shore of the Sea of Galilee where the ancient city gate has been unearthed, toward the south of the modern city, and at the summit of Mount Berenice, where a Byzantine church has been excavated.

The area covered by Tiberias is defined on one side by the lake. Remains of a city wall are still visible and can be traced, though likely in their Byzantine form, and have not yet been stratigraphically excavated, except for the gate on the southern side. The area encompassed by these walls, including a protrusion to protect the structures atop Mount Berenice, is just over 80 hectares. This does not include the area between the ancient city of Tiberias proper and Hammath-Tiberias, a stretch of land that was apparently not occupied in antiquity (*t. Meg* 4.3) even though the two sites were considered one (*y. 'Erub.* 22d). As at Sepphoris, one would expect Tiberias to

52. Yizhar Hirshfeld, *The Palestinian Dwelling in the Roman-Byzantine Period* (Jerusalem: The Franciscan Printing Press, 1995) 102–103.

53. Two of the excavators have suggested that during the Middle Roman Period, Sepphoris's population was between 10,000 and 12,000, and during the Late Roman Period between 14,000 and 18,000, based on a possible site size of at least 35 hectares, Weiss and Netzer, "Hellenistic and Roman Sepphoris," 33, 36. Safrai places a maximum of 32,000 on Sepphoris's inhabitants at its apex in the Late Roman and Byzantine Periods, using a very high coefficient of 300 to 400 persons per hectare, *The Economy of Roman Palestine*, 373–74. In previous estimates, I have calculated the population of Sepphoris somewhat higher than 8–12,000, using 60 hectares, "Places in Early Christianity" (Ph.D. diss, The Claremont Graduate School, 1993) 68–70. These figures have been adopted and modified by Horsley, *Archaeology, History, and Society in Galilee*, 44–45, and by Crossan, *The Birth of Christianity*, 218–222.

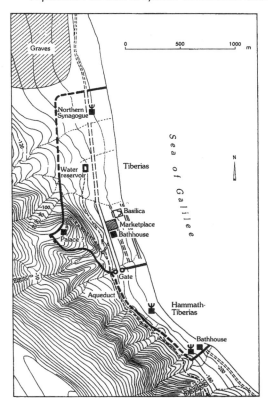

*Figure 3.4 Ancient Tiberias (Courtesy of Y. Hirschfeld)*

have grown over time, and cannot assume that the entire area encompassed by the walls was settled under Herodian rule. First-century Tiberias was smaller, probably no more than 60 hectares, and Gideon Foerster, one of its excavators, has suggested the Roman Period city to be around 30 hectares.[54] Since domestic areas are yet to be excavated at Tiberias, there is a lack of any hard evidence on Tiberias's population density in the first century. However, given that Tiberias was Antipas's second city, founded after he had rebuilt Sepphoris, its builders drew upon the same architectural tradition, and its

---

54. "Tiberias: Excavations in the South of the City," 1470. My calculations are based on Yizhar Hirshfeld's map, first published in "Tiberias: Preview of Coming Attractions," *BAR* 17.2 (1991) 46; a larger copy of the same map appears in "The 'Anchor Church' at the Summit of Mount Berenice near Tiberias," *Qadmoniot* 26 (1993) 120 [Hebrew]. A survey of the Roman Period city was made by Yohann H. Landau, "The Site of Tiberias," in *Eretz Kinnaroth* (Jerusalem: Jewish Palestine Exploration Society, 1950) 49 [Hebrew], cited in Michael Avi-Yonah, "The Foundation of Tiberias," *IEJ* 1 (1950–1951) 164–164; see also Magen Broshi, "The Population of Western Palestine," 4–5.

inhabitants had similar household structures. Tiberias's population density was like that at Sepphoris, between 150 and 250 persons per hectare. The upper parameters of Tiberias's population in the first century would then be 15,000 (60 x 250), and lacking sufficient stratigraphic excavations to determine the extent of the first-century site, its lower end was likely no less than 4,500 inhabitants (30 x 150). It is sensible to suggest that Tiberias's population was similar to Sepphoris and to work with an estimate for the Herodian city of between 6,000 and 12,000 inhabitants.

## The Populations of Galilean Villages

The magnitude of these two Herodian cities in the first century can be appreciated after a cursory glance at other Galilean towns, villages, or hamlets. None of the ruins of other Galilean sites cover areas of the same magnitude as Sepphoris and Tiberias. Even Japhia, which Josephus calls the largest village of Galilee (*Life* 235) measures well under 10 hectares. The walls at Yodefat, the best-preserved Galilean village, enclosed an area of just under 5 hectares.[55] The ruins of smaller Galilean villages, such as Gath-Hepher, reputed village of Jonah, measure 5 hectares or less; and the ruins of many Galilean hamlets or nucleated farms cover only 1 hectare, if that.[56] Gabara, which Josephus calls a polis and one of the most significant cities in Galilee, has yet to be located precisely somewhere in Upper Galilee, giving some indication of its actual diminutive size (*Life* 124). Again, except for Yodefat, which was destroyed in the first war with Rome and never resettled, it is doubtful that these areas were occupied during the first century in their entirety. Furthermore, most were not walled in the first century, a factor that ethnographic parallels show lowers the population density, since growth can be organically accommodated by new buildings on the periphery.[57] The first-century populations of Nazareth and Capernaum, sites that have been excavated and are of interest for the study of early Christianity, can be estimated with some certainty for the first century, thanks to their extensive excavations, which reveal that they are considerably smaller than the Herodian cities. At Capernaum, which will be analyzed in greater detail in chapter five, the extent of the site during the Early Roman Period measured no more than 17 hectares. At Nazareth, tombs and topography limit the area covered during the Early Roman Period to no more than 4 hectares.[58]

---

55. David Adan-Bayewitz and Mordechai Aviam, "Iotapata, Josephus, and the Siege of 67: Preliminary Report on the 1992–4 Seasons," *JRS* 10 (1997) 133.

56. Gal, *The Galilee in the Iron Age*, 12–35.

57. Josephus describes his activities in Galilee as fortifying the villages and cities of Galilee, many for the first time, *War* 2.573.

58. James F. Strange, "Nazareth," *ABD* 4:1050–51.

| Galilean Site | Max. Area in Ha. | Max. Population |
|---|---|---|
| Capernaum | No more than 17 | 1,700 |
| Tarichaea | 10 | 1,000 – 1,500 |
| Jodefat | 5 | 1,000 – 1,500 |
| Gath Hepher | 5 | 500 |
| Nazareth | 5 | 400 |

*Table 3.2 Areas and Populations of Galilean Villages*[59]

Agricultural Implications of Sepphoris and Tiberias's Growth

The key demographic characteristic of Sepphoris and Tiberias in antiquity is their dramatic growth between the Late Hellenistic and Early Roman Periods attributable to Antipas, from around 1,000 to at least 8,000 inhabitants at Sepphoris, and from zero to at least 8,000 at Tiberias. Obviously Sepphoris and Tiberias were politically important as Herod Antipas's capitals. According to Josephus, Herod Antipas rebuilt Sepphoris into the "ornament of Galilee" after its destruction by Varus in 4 B.C.E. (*Ant.* 18.27), and shortly thereafter founded Tiberias as its new capital (*Ant.* 18.37–38), though the capital alternated between the two throughout the first century. They were the cities from which Antipas ruled, where he housed his administrative apparatus (e.g., the ἀγορανόμοι lead weights from Sepphoris and Tiberias), and in which the local elites made their homes (e.g. the δεκαπρῶτοι, βουλή, ὑπάρχοι, and ἔπαρχος mentioned in *War* 2.615, *Ant.* 18.149, and *Life* 32–6, 271, 278, 296, 300, 381).[60] Josephus's account of the founding of Tiberias raises the question of the origin of these cities' populations and the causes of their rapid growth. Although he does not comment on how the

---

59. See the helpful data in Safrai, *The Economy of Roman Palestine*, 60–67; and the entries in *OEANE* and *NEAEHL*. The larger sites around Galilee, such as Bethsaida (about 10 hectares) and Gaba Hippeon (around 10 hectares) are not nearly as large as Sepphoris and Tiberias either, Rami Arav and John J. Rousseau, "The Bethsaïda Excavations: Historical and Archaeological Approaches," *The Future of Christianity: Essays in Honor of Helmut Koester* (ed. Birger Pearson; Minneapolis: Fortress Press, 1991) 77–106; Azriel Siegelmann, "The Identification of Gaba Hippeon, *PEQ* 116 (1984) 89–93; Zvi Gal, *Lower Galilee during the Iron Age* (ASOR Dissertation Series 8; Winona Lake: Eisenbrauns, 1992) 12–35. The figures in this chart are approximations based on recent surveys and estimated population density and differ, therefore, from Ben-David's schematic chart completed with the assistance of older reports, *Talmudische Ökonomie I*, 52.

60. A point stressed by Horsley, *Archaeology, History and Society in Galilee*, 43–87. On the lead weights, see Shraga Qedar, "Two Lead Weights of Herod Antipas and Agrippa II and the Early History of Tiberias," *Israel Numismatic Journal* 9 (1986–87) 29–35; and Yaakov Meshorer, "The Lead Weight," *BA* 49 (1986) 16–17.

rebuilt Sepphoris was repopulated after Varus deported its previous citizens, he does narrate some problems with populating Tiberias. According to Josephus's *Antiquities*, Antipas lured and coerced peasants from the surrounding Galilean villages and countryside to colonize Tiberias (18.37–38, οὐκ ὀλίγον δὲ καὶ τὸ Γαλιλαῖον ἦν). There is no archaeological evidence for large numbers of non-Jews living in the new Herodian cities. Josephus mentions that at Tiberias, some Greeks, likely Syro-Phoenicians from the coast or Tyrian Plain, were the target of the much larger Jewish population at the outbreak of hostilities in 66 C.E., when the Jewish citizens there joined with other rural Galileans to kill the Greeks, loot the palace, and burn the debt archives kept there (*Life* 66–67).[61]

Galilean villagers and rural peasants resettled in the Herodian cities, perhaps even migrating there after their lands were dispossessed; however, one should not envision the depopulation of rural sites to populate the urban centers. The villages around Sepphoris and Tiberias, indeed all across Galilee, likewise grew in the Early Roman Period at a time when many smaller sites were initially settled. The entire Galilee, both Upper and Lower, experienced demographic growth at this time.[62] The causes of this measurable population growth in Galilee were likely the relatively stable political situation under the Herodians and increased agricultural production fostered under centralized Herodian authority, which allowed birth rates to spiral higher.[63]

Sepphoris and Tiberias's population growth had an impact on the surrounding Galilean countryside. These cities were at the center of a major shift in Galilean demographics over the course of a single generation. This population growth, experienced across the entire Galilee and concentrated in Sepphoris and Tiberias, affected the countryside in profound ways. The archaeological evidence for rapid population growth at Sepphoris and Tiberias correlates with a shift in agricultural patterns across Galilee. The agricultural practices of the Galilee were stretched by Herod Antipas's rebuilding Sepphoris and building Tiberias, and landholding patterns realigned. The agricultural focus turned to feeding Sepphoris and Tiberias.

61. See Richard Horsley, "Bandits, Messiahs, and Longshoremen: Popular Unrest in Galilee around the Time of Jesus," in *SBLSP 1988* (ed. David Lull; Atlanta: Scholars Press, 1988) 183–199.

62. See the collection of data from a variety of surveys across Palestine in Safrai, *The Economy of Roman Palestine*, 436–442. A common feature accompanying urbanization across the Roman world was the increase in a region's settlement density after the building of a city, Merril Millet, "Roman Towns and their Territories: An Archaeological Perspective," in *City and Country in the Ancient World*, 169–189.

63. Bezael Bar-Kochba, "Manpower, Economics, and Internal Strife in the Hasmonean State," in Armées et fiscalité dans le monde antique (Paris: Editions du centre national de la recherche scientifique, 1977) 167–194); and Safrai, *The Economy of Roman Palestine*, 442–446.

Galilean society had been made up of a series of villages, hamlets, and farms, populated almost entirely with peasant families who tilled their own small plots of land. From the scant evidence in Galilee during this Late Hellenistic Period, Seán Freyne has shown that large royal estates existed only on the outskirts of Galilee, in the Jezreel Valley, north of Upper Galilee at Beth Anath, and along the coast.[64] Prior to the Roman Period, that is to say the founding of Sepphoris and Tiberias, not all of the arable land was being farmed in Galilee, and a biannual fallow could be practiced to reduce the chances of crop failure. Terraces and strip lynchets were yet to level many Galilean slopes into land suitable for plowing.[65] The average land holding necessary to feed a typical Galilean household of four to nine members at this time would have been between 4–6 hectares, without factoring in taxes.[66] Archaeological surveys and some papyri from elsewhere indicate that families typically parceled out their land into smaller plots, the result of inheritance and dowry practices.[67] Dispersing a family's plots over wide areas had numerous advantages to peasants: it aided self-sufficiency as it made available some plots on flatter terrain that were more suitable for grain and dry farming; some were on alluvial terrain for vegetables or legumes; and rockier sloping terrain could accommodate orchards and vines.[68] Diversification of products or polycropping also minimized the consequences of crop failure,

64. Although Freyne relies on Tscherikower to locate Beth Anath in Lower Galilee, an unlikely position, *Galilee from Alexander the Great to Hadrian*, 147 n. 15, 156; and similarly Albrecht Alt, "Galiläische Probleme," in *Kleine Schriften zur Geschichte des Volkes Israel II* (München: C. H. Beck'sche, 1959) 384–98. Victor Tscherikower's uncertainty was due to his equivocation over the location of the Kedesh mentioned, as either the Kedesh in Upper Galilee or Khirbet Kdish on the Sea of Galilee, *Palestine Under the Ptolemies. A Contribution to the Study of the Zenon Papyri, Mizraism IV–V* (New York: G. E. Stechert, 1937) 84 note 80. However, certainly the Kedesh at hand is that in Upper Galilee, 17 kilometers north of Hazor, where ample Hellenistic finds have been found, while Khirbet Kdish shows no Hellenistic occupation, Yohanan Aharoni, "Kedesh," *NEAEHL* 3:855–6; this location seems to fit the general locale of the site given in Josh 19:38, and Judges 1:3, see Félix-Marie Abel, "La Liste Géographique du Papyrus 71 du Zénon," *RB* 32 (1923) 409–15.

65. B. Golomb and Y. Kedar, "Ancient Agriculture in the Galilee Mountains," *IEJ* 21 (1971) 136–140; Ben-David has collected the rabbinic discussions on terracing, *Talmudische Ökonomie I*, 81–93.

66. Ben-David, *Talmudische Ökonomie I*, 135–141; Safrai, *The Economy of Roman Palestine*, 358–364; and Fiensy, *The Social History of Palestine*, 93–94.

67. Golomb and Kedar, "Ancient Agriculture in the Galilee Mountains" 136–40; Gildas Hamel, *Poverty and Charity in Roman Palestine, First Three Centuries C.E.* (Near Eastern Studies 23; Berkeley: University of California Press, 1990) 134–137; Magen Broshi, "Agriculture and Economy in Roman Palestine: Seven Notes on the Babatha Archive," *IEJ* 42 (1992) 230–240; Safrai *The Economy of Roman Palestine*, 355–370; and Freyne, "Jesus and the Urban Culture of Galilee," 608–609.

68. Magen Broshi has pointed to ethnoarchaeological parallel: "In 1935 there were 774,929 agricultural plots in Palestine, divided between 80,000–90,000 peasant

and spread the required labor more evenly over time, since even identical crops will not ripen at the same time in different soils and slopes. Polycropping could include letting such items as millet or lupine grow with little care, fodder not normally consumed but easily storable and digestible by humans in times of famine.[69] There is evidence that peasants foraged uncultivated areas for acorns and stored them for times of famine.[70] Aimed at minimal risk, families strove toward self-sufficiency in subsistence items by dispersing land holdings, diversifying products, and storing foodstuffs to protect against crop failure. Self-sufficiency was the goal of each peasant, and reciprocity among families, clans, and villagers was a primary means of exchange. In times of crisis, as Peter Garnsey says, the "first line of defence consisted of kinsmen, neighbors and friends in [their] own rural community."[71] Such conditions are described somewhat nostalgically in biblical imagery in 1 Maccabees: "They tilled their land in peace; the ground gave its increase, and the trees of the plains their fruit. . . . All the people sat under their own vines and fig trees, and there was none to make them afraid" (14:8, 12).

This situation was changed with Herod Antipas's rule in Galilee, a move perhaps already initiated under Herod the Great. The rise in the Galilee's population that accompanied the building of Sepphoris and Tiberias necessitated more intensive agricultural practices, whether by cultivating more land, letting less lie fallow, or otherwise farming it for higher yields. Overall, Galilee's economic emphasis shifted from peasant families striving for self-sufficiency with their surplus paid in kind to Hasmonean officials; to paying taxes and rents, in kind and increasingly in cash, to the Herodian rulers who lived in and ruled from the cities of Sepphoris and Tiberias. Instead of farming for their own necessities and trading for a few items in which they were deficient, peasant families were now responsible for a higher demand for taxes to support a growing administrative apparatus, a manufacturing sector, and construction crews. Although most of the available data on tax rates under the Herodians is anecdotal, it has been estimated at between one-third

---

families. This is an average of almost ten plots per family, without considering the *musha* that constituted some 25 percent of the land," "Agriculture and Economy in Roman Palestine," 240.

69. Peter Garnsey, *Famine and Food Supply in the Greco-Roman World* (Cambridge: Cambridge University Press, 1988) 43–55; for an ancient farmer's annual schedule, see the valuable chart in Safrai, *The Economy of Roman Palestine*, 366.

70. See e.g., Galen 6.620, who describes how acorns were stored as fodder for swine, and in times of famine first the animals were consumed, and then their fodder. This passage is of some note for the parable of the prodigal son, who is reduced to eating swine fodder, Luke 15:16.

71. *Famine and Food Supply*, 63.

and one-half of all produce and income.[72] Polycropping inevitably waned, as monocropping was required to produce higher yields and satisfy tax demands. More cash crops were sold for coinage with which peasants purchased many of their necessities. In other words, an asymmetrical exchange of goods increased. At best, peasant farmers could band together fragmented holdings to create economies of scale for grain, the most desirable produce, but more often, peasant land holdings were forced together into larger tracts by rulers or wealthy elites. Herod monetized his local economy to pay Roman taxes in currency; the sources consistently refer to Herod the Great and Antipas's income and tributes only in terms of precious metals.[73] This facilitated the trend of peasants selling their land to pay off their taxes in cash, and then staying on their land as tenants or indentured servants paying rent, or simply leaving their land to ply an artisan trade and eke out an existence.[74] In the process of increased tenancy and larger estates, a substantial number of rural peasants moved to the cities, where they remained involved in agricultural production as tenant farmers or day laborers.[75] Urban centers in antiquity provided a substantial labor force for agriculture, who could be exploited seasonally during harvest time; who harvested fields, orchards, and vineyards; and who brought the produce to Sepphoris and Tiberias for refinement and storage. The wine installations, olive presses, granaries, threshing floors, and millstones that have been found surrounding and even inside Sepphoris indicate as much.[76]

A study by David Fiensy on the Herodian economy notes that in spite of the difficulties in discerning whether land was owned or leased from the archaeological data, the trend points to a rise of larger holdings and leasing at the expense of small holdings. This confirms Shimon Applebaum's assessment that the impact of increased population in the first century "reduced the Jewish peasant unit of cultivation and endangered the cultivator's margin of livelihood."[77] This resulted in a more and more asymmetrical mode of

---

72. Ben-David estimates the rate at 33 percent, and considers the bulk of this to be due to the Temple taxes and various biblical tithes, *Talmudische Ökonomie I*, 136; and Oakman states that one-third would be the lower end of taxation, *Jesus and the Economic Questions*, 57–72.

73. Menahem Stern, "The Reign of Herod," in *The World History of the Jewish People* (First Series, Vol. 7; ed. Michael Avi-Yonah; Jerusalem: Massada, 1975) 92–97 [75–132]; and Oakman, *Jesus and the Economic Questions*, 69–72.

74. Heinz Kreissig, "Die Landwirtschaftliche Situation in Palästina vor dem judäischen Krieg," *Acta Antiqua* 17 (1969) 223–54.

75. See the helpful comments on the confusion of the term "peasants" among biblical scholars, Crossan, *The Birth of Christianity*, 216–218.

76. Strange, "Six Campaigns at Sepphoris," 343.

77. "Economic Life in Palestine," in *The Jewish People of the First Century II* (eds. Shemuel Safrai and Menachen Stern; Compendia Rerum Iudaicarum ad Novum

exchange, in which other indentured extended families or clan members were of less assistance than previously in times of crisis, and other tenants or day laborers in the village were of no help. Instead, wealthier villagers, urban landowners, or members of the ruling apparatus were solicited as magnanimous patrons: owners of much land could provide seasonal work for hire and allow families to stay on the land and work it, or members of the ruling apparatus could ease individuals' tax burdens in exchange for services and honor.[78]

Several archaeological surveys of the Galilee indicate the intensification of agricultural practices during the Roman Period. During earlier periods, Galilee was more heavily forested and contained many parcels of uncultivated lands, but by the Roman Period as much as 97 percent of all arable land was cultivated, and strip lynchets and terraces enabled the exploitation of almost every available plot of land in Galilee. Palynological studies have shown that in Roman Period Galilee the cultivation of olive trees eliminated the presence of wild trees such as oaks or terebinths.[79] In addition to the cultivation of more land, higher production levels were achieved by working larger tracts in valleys and on alluvial lands, with oxen and yokes, made possible by capital investment.[80]

Some data on feeding ancient populations concretizes the need for increased production in Galilee. The average per capita intake of grain, the basic stable of the Mediterranean diet in antiquity, is estimated at 250 kg per inhabitant. A good return on 150 kg seed per hectare in Galilee's fertile soil could yield an annual crop of 1,000–1,200 kg, of which 150 kg would have to be set aside for next year's seed. Given the necessity of a biennial fallow, and not accounting for any taxes in kind passed on outside Galilee, 1 hectare could supply grain for two people.[81] The best arable land around Sepphoris in the Beth Netofah Valley is around 5,000 hectares; along the Naḥal Zippori another 1,000 hectares are found; and the Tir'an Valley measures around 3,000 hectares.[82] This would supply grain for around 18,000 people per year.

Testamentum; Amsterdam: Van Gorcum, 1976) 691; see also Ben-David, *Talmudische Ökonomie I*, 138–141; and Oakman, *Jesus and the Economic Questions*, 77–80.

78. Garnsey, *Famine and Food Supply*, 56–63; and Freyne, "Jesus and the Urban Culture of Galilee," 606–610.

79. H. Baruch, "Shinuyei Tzomeach Be-ezor Kineret," *Rotem* 16 (1985) [Hebrew], cited in Safrai, *The Economy of Roman Palestine*, 441.

80. Golomb and Kedar have noted the pattern in the larger valleys of the Galilee similar to the *centuriae quadratae* laid out by Roman *agrimensores*, "Ancient Agriculture in Galilee," 137–139.

81. See Ben-David, *Talmudische Ökonomie I*, 106; Garnsey and Saller, *The Roman Empire*, 78–82; John K. Evans, "Wheat production and its social consequences in the Roman World," *CQ* 31 (1981), 432–3; Broshi, "The Population of Western Palestine," 7; Oakman, *Jesus and the Economic Questions*, 28; and Safrai, *The Economy of Roman Palestine*, 355.

82. Gal, *Lower Galilee During the Iron Age*, 3.

The Gennesaur Plain north of Tiberias and the arable land south measure around 8,000 hectares, supplying 16,000 people per year with grain. By analogy, the area of Pompeii's economic territory was around 16,000 hectares, with a total population of 36,000 for both rural areas and the city of Pompeii, the latter having between 8,000 and 10,000 inhabitants.[83] The fertility of these valleys was likely the main reason why Herod Antipas located his new city where he did. When one considers the presence of inhabitants in the villages and rural areas of the countryside, populations of between 8,000 and 12,000 each in Sepphoris and Tiberias were clearly the prime factors of Galilee's agronomy.

This assessment of the Herodian cities' consumptive demands on Galilean agriculture does not take into account the system of taxation, the extent to which Galileans paid the Temple tax and tithes, nor the rulers and landowning elites' tendency to store or hoard grain. The storing of grain by rulers and elites was a common practice in antiquity, and allowed them to sell or redistribute it to their subjects during crop failure or food shortages, or to other cities and regions during their crises. Josephus comments on the imperial granaries as a sore spot with the rural Galileans (*Life* 71, 118), and Acts 12:20 mentions Agrippa I's habit of selling grain to the coastal cities of Tyre and Sidon, which "depended on the King's country for food." Not all produce farmed on the land supplied its inhabitants. Whether Galileans, or Judean peasants, paid tithes and the Temple tax is a matter of some debate, as the questioning of Jesus in Mark 12:13–17 illustrates.[84] Although there is little clear evidence on tax rates and collection practices in Herodian Galilee or Palestine in late antiquity, it was likely somewhere between one-third to one-half of yields, distributed through the imperial and Herodian coffers.[85]

Urban Architecture, Manufacturing, and Trade at Sepphoris and Tiberias

Although agricultural products were the primary commodities and land the principal capital, the extent to which Antipas's rule increased exploitation and raised the asymmetrical balance of exchange can be gauged archaeologically in the extent of urban architecture, local manufacturing, and interregional trade.

The level of urban building projects is one archaeologically discernible factor in the equation to determine the level of exertion placed on the agriculture

83. Willem Jongman, *The Economy and Society of Pompeii* (Amsterdam: J. C. Gieben, 1988) 106–107, 112.

84. A positive view, that the taxes tended to be paid, is offered by Sanders, *Judaism: Practice and Belief*, 146–69; a more pessimistic view is given by Fiensy, *The Social History of Palestine*, 104.

85. See Broshi, "Agriculture and Economy in Roman Palestine," 240; Safrai, *The Roman Economy*, 359–62; Oakman, *Jesus and the Economic Questions*, 57–72; and Sanders, *Judaism: Practice and Belief*, 159–69.

of Galilee. At Sepphoris, some basic observations on the general arrangement of public architecture in the first century can be pieced together from the various excavations. Josephus described Antipas's Sepphoris as the "ornament of Galilee," a label that resonates in the archaeological record (*Ant.* 18.27). Considerable building activity is detectable throughout the first-century strata at Sepphoris. On the western slope of the acropolis, a massive retaining wall was constructed along which houses and a street were laid in a grid pattern. Along the southern slope a few walls on the same grid from the Early Roman Period have been excavated, despite considerable erosion and modern root damage. At the same time, buildings on a large level terrace to the east of the acropolis were laid out on a rigid orthogonal grid, commonly considered Sepphoris's lower market.[86] Much of this area has been rather extensively excavated, and two main perpendicular streets typical of Roman city planning, the north-south *cardo* and east-west *decumanus*, have been uncovered. These streets were in continual use for at least 500 years, and in spite of their repair and renovations over the years, the excavators remain confident that they were originally constructed around the time of Antipas, who laid the grid and the streets within which the city then grew.[87] The street had a width of 13.5 meters, and limestone stylobates lined the street proper and supported rows of columns to separate the street proper from the roofed sidewalks lined with shops.

The pavers in the street were laid diagonally in herringbone style, and deep ruts from wagons still cut into the street and testify to the sturdiness of the original foundation and pavement. The sidewalks were originally paved with simple monochrome mosaics, with more ornate mosaics surviving from later centuries.[88] Bits and pieces from other public structures have been found dating to the first century. Most of the well-known mosaics from Sepphoris date to later centuries, when the city reached its apex, but underneath these, elements from the first century have been found in line with these discoveries. For example, a basilica covering an area of 35 by 40 meters, with porches covering another 25 by 40 meters, has first-century elements. In style and layout it is similar to other administrative buildings or courts in the Roman world.

The building of Sepphoris was centrally planned in the first century, when Roman style architecture was newly introduced in Galilee. Its colonnaded market area, with paved streets and water channels, white plastered buildings with their red-tiled roofs, mosaic floors, and painted frescoes, all laid out in a grid system, was a novelty in Early Roman Galilee.[89]

---

86. On the markets of Sepphoris, see Stuart S. Miller, *Studies in the History and Traditions of Sepphoris* (Leiden: E.J. Brill, 1984) 29.

87. Weiss and Netzer, "Hellenistic and Roman Sepphoris," 32–33.

88. See Weiss and Netzer, "Hellenistic and Roman Sepphoris," 29–37.

89. Strange, "Some Implications of Archaeology," 31–41.

Although few areas have been excavated in Tiberias, one of the significant finds that bespeaks the style and magnitude of Tiberias's public architecture in the first century is the city's southern gate.[90] Facing the springs at Hammath Tiberias, the gate, which was built at the city's foundation, is a massive structure made of finely hewn basalt ashlars. Round towers 7 meters in diameter protruded from the gate complex, flanked by two niches and two pedestals for columns with rhomboids in relief. This imposing façade opened onto the north-south *cardo* that ran through the entire city. Best preserved from later periods, basalt pavers in herringbone style covered a 12-meter-wide street, flanked by 5-meter wide colonnades on either side, supported by granite columns, which led into small cubicle-like shops.[91] Though much less evidence exists for Tiberias than Sepphoris, several observations can be made: The *cardo* points to centralized city planning in Roman style and considerable investment in terms of labor and resources by the rulers; the gate points to the typical Roman predilection for facades, and more importantly, the desire to erect enclosures dividing space between insiders and outsiders.

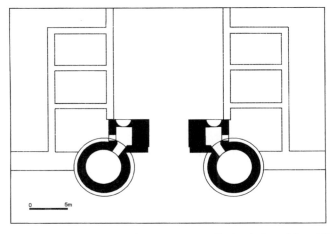

*Figure 3.5 The City Gate at Tiberias (adapted from NEAEHL)*

Sepphoris and Tiberias were centers of consumption for agricultural produce as well as raw materials for its architectural projects. Local limestone and basalt had to be quarried and hewn into ashlars appropriate for Herod Antipas's cities. Tessarae had to be struck for the mosaics covering the floors of both the private houses of the affluent and the public buildings

---

90. Gidion Foerster, "Tiberias: Excavations in the South of the City," *NEAHL* 4:1470–73
91. Hirshfeld, "Tiberias," *NEAEHL* 4:1467.

they sponsored.[92] Limestone had to be dug and processed for the frescoes that covered many walls, and plaster that covered many floors. Some items that were not readily available locally, such as marble sheeting, had to be imported, at an enormous cost, from outside Galilee.

It must be stressed that virtually no public architecture has been discovered at any of the other sites in Galilee. The general absence of pre-70 C.E. synagogues in Palestine has often been discussed in terms of synagogue-history, but the absence of public architecture in general in Galilee prior to 70 C.E.—other than the cities of Sepphoris and Tiberias—bears emphasis as well.[93] For the most part, buildings in villages and smaller settlements had thatch roofs and not tiles, were made of fieldstone and mortar instead of ashlar and fresco, and had beaten earth floors instead of mosaics or plaster, not to mention the complete absence of marble.

The Herodian cities also consumed manufactured goods for its citizens' daily life. There is evidence in Galilee that a variety of locally-made goods arose with the construction of Sepphoris and Tiberias. A chalk vessel manufacturing site near the village of Reina went into production as Sepphoris was built, some 4 km to the southeast, and 3 km north of Nazareth. The site is typical of local manufacturing centers in antiquity: it was more or less a cottage industry where members of a household gathered to shape stones around a quarry. Wasters were scattered around, but there is no evidence of a permanent industrial complex; apparently people worked in the open air or with temporary shelter.[94] A pottery manufacturing site 1½ km north of Sepphoris has been identified from an abundance of pottery wasters found. Likely, the village of Shikhin, mentioned in rabbinic literature as the satellite village of Sepphoris, was a major producer of bowls and jugs for the city of Sepphoris.[95]

Sepphoris and Tiberias also consumed wares from Galilean sites even farther removed. In an important study of pottery to that in Galilee, David

---

92. The famous Dionysos mosaic, dating to the early third century, was made up of tessarae of twenty-three different colors, most of them from local limestone. Some, however, seem to have been brought from farther away, Eric Meyers, Ehud Netzer, and Carol Meyers, *Sepphoris* (Winona Lake: Eisenbrauns, 1992) 42.

93. On the general lack of pre-70 synagogues, see Marilyn Chiat, "First-Century Synagogue Architecture: Methodological Problems," in *Ancient Synagogues: The State of Research* (ed. Joseph Gutman; Brown Judaic Studies 22; Chico, California: Scholars Press, 1981) 50–58; and Paul Flesher, "Palestinian Synagogues before 70 C.E.: A Review of the Evidence," in *Approaches to Ancient Judaism* (vol. 6; eds. Jacob Neusner and Ernst Frerichs; Atlanta: Scholars Press, 1989) 75–80.

94. Zvi Gal, "A Stone-Vessel Manufacturing Site in the Lower Galilee," *'Atiqot* 20 (1991) 25*–26*, 179–180.

95. Strange describes the site as a place "where ten or so families, or more, pursued a single industry," "Six Campaigns at Sepphoris," 351–35, 354.

Adan-Bayewitz traced the distribution of household pottery produced at Kefar Ḥananya, a small village in northern Galilee, some 25 km from Sepphoris. The distribution of the common kitchen ware in Galilee is predictable, given the high cost of overland transport, which lowered profits as distances increased: "in settlements near the manufacturing center virtually all the cooking ware is from that center, while in more distant settlements the relative quantities are inversely related to their distance from the center."[96] Kefar Ḥananya wares are virtually absent outside of a 25-km radius, yet they comprise roughly half of the common kitchenware of the city of Sepphoris, even though it is on the periphery of this 25-km radius, after which the ware drastically drops off. It is not that Sepphoris provided a lucrative market, compensating for the relatively lengthy overland transport, but more likely that the ruling authorities in Sepphoris commissioned Kefar Ḥananya to produce its household pottery. Many wares also found their way to Sepphoris as a means to transport gains, cereals, oils, or wine as tax or rent in kind. Sepphoris would have served as a secondary distribution point for the Kefar Ḥananya ware, which was redistributed, again perhaps filled with agricultural products from around Sepphoris.[97] There is evidence for Kefar Ḥananya wares in Hammat Tiberias, but because of the lack of excavations there is little evidence for them at Tiberias.[98] Very likely Tiberias had similar economic arrangements with local manufacturing sites as well, and its location on the lake would have hastened traffic with other sites on or near any shore of the lake. None of the Kefar Ḥananya ware antedates the founding of Sepphoris and Tiberias, so that their function as consumers must be seen as an important factor in local trade and production.

## Antipas's Urbanization in Perspective

It must be noted that neither Sepphoris nor Tiberias shows the same kind of appetite for materials, buildings, and particularly decorative elements that

---

96. David Adan-Bayewitz and Isadore Pearlman, "The Local Trade of Sepphoris in the Roman Period," *IEJ* 40 (1990) 170.

97. Adan-Bayewitz and Pearlman, "The Local Trade of Sepphoris," 170–171. Unlike a modern market economy which the Adan-Bayewitzes seem to assume, a redistributive or tributary political economy would be more likely in Galilee, see *Horsley, Archaeology, History, and Society*, 66–87.

98. Edwards suggests the importance of the lake for distribution to the Golan and across the Jordan Rift, see "The Socio-Economic and Cultural Ethos in the First Century," 57, esp. note 19, citing David Adan-Bayewitz, "The Pottery," "The Excavations of an Ancient Boat in the Sea of Galilee," *'Atiqot* 19 (1990) 89–96; and Charles Fritsch and Immanuel Ben-Dor, "The Link Marine Expedition to Israel, 1960," *BA* 24 (1961) 57–58.

symbolized Greco-Roman culture, compared to Caesarea Maritima or Scythopolis, the major cities in Palestine. Nor did they belong in the same category as these metropolises, in terms of site size, population, or agricultural demand. The ruins at Caesarea Maritima during the Roman period cover an area of nearly 100 hectares; those of Scythopolis are more than 100 hectares.[99] One should imagine populations of at least between 20,000 and 40,000 in each of these cities, double those of Sepphoris and Tiberias. Each also had at its disposal vast tracts of fertile land: Scythopolis controlled the plains south of the Sea of Galilee along the Jordan River and the eastern Jezreel Valley; Caesarea had access to the coastal plain and Shefelah and conducted maritime trade with Egypt.

In addition to their larger size and proximity to more arable land, both Caesarea and Scythopolis are known to have built quantitatively more and qualitatively better civic structures in the Greco-Roman urban parlance. Imported marble columns are ubiquitous at Caesarea and Scythopolis, an index of their wealth and ability to import massive items—30 yoke of oxen are needed to transport a single drum.[100] They are virtually absent at Sepphoris and Tiberias. Several smaller marble fragments for wall or floor sheeting have been found at Sepphoris, but more often *al dado* style frescoes have been uncovered, which imitated the green, red, and white marble patterns and can be produced with local materials. The architects at Sepphoris found visual mimicry more affordable. At the larger or coastal sites like Caesarea and Scythopolis, decorative arts in Greco-Roman style are plentiful, many coming from as far away as the Cape-Vathy quarry in northern Thasos.[101] Good proportions of marble artifacts from Roman Caesarea

---

99. Michael Avi-Yonah, "Palästina," *PWSup* XIII (München: Druckenmiller, 1973) cols. 373–74; and Claude R. Conder and Horatio H. Kitchener, *The Survey of Western Palestine II: Samaria* (London: Palestine Exploration Fund, 1882) 105.

100. Kevin Greene, *The Archaeology of the Roman Economy* (Berkeley: University of California Press, 1986) and Finley, *The Ancient Economy*, 126.

101. Rivka Gersht, "Dionysiac Sarcophagi from Caesarea Maritima," *IEJ* 41 (1991) 145–156; and "The Tyche of Caesarea Maritima," *PEQ* 116 (1984) 110–114. Tyche is also frequent on city coins, including those of Caesarea. Tyche can also be found on much later coins of Tiberias, George F. Hill, "Some Palestinian Cults in the Greco-Roman Age," in *Proceedings of the British Academy* 5 (1912) 3; Rivka Gersht, "The Reader of the Scroll From Caesarea Maritima," *Tel Aviv* 13 (1986) 67–70, Plate 4; Zeev Yeivin, "Bet Shean Project," *Excavations and Surveys in Israel 1987/1988* Vol. 6 (Jerusalem: The Israel Department of Antiquities and Museums, 1988) 7–45; F. Vitto, "Two Marble Heads of Goddesses from Tel Naharon–Scythopolis," 'Atiqot 20 (1991) 33–45; Zeev Pearl and Mordeckai Margaritz, "The Marble Source of the Tel Naharon–Scythopolis Heads," 'Atiqot 20 (1991) 46–47; and Moshe Fisher, "Figured Capitals in Roman Palestine. Marble Imports and Local Stones: Some Aspects of 'Imperial' and 'Provincial' Art," in *Archäologischer Anzeiger 1991* (Deutsches Archäologisches Institut; Berlin: Walter de Greuyter, 1991) 119–44.

Maritima, 5 out of 31, are also of Thasian marble.[102] It should come as no surprise that such specimens of imperial art have been uncovered at Caesarea, Palestine's major port, and Scythopolis, Palestine's largest and perhaps wealthiest city. But they have not been found at Sepphoris or Tiberias, nor at other inland Galilean sites.[103]

The absence of such features of the Greco-Roman decorative repertoire might be a matter of preference, a point discussed in the next chapter, but the cost factor should not be dismissed. Very few of the typical features of a Roman city have been found at Sepphoris; most date to after the more intense Romanization after the Bar Kochba War and the stationing of Roman legionaries at Maximianopolis (Legio).[104] The theater's date, though disputed in large part because of different pottery readings, may well be late first century; the dionysiac villa dates to the third century; and many features are simply lacking in the first century or have not been found yet: no temple, no gymnasium, no hippodrome, no *odeon*, no *nymphaeum*, no euergistic inscriptions.

There was relatively little international trade in the ancient Roman economy, and what existed was restricted to major urban sites. Wealthy cities or citizens were able to afford imported architectural materials and artifacts, as well as luxury items, from great distances, but, as this demand was realized, local shops (it is hardly proper to call them industries in our sense of the word), sought to fill the need. Capitalizing on the high cost of overland transport, local imitations competed with imports. For example, small vases containing ointments were imported from Lycia from the third century B.C.E. continuing into the first century C.E. to sites along the coast, and a few major inland sites. Initially these perfume or pharmaceutical bottles with a distinctive shape were imported into Palestine, but at a later period local imitations, produced likely at Tel Anafa north of the Sea of Galilee, begin to appear.[105] None, however, appear at Sepphoris.

---

102. Zeev Pearl, "Archaeological Marble in Israel—Chemical and Mineralogical Analysis," Ph.D. diss., Weizmann Institute of Science, Rehovot, 1989, cited in Pearl and Margaritz, "The Marble Source of the Tel Naharon–Scythopolis Heads," 47. Marble works of art tend to be found along the coast, or inland only in the major cities, L. Y. Rahmani, "Roman Miscellanea," *IEJ* 39 (1989) 66–75. The same can be said of the Hellenistic braziers in Israel, John Gunneweg and Isadore Pearlman, "Hellenistic Braziers From Israel: Results of Pottery Analysis," *IEJ* 34 (1984) 232–238.

103. The decorated sarcophagi from Beth She'arim, on the extremity of Galilee, are examples of later provincial art, though of course with themes adopted from imperial art; see Rachel Hachlili, *Ancient Jewish Art and Archaeology in the Land of Israel* (Leiden: E. J. Brill, 1988). Moshe Fisher, "Figured Capitals in Roman Palestine," 119–144.

104. Eric Meyers, "Jesus und seine galiläische Lebenswelt," *Zeitschrift für Neues Testament* 1 (1998) 27–39; and Zeev Safrai, "The Roman Army in Galilee," in *The Galilee in Late Antiquity*, 103–114.

105. Malka Hershkovitz, "Miniature Ointment Vases," *IEJ* 36 (1986) 50–51.

The archaeological picture of Sepphoris and Tiberias's economic importance, both in terms of local villages within its region and in terms of interregional trade, must be placed in perspective, as it relates to major centers in
the region. Ian Hopkins has plotted the major urban centers, minor urban
centers, towns, villages, and rural centers, and has shown how these form an
efficient network of economic and administrative interaction.[106] Major
urban centers throughout the Roman Empire are predictably spaced, and
incorporate a series of minor urban centers on the peripheries of their territories, with close economic and administrative ties to their surrounding
regions. The major urban centers in the Levant—Caesarea Maritima,
Scythopolis, and Tyre—form a rough triangle. Galilee lies beyond the immediate reach of each of these major urban centers. Only Scythopolis lies
within 25 kilometers of Galilee. But with the founding of Sepphoris and
Tiberias, no area of Galilee lies outside a 25-km radius of these new urban
centers.[107] Tiberias and Sepphoris must be seen as minor urban centers,
dominating the agricultural landscape of Galilee, but not large enough to
attract substantial international trade. The level of trade and agriculture did
not measure up to the major urban centers of Palestine such as Caesarea or
Scythopolis, not to mention Antioch or Alexandria.

## Some Implications for Historical Jesus Research

Setting aside the cultural and religious issues of Hellenism and Judaism, the
novelty of these cities in Galilee, in terms of their urban character, and the
socio-economic transformation of Galilee that Antipas introduced with them,
must be stressed. While much of the scholarly discussion on the urban character of Galilee is overblown, or certainly over simplified, as consumer centers
with 8–12,000 inhabitants, Sepphoris and Tiberias did shift both the agricultural and commercial focus of Galilee onto themselves.[108] Though not nearly as
large as Scythopolis, Caesarea, or Tyre, nor as wealthy, in their Galilean context,
they encapsulated Antipas's rule in terms of a shift from a traditional to a commercialized agrarian society. This placed an economic strain on Galilean peasants, added stress to families and challenged current values, and created new
rural-urban dynamics. Each of these factors is reflected in the Gospels.

---

106. Ian Hopkins, "The City Region in Roman Palestine," *PEQ* 112 (1980) 19–32.
107. Edwards notes that "If one takes R. MacMullen's fifteen-mile radius to markets seriously, then nearly every village in the Lower Galilee would fall within range
of the two major cities, Sepphoris and Tiberias," "The Socio-Economic and Cultural
Ethos in the First Century," 59.
108. See further my "Population Numbers, Urbanization, and Economics:
Galilean Archaeology and the Historical Jesus," 203–219; and Horsley, *Archaeology,
History, and Society in Galilee,* 43–65.

Sepphoris and Tiberias's Economic Strain on Galilee

The economic strain that Antipas's building of Sepphoris and Tiberias placed on the rest of Galilee is difficult to determine on an absolute scale, as is the resulting poverty level and sense of security. It is not necessary to envision an extreme crisis in Galilee—peasant life in antiquity was difficult enough and need not be exaggerated.[109] It is, however, important to stress that Antipas's urbanization of Galilee began a process in which the latter state was perceived as worse than the former by the vast majority; in other words, the peasants' relative state of deprivation, not their poverty in any absolute terms, is the decisive factor.

A blessing of the poor opens the beatitudes in the sermon (Q 6:20), followed by those who are hungry. It is not just the poor, however, but the very economic structures emerging in Galilee that lead to the poverty that recurs in the Gospels. Concern over debt, land division, and tenancy underlies much of the teachings of Jesus. The Lord's Prayer crystallizes the essential peasant concern by praying for the release from debt (Q 11:4), and Luke 12:58–59 expresses the realization that the courts provide no recourse for indebtedness. Instead, Luke ties Jesus' ministry to the biblical jubilee (Lev 25:8–12) and quotes Isaiah 6 to proclaim that Jesus brings "good news to the poor" and "release to the captives," as well as "let[s] the oppressed go free" (Luke 4:16–19, echoed in Luke 7:22). Disputes over land division typical of an agrarian society where land is becoming sparse underlie Luke 12:13, where a younger brother begs Jesus to persuade his brother to share the family inheritance. Jesus' teachings show not only an awareness of tenancy and estate life, but familiarity with the darker side of these practices and peasant concerns. Mark's parable of the tenants, and the Gospel of Thomas's less allegorical version, knows of the accountability of the tenants to their landlord (Mark 12:1), and the Matthean parable of the laborers in the vineyard presumes unemployed seasonal workers waiting for work at the marketplace (Matt 20:1–15). The lack of integrity (Luke 16:1–8) and abusive nature of *oikonomoi* (Matt 24:47–51) are also familiar features in the synoptic teachings.

Monetization and Reciprocity

Accompanying a concern over debt in the teachings of Jesus according to the Synoptic Gospels is a rejection of monetization in favor of the ideal of

---

109. Exaggerations can be found throughout Luise Schottroff and Wolfgang Stegemann, *Jesus von Nazareth, Hoffnung der Armen* (Stuttgart: Kohlhammer, 1978); and to some extent Richard Horsley's early work, such as *Jesus and the Spiral of Violence: Popular Jewish Resistance in Roman Palestine* (San Francisco: Harper-Collins, 1987).

reciprocity.[110] Money is not an uncommon phenomenon in the Gospels, and its use in the Gospels consistently points to an asymmetrical system of exchange.[111] Of the coinage mentioned, gold and silver denominations are envisioned as being hoarded by the rich, a practice that is condemned (Matt 23:16–17; Luke 15:8–9); the larger denominations of silver and bronze are mentioned in the context of paying off taxes or debt (Mark 12:15; Luke 7:41, 19:23; Matt 20:9, 27:10).[112] In terms of Jesus' interaction with coins, Jesus has to ask for a coin from the crowds in Mark 12:16—and comments that it will soon enough return to Caesar (Mark 12:17). Judas raises the shame of possessing a vial of perfume in Mark 14:5, an indication of their socio-economic status. In addition to the illusory nature of hoarding money (Q 12:33–34), a general scorn for greed and storing up for the future (Q 12:13–21), as well as serving Mammon (Q 16:13), are present at the earliest layers of the Jesus tradition.

In opposition to monetization, the teachings of Jesus espouse the ideal of reciprocity (Q 6:27–35, 9:57–61), a recurring theme at the heart of the Kingdom of God. Of note, however, is that this reciprocity is no longer sought at the level of one's family or village, but in the kingdom of God. Striking in the Jesus tradition are several sayings that undermine the household or family unit of birth (Q 9:59–60, 14:26, 12:51–53, 16:13, 16:18, and 17:26–27), in favor of the "true family" (Mark 3:31–35) and with the promise of new families and fields (Mark 10:23–31).[113] One significant exchange at the heart of the Jesus tradition is healing for food (Q 10; Mark 6), later preaching (1 Cor 9) or prophecy for food (*Didache* 13).[114]

Galilean Urban-Rural Relations

The cities of Sepphoris and Tiberias created a strain on the Galilean peasantry, in terms of land-holding patterns and kinship, but that the peasants singled out these urban centers as the source of their woes cannot be assumed, nor can one assume their isolation from these cities.[115] It is signif-

---

110. Freyne, "Jesus and the Urban Culture," 616–19.

111. Hanson and Oakman, *Palestine at the Time of Jesus*, 120–25.

112. The mission instructions in Mark 6:8 prohibit any bronze, while Matthew later reflects a more elite clientele when he forbids any gold, silver, or bronze, Matt 10:9.

113. Arland Jacobson, "Divided Families and Christian Origins," in *The Gospel Behind the Gospels: Current Studies on Q* (ed. Ronald Piper; Leiden: E. J. Brill, 1995) 361–380.

114. Crossan, *The Historical Jesus*, 341–45.

115. Though there is some anecdotal evidence that at times rural Galilean peasants directed their anger at these cities, hostility apparently was fueled by their debt to the ruling elite there, Horsley, *Archaeology, History, and Society in Galilee*, 43–65.

icant that these two cities are not singled out for condemnation by Jesus (unlike Capernaum, Bethsaida, and Chorazin, Q 10:11–14), and hence cannot be described as the locus of animosity for the Jesus movement, nor likely for Galilean society in general. One is inclined to assume that the inhabitants of Galilee had knowledge, perhaps firsthand and certainly secondhand, of Sepphoris and Tiberias, whether as agricultural suppliers or, less likely, through commercial contacts; perhaps to visit family and clan members who had moved there; or to visit the market, solicit services, or be hauled before court. In this context, an examination of the Gospels reveals traces of awareness and even interaction with these cities on the part of Jesus and his followers, in spite of the lack of mention of Sepphoris or Tiberias. In the mission discourse in Q, Jesus assumes his followers will go to *poleis* (Q 11:8,11), which, in spite of the lack of precision of this term in the New Testament, might in this case imply these Galilean cities. In contrast to John the Baptist's place in the wilderness, royal palaces are mentioned, likely alluding to Antipas's residence in Tiberias (Q 7:25). *Agorai* (Q 7:32, 11:43) are seen as the place where one encounters a variety of people, including one's enemies; and reminiscent of an urban context, plazas (Q 10:10, 13:26, 14:21) are mentioned as well. Other urban imagery, such as city gates (Q 13:24) and banks (Q 19:23) are present in Q and, more ominously, courts and prisons (Q 12:57–59) are to be feared.[116] These passages suggest that urban-rural contacts were not uncommon, which raises the question of whether Jesus can be placed in an exclusively village context, first around Nazareth and then around Capernaum, or whether he did, in fact, visit Tiberias or Sepphoris.

---

116. On the urban imagery in Q, and Q's location in Galilee based on urban, rural, and agricultural imagery, see my "The Social Map of Q," in *Conflict and Invention: Social and Literary Studies on Q* (ed. John Kloppenborg; Philadelphia: Trinity Press International, 1995) 17–36.

## PART TWO

CHAPTER 4

# Jesus and Sepphoris Revisited: Judaism and Hellenism

Whether Jesus visited the city of Sepphoris, Herod Antipas's first capital in Galilee, has generated considerable speculation. Sepphoris was Galilee's most significant city, whose centrality on the political scene was set by Gabinius, the Roman proconsul of Syria, who selected the Hasmonean settlement as the site of one of five Jewish councils in 63 B.C.E. (*Ant.* 14.91; *War* 1.170). Its geography and topography were suitable for both a Hasmonean military town and later Gabinius's regional center. It lies in the heart of Lower Galilee, perched on a hill "like a little bird" (Heb. *Zippori, b. Meg.* 6a), with a commanding view of the Beth Netofah Valley and traffic from the Sea of Galilee to Ptolemais and the Mediterranean. Herod the Great took the city from the last Hasmonean ruler Antigonus on his way to solidifying power in Jerusalem and built a royal palace and an armory there. Judas the Galilean, the son of the brigand Hezekiah whom Herod had put to death early in his reign, led an insurrection armed with weapons from Sepphoris's armory against Rome-backed rule after Herod's death (*Ant.* 17.271; and *War* 2.56). Supported widely across Galilee, Judas defied Roman taxation because it infringed on God's sovereign rule over Israel. The Roman legate Varus crushed the uprising in 4 B.C.E., and according to Josephus, burned Sepphoris to the ground and sold its inhabitants into slavery for their role in the rebellion (*Ant.* 17.288–89; and *War* 2.68–69). When Herod Antipas inherited Galilee, he launched a series of building projects imitating his father, starting with the rebuilding of Sepphoris into the "ornament (πρόσχημα) of all Galilee," which he renamed "Autonomous" (Ἀυτοκρατής), and made his capital (*Ant.* 18.27).[1] During the

---

1. On the meaning of πρoσχημα, see Stuart S. Miller, *Studies in the History and Traditions of Sepphoris* (Leiden: E. J. Brill, 1984) 57. Miller's work represents the best

first Jewish revolt, the citizens of Sepphoris took a pacifistic and pro-Roman stance, a point repeated by Josephus and attested in the numismatic record. Animosity among the rural Jews in Galilee toward their urban kin (whom Josephus calls their ὁμοφύλοι, War 3.32) led them to storm Sepphoris twice during the revolt, so that Vespasian had to send a Roman garrison for its protection.[2] Coins minted at Sepphoris in 67 C.E. read ΝΕΡΩΝΙΑΣ ΣΕΠΦΩΡΙΣ and bear the legend ΕΙΡΗΝΟΠΟΛΙΣ, "City of Peace," resonating with Josephus's description that the city's population "thinks peace" (εἰρηνίκα φρονοῦντες, War 3.31).[3] Sepphoris's pacifist stance was rewarded with close relations to Rome after the war: its bank and archives were granted expanded authority (Life 36–39) and it adopted the official name of Diocaesarea (i.e., dedicated to the imperial Zeus). In spite of this imperial and pagan designation, which appears on its coins and in pagan and later Christian authors, the Jewish sources continue to refer to the city with the Hebrew Zippori. The rabbinic corpus assumes it was overwhelmingly populated by Jews, and tells of its housing a leading rabbinic school founded by Judah Ha-nasi, who codified the Mishna at Sepphoris at the beginning of the third century. Legends also speak of his correspondence with and his special relationship as a spiritual mentor to a Roman emperor identified as Antonius (e.g., b. 'Abod. Zar. 10a–b, b. B. Mes. 35a), tales that arose from Sepphoris's close ties to Rome.

The city's political importance and its role in Galilean history render its absence in the New Testament notable. This omission appears puzzling because it lies only 5 kilometers from Jesus' hometown Nazareth, and most of the sites featured in the Gospels lie within a day's walk from Sepphoris: Cana (Horvat Qana) is only 5 kilometers further north, Nain (Givʿat Naʿim) 10 miles to the south, and Capernaum 30 kilometers to the east.

The significance of Sepphoris's absence in the tradition, and the city's importance to the study of Jesus and the Gospels, has been pursued in two distinct ways. On the one hand, the matter has been approached by speculating on whether Jesus actually visited Sepphoris, either during his youth or ministry. Sepphoris's absence in the Gospels has thus been explained as an

and most complete history of the city and is especially valuable because of his expertise on the rabbinic literature; his work replaced the earlier standard reference by Adolph Büchler, The Political and Social Leaders of the Jewish Community of Sepphoris in the Second and Third Centuries (London: Oxford University Press, 1909).

2. The accounts in Josephus are muddled, War 2.574–75, 3.61–62, and Life 373–80. A good discussion of these contradictions is found in Seán Freyne, Galilee from Alexander the Great to Hadrian, 323 B.C.E. to 135 C.E. (Notre Dame: University of Notre Dame Press, 1980) 124–128.

3. Yaakov Meshorer, "Sepphoris and Rome," in Greek Numismatics and Archaeology: Essays in Honor of Margaret Thompson (ed. Otto Morkholm and Nancy M. Waggoner; Wetteren, Belgium: Cultura, 1979) 160–162.

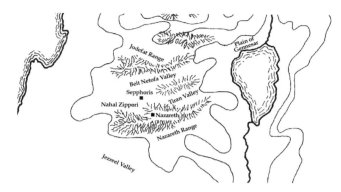

*Figure 4.1 Sephphoris in Lower Galilee*

accidental oversight of visits Jesus made to the city, a willful deletion of some events there from the tradition, or as the result of Jesus' intentional avoidance of the capital, for reasons that the Gospel writers do not elaborate. To approach the issue in terms of Jesus' personal journeys, however, is highly speculative and tends toward a psychological analysis of Jesus in ways that move beyond reasonable historical inquiry.[4] More recently, therefore, the question of Jesus and Sepphoris has been examined under the broader rubric of the city's impact on Galilee as a whole, and hence on Jesus and his movement indirectly. Sepphoris's possible role in fostering Hellenistic culture in Galilee, its socio-economic impact on the entire Galilee, and its position as Galilee's administrative center warrant attention as the specific local context of Jesus and the early Jesus movement.

Sepphoris has become a kind of test case for scholarly characterizations of the historical Jesus and the Gospel traditions. Those portraying him as a rural and Torah-abiding Jew tend to point out the absence of Sepphoris in the New Testament as evidence for his avoidance of a presumably Hellenistic and gentile city.[5] Scholars stressing Hellenistic or cosmopolitan traits in the Jesus tradition tend to identify Sepphoris as their source, believe Sepphoris's absence in the tradition to be accidental, and assume Jesus visited it during his youth and would have had no reason to avoid it during his ministry.[6]

4. Seán Freyne, "Jesus and the Urban Culture of Galilee," in *Texts and Contexts: Biblical Texts in Their Textual and Situational Contexts. Essays in Honor of Lars Hartman* (ed. Tord Fornberg and David Hellholm; Oslo: Scandinavian University Press, 1995) 604; and Wilibald Bösen, *Galiläa als Lebensraum und Wirkungsfeld Jesu* (Freiburg: Herder, 1985) 69–75.

5. See, for example, John P. Meier, *A Marginal Jew: Rethinking the Historical Jesus I* (New York: Doubleday, 1991) 283–4, 350–52; and E. P. Sanders, *The Historical Figure of Jesus* (London: Penguin, 1993) 104.

6. See, for example, Burton Mack, *The Lost Gospel: The Book of Q and Christian Origins* (San Francisco: HarperSanFrancisco, 1993) 57–62.

Lacking any clear evidence in the Gospels, the debate over Jesus and Sepphoris revolves around broader interpretations of his message and ministry and reconstructions of the Galilean background. Contested are the extent to which the city was Hellenistic and Gentile, socio-economic differences between urban and rural Galilee, and the nature of political control through Sepphoris. The growing archaeological evidence unearthed in and around Galilee is, unfortunately, only taken into consideration in an ad hoc manner, to bolster claims about the historical Jesus or to illustrate a point about his Galilean background. This chapter is an attempt to hold the discussion of Jesus and Sepphoris more accountable to the archaeological findings relating to Sepphoris over the past decades and to present the evidence on Sepphoris's character and impact on Galilee in such a way that Sepphoris's importance to the historical Jesus and the Gospels can be assessed. Since the middle of the 1980s, four different archaeological teams have been excavating the site. Eric and Carol Meyers have led the Sepphoris Regional Project concentrating on the Western domestic area of the acropolis, the Hebrew University team under Zeev Weiss and Ehud Netzer has excavated several areas around the theater and in the lower market area, the University of South Florida excavations led by James F. Strange have concentrated on the lower market around a basilica structure, and Tsvika Tzuk has cleared out the aqueduct east of the city for the Israel Antiquity Authority.[7] The results of these archaeological excavations permit a sketch of the character of Sepphoris's public and domestic spheres and allow a contrast with other Galilean sites, notably Jesus' hometown of Nazareth. This archaeological examination provides a more accurate description of the character and nature of the city than can be reconstructed from the literary sources, and indirectly answers the question of Jesus and Sepphoris. No traces of his presence or absence in Sepphoris can be detected in the archaeological finds, but they provide a more solid basis upon which his relation to the city can be imagined. Equally important, archaeology helps assess the city's impact on Galilee as a whole, the specific local context of Jesus, and the early Jesus movement.

## History of Scholarship

Jesus at Sepphoris

Prior to the advent of travelers to the Holy Land in the nineteenth century, New Testament scholarship seemed unaware of Sepphoris.[8] The centrality of Sepphoris in Galilee and its proximity to Nazareth were recognized only as

---

7. The results of the excavations have been summarized, without stratigraphic reports, in Rebecca Nagy et al., *Sepphoris in Galilee: Crosscurrents of Culture* (Winona Lake, Indiana: Eisenbrauns, 1996).

8. Stuart S. Miller, "Sepphoris, the Well Remembered City," *BA* 55 (1992) 74–83.

biblical scholars acquainted themselves with the lands of the Bible. Still before any archaeological excavations at the site, Gustaf Dalman wondered earlier this century about Jesus' possible visits to Sepphoris. He noticed the proximity of Nazareth to the capital of Galilee during Jesus' youth, assumed that the main road to Jerusalem from Sepphoris went through Nazareth, and took for granted that Jesus would have been personally familiar with Sepphoris. Dalman suggested that Jesus' parables drew upon images from his visits to Antipas's city, such as elite dining habits in the parable of the royal banquet (Matt 22:1–14) and banking and lending in the parable of the talents (Matt 25:14–30). Perhaps also Varus's razing the city had been seared in local memory, instilling a healthy respect for Roman rule, and fostering a disposition in the teachings of Jesus of passive resignation toward political rule.[9]

Two articles, written independently in the late 1920s under the influence of the history of religions school, explored the role of Sepphoris in shaping the broader cultural and religious milieu of Jesus. Walter Bauer's "Jesus der Galiläer" dealt with the character of Galilee as a whole, and examined Nazareth's proximity to Sepphoris. He stressed the latter's Hellenistic character and gentile population, which he thought influenced all Galilee as a way to distance Jesus from what he considered to be a legalistic "pharisaic" Judaism.[10] The article emphasized that Galilee's cultural and religious traditions were distinct from Judea's, and that its syncretism and un-Jewishness were aptly captured in the epigraph "Galilee of the Gentiles" (Is 8:23; 1 Macc 5:15; see also Matt 4:15). In spite of an interest in the broader world of Jesus, Bauer focused on Jesus' personal contacts with Sepphoris; he could not imagine why the Galilean Jesus would have avoided preaching or healing in Sepphoris, or, for that matter, in Tiberias, Gabara, and Taricheae, which he held to be further Hellenistic poleis in Galilee. Bauer was also inclined to minimize the threat Jesus posed to Herod Antipas, unlike John the Baptist, so Sepphoris would not have been avoided for political reasons. The omission of Sepphoris in the tradition must have been because Jesus' message did not resonate with its more urbane and cosmopolitan citizens, among whom he did not gain a following. In short, nothing noteworthy happened there to be preserved in the tradition. This argument *ad silencium* presupposes an apolitical Jesus, and more significantly, presumes that as a polis, Sepphoris was by definition heavily Hellenistic and Gentile.

In the first article devoted solely to the topic of "Jesus and Sepphoris," Shirley-Jackson Case accentuated the urban elements in Jesus' social world.[11]

---

9. Gustaf Dalman, *Orte und Wege Jesu*, (3rd ed.; Gütersloh: Bertelsmann, 1924) 68–69, 85–87.

10. Reprinted from the 1927 original in *Aufsätze und kleine Schriften* (ed. G. Strecker; Tübingen: J. C. B. Mohr [Paul Siebeck], 1967) 91–108.

11. Shirley-Jackson Case, "Jesus and Sepphoris," *JBL* 45 (1926) 14–22.

Like Bauer, he focused on Jesus' likely visits to Sepphoris, which would have been undertaken out of curiosity if not necessity, should he and Joseph have worked as carpenters on its construction under Antipas. The impact of Jesus' contacts with Sepphoris on his message was twofold: First, his mingling with crowds there engendered a more open and tolerant attitude toward strangers than was common in Case's caricature of Judaism. Second, even if Jesus did not frequently visit Sepphoris, he learned to recognize from its destruction in 4 B.C.E., as Dalman had also suggested, the futility of violent revolt against Rome.

Case's article inspired the first archaeological excavations at Sepphoris by Leroy Waterman in 1931, who sought to uncover concrete evidence of "the prime importance of Sepphoris as an outstanding factor in the early life of Jesus."[12] Unfortunately, the excavations lasted only one season, and were cut short by financial exigencies during the great depression. Waterman provided the first descriptions of cave tombs, the elaborate waterworks, an olive press, a house (incorrectly identified as a Christian basilica), and the theater.[13] The excavations made little impact on contemporaneous New Testament studies. Only a 1943 handbook on the archaeology of Palestine by Chester C. McCown, the president of the American Schools of Oriental Research, mentions the discovery of the theater. McCown lamented the regrettable lack of published ceramic evidence but agreed with the excavators that even if the theater's date cannot be determined stratigraphically, it could imaginably have been built at the earliest by Herod or Herod Antipas by historical inference.[14] The preoccupation in both Waterman's report and McCown's handbook reflects the prevailing interest of the time to identify archaeological discoveries dating with some veracity to the first century C.E., with which Jesus himself may have had contact.

Without any apparent familiarity with the excavations, the German archaeologist Albrecht Alt rebutted Bauer and Case's arguments that Jesus visited Sepphoris, and stressed the isolation of rural Galilee from the urban centers in and around it. Although not explicitly written to distance Jesus form Sepphoris, Alt implicitly insulated Jewish Nazareth from Hellenistic Sepphoris by combining topographical and geopolitical considerations. Nazareth, in his opinion, did not belong to Sepphoris's *chora*, and hence

---

12. Leroy Waterman et al., *Preliminary Report of the University of Michigan Excavations at Sepphoris, Palestine, in 1931* (Ann Arbor, Michigan: University of Michigan Press, 1937) v.

13. On the archaeological finds, see N. E. Manasseh, "Architecture and Topography," and for the date of the theater, see S. Yeivin, "Historical and Archaeological Notes," in *Preliminary Report of the University of Michigan Excavations at Sepphoris,* 29–30, esp. note 51.

14. *The Ladder of Progress in Palestine: A Story of Archaeological Adventure* (New York: Harper & Brothers, 1943) 263–266.

would not have been in its political or cultural sphere. Alt's description of the terrain placed a *Scheidewand,* or "partitioning wall," between the two sites. This topographical barrier was created in his mind by the ridge separating the Wadi el-Melek in the north from the Megiddo Plain to the south, a change in altitude of just under 200 meters, which he felt rendered social intercourse between Nazareans and Sepphoreans unlikely. Furthermore, Alt noted how some ancient authors, such as Eusebius, locate Nazareth 22 kilometers north of Maxiamianopolis, and not 5 kilometers south of Sepphoris/ Diocaesarea, which he supposed reflected Nazareth's political orientation toward the south (*Onomasticon* 140.1f). Finally, Alt argued that Japhia's leading role in the Jewish revolt implies it did not belong to the territory of pro-Roman Sepphoris, and if Japhia, 7 kilometers to the south, was not under its influence, neither would Nazareth have been.[15]

Alt's presentation is problematic on several counts. That Japhia revolted while Sepphoris did not tells us more about rural-urban relations and Sepphoris's character than Nazareth's administrative connections to Sepphoris. That Eusebius and others describe its distance from Maxiamianopolis says nothing about Nazareth's relationship to Sepphoris in the first century. Maxiamianopolis was built in the second century C.E. and eclipsed Sepphoris as the region's major city, and Eusebius of Caesarea naturally would have described Nazareth in relation to Maxiamianopolis, since from his geographical perspective and on his itineraries, Nazareth was past Maxiamianopolis. Underlying Alt's presentation is an attempt to minimize the possibility of Jesus visiting Sepphoris. To do so, Alt insinuates that Galilee consisted of both relatively autonomous rural areas and the small *chorai* of Sepphoris and Tiberias, rather than realizing that Antipas ruled over all Galilee and placed his ruling and administrative apparatus in these cities.[16] Equally problematic with his presentation is the presupposition that Sepphoris *qua* polis was essentially Gentile and Hellenistic, against which Jewish and rural Galilee in general and Jesus specifically needed shielding.

As interest in the historical Jesus waned in the wake of Bultmannian concern for Christology and the early Christian kerygma, New Testament scholarship remained in general disinterested in Sepphoris and other questions about the realia behind the Gospels. As curiosity about the social world of early Christianity was rekindled in the 1980s, and in particular with the

---

15. Albrecht Alt, "Die Stätten des Wirkens Jesu in Galiläa territorialgeschichtlich betrachtet," reprint of 1949 original in *Kleine Schriften zur Geschichte des Volkes Israels II* (München: C. H. Beck'sche, 1959) 441–47.

16. Centuries later the rabbis disputed whether some villages belonged to the city of Ptolemais or Sepphoris (e.g., *t. Git.* 1.1; *y. Git.*, 2.43g). However, there is no evidence from the time of Antipas to suggest that Sepphoris ruled areas independent of his control.

revival of historical Jesus research, attention returned to the Galilean setting of Jesus and the early Jesus traditions. In the discussion of Jesus' social world, the city of Sepphoris re-entered center stage just as new excavations were gearing up at the site in the mid-1980s. Richard Batey, on staff of the University of South Florida dig, published two articles and subsequently a more popular book, which stressed the importance of Sepphoris for Jesus' life and ministry. In the first article, Batey linked Jesus and Sepphoris by imagining him working there on its construction projects, as Case conjectured. Joseph and Jesus were carpenters (τεκτόν, Mark 6:3, Matt 13:55), who would have been in demand by Antipas's architects for the completion of their projects. The root of τεκτόν implies any kind of production, its semantic range includes the various craftsmen and skills involved in urban construction, and the word can not only be translated traditionally as "carpenter." Batey pointed to several sayings reflecting an artisan or construction worker's perspective: build on a solid foundation (Q 6:46–49), the collapse of the Tower of Siloam (Luke 13:4–5), a tower built in a vineyard (Mark 12:1), three days to rebuild the Temple (John 2:19), an easy yoke and light burden (Matt 11:30), and the mote and the beam (Matt 7:5). Of course this list does not substantiate the claim that Jesus worked at Sepphoris, but Batey pointed out that each saying is more poignant if in fact spoken by a construction worker. Batey surmised that even if Jesus did not actually work at Sepphoris, he still would have been acquainted with workers on Antipas's construction projects and their techniques. There was no reason to avoid the city, since, preferring Case's rather than Alt's topographical description, the main road from Sepphoris to Jerusalem led past Nazareth, and passage to anywhere in Galilee led past Sepphoris. There, Jesus ". . . would have experienced first hand life in a new city of elaborate Hellenistic design with its many newcomers, its cosmopolitan atmosphere, theatre, and royal court. On the streets and in the market places he would have interacted with people who participated in the commercial, political, religious, and cultural life in the capital—a life distinctly different from that in his own village." Furthermore, though acknowledging that Jews primarily inhabited Sepphoris, Batey believed that Jesus would have learned Greek through contacts with the Hellenistic polis's citizens. Regarding other aspects of Sepphoris's influence on Jesus, Batey noted how Jesus' more positive view of tax collectors (e.g., Matt 9:9) and Roman taxation in general (e.g., Mark 12:14) were rooted in a healthy respect for Roman rule, having learned a hard lesson from Judas the Galilean's revolt. Finally, Batey imagined that Jesus attended the theater in Sepphoris, a point addressed in his next article.[17]

---

17. R. Batey, "Is this not the Carpenter?" *NTS* 30 (1984) 249–258; "Jesus and the Theater," *NTS* 30 (1984) 563–574; and *Jesus and the Forgotten City* (Grand Rapids, Michigan: Baker, 1991).

In "Jesus and the Theater," Batey tried to answer the question of where Jesus might have become familiar with the term and concept ὑποκριτης, or stage actor, and how to account for the frequency of this word in the tradition. The answer, in short, was during Jesus' visits to the theater at Sepphoris.[18] In spite of the problematic date of the theater, Batey argued on historical, not archaeological, grounds that the theater was built by Antipas and stood at the time of Jesus. Admitting uncertainty over Jesus' actual presence at theatrical productions, Batey is sure that "Jesus and his audience were acquainted with professional actors," and "since actors were held in contempt by the more reactionary and conservative religious leaders, the comparison drawn by Jesus would have been all the more obnoxious." In addition to picking up the pejorative *hypocrite* there, the theater enriches our understanding of Jesus' message more generally, according to Batey. It heightens the likelihood of Jesus' familiarity with the Greek language; gives pause to reflect on how tragic heroes of Greek dramas, such as Oedipus, enhanced Jesus' self-image as the suffering servant; and provided exposure to great orations that sharpened his rhetorical skills.[19] A detailed critique of Batey's theses need not detain us here; it is sufficient to sketch some general criticisms.[20] From an archaeological perspective, too much Hellenistic cultural freight is placed upon an inferential dating of the theater instead of a stratigraphic dating, which at present points to the late first century C.E. From a redaction-critical perspective, Matthew's proclivity to add the term ὑποκριτής to his sources suggests "Matthew and the Theater" as the more suitable title. These specific criticisms aside, Batey's interest in both articles centered, like those of the previous generation, on Jesus actually visiting Sepphoris, and focused on the personal impact the city had on his later ministry and teaching.

Sepphoris's Impact on the Galilee of Jesus

As finds from Sepphoris's many excavations came to light in the 1980s, discussion over Jesus and Sepphoris moved in a new direction. The material

---

18. Benedict Schwank raised this question of Jesus' attendance in a more devotional manner, "Das Theater von Sepphoris und die Jugendjahre Jesus," *Erbe und Auftrag* 52 (1976) 199–206; see also "Die Neuen Ausgrabungen in Sepphoris," *BK* 42 (1987) 75–79.

19. "Jesus and the Theater," 563–74.

20. See Stuart S. Miller, "Sepphoris, the Well Remembered City," 74–83; Sanders, "Jesus' Relation to Sepphoris," in *Sepphoris in Galilee*, 75–79; and Freyne, "Jesus and the Urban Culture of Galilee," 604; Hengel has noted Batey's lack of clarity on the date as waffling, *The 'Hellenization' of Judaea in the First Century after Christ* (Philadelphia: Trinity Press International, 1989) 74 n. 90; and Lawrence Schiffman and Eric Meyers, *BA* 55 (1992) 105–7.

culture of Sepphoris and the finds from across Galilee transformed the question from whether Jesus ever visited Sepphoris to Sepphoris's impact on the Galilee of Jesus. Much of the impetus can be credited to studies on Galilean regionalism by Eric Meyers, who analyzed the distinct profiles of Upper and Lower Galilee's material culture, and introduced archaeology into a text-dominated field. Meyers's studies crossed over traditional disciplines and initiated dialogue between archaeologists, rabbinicists, historians of late antiquity, and New Testament scholars.[21] Sean Freyne's *Galilee* (1980), solidified its place on the map of New Testament studies, and his subsequent work led the way in integrating the archaeological data into New Testament scholarship.[22] Given their influence on the discipline, the question of Jesus and Sepphoris could no longer be posed in such a way that targeted only New Testament scholars. The meaning of Sepphoris and the significance of its excavations was no longer only about "the most important city of the life of Jesus," as it had been a generation ago, but subject to interdisciplinary dialogue. Any statement on Sepphoris and Jesus became accountable to the wider discussion on the nature of Lower Galilee and Sepphoris's role in shaping it and was subject to critique by archaeologists.

While a heightened awareness of archaeological data and other disciplines can be detected in recent New Testament scholarship, much of the debate over Sepphoris echoes the earlier dispute cast in terms of the city's Hellenistic character and its relation to the rest of Galilee's Jewish nature. The operative model is too often a simplistic antagonism between Judaism and Hellenism in which urban means Hellenistic and rural means Jewish. Some New Testament scholars continued to embrace, not unlike Alt, the cultural and religious divide between the Galilean villages and Sepphoris due to its Hellenistic character.[23] Others, not unlike Bauer, characterize Sepphoris and the Galilean cities as the very vehicles for Hellenizing all of Galilee.[24]

---

21. Eric Meyers, "Galilean Regionalism as a Factor in Historical Reconstruction," *BASOR* 220/221 (1975–76) 93–101; and "The Cultural Setting of Galilee: The Case of Regionalism and Early Judaism," *ANRW* 2.19.1 (1979) 686–70; see also the discussion, Richard Horsley, "Archaeology and the Villages of Upper Galilee: A Dialogue with Archaeologists," *BASOR* 297 (1995) 5–16, 27–8; and Eric Meyers, "An Archaeological Response to a New Testament Scholar," *BASOR* 297 (1995) 17–26.

22. With the full title, *Galilee from Alexander the Great to Hadrian 323 B.C.E. to 125 C.E.: A Study of Second Temple Judaism* (Notre Dame: Notre Dame University Press, 1980); and *Galilee, Jesus, and the Gospels: Literary Approaches and Historical Investigations* (Philadelphia: Fortress Press, 1988).

23. Such was Freyne's original thesis in *Galilee* with regard to the cities, repeated somewhat in *Galilee, Jesus, and the Gospels*, 139–140, but later restated in a more sophisticated manner in "Jesus and the Urban Culture of Galilee," 596–622. For a similar division, see also Hengel, *The 'Hellenization' of Judaea*, 74 n. 90.

24. J. Andrew Overman, "Who Were the First Urban Christians? Urbanization in Galilee in the First Century," in *SBLSP 1988* (ed. David Lull; Atlanta: Scholars Press,

Some have gone so far as to suggest that the building of Sepphoris as a polis in Galilee attracted Greco-Roman philosophical schools such as the Cynics.[25] However, to treat Hellenistic and Jewish, urban and rural, as mutually exclusive alternatives, is problematic. The persistence of indigenous traditions at urban sites throughout the Hellenized East casts serious doubt on the view that Hellenism was exclusively a cultural force antithetical to Judaism. According to Glen W. Bowersock, Hellenism "was a medium not necessarily antithetical to local or indigenous traditions," and even though many cities outwardly adopted the trappings of Greek or Roman urban culture, "indigenous forms of urbanization" expressed themselves in various ways.[26] Examples of indigenous forms of temples and architecture built in the style and materials typical of Hellenism in the Roman Period can be found nearby at Nabatean sites and cities of the Decapolis.[27] Rome was the primary vehicle for the East's urbanization and Hellenization, but it was surprisingly accommodating to various indigenous forms.[28]

Eric Meyers has suggested that much the same occurred at its infancy when Antipas built Sepphoris and Tiberias in Galilee. In his view, Sepphoris's essentially Jewish population, which consisted of a relatively large priestly component according to some literary clues, selectively adopted aspects of Hellenism, as Antipas introduced Roman architectural styles.[29] This process continued and intensified in the second century C.E.

1998) 160–168; and Howard Clark Kee, "Early Christianity in Galilee: Reassessing the Evidence from the Gospels," *The Galilee in Late Antiquity* (ed. Lee Levine; New York: The Jewish Theological Seminary of America, 1992) 3–22.

25. Gerald Downing has identified Sepphoris as the source where Jesus saw Cynics, "The Social Contexts of Jesus the Teacher: Construction or Reconstruction," *NTS* 33 (1987) 439–51; and *Christ and the Cynics: Jesus and Other Radical Preachers in First-Century Tradition* (JSOT Manuals 4; Sheffield: Sheffield Academic Press, 1988).

26. Glen W. Bowerstock, *Hellenism in Late Antiquity* (Ann Arbor: University of Michigan Press, 1990) 7; *Roman Arabia* (Cambridge: Harvard University Press, 1983); and "The Hellenism of Zenobia," in *Greek Connections* (ed. J. T. A. Koumoulides; Notre Dame: University of Notre Dame Press, 1987) 19–27.

27. Julian M. C. Bowsher, "Architecture and Religion in the Decapolis: A Numismatic Survey," *PEQ* 119 (1987) 62; David Graf, "The Nabataeans and the Decapolis," in *The Defence of the Roman and Byzantine East* (eds. Philip Freeman and David Kennedy; British Institute of Archaeology at Ankara Monography 8; Oxford: BAR, 1986) 785–796; Ernest Will, "L'urbanisation de la Jordanie aux époques hellénistique et romaine: conditions géographiques et ethniques," in *Studies in the History and Archaeology of Jordan II* (ed. Adnan Hadidi; Amman: Department of Antiquities, 1985 237–41; A. N. Barghouti, "Urbanization of Palestine and Jordan in Hellenistic and Roman Times," in *Studies in the History and Archaeology of Jordan II*, 209–227.

28. Shimon Applebaum, "Romanization and Indigenism in Judaea," in *Judaea in Hellenistic and Roman Times: Historical and Archaeological Essays* (Leiden: E. J. Brill, 1989) 155–65.

29. Meyers, "Roman Sepphoris," 325–6. The evidence for priests dates to later periods, most importantly from *y. Ta'an.* 4.68d and a fourth-century C.E. inscription

under direct Roman rule and with the permanent garrisoning of the *Legio VI Ferrata* in Maximianopolis. This process was not entirely antagonistic, according to Meyers, as ironically Antipas and Rome phased in Hellenism, which "unleashed a kind of creative synergism that enabled Judaism not only to survive the traumas of two catastrophic wars with Rome, but to prevail in a form and shape that constituted the essential framework of a classical Judaism. . . ."[30] One should be mindful that Sepphoris was pacifistic, pro-Roman is perhaps too strong, during the war and thereafter nevertheless served as one of the leading centers of rabbinic Judaism in late antiquity.

With a similar approach, James F. Strange emphasized how a Roman architectural "urban overlay" was grafted onto a Jewish base at Sepphoris beginning with Antipas." The Herodian ruler constructed a series of architectural structures with strategies that symbolized Roman power, themselves based on Hellenistic forms, which negotiated with Jewish sensibilities and symbols to create a blend at Sepphoris.[32] According to Strange, since metaphors and allusions to these symbols of Roman power appear in the earliest layers of the Gospels, "it is no longer possible to affirm the extreme, that the earliest Christian movement originated in a simple rural atmosphere." According to Strange, the Jesus movement from its beginning was urbanized and universal in outlook in Galilee, characteristics that were present due to the influence of Sepphoris and Tiberias. Strange's essay captures two important developments in the approach to Jesus and Sepphoris. For one, like Meyers, he acknowledged the complex interaction between Judaism and Hellenism and did not treat them solely as antagonists. It also represents an important shift in perspective in the study of Christian origins, in which the community that preserved the teachings of Jesus is the object of examination and to a lesser extent, a biographical or psychological examination of Jesus and his travels.

In a further helpful article, Douglas Edwards expanded the scope beyond cultural and religious conflicts and examined the broader question of urban-rural relations in Galilee. Without concentrating on Jesus and

found near Caesarea, Michael Avi-Yonah, "The Caesarea Inscription of the Twenty-four Priestly Courses," in *The Teachers' Yoke: Studies in Memory of Henry Trantham* (eds. E. Jerry Vardaman, et al. (Waco: Baylor University Press, 1964) 46–57; a thorough discussion is found in Miller, *Studies in the History and Tradition of Sepphoris*, 62–88, 120–127.

30. Eric Meyers, "The Challenge of Hellenism for Early Judaism and Christianity," *BA* 55 (1992) 84–91.

31. James F. Strange, "Some Implications of Archaeology for New Testament Studies," in *What Has Archaeology to Do with Faith?* (eds. James Charlesworth and Walter Weaver; Philadelphia: Trinity Press International) 23–59.

32. Strange draws heavily on John Stambaugh, *The Ancient Roman City, Ancient Society, and History* (Baltimore: John Hopkins University Press, 1988); and Colin Renfrew, *Approaches to Social Archaeology* (Cambridge: Harvard University Press, 1984).

Sepphoris, though with clear implications for Christian origins, Edwards focused on the movement of goods within Galilee and on trade networks outside of Galilee as revealed in the archaeological record. Only then did he turn to the administrative and cultural interaction between urban and rural areas.[33] Relying heavily on the distribution patterns of pottery fired at the Galilean village of Kefar Ḥananya, he stressed that the archaeological evidence as a whole points to considerable rural-urban interaction, so that the Jesus movement in the villages could not have operated in "cultural, political, or economic isolation from major urban areas."[34] Perhaps exceeding the limits of the archaeological data, Edwards further suggested that the material finds for rural-urban interaction imply less hostile attitudes among rural peasants toward the cities than is usually assumed. In other words, the urbanization of Galilee did not create a dire situation for the Galilean peasantry, but generated reciprocity between city and country; cities in antiquity and Sepphoris in particular were not parasitic, according to Edwards, but fostered a symbiosis that benefited the rural inhabitants as well.[35]

Like Edwards, Richard Horsley focused on socio-economic issues in *Archaeology, History, and Society in Galilee*, but arrived at diametrically opposite conclusions.[36] Horsley stressed how political structures determined ancient rural-urban relations, which must be considered when interpreting the archaeological data relating to Galilee and Sepphoris. Given the ancient city's role in administering taxation in a closed political economy, unlike modern open market economies, Horsley suggests that "reaction and resistance outweighed acculturation and assimilation" as far as the rural Galileans' perception of Sepphoris and Tiberias was concerned.[37] Although rural Galileans, typified in the early Jesus traditions, had images of what went on in the cities, they were often hostile toward the urban elites and cities in general, a point that is illustrated by Josephus's account of the villagers storming

---

33. "First Century Urban/Rural Relations in Lower Galilee: Exploring the Archaeological and Literary Evidence," *SBLSP 1988* (ed. David Lull; Atlanta: Scholars Press, 1988) 169–182; and "The Socio–Economic and Cultural Ethos of the Lower Galilee in the First Century: Implications for the Nascent Jesus Movement," in *The Galilee in Late Antiquity*, 53–73.

34. Edwards, "The Socio-Economic and Cultural Ethos of the Lower Galilee," 72.

35. Edwards relies heavily on Keith Hopkins, "Economic Growth in Towns in Classical Antiquity," in *Towns in Societies: Essays in Economic History and Historical Sociology* (eds. Philip Abrams and E. A. Wigley; Cambridge: University Press, 1978) 35–77.

36. Horsley, *Archaeology, History, and Society in Galilee: The Social Context of Jesus and the Rabbis* (Valley Forge, Pennsylvania: Trinity Press International, 1998).

37. A point that reinforces his earlier work on social banditry in Palestine, which arose in part out of an increase in exploitation, "Ancient Jewish Banditry and the Revolt against Rome, A.D. 66–70," *CBQ* 43 (1981) 409–432; and *Jesus and the Spiral of Violence: Popular Jewish Resistance in Roman Palestine* (San Francisco: Harper & Row, 1987).

Sepphoris (e.g., *Life* 30; 39; 395-80; see also 126–27).[38] Jesus and his move-ment can be located in the Galilean villages, and they represent a community whose behavior both undermined and symbolically challenged the urban and Roman client-king Antipas's political and economic rule.

Seán Freyne has sought to understand the implications of socio-economic factors resulting in Sepphoris's rebuilding and Herod Antipas's rule on cul-tural and religious attitudes. In trying to understand urban-rural relations in Galilee, he has contrasted the peasants' perception of Jerusalem, what he calls an orthogenetic type city, and Sepphoris, what he calls a heterogenetic type city.[39] Freyne notes how the newly founded city was unable to compete with the older and more pervasive relationship with Jerusalem, to whom Galileans were symbolically attached through a series of myths, traditions, and religious views. In contrast, Sepphoris's relationship with the Galilean peasants was based on pragmatic administrative functions, and was openly exploitative and coercive without any accompanying myth vying for the vil-lagers' loyalties. For this reason, though both rural Galilee and urban Sepphoris were inhabited by Jews, Freyne stresses their distinctness in spite of their close proximity, and concludes: "Each had its own identity, values, and norms, despite a degree of influence that each had on the other."[40] Freyne integrates the available archaeological evidence at Sepphoris and Tiberias, along with the rest of Galilee, into an analysis of their impact on Galilee. Although intrigued by the absence of Sepphoris in the tradition, Freyne avoids "psychologising Jesus after the manner of the nineteenth-century liberal lives," as he examines the role of Sepphoris in the Jesus move-ment. The key role Sepphoris and Tiberias played was that they were "new foundations, and as such they symbolised and embodied rapid social change in Galilee as a whole under Antipas." Although he admits that some evi-dence, especially the distribution of Kefar Ḥananya wares across Galilee, might imply some cooperation between Galilean villages and cities, he is less sanguine about this interaction than Edwards. Indeed, Freyne argues that Herod's building of two urban centers necessitated more agricultural pro-duction across Galilee, in which Antipas and the Roman-backed ruling elites extracted the resources from the countryside in an increasingly asymmetri-cal exchange of goods, coinage, and labor. The values of Antipas's new econ-omy, embodied in the two newly constructed cities, are criticized in the Jesus tradition without explicitly mentioning either city (e.g., Q 12:33–34; 16:13). Herod's striving for Roman-backed kingship and his rule in general are

---

38. Horsley, *Archaeology, History, and Society in Galilee: The Social Context of Jesus and the Rabbis* (Valley Forge, Pennsylvania: Trinity Press International, 1998) esp. 118–130.

39. "Urban-Rural Relations in First-Century Galilee: Some Suggestions from the Literary Sources," in *The Galilee in Late Antiquity*, 75–91.

40. "Urban-Rural Relations in First-Century Galilee," 90.

contrasted with the kingdom of God, which relies on love, forgiveness of debt, and reciprocity (e.g., Q 6:27–35).[41]

## Sepphoris and Jesus—The Basic Issues

The discussion over Sepphoris's role in the early Christian tradition has matured over the century. Concern has shifted from determining its place in the itinerary of Jesus' ministry to an interest over its impact on Galilee as a whole. Sepphoris's importance is no longer limited to whether Jesus visited or avoided it, but more broadly in terms of its shaping of Galilee as the religious, cultural, economic, and social milieu for early Christianity. How Sepphoris affected Galilee, and how this impact is addressed in Jesus' teachings as recorded by his followers, is the principal concern. In spite of this shift, three topics persist: 1) In the religious and cultural sphere, what was Sepphoris's role in the complex interactions between Hellenism and Judaism, and can Jesus be imagined in such a city? 2) In the socio-economic sphere, did Sepphoris's accommodation of an urban elite alienate the rural peasantry, or did it provide economic and social opportunities, and how is this reflected in the teachings of Jesus? 3) In the political sphere, to what extent was Herod Antipas's reign over Galilee a foil for Jesus' kingdom teachings, and would the Antipas ruling apparatus in Sepphoris threaten Jesus?

Discussion of each of these issues can be enlightened by the archaeological discoveries at and around Sepphoris. Aspects of Sepphoris's character as revealed by archaeology bring to the fore issues pertinent to Jesus' ministry and teachings that are often neglected. After a brief overview of the topography and political geography of Sepphoris, especially as it relates to Jesus' hometown Nazareth, features of Sepphoris's public and private space will be used to characterize Herod's first capital. By looking at the public space at Sepphoris, the civic sphere and communal structures, whose forms and styles are determined by the ruler and social elites, are considered. Aspects of public space reveal in particular the ruling classes' cultural leanings, their socio-economic standing, and the extent of their political control of the region's resources. Private space, on the other hand, consists of the domestic sphere, the patterns in the material culture in dwellings and homes that were determined by the populace, at least as far as socio-economic levels permitted. Aspects of private space reveal in particular issues of ethnicity and socio-economic standing.

---

41. "Jesus and the Urban Culture of Galilee," 596–622. A similar picture is sketched in J. D. Crossan, *The Birth of Christianity*, 209–235. It is this process that I also described in chapter two. Martin Goodman sees the increasingly indebted rural peasantry at the root of the revolt, "The First Jewish Revolt: Social Conflict and the Problem of Debt," *JJS* 33 (1982) 417–27.

## Sepphoris and Nazareth: Topographical
## and Political Considerations

The magnitude of Sepphoris as a city and its urban character can be delimited by historical geography. Urban areas in the ancient world needed a perennial water source and abundant agricultural land, with nearby trade routes and defensive topography playing a secondary role. Ideal conditions for major urban sites existed in Northern Palestine outside Galilee, in the Huleh Valley, the Jezreel Valley, and along the coast. The largest urban sites had always been north of Galilee at Hazor or at the springs of the Jordan at Dan, along the coast at Acco and Dor, and to the south at Megiddo and Beth-Shean/Scythopolis. Galilee's four east-west running valleys were much smaller, though they had a high annual rainfall and tended to be occupied by lesser urban sites, such as Tel Hannaton.[42] Antipas chose Sepphoris as his primary city because of its defensible position overlooking the largest Galilean valley, the Beth Netofah just to the north, and its proximity to the perennial springs at 'Ein Zippori to the south. It was also along the main east-west road through Galilee. The Beth Netofah valley and the fertile land along the Nahal Zippori could supply ample grain for a minor city, and the hills around the area including the Nazareth ranges to the south were ideal for olive trees and vineyards. However, these areas were neither vast enough nor fertile enough to support as large a population as the sites such as Scythopolis or Caesarea.

Topographical and political considerations, particularly in the borders of Galilee, indicating that Nazareth was oriented toward Sepphoris, come into play. Nazareth lies 5 kilometers to the south of Sepphoris and can be reached after descending the acropolis at Sepphoris, crossing the Nahal Zippori, and then making a nearly 200-meter ascent up the Nazareth ridge. The climb, however, is not as steep as Alt's term "Scheidewand" ("partitioning wall") suggests, since the path cuts at an angle along the slope. Once in Nazareth, however, the steep descent south on the Nazareth ridge precludes any notion that Nazarenes went down into the Jezreel Valley to work fields there. Nazareth itself lies at around 500 meters above sea level, and, just a short jaunt to the south, the Jezreel Plain lies at 150 meters, a much steeper incline than toward Sepphoris. There are other reasons to suppose that Nazareth was oriented toward Sepphoris as well. The Jezreel Valley was the best and most easily plowed land and traditionally was either filled with royal estates of whatever ruler or belonged to the large urban sites at Beth-Shean/Scythopolis, later Maximianopolis (Legio), or Megiddo.

Furthermore, the Jezreel Valley was not part of Antipas's Galilee. Josephus indicates somewhat vaguely that the border of Galilee was "along

---

42. Gal, *The Lower Galilee*, 23.

Samaria to Scythopolis and to the Jordan" (*War* 3.37), so maps too often interpret this by including large portions the Jezreel Valley inside Galilee's territory and draw the line of Galilee's border nearly to the city of Scythopolis and then to the Jordan.[43] However, the southernmost villages that Josephus describes as Galilean—Simonias (*Life* 24), Japhia (*War* 2.573; 3.289), Xaloth (near Mount Tabor, *War* 3.3), and Dabaritta (*War* 2.595; *Life* 62)—form an east-west line that extends along the topographical barrier of the Nazareth Ridge, and there is no evidence that Galilee's borders protrude into the Jezreel Valley.[44] Antipas's territory did not extend into the Jezreel Valley, and the villages along on the Nazareth Ridge, including Nazareth, were the southernmost in his territory and were administered through and politically oriented to Sepphoris, some 5 kilometers to the north. To sustain a population of its size, Sepphoris would have counted on the agricultural production of villages and hamlets all along the Naḥal Zippori and Nazareth Ridge.

*Figure 4.2 Beth Netofah Valley from Sepphoris Acropolis*

43. See, for example, Hanson and Oakman, *Palestine in the Time of Jesus*, x.

44. Félix-Marie Abel advocated this as the boundary of Galilee some time ago, *Géographie de la Palestine I: Géographie physique et historique* (2nd ed; Paris: Librairie Lecoffre, 1938), 154, 158, Map ix; see also Wilhelm Oehler, "Die Ortschaften und Grenzen Galiläas nach Josephus," *ZDPV* 28 (1905) 1–26, 49–74; and the helpful discussion and maps in Bösen, *Galiläa*, 24–28.

Another important topographical consideration relates to the network of regional and interregional roads. Contrary to Dalman and Batey's assertion, there is no evidence of a major Roman road extending from Sepphoris, through Nazareth, and on to Jerusalem. The evidence for an interregional Roman road from Sepphoris to Jerusalem through the central hill country and past Nazareth is late or post-Hadrianic and dates after the Bar Kochba Revolt at a time after Maximianopolis was built.[45] In the earlier periods, the main regional roads went from Ptolemais to Tiberias past Sepphoris, and, to travel to Jerusalem, Nazareans would have linked up with this major road around Sepphoris, traveled to the Sea of Galilee, and then along to Jordan toward Jericho.

## The Archaeology of Public Space at Sepphoris

The various excavations at Sepphoris have uncovered sufficient areas to provide an idea of the growth at Sepphoris in the Early Roman Period and the general arrangement of its public architecture. Only a few sherds and small finds without any accompanying architecture date to the Persian and Early Hellenistic Periods, indicating that the site was a small outpost or village during this time. Like many other Galilean sites that were settled by Jews under Hasmonean rule, Sepphoris's population grew in the first century B.C.E., perhaps to around 1,000 people living on the summit. Evidence across the site of city planning begins when an orthogonal grid adjusting to the contours of the terrain was imposed on the topography. No widespread evidence of destruction has been found from the turn of the millennium attributable to the Roman Legate Varus, rendering Josephus's description of its magnitude suspect (*Ant.* 17.288–89; and *War* 2.68–69). His tendency to exaggerate Roman might and the repercussions of rebellion must be considered when interpreting this passage.[46] On the other hand, Josephus's description of the rebuilding of Sepphoris by Antipas as the "ornament of all Galilee" (*Ant.* 18.27) resonates with the archaeological record. Dating to the beginning of Antipas's rule in Galilee, considerable building activity is discernible across the site, when the city grew to a population of between 8,000 to 12,000.[47] On the western slope of the acropolis, excavators have unearthed a massive retaining wall constructed along an earlier military structure, an alley and street in line with the retaining wall, and two or three domestic units perpendicular to these. At the same time, a rigid orthogonal framework was imposed on a plain to the east of the acropolis, bisected by two

---

45. Michael Avi-Yonah, "The Development of the Roman Road System in Palestine," *IEJ* 1 (1950–51) 57.

46. Meyers, "Sepphoris on the Eve of the Great Revolt (67–68 C.E.): Archaeology and Josephus," 132.

47. See pages 77–80.

perpendicular streets, the north-south cardo and east-west decumanus, the typical pattern of Roman urban construction.[48] The coins and sherds at the lowest level of the grid point to Antipas as having begun its construction.[49]

Most of the public structures in the grid, including many of the site's well-known mosaics, are best preserved in their Late Roman and Byzantine phases. Underneath these, enough bits and pieces from the Early Roman Period survive to provide a sketch of Antipas's city. One of the most imposing features was the *cardo*, 13.5 meters in width.[50] The hard limestone pavers of the street cover a sewage system and were laid diagonally in herringbone style, sturdy enough to survive five hundred years of wagon wheels that cut ruts into the street. Limestone stylobates lined the street proper and supported rows of columns that cordoned off roofed sidewalks originally paved with simple white mosaics and lined with shops. The columns were of local limestone and granite, not expensive imported marble, and the ashlars of the shops' facades show no evidence of marble sheeting, but were simply plastered over with whitewash and shaped with stucco, ranking it in the second tier of urban parlance.[51]

Another impressive structure excavated in the lower market is a basilica with many first-century elements intact. The interior basilica covered an area of 35 by 40 meters and its porches another 25 by 40 meters. Structurally, the building had a central nave and two aisles separated by columns; stylistically, it had a mosaic floor, frescoed walls, and marble-lined pools; and functionally, it served as some kind of administrative building, possibly a market or even a court. In its later form, an *oecus* or *triclinium* dining area, and several smaller rooms built like shops suggest that it might have been used as an indoor mall, perhaps for the sale of luxury items; and portions of it might have served as meeting or conference rooms for rulers. In either case, it testifies to central planning and control, as well as a high level of maintenance.[52]

48. Stambaugh, *The Ancient Roman City*, 243–54; and Josian Rykwert, *The Idea of a Town: The Anthropology of Urban Form in Rome, Italy, and the Roman World* (London: Faber & Faber, 1976).

49. Zeev Weiss and Ehud Netzer, "Hellenistic and Roman Sepphoris," *Sepphoris in Galilee*, 32–34; Strange, "Six Campaigns at Sepphoris," 339–355.

50. At larger Mediterranean cities, the width of the *cardo* or *decumanus* could be as great as 22 meters, Magen Broshi, "The Standards of Street Widths in the Roman Byzantine Period," *IEJ* 27 (1977) 232–5.

51. The practical and utilitarian approach to public architecture was characteristic also of Herod the Great's projects, which frequently masked internal construction with facades, Ehud Netzer, "Herod's Building Projects: State Necessity of Personal Need," in *Biblical Archaeology Today, 1990, Proceedings of the Second International Congress on Biblical Archaeology* (eds. Avraham Biran and Joseph Aviram; Jerusalem: Israel Exploration Society, 1993) 48–61.

52. James F. Strange, "The Eastern Basilica Building," in *Sepphoris in Galilee*, 117–121; and "Six Campaigns at Sepphoris: The University of South Florida Excavations, 1983–1989, in *The Galilee in Late Antiquity*, 339–355.

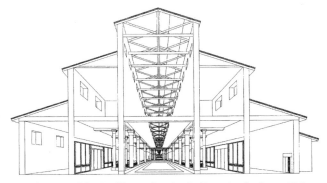

*Figure 4.3 The Basilica at Sepphoris (Drawing by James F. Strange, Dir., The University of South Florida Excavations at Sepphoris)*

The theater, dating to the latter half of the first century C.E., lies on the northern side of the city overlooking the Beth Netofah valley. Rather than being constructed from the ground up, as was typical of Roman-style theaters, its builders took advantage of the topography and chiseled the lower portions of the auditorium's seating (*cavea*) into the natural cavity on the northern slope of the acropolis, similar to theaters in classical Greece. Otherwise, Sepphoris's theater was akin to Roman types throughout the Empire: vaults and arches supported the upper tiers of the *cavea*, passage into the theater from the outside to the mid-level seating was through *vomitoria*, and it seems to have been closed off by an imposing *scaenae frons*.[53] One of the more modest theaters on the Eastern Mediterranean, its diameter was just over 70 meters for a seating capacity of around 4,000.

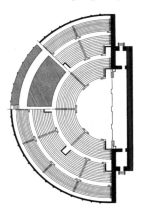

*Figure 4.4 The Theater at Sepphoris (Waterman)*

53. Arthur Segal, *Theaters in Roman Palestine and Provincia Arabia* (Mnemosyne, Bibliotheca Classica Batava Supplementum 120; Leiden: E. J. Brill, 1995).

The diminutive size of the theater is not so much related to the size of Sepphoris's population as it is to the city's relative wealth. Much of the structure's interstices were composed of fieldstones and packed dirt, with only a façade of well-hewn limestone ashlars. The fact that the lower auditorium was built into the hill also reveals the builder's concern to cut expenses, as does the complete lack of marble and fluted columns; stucco, plaster, and fresco, however, covered the less than ideal workmanship.

The debate over the date of the theater encapsulates a basic problem in coupling archaeology with historical Jesus research. Arguing that Jesus attended the theater necessitates an early date.[54] However, the date cannot be deduced historically by arguing that Antipas was likely to build a theater; rather, the structure must be dated stratigraphically. The sherds, under a cavity that was filled when one of the *vomitoria* was constructed, include types that date to the latter half of the first century C.E. Ehud Netzer and Zeer Weiss, the excavators of portions of the *scaenae frons*, likewise claim a date to the latter half of the first century.[55] The results of stratigraphic excavation must be taken seriously, and though it is clear that Antipas introduced Roman style architecture and Hellenistic based structures, this process continued after his death, and even accelerated after the Jewish Revolt and the stationing of the Legion in Maximianopolis.[56]

As an aside, if the theater, of Sepphoris or elsewhere, is of relevance to the Jesus traditions, it is neither as the source of hypocrites nor as the vehicle for classical Greek culture. Provincial theaters usually provided baser forms of entertainment, with jugglers and acrobats, mimes and pantomimes, farces, and more vulgar spectacles.[57] The theater may, however, have been one of the symbols of the Roman Empire's rigid social stratification under attack in the teachings of Jesus. Unlike theaters of the classical Greek polis, with open seating for all citizens, in the Roman Period, the best seats near or even on the orchestra had backrests and were often inscribed with the leading families' names, as at Neapolis/Shechem. The social elites also entered exclusively and separately through the *parodoi*, while the lower classes streamed

54. So, for example, Batey, "Jesus and the Theater," 563–74; and Schwank, "Das Theater von Sepphoris," 199–206.

55. Weiss and Netzer, "Hellenistic and Roman Sepphoris," in *Sepphoris in Galilee*, 32. William F. Albright had dated the theater to the second century based on architectural style, "Review of Waterman's Preliminary Report on the 1931 Excavations," *Classical Weekly* 21 (1938) 148.

56. Meyers, "Roman Sepphoris in Light of New Archaeological Evidence," in *The Galilee in Late Antiquity*, 321–338.

57. Contra Batey, "Jesus and the Theater." Mary T. Boatwright, "Theaters in the Roman Empire," *BA* 53 (1990) 184–192; Richard C. Beacham, *The Roman Theater and Its Audience* (Cambridge: Harvard University Press, 1992) 150; and Daniel Sperber, *The City in Roman Palestine* (New York: Oxford University Press, 1998) 79–85.

through the *vomitoria*.[58] In this way the theater visibly announced the social hierarchy and magnified class distinctions, practices under attack in the Gospels (e.g., Q 11:43; Mark 10:41–45; Luke 14:11; 18:14).

Very little epigraphic evidence from Sepphoris dates to the earlier periods, and no euergtistic inscriptions have been uncovered from the Early Roman Period boasting of a patron's munificence, a commonplace of civic life in the Roman world. Two inscriptions, however, one an *ostracon* dating to the Late Hellenistic Period and the other an inscribed weight from the Early Roman Period, are of relevance. The *ostracon* is on a storage jar fragment and reads '*pmlslsh* painted in red Hebrew block letters, a translation of the Greek ἐπιμελητής "manager, overseer, or treasurer."[59] The jar likely contained grain, olive oil, or wine that had been taxed in kind and handed over to the ἐπιμελητής who wrote in Hebrew letters but had adopted a Greek administrative title.[60] The other inscribed item is a lead market weight with Greek writing.[61] Dating to the first century C.E., one side lists the amount of the weight (HMI–ΛITPIN) surrounded by schematic drawings of a colonnaded street signifying the *agora*, and the other side's inscription in Greek datable to the first century C.E. reads:[62]

| | |
|---|---|
| ΑΓΟΑΝΟΜΟ | Under the market |
| ΥΤΩΝ ΣΙΜΩΝΟ | inspection of Simon |
| ΑΙΑΝΟΥ | son of Aianos... |
| ΙΟΥΣΤΟΣ | son of Justus |
| [Υ]ΙΟΥ | |

The names of the ἀγορανόμοι or "market inspectors," who sold permits, ensured quality, or controlled weights, are distinctly Jewish. In this case they set the standard of a half litra, a common unit of weight in the Roman world (36 ounces or 1,018 grams).[63] The weight combines a Roman/Latin

---

58. Paul Zanker, *The Power of Images in the Age of Augustus* (Ann Arbor, Michigan: University of Michigan Press, 1990) 147–53; David Small, "Social Correlation to the Greek Cavea in the Roman Period," in *Roman Architecture in the Greek World* (eds. Sarah Macready and F. Thompson; London, 1987) 85–93; and Jerzy Kolendo, "La répartition des places aux spectacles et le stratification sociale dans l'empire romain," *Ktema* 6 (1981) 301ff.

59. *Sepphoris in Galilee*, 170

60. See the helpful comments by Meyers, "Sepphoris on the Eve of the Great Revolt," 130–131.

61. *Sepphoris in Galilee* 201; and Yaakov Meshorer, "Preliminary Report: The Lead Weight," *BA* 49 (1986) 16–17.

62. Translated by Meshorer , "Preliminary Report: The Lead Weight," 17.

63. On the duties of the *agoranomos* as reflected primarily in the rabbinic literature, see Sperber, *The City in Roman Palestine*, 32–47.

measure, written in Greek script, testifying to Jews controlling important administrative matters in Sepphoris, a pattern for which there is also archaeological documentation from Tiberias.[64]

The coins of Sepphoris likewise show a blending of cultures. Herod Antipas minted the first coins at Sepphoris; however, his position procured the privilege of coinage by Rome, rather than the city itself. Antipas's coins eschewed his image and tended to contain symbols that Jews considered appropriate, but which were not necessarily foreign to the wider Greco-Roman world, such as reeds, palm branches, and palm trees. During the revolt, the city minted bronze coins with crossed double cornucopia on the obverse, a typical Jewish numismatic symbol.[65] Instead of the emperor's image, only the name *Caesar Nero Claudius* is written in large letters. The reverse's legend reads:

ΕΠΙ ΟΥΕΣΠΑΣΙΑΝΟΥ/ΕΙΡΗΝΟΠΟΛΙ/ΝΕΡΩΝΙΑ/ΣΕΠΦΩ
"under Vespasian, in Eirenopolis—Neronias—Sepphoris"

Struck in 68 C.E., the coin announced the city's pacifistic stance and refusal to rebel against Rome, and even added the new names *Neronias* and *City of Peace* (εἰρηνοπόλις).[66] The same Greek inscription is found encircled by a wreath on another issue in the same year, whose reverse is imprinted with the large Latin letters "S" and "C," the characteristic insignia of S[enatus] C[onsulto], the Roman Senate. These coins were aniconic and in that sense typically Jewish, albeit in Greek and bowing to Roman rule. Herod Antipas was politically shrewd enough to know where to draw the line with his subjects, and later the inhabitants of Sepphoris were savvy enough to proclaim their intentions, bowing to Vespasian and Nero without abandoning Jewish religious sensibilities on their city-coins. Somewhat later, the first Emperor's bust on Sepphoris's coins was that of Trajan, though typically Jewish symbols such as the palm tree, *caduceus*, or barley corn accompanied it on the reverse, contributing to their characterization as "Jewish-Roman." Only under Antonius Pius (138–61 C.E.) is the emperor's image accompanied by a pagan symbol, Tyche inside a temple, at which time the city's name is no longer *Sepphoris* derived from Hebrew, but *Diocaesarea*, "dedicated to the Imperial Zeus," the name adopted in later pagan and

---

64. Shraga Qedar, "Two Lead Weights of Herod Antipas and Agrippa II and the Early History of Tiberias," *Israel Numismatic Journal* 9 (1986–87) 29–35.

65. Yaakov Meshorer, "Jewish Symbols on Roman Coins Struck in Eretz Israel," *Israel Museum News* 14 (1978) 60–63.

66. Meshorer, "Sepphoris and Rome," 159–71; and Colin M. Kraay, "Jewish Friends and Allies of Rome," *American Numismatic Society Museum Notes* 25 (1980) 53–57.

Christian literature. The early coins of Sepphoris befit a Jewish population, and the gradual increase over time in Roman and pagan elements ultimately push aside the distinct Jewish symbols.

## Public Space at Scythopolis and Caesarea Maritima

Sepphoris's character becomes clearer when its coins, inscriptions, and public architecture in general are compared to those of Palestine's major gentile cities. The city of Scythopolis, with a sizable Jewish minority, was granted the right to mint coins in 63 B.C.E., right after Pompey conquered the region. Already the first coins struck at Scythopolis bear the portrait of Gabinius, the Roman proconsul who divided the region into districts, and who had also made Sepphoris the seat of the Galilean district's council (*Ant.* 14.91; *War* 1.170). The legends on these coins call the city "Gabinis-Nysa" in honor of Gabinius and dedicated to Dionysos's nurse, whose mythical burial was near Beth-Shean. She appears on many coins, often inside a temple and sometimes holding the infant Dionysos, who otherwise is prominently featured on other coins of Scythopolis. At Caesarea, the first coins minted by Herod the Great were typically cautious. As "King of the Jews," he avoided human images even at this primarily gentile city, preferring to depict a galley and anchor on opposite sides. But under Agrippa I the coins of Caesarea featured Tyche the city-goddess holding a rudder. During the Jewish War in 68 C.E., Caesarea struck coins in Nero's rule bearing the image of the general Vespasian, and after the War the city's status was elevated to that of a colony, reflected in coins that read *Colonia Prima Flavia Augusta Caesarea*. The many coins of Caesarea in this period contained numerous pagan deities, Tyche, Serapis, Minerva, Dionysos, Poseidon, and Nike.[67]

The coins reveal Scythopolis and Caesarea Maritima's more elevated status and more pagan character, traits that the inscriptions found in these cities bear out. The sheer number of inscriptions at each site point to higher levels of Greek literacy, as well as broader civic participation in building and maintaining the city. In contrast to Sepphoris, numerous inscriptions have been uncovered at Scythopolis, many of them from the Early Roman Period. All are in Greek, and many boast of a sponsor's erection or maintenance of a civic building. At Caesarea on the Sea abundant epigraphic evidence from the Roman Periods show Greek to be common, with some Latin as well. Many are euergistic, such as the inscription discovered on the back of a seat in the theater, which tells of Pontius Pilate's gift for the *Tiberium* built in honor of the Emperor. These inscriptions illustrate a higher visibility on the

---

67. Yaakov Meshorer, *City-Coins of Eretz-Israel and the Decapolis in the Roman Period* (Jerusalem: The Israel Museum, 1985) 20–21, 40–42.

part of the ruling elite in shaping civic life and their desire to compete for honor for their efforts.

The public architecture of these cities shows greater wealth on behalf of the elites in the way in which civic buildings were constructed. Multiple drummed marble columns are frequent; white marble from Turkey and Greece, and red granite from the Nile, show an ability to import bulky and expensive materials from far away. The structures themselves were also more massive and generally made of better fitting stones than are found at both Sepphoris and Tiberias. They also included many more overtly pagan elements, whether temples, statues, or decorative items. Caesarea was unabashedly Romophilic in its architecture, with the massive Temple to the Emperor, the *Augusteum*, as the city's central building. The temple with statues of Augustus and Roma was 23 by 7 meters, and a 1-meter-long foot has been found along with other statues and sarcophagi decorated with mythological themes. The theater seated more than 5,000, was built from the ground up, and was richly covered with various colored marble sheets. Thousands of columns of pink granite from Aswan are scattered across the site. The amphitheater was larger than the Coliseum in Rome. There were also vast public bath complexes for the elites.

Scythopolis likewise eclipses Sepphoris in its public architecture and pagan character. The theater was one of the largest in Palestine discovered to date, built with a core of basalt stones and decorated with marble and white limestone. The white-marble temple dedicated to Dionysos typifies the acceptance of the Greco-Roman pantheon in Scythopolis, which often cloaked its Semitic deities in Greco-Roman style and with Greco-Roman names; for example, the local *Baalshamim* became *Zeus Akraios*.[68] The archaeological testimony of Caesarea Maritima and Scythopolis stands in stark contrast to Sepphoris and Judaism in general, which did not adopt anything from the pantheon for its divinity.

Compared to Scythopolis and Caesarea, the archaeology of Sepphoris's public space was clearly on a lower tier socio-economically. It could not afford marble or imported columns, and it was more hesitant and selective in embracing of Greco-Roman elements. Although Herod Antipas introduced Greco-Roman urban architecture into Galilee, Sepphoris retained its Jewish character more pronouncedly, without statues or temples. It is fair to characterize urbanization in its infancy under Herod Antipas. The local elites were reluctant to adopt foreign beliefs and were intent on maintaining their religious convictions, though they sought out the socio-economic benefits that accompanied Roman urbanization.

---

68. Yoram Tsafrir, "More Evidence for the Cult of Zeus Akraios at Beth-She'an," in *Eretz-Israel* 19 (Jerusalem: Israel Exploration Society, 1987) 81 [English summary] 282–283 [Hebrew].

The Archaeology of Private Space at Sepphoris

Two houses at Sepphoris help elucidate the archaeology of its private space. One is Unit II on the acropolis's western domestic quarters, which was excavated by the Sepphoris Regional Project over several seasons in the mid-1990s, and the other is the well-known Dionysiac villa, excavated in the mid-1980s.[69] Unit II was constructed at the beginning of the Early Roman Period as part of Antipas's rebuilding projects and continued in use with some modifications until the Late Roman Period. Partial destruction by fire in the latter half of the first century C.E. permits a picture of several rooms of the house. Judging from the Early Roman strata of other domestic units in the area, Unit II is representative of this more affluent neighborhood near the top of the acropolis.

*Figure 4.5 Western Acropolis (Courtesy Duke University, Sepphoris Regional Project)*

Unit II is the uppermost of several houses perpendicular to a 3-meter-wide street along the western slope of the acropolis. The layout of the 150-m² house is one of several typical dwellings in Roman Palestine. It is an inner courtyard house without columns, common among wealthier families in urban areas of the region.[70] Like most houses in Galilee, Unit II's courtyard was concealed and not visible from either the street to the north or the alleyway to the west. The walls stood atop bedrock and boulder foundations, and its lower courses were made of hewn limestone, evenly shaped in regular sizes by skilled craftsmen. The 70-centimeter-wide outside walls were

---

69. I was the area supervisor during the excavations under the direction of Eric Meyers.

70. Using Yizhar Hirshfeld's classification, *The Palestinian Dwelling in the Roman-Byzantine Period* (Jerusalem: Franciscan Printing, 1995) 57–97, 109.

arranged in header-stretcher technique and could have easily supported a second story. A large cistern opened into the courtyard, and several others scattered throughout the house disclose the inhabitants' desire and ability to store their own water. A small wine processing area to the south of the house and smaller unplastered cisterns hewn into bedrock likely served as dry grain storage or cool storage for wine. Some rooms in the house were covered with *al secco* fresco, a cheaper and less complicated style that is painted after the plaster dried. The designs were simple floral or geometric patterns, as well as green and red rectangles imitating marble paneling in *al daddo* style.[71] The frescoed rooms had smooth plaster floors, as did the courtyard, and patches of mosaic tessarae were discovered *ex situ* in the fill of another room whose Early Roman phase was destroyed beyond recovery. The kitchen area and other rooms, however, were covered with a beaten earth floor.

In addition to the fresco and mosaic, several other artifacts are reflective of the first-century inhabitants' relative wealth.[72] Fragments of an expensive molded glass cup, a hanging lamp, and an incense bowl are among the finds from the Early Roman strata, as are finely carved bone pins and a makeup spatula. The inhabitants were not extravagantly wealthy—the cosmetic items were bone and not ivory, and the ceramics were common wares from the Galilean villages of Shikhin nearby and Kefar Hananya: water jars jugs, cooking pots, and casserole cookers. Only a very few fine wares were present, and more expensive *terra sigilatta* serving bowls or plates were absent, as were imported wine amphora with stamped handles, in stark contrast to elite urban houses of the Decapolis or along the coast.[73] Unit II and the buildings on the western side of the acropolis show an awareness of Roman architectural styles prevalent across the broader Mediterranean world, but the implements of the social elite were not adopted in full or were not affordable.[74]

---

71. The fresco is reminiscent of the Pompeiian second style, very similar to that of the Palatial or Great Mansion in the Herodian Quarter in Jerusalem, Nahman Avigad, *Discovering Jerusalem* (Nashville, Tennessee: Nelson, 1980) 95–120; similar frescoes have also been found in elite houses at Jodefat and Gamla.

72. See the valuable comments on the spread of status indicators in architectural contexts in Andrew Wallace–Hadrill, *Houses and Society in Pompeii and Herculaneum* (Princeton: Princeton University Press, 1994) 143–74.

73. Waterman's excavation found a single stamped Rhodian jar handle, Yeivin, "History and Archaeology," in *Preliminary Report of the University of Michigan Excavation at Sepphoris,* 27; the excavations directed by the Meyerses have unearthed in nine seasons a single stamped wine amphora handle.

74. Especially when compared with houses in Italy, see Wallace-Hadrill, *Houses and Society in Pompeii and Herculaneum*; the villas along the coast, Shimon Applebaum, "The Roman Villa in Judaea: A Problem," in *Judaea in Hellenistic and Roman Times: Historical and Archaeological Essays* (Leiden: E. J. Brill, 1989) 124–131; or even the villa at Tel Anafa, Sharon Herbert, *Tel Anafa I. Final Report on Ten Years of Excavation at a Hellenistic and Roman Settlement in Northern Israel* (JRA Supplemental Series 10.1; Ann Arbor, Michigan: Kelsey Museum of Archaeology, 1994).

Finds inside Unit II attest to the occupants' Jewish ethnicity and religion. It contains four stepped pools identified as *miqwaoth*; two might have been added in the Middle Roman Period when the other two went out of use at the end of the Early Roman Period. Each was chiseled into bedrock and plastered with descending steps, and was large enough for people to immerse themselves entirely. Each was flanked by a cistern of varying size, one of which was connected to the stepped pool by a channel still intact. Whether the exact function of these stepped pools can be deduced, or their precise relation to ritual purity determined, should not undermine their identification as uniquely Jewish water installations.

*Figure 4.6* Miqveh *at Sepphoris (Courtesy Duke University, Sepphoris Regional Project)*

The lack of pork in the bone remains also points to the Jewish ethnicity of the house's inhabitants. Over 450 animal bone fragments have been found in the kitchen area alone, of which only four are possibly pork, statistically considered nil.[75] Furthermore, more than a dozen fragments from stone vessels have been recovered in Unit II. Like the *miqwaoth*, the use of chalk or soft limestone vessels can be tied to Jewish beliefs in ritual purity, since the Mishnah describes stone as a material impervious to impurity (*Kelim* 10:1; *Ohol.* 5:5; *Para* 5:5). In particular, the presence of many lids and stoppers made of stone suggests conformity to the Mishnaic ruling that ceramic vessels become unclean through their openings, which can be prevented with

75. The zooarchaeologist for the excavation is Bill Grantham of Troy State University in Alabama; see also Brian Hesse and Paula Wapnish, "Can Pig Remains Be Used for Ethnic Diagnosis in the Ancient Near East," in *The Archaeology of Israel. Constructing the Past, Interpreting the Present*, 238–270.

coverings of stone (*Kelim* 2:5). Regardless of their owners' intent, chalk bowls, mugs, and cups are present in areas populated by Jews—Judea, Golan, and Galilee—but generally absent in Samaria, along the Coast, or in Transjordan. Among the stone vessels in the western domestic quarters are several fragments of large *kalynx*-type jars, barrel-shaped and turned on a large lathe, which were luxury items and are typically found in wealthier Jewish homes. Unit II's decorations were completely aniconic, and a lamp with a menorah on its disc typifies the occupants' Jewish identity, even if the lamp dates to the next stratigraphic phase of the house.

This pattern persists throughout the domestic quarters, which appears to be inhabited exclusively by Jews. More than 20 stepped pools have been found, most of them likely *miqwaoth*; more than 120 chalk vessel fragments have been excavated; and pork, virtually absent across this area during the Roman Period, does not appear until the Byzantine Period. Though none have been found in the Early Roman strata of Unit II, ceramic incense shovels like those appearing on synagogue mosaics have also been unearthed across the western domestic quarters.[76] Although the area is generally aniconic, a few items indicative of paganism have been uncovered, such as miniature statues of Prometheus and Pan in a Middle Roman context, and a small medallion depicting a Dionysiac scene in a Late Hellenistic context.[77] It is not unimaginable that such small decorative items belonged to Jews, though it must be stressed that the first two items were found in layers of detritus, and that the latter item was found outside a house in an open area.

The second house under consideration, the so-called Dionysiac villa, was constructed south of the theater at the end of second or early third century C.E. The size of the house, some 40 meters long and 23 meters wide (920m²), necessitated the leveling off of bedrock to the building's west and the raising of a dirt platform for its southern extent. The house was built with a central peristyle courtyard opening to the south, and with a splendid banquet or dining hall (*triclinium*) off to the north of the courtyard, with smaller bedrooms, service rooms, storage rooms, and bathrooms on the periphery.

Constructed of large limestone ashlars, numerous floral and geometric fresco fragments testify that the interior walls were colored with wall paintings. Simple white and black mosaics with some geometric patterns spread

76. *Sepphoris in Galilee*, catalogue numbers 78 and 79, pages 205–206; Mordecai Narkiss, "The Snuff-Shovel as a Jewish Symbol," *JPOS* 15 (1935) 14–28; Erwin Goodenough, *Jewish Symbols in the Greco-Roman Period* Vol. 3 (New York: Pantheon Books, 1953–68) Figs. 293, 334–7; and Rachel Hachlili, *Ancient Jewish Art and Archaeology in the Land of Israel* (Lieden: E. J. Brill, 1988) 257–66.

77. Catalogue numbers 17, 18, and 21 in *Sepphoris in Galilee*. The small bronze bull (Serapis?) and altar found in detritus of a cistern date to the fourth century, Strange, "Six Campaigns at Excavation," 344–45.

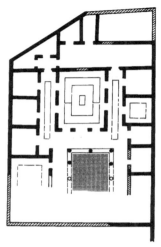

*Figure 4.7 The Dionysiac Villa at Sepphoris (after Meyers, Netzer, and Meyers, 1992)*

over the hallways and side rooms of the house, and the privy and running water were adorned with the appropriate lettering ΥΓΕΙ, "health!" The most exquisite mosaic floor covered the *triclinium*, exceptional in artistic quality at the site and all of Galilee. The *triclinium*'s design and the mosaic's theme were common in elite houses of the Roman world.[78] The 7 x 5.5-meter mosaic with more than 20 different-colored tessarae was divided into three areas: a U-shaped area with white tessarae and "gamma" marks, symbolizing the placement of the three couches (τρι–κλίνη) for reclining; a colorful U-shaped area depicting processional scenes, some of which were damaged and repaired in antiquity; and a central rectangular area featuring a series of panels celebrating the life of Dionysos and joys of the vine.

Little in the mosaic reflects cultic elements or the mysteries of the wine god; rather, the central panel typifies the ambiance the mosaic sought to convey, a drinking bout between Herakles and Dionysos. In flanking panels, Dionysos is declared the victor (with the inscription ΠΟΜΠΗ) reclining in his chariot and casting a glance onto the next panel, where the puking Herakles (ΜΕΘΗ) is being helped by a satyr and maenad. Other panels rejoice in the fruit of the vine, such as the trampling of grapes (ΛΗΝΟ–ΒΑΤΗ) and a village festival (ΚΩΜΟΣ). Some panels recall legends of Dionysos, such as the washing of Dionysos by the nurses who hid him (ΔΙΟΝΥΣΟΥ ΛΟΥΤΡΑ), the revealing of the vine's mystery to the shepherds

---

78. Christine Kondoleon, *Domestic and Divine: Roman Mosaics in the House of Dionysos* (Ithaca: Cornell University Press) 1994; and Glen W. Bowersock, *Hellenism in Late Antiquity* (Ann Arbor: The University of Michigan Press, 1990) 41–53.

(ΠΟΙΜΝΑΙ), and his marriage to Ariadne (ΥΜΕΝΑΙΟΣ). Interspersed with medallions, bucolic processions of peasants are portrayed joyfully handing over their harvest, including grapes, fruit, chickens, and ducks. Facing the host's seat is a portrait of a beautiful woman (Ariadne or the matron of the house?), which the excavators have dubbed "the Mona Lisa of the Galilee."[79]

The Roman artistic motifs and celebration of the pagan deity Dionysos insinuate that the villa belonged to a Roman official; however, a Jewish owner cannot be precluded, given that by the third and fourth centuries even synagogues were adopting similar motifs and apparently pagan themes. Aside from what the Dionysos mosaic tells us about the owner's religious leanings, it and the layout of the house betray the owner's wealth and interest in publicizing his extravagance. While the traditional closed courtyard house concealed the daily life of its occupants in privacy, the peristyle house's atrium puts on a conspicuous show for the passerby, bolstering the idea of social stratification. The very design of a peristyle house reinforced notions of "in" and "out," by making visible to outsiders the splendor of the atrium's mosaics, frescoed walls, fluted columns, and gardens.[80] The social hierarchy was further reinforced for those invited into the *triclinium*. The layout of the mosaic privileged three diners, the host and the guests of honor to his right and left, whose couches were marked off on the large white U-shape by *gamma* marks, with the remaining diners crowding around the white tessaraed areas in descending social order (as is assumed in Luke 14:7–11).[81]

Even though exceptional at the site and over a century after the time period under consideration, the Dionysiac villa represents an important point on the trajectory of elite domestic architecture at Sepphoris. Built in the early first century C.E., Unit II was an enclosed courtyard protecting the privacy of the family's daily activities, but it had adopted decorative elements such as fresco and mosaic that marked its prominence on the social scale. The luxury items and styles were adopted inside the house, but not yet fully displayed to outsiders. A contemporaneous house across the street, however, was built in peristyle, showing that already some Jewish families in the first century at Sepphoris were adopting more fully the Roman style of displaying one's wealth architecturally in pretentious ways.[82] The Dionysiac villa shows the extent to which ostentation had risen in the city by the third century C.E.

---

79. Eric Meyers, Ehud Netzer, and Carol Meyers, "Artistry in Stone: The Mosaics of Ancient Sepphoris," *BA* 50 (1987) 223–31.

80. Wallace-Hadrill, *Houses and Society in Pompeii and Herculaneum*, esp. 143–74.

81. This dining tradition, where two guests of honor flank the host, is presupposed also in James and John's request for a privileged seat in Mark 10:35–45.

82. The structure was partially excavated by Waterman, and originally identified as a Christian basilica because of its columns, Manasseh, "Architecture and Topography," in *Preliminary Report of the University of Michigan Excavations at*

The archaeology of private space at Sepphoris is overwhelmingly Jewish in its religious and ethnic indicators. Some small household items reminiscent of pagan mythological themes are interspersed among the houses, and by the late second century a mosaic dedicated to Dionysiac themes was built in an elite house. More significantly, in Jewish homes excavated, an increase in luxury and status items can be seen, and in some this wealth and status differentiation was beginning to be put on display in the pretentious fashions of Roman architecture.

## The Archaeology of Nazareth

The finds from the village of Nazareth, some 5 kilometers to the south of Sepphoris, provide a stark contrast with those of Sepphoris, and a brief comparison sheds some light on the question of Jesus' presence or absence at Sepphoris. Massive church-building activities beginning after the conversion of the Empire obscure much of the evidence for the material culture of first-century C.E. Nazareth. The mosaics, graffiti, and basilica structure of the later periods of the Church of the Annunciation and of Saint Joseph arose at a time when imperial funds and outside pilgrims came into Nazareth.[83] The village in the first century, however, was much more modest and simple, and agricultural, and was confined to an area of around 4 hectares, composed of an area around the Church of the Annunciation, under lands some 100 meters to the west now occupied by the Sisters of Nazareth. Roman and Byzantine Period tombs to the west and east of the Church of the Annunciation delimit the size of the site and suggest a population of less than 400 people.[84]

The modest architecture and scant building projects from the earlier period leave little evidence, though the site was clearly not planned in an orthogonal manner, nor is there any trace of a paved street across the entire site. Notable in this sense is what has not been found. There is no evidence of any public structures from the Early Roman Period. There is no marble nor mosaics nor frescoes from the period prior to Christian construction in the post-Constantinian period. There are no public inscriptions whatsoever, instructive of the level of illiteracy and lack of elite sponsors. The only

---

*Sepphoris*, 4–6; under the direction of Strange portions were re-excavated, leading to a reinterpretation of the building as a domestic, "Six Campaigns at Sepphoris," 344–47. Its *miqwaoth* point to Jewish inhabitants.

83. For the later evidence, Joan Taylor, *Christians and the Holy Places: The Myth of Jewish-Christian Origins* (Oxford: Clarendon Press, 1993) 230–33.

84. James F. Strange, "Nazareth," *ABD* 4:1050–51. On the location of the tombs, see Clemens Kopp, "Beiträge zur Geschichte Nazareths," *JPOS* 18 (1938) 191–228.

inscription from pre-Christian period is an Aramaic funerary inscription found in the tombs (*CII* 2.988). And Nazareth did not, of course, mint coins, few of which were found during the Franciscan excavations.

In terms of private space, one of the notable problems is that the later Christian constructions have obliterated any evidence of homes other than the subterranean cisterns, storage bins, and caves. The fact that so little has been found leads to the conclusion that the houses themselves were rather poorly made of fieldstones and mud, with thatched roofs and coverings over caves. The entire area seems to have been preoccupied with agricultural activities. On the outskirts of the village, traces of terracing have been found, as has evidence of a vineyard tower. Inside the village, wine-pressing vats with straining depressions, fermenting vats, and depressions to hold storage jars, along with grinding stones and silos are complemented by simple locally made pottery and household items, without any trace of imported or fine wares from the earlier periods. There are also no luxury items of any kind, though a few stone vessel fragments have been found.

The pejorative question, can anything good come out of Nazareth (John 1:46), seems apt. It was a small Jewish village, without any political significance, preoccupied with agriculture and, no doubt, taxation.

## Jesus and Sepphoris

We conclude with a reassessment of the question of Jesus and Sepphoris, and Sepphoris's influence on the Galilee of Jesus. Whether Jesus himself was ever in Sepphoris, during either his youth or ministry, cannot be settled with certainty. Of his youth we know nothing short of his growing up in Nazareth as a (τεκτόν carpenter, Mark 6:3).[85] It is probable that a villager in antiquity, specifically a Galilean from the artisan class, visited nearby cities, but this is beyond proof. What is unlikely is that villagers worked in cities, since, unlike today, the general flow of labor was from the city to the countryside, and cities tended to have enough unemployed workers. However, it is not unlikely that Galilean villagers visited Sepphoris on some occasions, such as for the market or during festivals, and certainly there was much hearsay about Sepphoris in hamlets like Nazareth from the more mobile of society, like itinerant peddlers. The fact that the tradition shows an awareness of urban features, such as a colonnaded street (πλατεῖα, Luke/Q 14:21), a city gate (πύλη, Q 13:23–24), and markets (ἀγορά, Q 7:31–32) lends credibility to the position that rural Galileans were aware of Sepphoris. Some passages show more than just awareness, hinting at the villagers' weariness toward the

---

85. Matthew and Luke distance Jesus further from manual labor, the former by describing him as a son of a τεκτόν (Matt 13:55), and the latter by describing him simply as the son of Joseph without any mention of his occupation or status (Luke 4:22).

cities, such as fear of courts (Q 12:57–59) and conflicts in the agora (Q 7:31–35; 11:43).[86] Consequently, even though visits to Sepphoris on the part of Galilean villagers were likely, they represented the crossing over of political, socio-economic, perhaps even cultural boundaries, as the archaeological comparisons of Nazareth and Sepphoris serve to remind us.[87]

The debate over whether Jesus visited Sepphoris as part of his ministry, or whether its omission in the tradition reflects a programmatic avoidance of the two Herodian cities, turns on one's characterization of Jesus and his teachings generally. Perhaps one should be reluctant to read too much into the omission of Sepphoris in the tradition since its absence only raises the possibility of Jesus' avoiding it. However startling Sepphoris's omission seems, especially to those who have spent so much time excavating its ruins, theories extrapolating on its absence in the New Testament rest on shaky ground. His itinerary cannot be reconstructed from the place names mentioned in the tradition alone. There are only nine place names in the sayings source Q, and five of them take on a mythological character and are not necessarily indicative of Jesus' presence there (Tyre and Sidon in Q 10:13–15; Jerusalem in Q 13:34; Sodom in Q 10:12; and Nineveh Q 11:32). The Gospel of Mark presents more geographical information about Jesus' Galilean ministry, and portrays Jesus' avoidance of the poleis proper in favor of their chorai.[88] In spite of Mark's redactional interest in polarizing city and country, there may be some historical validity to Jesus' avoidance of the larger gentile cities around Galilee, such as Tyre (Mark 7:24, 31), Caesarea Philippi (Mark 8:27), or the Decapolis (Mark 7:31; 6:53), but whether this avoidance parallels his relationship with Jewish Sepphoris is questionable. Likewise, whether Jesus and his disciples' close connections to Bethsaida have analogies with his relationship to Sepphoris is unsure. The excavations at Bethsaida have uncovered a rather diminutive and inelegant polis, and the extent of its Jewish and Gentile leanings are yet to be fully determined.[89]

---

86. Jonathan L. Reed, "The Social Map of Q," in *Conflict and Invention: Social and Literary Studies on Q* (ed. J. Kloppenborg; Philadelphia: Trinity Press International, 1995) 17–36.

87. A point stressed by Freyne, "Urban-Rural Relations in First-Century Galilee," 88–90; and "Jesus and the Urban Culture of Galilee," 604–11. Shimon Applebaum has suggested that there was antagonism based on "conservative, Aramaic-speaking rural areas and Hellenistically-oriented urban areas", "Judaea as a Roman Province: The Countryside as a Political and Economic Factor," *ANRW* II.8, eds. Wolfgang Haase and Hildegard Temporini (Berlin: Walter de Gruyter, 1977) 371.

88. Freyne, *Galilee, Jesus, and the Gospels*, 33–63; Thomas Schmeller, "Jesus im Umland Galilläas," *BZ* 38 (1994) 44–65; and Friedrich Lang, "'Über Sidon mitten ins Gebiet der Dekapolis.' Geographie und Theologie in Markus 7,31," *ZDPV* 94 (1978) 145–60.

89. Rami Arav and Richard Freund, *Bethsaida: A City by the Northern Shore of the Sea of Galilee* (Bethsaida Excavations Project I; Kirkesville, Missouri: Thomas Jefferson University Press, 1995).

The archaeology of Sepphoris's public and private space, when compared to Nazareth and other cities in Northern Palestine, sheds considerable light on the debate over Sepphoris's omission in the Gospels. The possibility that Jesus programmatically avoided Sepphoris can only be discussed with the aforementioned archaeology in mind. But, more generally, Christian origins and the Gospel traditions can only be understood with Sepphoris's influence on Galilee as the background.

Sepphoris and Ethnicity and Culture—Judaism and Hellenism

Archaeological evidence from surveys and excavations indicates that Judeans colonized a sparsely inhabited Galilee during the Late Hellenistic Period under Maccabean rule, including Sepphoris. The pattern of Galilee and Sepphoris's material culture parallels that of Judea. In terms of religious and ethnic indicators, continuity exists between Galilean villages, such as Yodefat, Capernaum, and Nazareth, and the city of Sepphoris. In both the Galilean city and villages, pork was avoided, miqwaoth are found, stone vessels were present, and burial was in kôchim shafted tombs with ossuaries. The overwhelming majority of Sepphoris inhabitants were, like the rural Galileans, Jews. The coins and inscriptions from Sepphoris verify that Jews ranked in the highest civic circles in the first century.

Hellenistic influences on Judaism can be imagined on a continuum, with the rural peasantry showing the least influences on one extreme, and the more urban and socio-economically elite Jews on an ascending scale of Hellenization. There is no doubt that the urban elites in Sepphoris were more "Hellenized" than rural Galileans. Much of their life functioned in Greek and they were likely at ease in a bilingual atmosphere, whereas rural areas tended to be pronouncedly Aramaic. However, more Greek does not imply un-Jewish, as Hellenism and the Greek language provided Semitic peoples and Jews a vehicle and framework to express their local traditions in a universally comprehensible way, as well as to administer their affairs.[90] It is not surprising, then, that items such as pagan statues, architecture, inscriptions, or coins were not present in the Early Roman Period, since Herod Antipas laid Roman-Hellenistic architectural style and structures over a Jewish base, and adhered to suitably Jewish standards.[91]

90. Bowersock, *Hellenism in Late Antiquity*, 1–13. Already at an early stage, Jewish histories (e.g., by Eupolemus and Jason the Cyrene) were written in Greek in Palestine by the cultural elites, see Martin Hengel, *The Hellenization of Judaea*, 88–102; on the spoken language as Aramaic in Galilee, see Horsley, *Archaeology, History, and Society in Galilee*, 162–71.

91. See Peter Richardson, *Herod the Great: King of the Jews and Friend of the Romans* (Columbia: University of South Carolina Press, 1996).

In this light, Alt and others' position that Sepphoris was isolated from Galilee due to religious and cultural differences, and that Jesus would have avoided this allegedly Gentile, pagan, or Hellenistic city, rests on false assumptions about the character of Sepphoris. At the time of Jesus, the only pagan elements are a few small household items; more than a century later, the Dionysiac mosaic is inside a villa; and only later is such mythological imagery in public architecture. But by the Byzantine Period, even synagogues, such as at Beth Alpha or Sepphoris, had zodiacs containing overt mythological images.

Theories accentuating Greek education or Cynic philosophical schools at Sepphoris are equally implausible. It must be remembered that when Gabinius made Sepphoris the seat of the regional council in 57–55 B.C.E., it was for Jews to rule their affairs on Rome's behalf.[92] There was neither a Roman garrison nor a Roman administrative apparatus at Sepphoris until much later. Even though Antipas might have employed a handful of Gentile and even Roman architects and engineers in building Sepphoris, one reason for his building projects was to provide work for local Jewish men as a preventative to banditry, not the immigration of Gentiles.[93] Sepphoris was not home to a significant number of Gentiles, Romans, or Greeks, and the presence of Greco-Roman philosophical schools is highly unlikely. The material culture of Sepphoris mitigates against attributing Jesus' avoidance of Sepphoris to ethnic or religious differences, as it does casting the impact of Sepphoris on Galilee in terms of gentile, pagan, or Hellenistic differences.

Would Jesus have avoided Sepphoris because it was too Hellenistic? It seems doubtful. Nothing in his teachings relates to overtly Hellenistic aspects of life, such as iconography, nude bathing and circumcision, or the use of Greek. If one were to argue that more Hellenized Jews, however defined, populated Sepphoris, one still must wrestle with the fact that the tradition does not at all criticize Hellenized forms of Judaism. Indeed, the fact that even the earliest traditions are in Greek warns against imagining too large a gap between an Aramaic-speaking Jesus and Greek-speaking Sepphoris.[94] Furthermore, the evangelists record numerous encounters with Gentiles, such as the Gerasene demoniac (Mark 5:1) and the Syro-Phoenician

---

92. *Ant.* 14.91.

93. Sanders, "Jesus' Relation to Sepphoris," 76–77; who also points out that Josephus explicitly mentions the fear of large bodies of unemployed men as one of the underlying motives for Herod the Great's continued building/employment projects, *Antiquities* 20.219–22.

94. The fact that even Q was written in Greek, as was Mark and all the other early Christian traditions, warns against this, Heinz Gunther, "The Sayings Gospel Q and the Quest for Aramaic Sources: Rethinking Christian Origins," *Early Christianity, Q, and Jesus* (eds. John Kloppenborg and Leif Vaage; *Semeia* 55; Atlanta: Scholars Press, 1992) 41–76.

woman (Mark 7:24–30), and even shade Gentiles in a positive light to shame Jews, such as the Capernaum centurion (Luke 7:1–10//Matt 8:5–13; John 4:46–54) or the citizens of Tyre and Sidon (Q 10:11–13). These encounters with Gentiles on the fringes of Galilee render unlikely Jesus' avoidance of Hellenized Jews in Sepphoris.

Sepphoris and Socio-Economics, Status, and Wealth

Even though Sepphoris was more Hellenized than rural Galilee, enough continuity existed between rural and urban Judaism in Galilee to cast doubt on religion or ethnicity as a reason for Jesus' avoidance of Sepphoris. Were there, perhaps, socio-economic differences that led Jesus to avoid Sepphoris? Antipas's rebuilding of Sepphoris necessitated intensification of agrarian production, which raised the standards of living and availability of luxury items for elites in urban areas such as Sepphoris, but at the expense of rural peasants. The disparity between the urban elites and peasantry was not as radical as at sites such as Scythopolis or Caesarea, but the relative wealth at Sepphoris was manifestly greater than that of rural Galileans, and becoming more visible after Sepphoris and Tiberias were built. Gates, facades, vistas, and colonnaded streets made with fresco, plaster, and mosaics communicated the distinctions between the Galilean cities and villages. Similar distinctions existed in the domestic realm as well, and even some religious features distinguished the urban dwellers from the villagers: each house on the acropolis had private *miqwaoth*, as opposed to communal *miqwaoth* at villages or simply the Sea of Galilee; ornate, large lathed stone vessels were common at Sepphoris and a status symbol, but not present in village settings.

Much in the teachings of Jesus attacks the increased visibility between the haves and have-nots. The Inaugural Sermon in Q's opening beatitude blesses the poor and gives them the Kingdom; Matthew's added beatitude even states that the meek "will inherit the earth" (Matt 5:5, with land the basis of wealth); and Luke's subsequent cursing of the rich makes the contrast between wealthy and poor even more pronounced.[95] At the same time, the teachings of Jesus cannot be described anachronistically as a revolutionary social program, since the Gospels show more concern with human relations than social classes, even among the elite. While Jesus was certainly from the lower classes and their advocate as well as that of the poor, his dining habits

---

95. See further, Douglas Oakman, *Jesus and the Economic Questions of His Day* (Studies in the Bible and Early Christianity 8; Lewiston, New York: Edwin Mellen, 95–220); on Luke, see Philip Esler, *Community and Gospel in Luke-Acts: The Social and Political Motivations of Lucan Theology* (Society for New Testament Studies 59; Cambridge: Cambridge University Press, 1987); and also Luise Schottroff and Wolfgang Stegemann, *Jesus and the Hope of the Poor* (Maryknoll, New York: Orbis, 1986).

led to the accusation, which he does not deny, that Jesus was a "friend of tax collectors and sinners" (Q 7:34).[96] Otherwise, the wealthy are not entirely absent in his audience, such as the rich young man (Mark 10:17–22) or the tax collector (Mark 2:13–17). In fact, Luke 8:3 even mentions a Joanna, the wife of Herod Antipas's steward Chuza, who was part of Jesus' traveling retinue, whose home was very likely in Sepphoris or Tiberias. That Jesus avoided Sepphoris because he was more at home among the larger, lower spectrum of society seems perhaps more plausible than that he avoided it for religious reasons, but not entirely convincing. Paradoxically, the very place where his encounters with the wealthier citizens (tax collectors) could have occurred may have been Sepphoris.

## Sepphoris and Antipas's Political-Administrative Rule

If Jesus did not avoid Sepphoris for religious, ethnic, or economic reasons, perhaps he did so on political grounds. Political reasons for Jesus' possible avoidance of Sepphoris remain to be considered; though unlike ethnicity, religion, or socio-economics, the political sphere leaves few traces in the archaeological record. However, the apparent flow of wealth from the rural areas to the cities and the cities' function as distributor of goods, with structures symbolic of political control, like gates, basilicas, and walls, shows that political power concentrated in the cities.[97]

There are reasons to believe that Jesus avoided Sepphoris, and even some passages in the Gospels that hint at his avoidance of Antipas. Jesus was certain to have known of the Baptist's imprisonment. That John baptized Jesus is as historically credible as anything in the Gospels, so that Jesus' interest in the fate of the Baptist is certain, aside from simply being aware of such a widely publicized event, even if the Gospel's account of his prison communiqués is fabricated (Matt 11:2). Furthermore, Luke 13:31–33, though this is likely a Lukan construction, expressly states that Jesus evaded "that fox" Antipas, who was intent on killing him. Luke resumes this thread in his version of the trial, though by then Antipas is less hostile and more curious about Jesus whom he had never met (Luke 23:6–12). Given the fate of John the Baptist, Jesus had every reason to avoid the seats of Herodian power in Galilee at Sepphoris and Tiberias.

Two passages from the earliest layers of the tradition even hint at criticism of Herod Antipas. Gerd Theissen has argued rather convincingly that the "reed" in Q 7:24 should be interpreted emblematically as referring to Antipas, contrasting John with his executioner living in "soft robes" and

---

96. Janos Bolyki, *Jesu Tischgemeinschaften* (WUNT ser. 2, vol. 96; Tübingen: J. C. B. Mohr [Paul Siebeck], 1998); see also Crossan, *The Historical Jesus*, 259–64.
97. Strange, "Some Implications of Archaeology, " 23–59.

"royal palaces," with Tiberias and perhaps also Sepphoris in mind.[98] Given Jesus' reference to Antipas as a fox in Luke 13:31 and that his capital's name in Hebrew means "little bird" (*Zippori*), it is not unlikely that Jesus contrasts himself with Antipas in Q "foxes have holes and birds of the sky have nests, but the Son of man has nowhere to lay his head."

In sum, it is likely that Jesus on occasion ventured into Sepphoris during his youth; it was neither too Gentile nor too Hellenistic, but simply more affluent, more Hellenized, and more cosmopolitan. The tradition is clear that he was cautious with regard to Antipas, so that there were reasons to avoid Sepphoris and Tiberias during his ministry. It might be that moving from Nazareth to Sepphoris represented too drastic a step in wealth and accommodation to Hellenism for his message; but, if anything, it would have been Antipas's power that kept him from Sepphoris during his ministry. His choice of Capernaum, a larger village than Nazareth on the periphery of Antipas's power with easy access to the other side of the lake, was thus more suitable.

---

98. "Das 'schwankende Rohr' (Mt 11,7) und die Gründungsmünzen von Tiberias," *ZDPV* 101 (1985) 43–55.

CHAPTER 5

# Jesus and Capernaum: Archaeological and Gospel Stratigraphy

Unlike Sepphoris, Capernaum appears frequently in the New Testament. The various strands of the Jesus tradition converge to portray it and the northwest shore of the Sea of Galilee as the center of Jesus' ministry. The sayings source Q's story of the healing of the centurion's servant is conspicuous as the only act or saying of Jesus located in a named place, Capernaum (Q 7:1). The Gospel of Mark depicts Capernaum as the hub of Jesus' ministry. His first miracle, the healing of a man with an unclean spirit, takes place in its synagogue (Mark 1:21), and thereafter Jesus is described as being "at home" (ἐν οἴκῳ) in Capernaum (Mark 2:1, 9:33). Matthew assumes Jesus' residence was in Capernaum; he says that Jesus "settled down" there (κατῴκησεν Matt 4:13 // Mark 1:21), and calls it "his own city" (τὴν ἰδίαν πόλιν, Matt 9:1 // Mark 2:1). Luke likewise attests to Jesus' special relationship with Capernaum when Jesus predicts that the inhabitants of Nazareth will request that the miracles done at Capernaum be done in his hometown (Luke 4:23).[1] The Gospel of John concurs with the synoptics' picture of Capernaum's centrality. Jesus stayed there for a few days after the miracle in Cana (2:12), healed the centurion's child there (4:46), withdrew to and was sought by the crowds in Capernaum (6:17, 24), and taught in its synagogue (John 6:59).[2]

---

1. Luke obviously is indebted to his source Mark here, Ulrich Busse, *Das Nazareth-Manifest Jesu. Eine Einführung in das lukanische Jesusbild nach Lk 4,16–30* (Stuttgarter Bibelstudien 91; Stuttgart: Verlag Katholisches Bibelwerk, 1978) 62–67. However, Luke has Jesus predict the reaction of Nazareth's citizens in a way that makes Capernaum's centrality for Jesus' miracles obvious, Wilibald Bösen, *Galiläa als Lebensraum und Wirkungsfeld Jesu* (Freiburg: Herder, 1985) 83–84.

2. It is significant that four of the five occurrences of Capernaum in John are from the putative signs source. Without begging the question of its existence, John

Despite Capernaum's frequent mention in the New Testament, second only to Jerusalem, the Gospels offer little information about its character. They indicate that fishermen lived there (e.g., Matt 4:12–22), that a tollhouse was there (Mark 2:13–14, apparently in Capernaum, see Mark 2:1), and that a "centurion" (ἑκατοντάρχος) was garrisoned there (Q 7:1–10; John 4:46–54). Q 10:13–15 suggests by inference that Capernaum was Jewish when it condemns its lack of repentance unfavorably with gentile cities. The presence of crowds seeking Jesus (e.g., Mark 2:1) could imply that it was in an easily accessible or well-populated area. Even though it is called a polis in the Gospels (Matt 9:1, 11:20; Mark 1:33; and Luke 4:31), they do not elaborate on Capernaum's size, constitution, civic buildings, socio-economics, or population in a way that makes the implications of its being a polis clear.

## Literary Evidence and the Identification of Capernaum

The lack of Capernaum's mention in literature from earlier periods betrays its insignificance. Neither the Hebrew Bible nor other literature prior to Jesus mentions it, and Josephus only refers to it as the village (κώμη) to which he was taken after falling off his horse near Bethsaida (*Life* 72).[3] He also remarks that the locals called the spring in the Gennesar Plain, Capernaum (Κεφαρνόκος in the manuscripts, *War* 3.519). The rabbinic literature mentions Capernaum, *Kfar Nahum* or "village of Nahum," as a locale for *minim*, a term signifying those who questioned rabbinic Judaism, whether Gnostic, pagan, Christian, or otherwise dissident. Although a *min* in the rabbinic literature can not be equated with a Jewish Christian, as some scholars tend to assume, perhaps the min associated with Capernaum in *Midr. Qoh.* 1.8 and 7.26 were, since the issue centers around keeping the Sabbath.[4] However,

---

4:46–54 shows some redactional strokes that stylistically blend the traditional story into John's narrative, see Uwe Wenger, *Der Hauptmann von Kafarnaum* (WUNT ser. 2 vol.14; Tübingen: J. C. B. Mohr [Paul Siebeck], 1985) 22–32; on John's integration of traditional materials into a coherent whole and the question of sources, see Martin Hengel, *The Johannine Question* (Philadelphia: Trinity Press International, 1989) 74–108.

3. On the spelling of Capernaum in the manuscripts, see Félix-Marie Abel, "Le nom de Capharnaum," *JPOS* 8 (1928) 24–34; and Eric Bishop, "Jesus and Capernaum," *CBQ* 14 (1953) 427–37.

4. Ray Pritz, *Nazarene Jewish Christianity: From the End of the New Testament Period Until Its Disappearance in the Fourth Century* (Leiden: E. J. Brill, 1988) 49–50. On the minim, see Shaye J. D. Cohen, "A Virgin Defiled: Some Rabbinic and Christian Views on the Origins of Heresy," *USQR* 36 (1980) 3; Stuart S. Miller has convincingly argued that in the case of Sepphoris, minim have been too readily assumed to be Jewish Christian, "The Minim of Sepphoris Reconsidered," *HTR* 86 (1993) 377–402; and "Further Thoughts on the Minim of Sepphoris," in *Proceedings of the Eleventh World Congress of Jewish Studies B.1* (Jerusalem: World Union of Jewish Studies, 1994) 1–8.

neither the term nor the passages support the notion of a Jewish-Christian community in Capernaum, and much less its portrayal as a Jewish-Christian village.[5] After Constantine made Christianity the official religion of the Empire, Capernaum became more prominent in the literature. Epiphanias reports that toward the end of Constantine's reign (306–337 C.E.), the high-ranking Jewish convert Joseph of Tiberias built churches under imperial sanction throughout Galilee, including Capernaum (*PG* 41:409–27).[6] Beginning in the Byzantine Period, Christian pilgrims frequently refer to Capernaum, though most surprisingly list it as a minor stop on their itineraries. Usually described simply as a village, the only distinguishing features the pious commented on are the basilica built over the house of Saint Peter and the synagogue where Jesus ministered.[7]

Other than the Gospels themselves, therefore, no literary evidence provides information about first-century C.E. Capernaum, since the rabbinic and Christian literature dates to after Christianity's impact on Capernaum and after it is perceived as a holy site. The lack of adequate literary descriptions places the burden of determining Capernaum's character at the time of Jesus squarely on the shoulders of archaeology. Fortunately, after its identification at Tel Ḥum on the northern shore of the Sea of Galilee in the nineteenth century, Capernaum has been heavily excavated. Because of its status as a Christian holy place, most excavations focused on the basilica and the synagogue and, typical of biblical archaeology at the time, centered on confirming or denying the chronology of the synagogue and the validity of the church on top of Peter's house.

The ruins of the synagogue at Tel Ḥum were first discovered in 1838 by the American explorer and biblical scholar Edward Robinson, who at the time located Capernaum a few kilometers to the southwest at Khirbet

---

5. See Joan Taylor's criticisms of theories of Jewish Christianity in Capernaum, *Christians and the Holy Places: The Myth of Jewish-Christian Origins* (Oxford: Clarendon Press, 1993).

6. Epiphanius rambles a bit and is otherwise problematic, so any correlation between Joseph's activities and the *insula sacra* remains tentative, Joseph Blenkinsopp, "The Literary Evidence," in *Excavations at Capernaum 1* (Vasilios Tzaferis; Winona Lake, Indiana: Eisenbrauns, 1989) 204–206.

7. Egeria, who visited Palestine between 381 and 384 C.E., describes a church that "has been made out of the house of the prince of the apostles, the original walls of which are still standing today" (CSEL 39:112). However, this statement is not in Egeria's itinerary, but attributed to her by Bede's eighth-century *De Locis Sacris*, a popular medieval travel guide to the Holy Land. Whether it accurately reflects her visit to the house-church (Stratum II, so Virgilio Corbo, *Cafarnao 1: Gli edifici della città* [Studium Biblicum Franciscanum 19; Jerusalem: Franciscan Printing Press, 1975], 71–74), or is embellished by Bede or his sources with the later octagonal church (Stratum III) in mind, is difficult to determine. Blenkinsopp discounts the evidence in Bede, "The Literary Evidence," 205; and Robert North thinks the evidence is inconclusive, "Discoveries at Capernaum," *Bib* 58 (1977) 425–26.

Minya.[8] Only later, in 1866, did the British engineer Captain Charles Wilson properly identify Tel Ḥum as Capernaum, and made some soundings in the remains of the synagogue.[9] Shortly thereafter, the Franciscan Custodians of the Holy Land purchased much of the land around the ruins, and the eastern third of the site later became the property of the Greek Orthodox Patriarchate of Jerusalem. The synagogue was examined and surveyed in 1905 by the German archaeologists Heinrich Kohl and Carl Watzinger, and shortly after the First World War the Franciscan Gaudenzio Orfali worked on and partially restored the synagogue, which he took to be the very structure built by the centurion in which Jesus ministered.[10] He also unearthed the remains of an octagonal church just south of the synagogue. The Franciscan Fathers Virgilio Corbo and Stanislao Loffreda resumed excavations in and around the synagogue and church from 1968–85, and published results that stirred up considerable controversy.[11] On the one hand, by presenting clear stratigraphic evidence that the synagogue dates to the fifth century C.E., they upset entrenched notions among Israeli archaeologists on the development of synagogue styles.[12] On the other hand, their report on Saint Peter's house, in particular some overtly Christian readings of the graffiti, has been criticized as tendentious.[13]

---

8. Edward Robinson, *Later Biblical Researches in Palestine and in the Adjacent Regions: A Journal of the Travels in the Year 1952, Volume 3* (Boston: Crocker and Brewster, 1857) 348–58; and *Biblical Researches in Palestine and in the Adjacent Regions: A Journal of Travels in the Year 1838, Volume 2* (Boston: Crocker and Brewster, 1868) 403–5. The excavations at Khirbet Minyeh reveal it was an Islamic palace, with nothing at the site antedating the Arab Period, A. M. Schneider, "Ḥirbet El-Minje am See Genesareth," *Annales archéologiques de Syrie* 2 (1952) 23–45; and O. Grabar, et al., "Sondages à Khirbet el-Minyeh," *IEJ* 10 (1960) 226–43.

9. Charles Wilson, *The Recovery of Jerusalem: A Narrative of Exploration and Discovery in the City and the Holy Land* (London: R. Bentley, 1871) 342. John Laughlin most recently has argued convincingly that Tel Hum is Capernaum, "The Identification of the Site," in *Capernaum I*, 191–199.

10. Heinrich Kohl and Carl Watzinger, *Die antiken Synagogen in Galilaea* (Leipzig: Hinrichs, 1916) 204; Gaudenzio Orfali, *Capharnaum et ses ruines d'après les fouilles accomplies à Tell-Houm par la Custodie Franciscaine de Terre Sainte, 1905–1921* (Paris: A. Picard, 1922).

11. Corbo, *Cafarnao I*; Stanislao Loffreda, *Cafarnao II: La ceramica* (Studium Biblicum Franciscanum 19; Jerusalem: Franciscan Printing Press, 1974); Augusto Spijkerman, *Cafarnao III: Catalogo della monete della città* (Studium Biblicum Franciscanum 19; Jerusalem: Franciscan Printing Press, 1975); and Emmanuel Testa, *Cafarnao IV: I graffiti della casa di S. Pietro* (Studium Biblicum Franciscanum 19; Jerusalem: Franciscan Printing Press, 1972).

12. Gideon Foerster, "Notes on Recent Excavations at Capernaum," *IEJ* 21 (1971) 207–11; and Stanislao Loffreda, "The Late Chronology of the Synagogue of Capernaum," *IEJ* 23 (1973) 37–42.

13. Taylor, *Christians and the Holy Places*, 284–88; James F. Strange, "The Capernaum and Herodium Publications," *BASOR* 226 (1977) 65–73.

These controversies—over method, synagogue typology, and the validity of Peter's house under the basilica—should not sidetrack our examination of first-century C.E. Capernaum. These questions are of marginal concern to the nature and character of Capernaum at the time of Jesus. Whether the current synagogue dates to the third or fifth century C.E. is a moot point, and whether the few foundation walls underneath the white limestone structure were the synagogue of Jesus are of little relevance, since these isolated walls provide no significant data about the alleged earlier synagogue's character and function. In the same way, whether the stratigraphy of the so-called *insula sacra*, altered from a private room (Stratum I, first century B.C.E.) into a shrine (Stratum II, either early second or third century C.E.) and later encircled by an octagonal basilica (Stratum III, fifth century C.E.), can certify that the house belonged to Peter is of little relevance.[14] What this spot commemorates, and whether there is any validity to its sacred status, is less important than is the evidence revealed at the lowest levels of stratigraphy about the kinds of lives experienced by the people in first-century C.E. Capernaum. Like the later literary evidence for Capernaum, which supplies no relevant information, so too the later archaeological strata from the Late Roman and Byzantine Periods have little bearing on the study of the historical Jesus and the Gospel traditions. The pressing question is not where Jesus was in Capernaum, but what the Capernaum of Jesus was like.

In examining the archaeological evidence for reconstructing Early Roman Capernaum, the various features accentuated in the New Testament—that it was a small fishing village, border town on the lake, and called a polis—need to be assessed. The diverse claims by scholars about Capernaum also call for critical evaluation. Whether it was a small village, "un village modeste," in Bellarmino Bagatti's words, or a town of 12,000–15,000 inhabitants, or even a city showing that Jesus' Galilee was "as urbanized and urbane as anywhere else in the empire"[15] needs to be appraised with the available archaeological evidence. The implications of the material culture for the study of the historical Jesus, in particular any light it

---

14. Taylor provides the most cogent discussion of the issues, with a somewhat pessimistic evaluation of the house's "sacred" status, *Christians and the Holy Places*, 293–94.

15. Bellarmino Baggati, "Capharnaum," *MB* 27 (1983) 9. The figure of 1,000 inhabitants is also given in Stanislao Loffreda's tour book *A Visit to Capernaum* (Jerusalem: Franciscan Press, 1972) 20. James F. Strange earlier estimated a population of at most 1,000, *IDBSup*, 140. Eric Meyers and James F. Strange, *Archaeology, the Rabbis, and Early Christianity* (Nashville: Abingdon, 1981) 58. J. Andrew Overman, "Who were the First Urban Christians?" in *Society of Biblical Literature Seminar Papers 1988* (ed. David Lull; Atlanta: Scholars Press, 1988) 168. F. Gerald Downing has suggested that an urbane atmosphere renders Cynic parallels with Jesus more plausible, *Christ and the Cynics* (JSOT Manuals 4; Sheffield: JSOT Press, 1988) x.

sheds on Capernaum as the hub of his ministry, as well as the Gospel traditions' portrayal of Capernaum, is the focus of this study. With this goal in mind, the topography and settlement history of Capernaum will first be surveyed, then the structures relating to its public space will be sketched, and finally the construction and artifacts within private domestic space will be examined. The implications for our understanding of Jesus' ministry in Capernaum's vicinity vis-à-vis questions of ethnicity, socio-economic status, and political boundaries, as well as the Gospel traditions' labeling it a polis, will conclude this study.

## Topographical and Political Considerations

Capernaum lies on the northwestern shore of the Sea of Galilee, some 200 meters below sea level, in a climate conducive to hot summers and mild winters. Geologically, the region is basalt, with fertile soil but whose ubiquitous black lava stones and boulders create arduous agricultural conditions. Plowing fields for any kind of grain is cumbersome, though over the generations small, cleared areas have allowed peasants to eke out some wheat and cereal. Likewise, many kinds of trees have difficulty taking root in this terrain, though it is suitable for olive trees and vineyards. To the west of Capernaum, just over the ridge at Tel Chinnereth in the Gennesar Plain, lies some of the finest agricultural land in Palestine. Josephus praises this productive strip of alluvial soil on the northwest shore of the Sea of Galilee, ". . . for there is not a plant which its fertile soil refuses, and its cultivators grow them all. . . . In addition to its genial air, it is also irrigated by a most fertile spring, which the natives call 'Capharnaum'" (*War* 3.516–9). Capernaum also benefited from its proximity to the lake, which provided a perennial water source and fishing opportunities to supplement the dietary needs of its inhabitants.[16]

In the earlier periods, the significant sites on the northern side of the Sea of Galilee flanked the spot where Capernaum was later settled, at Tel Chinnereth 3 kilometers to the west, and Bethsaida 5 kilometers to the east.[17] At Capernaum, only faint traces of occupation from the Middle Bronze Age (2,200–1,550 B.C.E.) and Iron I Periods (1,200–1,000 B.C.E.) have been

---

16. Wilhelm Wuellner, *The Meaning of "Fisher of Men"* (Philadelphia: Westminster, 1967); and K. C. Hanson and Douglas Oakman, *Palestine in the Time of Jesus: Social Structures and Social Conflicts* (Minneapolis: Fortress, 1998) 106–110.

17. Volkmar Fritz, *Kinneret, Ergebnisse der Ausgrabungen auf dem Tell el-'Oreme am See Gennesaret 1982–1985* (Wiesbaden: Otto Harrassowitz, 1990) 18; and Rami Arav, "The Bethsaida Excavations: Preliminary Report, 1987–1993," in *Bethsaida: A City by the North Shore of the Sea of Galilee* (eds. Rami Arav and Richard Freund; Kirksville, Missouri: Thomas Jefferson University Press, 1995) 3–64.

uncovered, and the latter's scant evidence is insufficient to determine whether the occupants were Israelites, though the Hebrew Bible assigns the land west of the Jordan River and Sea of Galilee to the tribe of Naftali (Joshua 13:29–39). There is no occupational evidence whatsoever for the Iron II–Iron III Ages at Capernaum (1,000–587 B.C.E.). Surveys and excavations across Galilee have shown that the Assyrians depopulated the area in the latter half of the eighth century B.C.E. The absence of any occupation during this period explains Capernaum's omission in the Hebrew Bible and invalidates attempts to connect the site's name with the seventh-century prophet Nahum.[18] A few sherds from the Persian and Early Hellenistic Periods (fourth to second centuries B.C.E.) suggest a modest encampment or travelers passing through, but the first significant remains accompanied by architectural features date to the Late Hellenistic Period, at the end of the second century B.C.E.[19] The increase in Capernaum's material culture and its emergence as a village in the Late Hellenistic Period correspond with the overall rise of settlements in the north tied to the Maccabean expansion or colonization of Galilee. Under Aristobolus I (104–3 B.C.E.) and his heirs, the Maccabees began to establish Jewish settlements in Galilee, and after defeating several of the Eastern Decapolis cities such as Hippos and Gadara, established some Jewish enclaves to the east of the Jordan, most notably Gamla and Horvat Kanaf.[20] Along with the other villages northwest of the Sea of Galilee, Capernaum formed a bridge of Jewish settlements ranging from Upper and Lower Galilee across the Jordan into the Golan, which itself was surrounded by gentile settlements and cities. To the north, Itureans inhabited the mountainous regions of the Hauran and at the foot of Mount Hermon, and Syro-Phoenicians (Tyrians) had settled in the Huleh Valley and north of the Upper Galilee; on the eastern shore of the lake were the territories of the Decapolis cities of Hippos and Gadara.[21]

---

18. Clemens Kopp, *Die Heiligen Stätten der Evangelien* (Regensburg: Friendrich Pustet, 1959) 220–22.

19. Stanislao Loffreda, *OEANE* 1:418. Corbo, based on the numismatic finds, thinks a date for the founding of Capernaum prior to 200 B.C.E. is impossible; given the presence of so many Jannaean coins early in the profile, it is reasonable to connect the founding of the site with the Hasmoneans, *Cafarnao* I, 215.

20. Danny Syon, "Gamla: Portrait of a Rebellion," *BAR* 18 (Jan.–Feb., 1992) 23–24; and Zvi Maoz, "Horvat Kanaf," *NEAEHL* 3:847–50. For the developments in the region in the early first century B.C.E., see Andrea Berlin, "Between Large Forces: Palestine in the Hellenistic Period," *BA* 60 (1997) 36–43.

21. On the Itureans' sites, see Shimon Dar, *Settlements and Cult Sites on Mount Hermon, Israel: Ituraean Culture in the Hellenistic and Roman Periods* (BARIS 89; London: BAR, 1993) 200, 210; and M. Hartal, *Northern Golan Heights. The Archaeological Survey as a Source of Regional History* (Qatzrin: Israel Department of Antiquities and Museums, 1989). On the Phoenician settlements in the Huleh Valley and toward the coast, see Andrea Berlin, "From Monarchy to Markets: The

During Herod the Great's reign, these diverse ethnic groups and cities to the north and east of the lake were united into a single political kingdom. But after Herod's death, Caesar restored autonomy to the Decapolis cities of Hippos and Gadara, and they remained under the protectorate of the Syrian Legion, which exacerbated Jewish-gentile relations to the point of open hostilities during the Revolt.[22] Philip inherited the area with mixed ethnic populations of Greeks, Itureans, Syro-Phoenicians, and Jews to the east of the Jordan, and Antipas received the entirely Jewish Galilee (*War* 2.94–100). This division made the Jordan's natural boundary also the political border between Philip and Antipas's territories, rendering Capernaum the closest site in Antipas's territory to Philip's, some 4 kilometers from the Jordan River. The Jewish villages and the Jewish inhabitants of Bethsaida in Philip's realm were still culturally oriented toward Galilee, and one must imagine considerable interaction between the two areas.[23] Antipas's founding of Tiberias in 18/19 C.E. and Philip's re-founding of Bethsaida as Julias in 30 C.E. increased interregional traffic, which flowed through Capernaum and enhanced its role in the local economy.[24]

Capernaum's increased role in local traffic and trade networks notwithstanding, the misconception that the *via maris* and sizable international trade went through or past Capernaum must be corrected.[25] Historically, the two major international trade routes through the Levant were the aforementioned *via maris* and the inland King's Highway. The former accompanied the grain trade by boat from Egypt in the Roman Period, which went along the Palestinian coast and then branched inland at Tyre to Damascus. The King's Highway went inland from the Red Sea along the Transjordan

Phoenicians in Hellenistic Palestine," *BASOR* 306 (1997) 75–88. On the Decapolis, see H. Bietenhard, "Die syrische Dekapolis von Pompeius bis Traian," *ANRW* II/8 (1977) 220–261.

22. Josephus reports violent clashes between Philadelphians and the Jews over a village under Fadus's rule in 44 C.E. (*Ant.* 20.2) and again bloodshed at the outbreak of the war (*War* 2.458–59). See more generally Ayre Kasher, *Jews, Idumaeans, and Ancient Arabs: Relations of the Jews in Eretz-Israel with the Nations of the Frontier and the Desert during the Hellenistic and Roman Era (332 B.C.E.–70 C.E.)* (TSAJ 19; Tübingen: J. C. B. Mohr [Paul Siebeck], 1988).

23. On the Jewish population in Philip's territory, see Michael Avi-Yonah, "Historical Geography of Palestine," in *The Jewish People in the First Century I* (eds. Shemuel Safrai and Menachem Stern; Amsterdam: Van Gorcum, 1974) 94. The fact that many of Jesus' followers came from Bethsaida is also telling (John 1:44; 12:21).

24. Michael Avi-Yonah, "The Foundation of Tiberias," *IEJ* 1 (1950) 160–69.

25. Michael Avi-Yonah noted the Gospels mention of a toll house at Capernaum, and suggested that perhaps a significant route went through Capernaum, *The Holy Land* (Grand Rapids, Michigan: Baker Books, 1966) 138; and *Gazetteer of Roman Palestine* (Qedem 5; Jerusalem: Hebrew University, 1976), 46; this is often mischaracterized as "off the *via maris*."

Plateau to Damascus and then on eastward, and during the Roman Period went through the Nabatean trade cities, toward which the Decapolis cities were oriented as well. These routes bypassed Galilee entirely, and neither route went through Capernaum. Important branches connecting the Kings Highway with the coast went along the east of the Sea of Galilee through Scythopolis and across the Jezreel Valley to the coast.[26] Herod the Great's construction of a major port at Caesarea Maritima accelerated traffic on these branches through his territory toward the new port, a move that possibly also increased the traffic through Capernaum beginning in the first century C.E.

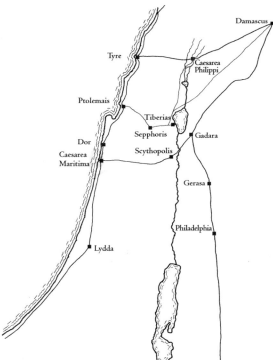

*Figure 5.1 Regional and Interregional Roads*

---

26. On the road through the Golan possibly thorough Hippos, Gadara, and south of the lake to Scythopolis, see Gottlieb Schumacher, *The Jaulan: Surveyed for the German Society for the Exploration of the Holy Land* (London: R. Bentley, 1888) 63–64; Peter Thompsen, "Die römischen Meilensteinen der Provinzen Syria, Arabia und Palaestina," *ZDPV* 40 (1917) 33–34; and Michael Avi Yonah, *The Holy Land From the Persian to the Arab Conquest: A Historical Geography* (Grand Rapids, Michigan: Baker Books, 1977) 187.

The building of Tiberias in 18/19 C.E., and the project of rebuilding Bethsaida as Julias in 30 C.E., certainly increased regional trade along the lake through Capernaum. Interregional traffic from the north and east, including the Huleh Valley and the Decapolis, may have also came from Bethsaida through Capernaum to Tiberias, then via Sepphoris to one of the Mediterranean ports like Ptolemais or even Caesarea Maritima. This pattern accompanied the newly founded cities by the Herodian dynasty in and around Galilee in the first half of the first century C.E.[27] In the Early Roman Period, then, Capernaum began to experience traffic in addition to the contacts and trade between the Jews in the Golan and Galilee, for which there is considerable archaeological evidence.[28] With the emergence of Bethsaida/Julias, Tiberias, and Sepphoris, Gentiles from Philip's realm and perhaps beyond would have increasingly traveled through Capernaum as a more convenient path toward the coast.

While Capernaum had more interregional contacts than most Galilean villages, in addition to its fishers' chance meetings on the lake or emergency landings at a foreign anchorage, it was not on a major international trade route. The well-paved and -marked Roman roads in this area do not date until the early second century C.E., and were built as part of Hadrian's road system in the east, as the milestone at Capernaum indicates. The *via maris*, however, did not bisect Capernaum, and there is no evidence for significant international trade going through it at the time of Jesus. It would have witnessed considerable regional and some interregional traffic, which would become a prominent feature of its character during the first half of the first century C.E.

## The Archaeology of Public Space at Capernaum

The discussion of the archaeological remains has been preoccupied with two dates and places—the chronology of the synagogue and whether earlier

---

27. It is likely that these cities realigned local trade patterns, from the long-standing local paths, which went from the Golan along the tip of the lake through Chorazin, through the wadi north of the Arbel cliffs, and on through the Beth Netofah Valley through Cana, Yodefat and on to Ptolemais. This road was not paved, and the Roman Legions improved and straightened it on their way from Ptolemais to Jodefat (Josephus, *War* 3.110–34). Coin profiles indicate that Ptolemais waned in importance after Caesarea Maritima was built; Donald Ariel, "A Survey of Coin Finds in Jerusalem," *LA* 32 (1982) 292.

28. David Adan-Bayewitz and Isadore Perlman, "Local Pottery Provenience Studies: A Role for Clay Analysis," *Archaeometry* 27 (1985) 206; "The Pottery," in Shelly Wachsmann, *The Excavations of an Ancient Boat in the Sea of Galilee* ('Atiqot 19 [English Series]; Jerusalem: Israel Antiquities Authority, 1990) 89–96; Charles Fritsch and Immanuel Ben-Dor, "The Link Marine Expedition to Israel, 1960," *BA* 24 (1961) 57–58.

remains represent a synagogue from the time of Jesus, and the location of the basilica over the alleged site of Peter's house.[29] A myopic focus on these two holy sites prevents a more synchronic and holistic description of Capernaum in the Early Roman Period, which is of crucial importance for historical Jesus research.[30] Our concern with Capernaum's public space expands beyond these two sites and seeks to assess the population size of Capernaum, its layout and the extent of centralized planning, the number of public building projects, and evidence for elite sponsorship of civic buildings.

Although the precise number of inhabitants would have been of little concern to ancients in assessing the character of Capernaum, modern estimates on a wide spectrum ranging from 1,000 all the way to 25,000 inhabitants compete for diverse portrayals of the site. Reliable evidence for the size of Capernaum is not found in any literary texts. Josephus's description that "even the villages are all so densely populated that the smallest contains above 15,000 inhabitants" (*War* 3.43) is of no relevance since his absurd population numbers are grossly exaggerated.[31] Capernaum's population in antiquity can, however, be assessed from the archaeological record by examining the extent of its ruins and the density of its living quarters, that is to say, by multiplying the number of hectares of the site by the likely number of people per hectare.[37] Meyers and Strange used this technique to arrive at the frequently cited population estimate of 12,000–15,000 for Capernaum.[33] They relied, however, on a description of the ruins by Captain Charles Wilson of the British Army, who reported in 1871 that: "The whole area, half a mile in length by a quarter in breadth [750 by 375 meters, or just under 30 hectares] was thickly covered with the ruined walls of private houses. . . ."[34]

---

29. See, e.g., Gustaf Dalman, *Orte und Wege Jesus* (3rd ed.; Gütersloh: Bertelsmann, 1924) 149–65.

30. Already noted by Chester C. McCown with regard to Orfali's work at the site: "On another score their [the Franciscans] sentimental interest in the synagogue is obstructive of scientific progress. Their property is ideal for the investigation of the character of a Jewish village in Galilee," *The Ladder of Progress in Palestine* (New York: Harper and Brothers, 1943) 270.

31. Anthony Byatt, "Josephus and Population Numbers in First Century Palestine," *PEQ* 105 (1973) 52.

32. The basic correlation between population size and settlement area has been demonstrated by various studies. See, e.g., William Sumner, "Estimating Population by Analogy: An Example," in *Ethnoarchaeology: Implications of Ethnography for Archaeology* (ed. Carol Kramer; New York: Columbia University Press, 1979) 168; Yigal Shiloh, "The Population of Iron Age Palestine in the Light of a Sample Analysis of Urban Plans, Areas, and Population Density," *BASOR* 239 (1980) 25–35; and Jeffrey Zorn, "Estimating the Population Size of Ancient Settlements: Methods, Problems, Solutions, and a Case Study," *BASOR* 295 (1994) 31–48.

33. Archaeology, the Rabbis and Early Christianity (Nashville: Abingdon, 1981) 58.

34. Meyers and Strange cite Charles Wilson, *Recovery of Jerusalem: A Narrative of Exploration and Discovery in the City and the Holy Land* (London: Richard Bentley

They then multiplied the coefficient of 400 to 500 persons per hectare by 30, to arrive at a population between 12,000 and 15,000 inhabitants.[35] Two variables, however, need to be scrutinized: the extent of the site's ruins, and the density of living quarters.

*Figure 5.2 North-west Shore of the Sea of Galilee*

The maximum northern extent of ancient Capernaum is determined by burials some 300 meters off the shore, consisting of several sarcophagi housed in an underground mausoleum from the Late Roman Period. In light of the common practice of burying the dead outside inhabited areas, these tombs delimit the northernmost parameter of the site. The lake determines the southern extent of the site's ruins, and though there is reason to believe that the water level of the lake was lower in antiquity, the remains of an ancient promenade provide a firm boundary and discount notions that the ruins extended underneath the modern water level. The promenade also helps determine the eastern and western limits of Capernaum. Although the

& Son, 1871) 269, 345. Captain Wilson makes no claim to accuracy, i.e., he is not reporting on a scientific survey.

35. The coefficient of 400 to 500 is not explicitly stated in Strange and Meyers. It is given by Magen Broshi, "The Population of Western Palestine," 1. But Broshi stresses that "this figure represents the maximum density in built-up areas" (1). Furthermore, in his calculations Broshi deduces one quarter of the area to account for "public and open spaces" (5).

harbor facilities connected to the promenade extend some 800 meters along the shore, Capernaum's ruins are visibly shorter and increasingly so as one moves away from the lake.[36] Not all of the ruins, however, were occupied in the first century C.E. and none of the easternmost antedate the seventh century C.E. Excavations by Vasilios Tzaferis on the Greek Orthodox property have determined that Capernaum's center shifted eastward at the close of the Byzantine Period. At the transition between the Byzantine and Early Arab Periods, ". . . a new town of entirely different plan was constructed, east of the earlier town. . . . Capernaum of the 7th century A.D. lay mostly in previously unsettled areas spreading north and east of the synagogue area."[37] These areas cannot be included in estimates of Capernaum at earlier times. Excluding these, the settled area, which was occupied by the end of the Roman Period, is ". . . limited to a short, narrow strip" along the sea measuring no more than 350 by 500 meters, an area of 17 hectares.[38] The area that was inhabited during the Early Roman Period is even less, perhaps as low as 6 hectares, the portion across which the Franciscan excavator S. Lofredda has located Early Roman ceramics.

The density of living quarters at Capernaum during the first century C.E. would be less than contemporaneous walled sites, such as the cities of Tiberias or Sepphoris, or even the larger walled villages of Yodefat or Gamla.[39] Without a city wall to drive the population density upward, new buildings could easily be added on Capernaum's periphery given the topography, as was the case during the seventh century C.E. The extant domestic walls and foundations were crudely made of mud-packed basalt fieldstones, and would not have supported second stories, pushing the population density lower.[40] Perhaps some houses at Capernaum had a second floor over a portion of the house, but they were not what could be considered multiple-storied houses.[41] Add to this the common practice of using portions of the

36. Mendel Nun, *Sea of Galilee: Newly Discovered Harbours From New Testament Days* (rev. ed.; Ein Gev: Kinnereth Sailing, 1989) 25–26.

37. Tzaferis, "Historical Summary," in *Excavations at Capernaum 1*, 216; see also 2–3, 4 (for Area C) 9 (for Area D).

38. Tzaferis, *Excavations at Capernaum*, 216. This is close to the area of 200 meters x 500 meters given by the various Franciscan authors. And even here one cannot be sure that the entire area was inhabited during the Roman Period.

39. Capernaum was not on the list of walled cities listed in *m. 'Arak.* 9.6, as was Gamla (even though these were attributed to the time of Joshua, this is obviously an anachronism). Both Josephus and the excavations point to a densely populated Gamla, where the steep slopes and city wall necessitated staggered housing, *War*, 4.27; and Syon, "Gamla: Portrait of a Rebellion," 20–37.

40. Virgilio Corbo, "Aspetti Urbanistici di Cafarnao," *LA* 21 (1971) 272.

41. Analogous to the type found throughout Southern Syria and Northern Galilee, Tzaferis, *Excavations at Capernaum I*, 217, esp. note 12. Howard Crosby Butler, *Ancient Architecture in Syria, Division II, Section A: Southern Syria* (Leiden: E. J. Brill, 1907) 120–123; Corbo, *Cafarnao I*, 171–212.

ground floor for livestock, and the population density was much lower than at urban sites. Based on the type and distribution of buildings, Capernaum's density could not have exceeded 150 persons per hectare, and was likely around 100 persons per hectare. Since the minimum size of first-century C.E. Capernaum's area was 6 hectares, and unlikely more than 10 hectares, the population of Capernaum at the time of Jesus would have been between 600 and 1,500 inhabitants. Compared to the major Galilean cities of Sepphoris and Tiberias, which had between 8,000 and 12,000 inhabitants, Capernaum's population size was modest. At the same time, compared to the many Galilean hamlets made up of several extended families and small villages such as Nazareth with fewer than 400 inhabitants, Capernaum would have been viewed as one of the larger villages.[42]

Capernaum's layout in the first century is typical of contemporaneous Jewish villages in that it lacks centralized planning. Although described in some of the secondary literature as orthogonal or "Schachbrettartig" in its arrangement, a closer look at the plan reveals organic growth.[43] Most of the houses at Capernaum are clustered by threes and fours around a shared courtyard, making up blocks of approximately 40 by 40 meters.[44] The publications of the Franciscan excavators designate these blocks, including that formed by the Church of Saint Peter, with the potentially misleading nomenclature *insulae*.[45] This term, however, and the description of block units, should not be misconstrued as indicative of centralized planning on a grid system, as is apparent in classical Roman cities and to a considerable degree also at

---

42. Ranges of population based on the terms *kefar*, *'ir*, and *kerakh* in the rabbinic literature have been proposed by Zeev Safrai, *The Economy of Roman Palestine* (London: Routledge, 1994) 17–103; and Ayre Ben–David, *Talumdische Ökonomie I* (Hildesheim: Georg Olms, 1978) 48–57. Martin Goodman prudently suggests, however, that they are not good indicators of site size, *State and Society in Roman Galilee*, A.D. *132–212* (Totowa, New Jersey: Rowman & Allanheld, 1983) 28–29.

43. Meyers and Strange noted how the houses tended to cluster around courtyards in 40 by 40 meter blocks, *Archaeology, the Rabbis and Early Christianity*, 58. This phenomenon has been taken to imply orthogonal city planning by some, e.g., Overman, "Who Were the First Urban Christians?" 162; and Bösen, *Galiläa*, 77.

44. The more popular tourist book prepared by Loffreda can give the impression that the site is intentionally laid out in blocks, *A Visit to Capernaum* (Jerusalem: Franciscan Printing Press, 1976), 10. A careful look of the map, however, especially taking the stratigraphy into consideration, shows walls slanting off perpendicular angles.

45. The term is inconsistently used by archaeologists working in the Mediterranean world. At times it simply means any unit surrounded on four sides by streets, as here or at Pompeii; otherwise, and predominantly, *insula* refers to a multi-story and multi-occupancy apartment complex, as at Ostia, see Andrew Wallace-Hadrill, *Houses and Society in Pompeii and Herculaneum* (Princeton: Princeton University Press, 1994) 132.

Antipas's Sepphoris and Tiberias. Nor should the term be taken to imply the presence of multiple-storied apartment-style housing at Capernaum.[46] A closer look at the excavators' plans reveals that the fifth-century C.E. synagogue and basilica complex imposed the most orderly perpendicular blocks onto the site's plan. Yet even they are not exactly parallel, nor are the extant walls from the Early Roman Period, which are built in uneven lines that make up "blocks" of varied sizes. The driving force in Capernaum's layout was not centralized planning, but rather domestic growth around courtyards, which were encircled as members of extended families added houses, walls, or storage rooms.[47] The spaces left between the domestic clusters for passageways and streets ran in slightly crooked and curved lines through Capernaum.

Furthermore, there is no evidence for two intersecting thoroughfares, either a *decumanus* or a *cardo maximus*, and none of the streets was paved with slabs, much less lined with columns or porticoes. The excavated streets' average width of 2–3 meters was much smaller than those at urban sites, being what the rabbinic literature refers to as *semita*, and not the wider urban streets or *platia* (from the Greek πλατεῖα).[48] None had channels for running water or sewage, which must have been tossed in the alleyways. Instead, the roads in Capernaum bend at the various clusters of houses, and were made of packed earth and dirt, dusty in the dry hot seasons and muddy in the short rainy seasons, but smelly throughout.

The dearth of civic buildings in the earlier periods underscores the village-like character of Capernaum's public space. There is no evidence for defen-

---

46. Such *insulae* are in fact entirely absent in Palestine; there are several from the Late-Roman to Byzantine Periods east of the Jordan, at Umm el-Jimal, Pella, and Gerasa, Yizhar Hirschfeld, *The Palestinian Dwelling in the Roman-Byzantine Period* (Jerusalem: Franciscan Printing Press, 1995) 45–50.

47. Contra James F. Strange, who describes Capernaum as one of the cities in the region, along with Antipatris, Caesarea, Sepphoris, Sebaste, Petra, and Gerasa, as having a hippodamian geometric grid, "Some Implications of Archaeology for New Testament Studies," in *What Has Archaeology to Do with Faith* (eds. James Charlesworth and Walter Weaver; Valley Forge, Pennsylvania: Trinity Press International, 1992) 36. Gideon Foerster has criticized Strange et al for suggesting Meiron was built on a Roman-style block plan, "Excavations at Ancient Meiron," *IEJ* 37 (1987) 266.

48. Daniel Sperber, *The City in Roman Palestine* (Oxford: Oxford University Press, 1998) 104, 176–77; see also Samuel Krauss, *Griechische und Lateinische Lehnwörter im Talmud, Midrasch, und Targum 2* (Berlin: S. Calvary, 1898–9) 385. The observations of Magen Broshi on the system of standards of streets in the Near East is instructive: for a long period, a ratio of 18:24:36 feet (with local variants of the *podes*) existed for cities' streets, "though naturally the standard was only used in planned cities . . .," "Standards of Street Widths in the Roman-Byzantine Period," *IEJ* 27 (1977) 232–235. No such regularity exists at Capernaum, indicative of its organic growth and development.

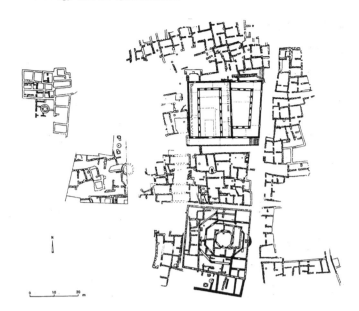

*Figure 5.3 The Insulae of Capernaum (Courtesy Franciscan Printing Press)*

sive fortifications or walls, observed by even the earliest visitors to the site.[49] There were no civic structures enjoyed by the urban elites throughout the Roman world, such as a hippodrome, amphitheater, theater, or even a smaller *odeon*. There is likewise no evidence for a basilica used as a court of justice, council, or for commercial activities. However, if the Early Roman walls under the fifth-century C.E. limestone synagogue represent the foundations of an earlier synagogue, it would have served both civic and religious functions, inseparable realms in Jewish village life.[50] That a synagogue building, perhaps similar to the nearby first-century synagogue at Gamla, once stood in Capernaum cannot really be confirmed by the Gospel references to

---

49. As the pilgrim Giacomo da Verona noted in 1335, Corbo, *Cafarnao 1*, 21; and Dalman some six centuries later, *Orte und Wege Jesus*, 149–50

50. James F. Strange and Hershel Shanks, "Synagogue Where Jesus Preached Found at Capernaum," *BAR* 9 (1983) 24–31. There is considerable evidence that the earliest synagogues in Palestine in the first century were not dedicated solely to religious purposes, see Moshe Dothan, "Research on Ancient Synagogues in the Land of Israel," in *Recent Archaeology in the Land of Israel* (eds. Benjamin Mazar and Hershel Shanks; Jerusalem: Israel Exploration Society, 1984) 89–96; Richard Horsley has suggested that in the earlier periods, συαγωγη referred more to the assembly than to a structure, *Archaeology, History, and Society in Galilee: the Social Context of Jesus and the Rabbis* (Valley Forge: Trinity Press International, 1996) 131–53; see also Sidney Hoenig, "The Ancient City-Square: Forerunner of the Synagogue," *ANRW* 2.19.1 (1979) 448–476.

a synagogue (e.g., Mark 1:21, John 6:59), since the term refers primarily to a gathering and only secondarily to a structure in the earlier periods in Palestine. It is notable that of all the Gospel accounts, only the Lukan version of the centurion story implies a synagogue structure, built with his benevolence for the Jews (Luke 7:5); but Luke narrates the events from outside Palestine, where Diaspora communities more clearly used this term (and προσευχή) for an actual structure.[51] The archaeological excavations to date have uncovered no overtly pagan artifacts associated with shrines or temples at Capernaum. Nor is there even any kind of evidence for structures relating to the agora, such as shops or storage facilities. Presumably market days were held in tents or booths on the open unpaved areas along the shore, between the domestic quarters and the harbor. In terms of the harbor facilities, the remains indicate simple fieldstone jetties functioning as breakwaters and anchorages.[52]

Sometime early in the second century C.E., a small Roman-style bathhouse was constructed in a newly developed area to the east of the town. This 8 x 20 meter structure was constructed in a quality unlike any other at the site: a brick and tile hypocaust system with flues underneath was covered by a thick waterproof mortar and concrete floor, the walls were constructed of uniformly cut stones, carefully leveled courses, and with ample mortar.[53] The bathhouse's division into four chambers—a *frigidarium, tepidarium, caldarium,* and *apodyterium*—is typical of the row-type bathhouse built by the Roman Legions on the western *limes* during the second century.[54] This presence of this Roman *balneum*, however, does not suggest that public bathing in Roman-urban style was practiced at Capernaum, but instead indicates that a Roman occupying force stationed there in the second century C.E. wanted to bathe in Roman style.[55]

51. Martin Hengel, "*Proseuche* und *Synagoge*: Jüdische Gemeinde, Gotteshaus, und Gottesdienst in der Diaspora und in Palaestina," in *Tradition und Glaube: das frühe Christentum in seiner Umwelt. Festgabe für Karl Georg Kuhn zum 65. Geburtstag* (eds. Gret Jeremias, Heinz-Wolfgang Kuhn, and Harmut Stegemann; Göttingen: Vanderhoeck and Ruprecht, 1971) 157–84.

52. Nun, *Sea of Galilee*, 25.

53. James Russel, "The Roman Bathhouse at Capernaum," unpublished paper delivered at the 1988 annual meeting of the American Schools of Oriental Research in Boston. See also John Laughlin, "Capernaum: From Jesus' Time and After," *BAR* 19 (Sept./Oct. 1993) 56–59.

54. The structure at Capernaum is very similar to the Roman bathhouse at En Gedi dated likewise to Hadrian's activities in the East, Benjamin Mazar and Immanuel Dunayevsky, "En-Gedi: Fourth and Fifth Seasons of Excavations. Preliminary Report," *IEJ* 17 (1967) 142–3; and Benjamin Mazar, "En Gedi," *NEAEHL* 2:404–405.

55. On Jews and such practices, see Ronny Reich, "The Hot Bath-House (*balneum*), the *Miqweh*, and the Jewish Community in the Second Temple Period," *JJS* 39 (1988) 102–107; Goodman has noted the aversion to Roman-style public bathing in Galilean villages, unlike at urban sites, *State and Society in Roman Galilee,* 28, 33, 74–5, 83–4.

The evidence for Roman Legionnaires at Capernaum, however, cannot be connected with the Gospel's centurion and Jesus' ministry a century earlier.[56] The evidence dates their presence at Capernaum to well after the First Revolt, to the time after Roman soldiers began working on the Emperor Hadrian's road building in the east, a point supported by the Roman milestone in Latin found near Capernaum bearing the Emperor Hadrian's name:

IMP(erator)
C[A]E[S]AR DIVI
[TRAIA]NI PAR(thici)
F(ilius)[DIVI NERVAE][N]EP(os)TRAI
[ANUS][HA]DRIANUS AUG(ustus)

There is otherwise little epigraphic evidence from Capernaum, which corroborates the general absence of public structures common in urban settings. The complete lack of first-century C.E. public, and private, inscriptions betrays Capernaum's modest stature at that time. Public inscriptions were an important aspect of Greco-Roman city life, and proclamations of this or that benefactor were incised on all sorts of public surfaces: pavements, columns, fountains, and statues; they were the billboards of ancient city life.[57] Euergetism, the expenditure by private individuals on public building projects, left its mark on stone in the ubiquitous honorific inscriptions unearthed in cities of the Mediterranean littoral, including the Palestinian cities of Caesarea Maritima and Scythopolis.[58] Only two honorific inscriptions have been found in heavily excavated Capernaum, and both come from inside the Byzantine Period synagogue, one on a column and one on a lintel. One is in Greek, somewhat rare on later synagogues, and the other in Aramaic, as were most of the synagogue inscriptions from this period in Palestine. Both contain Jewish names: Herod (son of?) Halphai are on the former, and the other names a Halfo, son of Zebida, son of John.[59] This evidence, however, can only cautiously be used to assess the language at Capernaum in the earlier periods, but that the absence of inscriptions intimates a predominately illiterate village merits consideration.

Without a grid bespeaking centralized planning and without structures typical of Greco-Roman cities, Capernaum also lacked the usual style of

56. Russell, "The Roman Bathhouse at Capernaum;" and Horsley, *Archaeology, History, and Society*, 115.

57. John Stambaugh, *The Ancient Roman City* (Baltimore: Johns Hopkins University Press, 1988) 141.

58. See Peter Garnsey and Richard Saller, *The Roman Empire: Economy, Society and Culture* (Berkeley: University of California Press, 1987) 33–34.

59. Eleazar L. Sukenik, *Ancient Synagogues in Palestine and Greece* (London: The British Academy, 1934) 71–72; *NEAEHL* 1:294.

arranging buildings at urban sites: there was no axial ordering, no enclosing walls or imposing facades, nor were vistas creating by arranging structures. Neither have any of the materials associated with these and the social elites been unearthed at Capernaum: there are no plaster surfaces, no decorative frescoes, no marble of any kind, no patches nor even tessarae stones, and no red ceramic roof-tiles in Roman Period contexts.

## The Archaeology of Private Space at Capernaum

The domestic complexes at Capernaum are typical of Jewish villages in Roman Palestine and conform to the houses excavated in eastern Galilee and southern Golan built with local dark basalt. Each of the complexes excavated at Capernaum was laid out with several abutting units encircling a court-yard, which was shared by the inhabitants of the domestic units, perhaps an extended family. The houses, storage facilities, and enclosure walls shielded the courtyard, which apparently only had one entrance. The few windows in the houses were up near the roof, designed not for views but with lighting and ventilation in mind. The restricted access to the courtyard and the windows' obstructed views indicate that the inhabitants valued security and a sense of seclusion from outsiders and street life (see, e.g., Mark 1:33 and 2:2), in contrast to Roman villas and urban elite houses in Jerusalem or Sepphoris, for example, which ostentatiously unveiled their wealth to outsiders and passersby.[60] Inside the courtyard at Capernaum, parts of *tabun* ovens survive, fishhooks are strewn about, and agricultural implements are scattered about, such as grinding stones, presses, and loom weights, illustrating how the families' work and lives centered around the courtyard.

One feature that has not been excavated to date at Capernaum is a *miqweh*. This absence is not that surprising, however, considering that *miqwaoth* found in private houses have been in wealthier urban homes (e.g., Sepphoris and Jerusalem).[61] In village settings or rural areas they tend to be

60. For the Dionysiac villa at Sepphoris, see Eric Meyers, Ehud Netzer, and Carol Meyers, "Artistry in Stone: The Mosaics of Ancient Sepphoris," *BA* 50 (1987) 223–31; "A Mansion in the Sepphoris Acropolis and Its Splendid Mosaic," *Qadmoniot* 21 (1988) 87–92 [Hebrew]; Carol Meyers, Eric Meyers, Ehud Netzer, and Zeev Weiss, "The Dionysos Mosaic," in *Sepphoris in Galilee*, 111–115; Rina Talgam and Zeev Weiss, "'The Life of Dionysos' in the Mosaic Floor of Sepphoris," *Qadmoniot* 21 (1988) 93–99 [Hebrew]. For the palatial mansion in Jerusalem, see Nahman Avigad, *Discovering Jerusalem* (Nashville, Tennessee: Nelson, 1980) 95–120; on the use of luxury to communicate status in domestic architecture, see Wallace-Hadrill, *Houses and Society in Pompeii and Herculaneum*, 143–174.

61. In addition to their presence at elite houses in urban settings, *miqwaoth* are also found in Hasmonean royal-priestly palaces at Jericho, and the Herodian palaces at Herodium, Jericho, and Masada. See the valuable comments by E. P. Sanders,

public in nature, either attached to synagogues (e.g., Gamla and Chorazin) or near olive press installations (e.g., Manṣur el-ʿAqeb).[62] For this reason the absence of *miqwaoth* in private houses at Capernaum is less telling of ethnicity than socio-economic status; a *miqweh* in a private house indicates the relatively high socio-economic status of its Jewish inhabitants, but the absence of *miqwaoth* in private houses does not correlate with non-Jewish inhabitants. Furthermore, considering that the Sea of Galilee provided halachically suitable water for ritual bathing ("living water," Lev 15:13; *m. Miqw.* 1.1, 1.6), one suspects that the arduous task of digging through basalt ground would diminish a family's interest in having a private *miqweh*.[63]

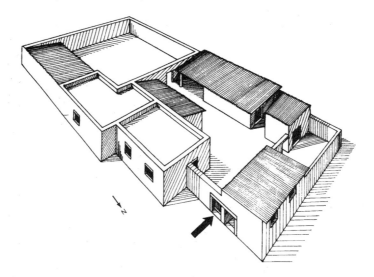

*Figure 5.4 First Century "Saint Peter's House" (Meyers and Strange, 1983)*

*Jewish Law from Jesus to the Mishnah: Five Studies* (Philadelphia: Trinity Press International, 1990) 215–16; and *Judaism: Practice and Belief 63 B.C.E.–66 C.E.* (Philadelphia: Trinity Press International, 1992) 222–29; two have also been found in a fortified courtyard house at Horvat Salit, which belonged to a great estate owner of the first and second century C.E., Hirshfeld, *The Palestinian Dwelling*, 71–2; first reported in D. Alon, "Horvat Salit (Kh. Salantah)," *ESI* 5 (1986) 94–96.

62. Ronny Reich, "Ritual Baths," *OEANE* 4.430–31; and Yizhar Hirshfeld and Rivka Birger-Calderon, "Early Roman and Byzantine Estates Near Caesarea," *IEJ* 41 (1991) 81–111.

63. A glimpse at Reich's map in his dissertation reveals a noticeable absence around the shore of the lake, except for Tiberias, "*Miqvaot* (Jewish Ritual Immersion Baths) in Eretz-Israel in the Second Temple Period and the Mishnah and Talmud Periods," Ph.D. dissertation, Hebrew University Jerusalem, 1990 [Hebrew with English summary].

Judging from the remains of the walls, Capernaum's houses were constructed without the benefit of a skilled craftsman's techniques or tools. Perhaps an experienced elder from the village assisted in the design, lent some rudimentary tools, and performed the more difficult tasks with the household, friends, or neighbors providing the labor. [64] But the general construction was very low in quality. The simple foundations consisted of large basalt boulders; the surviving lower courses were of unhewn fieldstones aligned together and packed with mud or clay and smaller stones in the interstices; and the faces of the walls were smeared with clay, mud, or even dung mixed with straw for insulation. Lacking also in the Early Roman strata of each of the domestic units are any signs of plaster or fresco; not to mention mosaics, as no tessarae have been found in domestic contexts. Indeed, it was the plaster and fresco in the *insula sacra* from a later period that stood in stark contrast to the other rooms that led to its identification as non-domestic space, a house church or a shrine, in which Christian graffiti was later etched. If *insula* 2 is taken to be typical, then the main entrances to the courtyard did have a hewn threshold and ashlar doorjambs with a locking mechanism for a wooden door, but it was not near the quality and sturdiness of the monolithic door frames at either the "House of the Lintel" in the Upper Galilean village of Merion or at a house in the Galilean village of Horvat Susita, much less the urban houses at Sepphoris (e.g., Unit II) or the Herodian Quarters in Jerusalem (e.g., the Palatial Mansion).[65] The internal doorways were crudely made of fieldstones with simple wood beams framing the entry without any apparent closing mechanism; they may have been covered with straw mats or curtains.[66] Though no roofs have survived *in situ*, the lack of stones shaped as arch or vault pieces, the very few *ex situ* large basalt beams supporting partial roofs as at Bethsaida and Chorazin, and the complete absence of roof tiles, means that the roofs were of thatched reeds. Wooden ceiling beams supported a thick bed of reeds, which protected the beams from dampness, and the whole was covered with packed mud for additional insulation (*m. Kelim* 20:5).[67] It is therefore clear and has often been observed that in the story of the paralytic, Luke's "through the tiles" (5:19) is less appropriate to the actual milieu than Mark's more probable "that they dug through the roof" (2:5), which made no sense in Luke's urban setting where roof tiles were common.[68]

---

64. Hirshfeld has noted numerous ethnographic parallels that are instructive, *The Palestinian Dwelling*, 112–15.

65. Corbo, *Cafarnao* I, 177, Meyers, *Excavations at Ancient Meiron. Upper Galilee. Israel 1971–72, 1974–75, 1977* (Cambridge, Massachusetts: ASOR, 1981) 39; and Hirshfeld, *The Palestinian Dwelling*, 249–255.

66. I.e, the *paphilionot* in the rabbinic literature, Hirshfeld, *The Palestinian Dwelling*, 254–55.

67. Hirshfeld, *The Palestinian Dwelling*, 237–9.

68. E.g., Chester C. McCown, "Luke's Translation of Semitic into Hellenistic Custom," *JBL* 58 (1939) 213–36; and Dalman, *Orte und Wege Jesu*, 78; James

The material culture inside the rooms from the Late Hellenistic and Early Roman Periods bespeaks a simple existence that one would expect in a fishing and agricultural village. The pottery is mostly common, much of it from the Upper Galilean village of Kefar Ḥananya, and the lamps were of the simple undecorated Herodian types, without any imports.[69] There are no signs of wealth, such as imported wine vessels or *unguentaria* for perfumes, and almost no finely decorated vessels or even simple glass.[70] One group of artifacts common to each and every domestic unit, however, was the chalk or so-called Herodian stone vessels. Though the chalk vessels are indicative of Jewish ethnicity, the fact that almost all at Capernaum were either handmade or turned on a small lathe bespeaks the inhabitants' lower socio-economic status, or inability to afford the more expensive large, lathe-turned vessels.[71]

## Jesus in Capernaum

Without a full investigation of the place and time of each of the Gospels and the ways in which their narrative worlds shape the picture in Galilee, full justice cannot be done to their various portrayals of Jesus and Capernaum.[72] What follows, therefore, are only some summary observations of relevant issues in the archeological record at Capernaum, and tentative suggestions regarding the historical Jesus, without delving into the details of each Gospel's own integrity, social world, and created narrative world.

Charlesworth, *Jesus Within Judaism: New Light From Exciting Archaeological Excavations* (New York: Doubleday, 1988) 109–115.

69. It is notable that after the conversion of the Empire, Capernaum was "flooded with elegant wares from Africa, Greece, and Cyprus," Loffreda, *OEANE* 1:418; see the "typo TS" (*terra pseudo-sigillata*) in Loffreda, *Cafarnao 2*, 65–88. Ironically, the earlier road building by Hadrian paved the way for this influx.

70. The signs of wealth described by Laughlin in the eastern portion of the ruins (mostly plaster) date to the second century C.E., and are only found in or next to the bathhouse, and are in fact contrasted with the remaining houses, "Capernaum at the Time of Jesus," 57.

71. Orfali has noted the large stone (cultic?) vessels before the synagogue, *Capharnaum et ses ruines*, 56; see also the misleading discussion by Dalman, who presupposes that these served ritual purposes, *Orte und Wege Jesu*, 156. These are the roughly hewn limestone basins displayed at the site, and not *kalal* style large lathe chalk vessels associated with ritual purity found at Jerusalem and elsewhere, see the photo in Roland Deines, *Jüdische Steingefässe und pharisäische Frömmigkeit: Ein archäologisch-historischer Beitrag zum Verständis von Joh 2,6 und der jüdischen Reinheitshalacha zur Zeit Jesu* (WUNT 2.52; Tübingen, J. B. C. Mohr [Paul Siebeck], 1993) photo 1b.

72. On their views of Galilee, see Freyne, *Galilee, Jesus, and the Gospels*, 33–132.

The Ethnic and Religious Character of Capernaum

The archaeological evidence indicates that Capernaum was a Jewish village, a point apparent in the literary evidence. The fact that the rabbinic literature locates *minim* at Capernaum means that it was a Jewish village where heretics stood out. Likewise, Epiphanius's account of Joseph building a church there—as a convert he built primarily at Jewish sites—as well as the later Jewish and Christian pilgrim literature, attests to its Jewish character. The archaeology confirms this, first, by uncovering the site's foundation as a village in the Late Hellenistic Period, which coincides with the widespread Jewish settlement of Galilee and parts of the Golan. Second, the similarities in terms of material culture with Jewish sites in Galilee and the Golan, and evidence for trade connections between them, substantiate the Jewish ethnicity of Capernaum. In particular, the presence of stone vessels, found in each of the domestic units excavated at Capernaum, are telling in this matter, as is the presence of the synagogue for a later period. One should envision, then, that in moving from Nazareth to Capernaum, Jesus went from a small Jewish settlement to a larger, but still Jewish, village.

Nevertheless, the question arises whether Capernaum had a more substantial gentile presence. On the whole, there is no evidence for mixed villages in either Galilee or the Golan, as even the cities in Galilee were predominately Jewish. The larger gentile cities around Galilee, notably those of the nearby Decapolis, had mixed populations with substantial Jewish minorities (*War* 2.457–86). But there is no evidence for the opposite in the Early Roman Period, namely that the Jewish cities had substantial gentile minorities, and it is even more unlikely that Jewish villages would have had them. The centurion mentioned in Q 7:1–10, however, poses the question of a gentile minority at Capernaum in a concrete manner.[73] The term, ἑκατοντάρχος, literally means "leader of one hundred" (Latin = *centurio*), and is typically used for officers serving in Roman Legions, including their roles as building supervisors, tax collectors, or police guards.[74] However,

---

73. In John 4:46–54, this issue is not raised, as the official (βασιλικός) is apparently a Jew, Martin Hengel, *The Johannine Question* (Philadelphia: Trinity Press International, 1989) 168 n. 48, 217 n. 92. Rudolf Bultmann thought that John changed the βασιλικός into an ἑκατοντάρχος to make him a Jew, *The Gospel of John* (Philadelphia: Westminster, 1971) 206; however, John makes no issue of the ethnicity of the official, so that if any changes were made in the tradition, it was in the Q version, where the story's conclusion hinges on the official being a Gentile, John Kloppenborg, *The Formation of Q: Trajectories in Ancient Wisdom Collections* (Studies in Antiquity and Christianity; Philadelphia: Fortress, 1987) 120.

74. Wenger, *Der Hauptman von Kafernaum*, 60–72; though the evidence for their use as tax collectors is after the second century, Daniel Sperber, "The Centurion as a Tax-Collector," *Latomus* 28 (1969) 186–88.

because Herod Antipas adopted the common Greek terms used for Roman administrators and officials (e.g. the χιλίαρχοι and σπεκουλάτωρ in Mark 6:21, 27), Q 7:1–10 does not substantiate that a detachment of Roman Legionnaires was at Capernaum.[75] In fact, it is historically implausible to suggest that a Roman Centurion and upwards of 100 Roman Legionnaires were stationed at Capernaum. Roman troops only periodically passed though Galilee, such as to quell the revolt at Sepphoris upon Herod's death, but no troops were stationed in Herod's kingdom or his son Antipas's tetrarchy. This is clear when, after King Aretas IV's Arab troops defeated Antipas's army in Perea because he divorced the king's daughter, hostilities ceased as soon as Vitellius, the Roman governor of Syria, retrieved his Legions from a Parthian campaign and began to march on Aretas, who immediately fled in fear of a direct conflict with Rome. Furthermore, Josephus expressly says that the Roman Legion at Antipas's request circumvented travel through Jewish territories because the Legion's standards offended their sensibilities (*Ant.* 18.121–22). In the first century, the *Legio X Fretensis* was stationed in nearby Syria and protected the Decapolis, but it was not until the second century C.E. that Legions were permanently stationed near Galilee at Legio.[76]

The ἑκατοντάρχος of Q 7:1–10 was likely an official in Antipas's administrative and military apparatus, which apparently also included non-Jews, for whose position Roman terminology had been adopted.[77] Antipas was on good terms with his neighbor and brother Philip, the Decapolis region was protected by the Legions stationed in Syria, and any hostilities with Aretas were limited to Perea, so that there was little need to have Galilee fortified and defended with gentile mercenaries, of whom the archaeology of the border site Capernaum shows no trace. Instead, Capernaum was mostly a Jewish town, with an exceptional gentile official or two, who would have stood out (Q 10:13–15).

Nevertheless, Capernaum's location offered considerably more opportunities for contact with Gentiles and was more accessible to gentile sites than most Galilean villages, particularly the small settlement of Nazareth. For one, the Decapolis was just across the lake, and even though the cities of

---

75. Adrian N. Sherwin-White, *Roman Society and Roman Law in the New Testament* (Oxford: Oxford University Press, 1963) 137; and Harold Hoehner, *Herod Antipas* (Cambridge: Cambridge University Press, 1972) 119–20.

76. Zeev Safrai, "The Roman Army in the Galilee," in *The Galilee in Late Antiquity*, 103–114.

77. Alternately, Wenger has suggested that Q's change of the original βασιλικός (so John 4:46–54) to ἑκατοντάρχος shows that the story had adapted itself to the new geographical milieu of Q (Syria or Judea?) where Roman occupation was in effect, *Der Hauptmann von Kafernaum*, 72 note 84; or assuming a rather late date for Q, one could argue that it reflected a time when Roman troops were in Galilee around the first revolt.

Hippos and Gadara lay inland, their territories extended to the lake and each had harbor facilities on the shore. The frequent crossings "to the other side" in the Gospels insinuate that Jesus came into contact with Gentiles, though it is notable that the tradition restricts his visits to the *chora*, and not to the cities themselves.[78] Most telling story in this regard is the demoniac possessed by "Legion" in the territory of a Decapolis city (Mark 5:1–20). As Gerd Theissen has noted, the role of the swine in the story points to ethnic tensions between Jews and Gentiles in the region, and the naming of the demon "Legion" reveals the political aspect of the conflict: it was the *Legio X Fretensis*, whose standard included the image of the boar, that protected the cities on the eastern shore after they were taken from the Herodian kingdom and had their autonomy restored.[79] Certainly the presence of Legions nearby, who sided with the Decapolis, was not welcomed by Jews. This is even more the case if Mark was written during or after the Jewish Revolt. Although the pericope does not overtly debate the question of ethnicity, the underlying ethnic tensions are not resolved: the swine are dead, Legion is gone, and Jesus is asked to leave.

Similar tensions are apparent in Mark's portrayal of Jesus' circuit north to the villages of Caesarea Philippi in his contacts with Syro-Phoenicians (Mark 7). Tyrian territory and Syro-Phoenician settlements were closer to Galilee than is often recognized. Kedesh, a key Tyrian site on its border with Upper Galilee, was only 25 km north of Capernaum, and archaeological evidence of Syro-Phoenician settlements has been uncovered at several sites in the Huleh Valley, and isolated evidence has been found even in southern Golan.[80]

The general economic orientation of Upper and Lower Galilee toward Tyre during this period has been noted in terms of numismatic profiles and trade.[81] However, in addition to this evidence, the proximity of Phoenician inland settlements all along Galilee's northern border, into the Huleh Valley,

---

78. Visits to Bethsaida and other Jewish sites on the northeastern shore would have been considered trips "to the other side" (see Mark 6:45). That Jesus goes only to the regions of the cities, and not the cities themselves, has been pointed out by Freyne, *Galilee, Jesus, and the Gospels,* 139–40.

79. Theissen, *The Gospels in Context,* 105–111.

80. Notably Tel Anafa and Tel Wawiyat, Berlin, "From Monarchy to Markets," 82–83.

81. Eric Meyers first raised the archaeological ties between Upper Galilee and Tyre, including the evidence from John of Gishala's trade in kosher oil to Jews of Tyrian territory, "The Cultural Setting of Galilee: The Case of Regionalism and Early Judaism," *ANRW* 2.19.1 (1979) 700; and "Galilean Regionalism: A Reappraisal," in *Approaches to Ancient Judaism. Volume 5* (ed. William Green; Atlanta: Scholars Press, 1985) 123. See also Richard Hanson, *Tyrian Influence in the Upper Galilee: Meiron Excavation Project 2* (Cambridge, Massachusetts: ASOR 1980). Horsley's critique raises important issues but does not seriously challenge the basic observations, *Archaeology, History, and Society in Galilee,* 102–103.

around the springs of the Jordan, and even the Golan, suggests much more cultural contact, and tensions, between villages on Galilee's periphery. The path from Capernaum to some of the villages of Caesarea Philippi led through Phoenician territories and villages, and although Jesus' travels in Mark serve a theological purpose in associating Jesus with the gentile mission, the milieu underlying the story—Jews and Gentiles in close proximity—is historically plausible. Jesus' healing of the Syro-Phoenician's daughter (Mark 7:24–30) seems to open the door for more positive relations, but it does not entirely resolve the underlying tensions, nor did it eradicate the stereotypes of the "others" (leading Luke to delete the story entirely).[82] In the same way, the condemnation against Capernaum (Q 10:13–15) rubs salt into the wound by invoking the Syro-Phoenician cities of Tyre and Sidon to shame the inhabitants of Capernaum.

To sum up, even though Capernaum was a Jewish village, its proximity to gentile areas to the east and north left its mark in the Gospels in terms of underlying ethnic tensions.

### Socio-Economic Character of Capernaum

In addition to its Jewish character, the archaeological record makes it clear that chiefly the lower levels of society inhabited Capernaum, like most villages in antiquity. The evidence for wealth at the site, notably the splendid fifth-century C.E. limestone synagogue and imported fine wares, dates to after the influx of pilgrims to the Holy Land, which brought some revenue to Capernaum. In earlier times, however, the inhabitants of Capernaum show no ability to afford luxury items such as imported pottery, *unguentaria*, jewelry, or large lathe stone vessels; but they eked out a living from the nearby fields, vineyards, or fishing on the lake. Any surplus generated from these activities did not stay in the village; there is no evidence of elite houses at the site. Instead, it went to Antipas's coffers or landlords among the elite living in Tiberias and Sepphoris. Some of the peasants at Capernaum may have been better off than others; some fishers may have owned their boats and dealt directly with tax collectors; others were dispossessed peasants who hired themselves out as day laborers.

---

82. Theologically journey is often taken as Jesus inaugurating the gentile mission, see Friedrich Lang, "Über Sidon mitten ins Gebiet der Dekapolis. Geographie und Theologie in Markus 7,31," *ZDPV* 94 (1978) 145–59. On the situation more generally and the applicability of the term "Syro-Phoenician," see Theissen, *The Gospels in Context*, 61–80, 244–47, and Thomas Schmeller, "Jesus im Umland Galiläas. Zu den markinischen Berichten vom Aufenthalt Jesu in den Gebieten von Tyros, Caesarea Philippi und der Dekapolis," *BZ* NF 38 (1994) 44–66.

Fishing was no guarantee for economic windfall, as has often been suggested.[83] For every family engaged in fishing or drying fish, there was a tax collector or official who sold the rights to fish and demanded a hefty return.[84] The fact that Zebedee, the father of James and John, worked with hired hands (μισθωτοί) in no way indicates wealth on his part or a significant entrepreneurial fishing enterprise (Mark 1:20). Rather, it points to the common practice of seasonal, daily, or hourly hiring of peasants dispossessed from their land who sought to eke out a living in the larger villages and cities. Certainly, among the literary elite, fishing was not a worthy pursuit; it was one of the practices that Plato excluded from proper *paideia* (*Laws* 823b) and, in general, was deemed a despicable, smelly profession.

There is no evidence in the archaeological record suggesting that any individuals lived affluent lives in Capernaum, nor is there any evidence for social elites displaying their civic responsibility at Capernaum by sponsoring public buildings, as the wealthy did at Scythopolis, Caesarea, Sepphoris, and Tiberias. There were no mosaics, no frescoes, no marble. Officials and the tax collectors would have usurped whatever wealth was in Capernaum, a point of resentment among the villagers. One suspects that Capernaum was a slight step up from Nazareth on the socio-economic ladder, but perhaps only insofar as some low-level bureaucrats or officials with a modicum of wealth lived there. Travelers passing through Capernaum on the regional trade network included affluent merchants, Herodian officials, or ostentatious elites. In this sense, the people of Capernaum would have had greater exposure to the visible signs of wealth than those at Nazareth, but at the same time, these conditions likely also attracted beggars, cripples, and prostitutes, who find their homes in the stories of the Gospels.

The Political Situation on the Lake's Northwest Shore

The increased traffic lanes at Capernaum raises the question of whether Jesus' presence there has any connection to the Galilean political scene. If Jesus avoided Sepphoris and Tiberias because they were the seats of Antipas's

83. Kee, "Early Christianity in the Galilee: Reassessing the Evidence," in *The Galilee in Late Antiquity*, 16. Freyne once suggested that Galilee and particularly Capernaum were less receptive to Jesus' message of simplicity because it was a more well-to-do town, *Galilee, Jesus, and the Gospels*, 160–61. His argument is mainly inferential, and relies on the observation that many of the poor mentioned in the Gospels are located in Jerusalem or on Jesus' way there, and not in Galilee. It is not based on a description, archaeological or literary, of Galilee or Capernaum itself.

84. Wuellner, *The Meaning of "Fishers of Men,"* 23–25; and Oakman and Hanson, *Palestine in the Time of Jesus*, 106–110.

power, then conducting his activities in and around Capernaum and the northern shore of the Sea of Galilee would be appropriate, since it was on the periphery of Antipas's tetrarchy. Notwithstanding the possible presence of a centurion (ἑκατοντάρχος or simply a royal official, βασιλικος) serving in the Herodian retinue, Capernaum was adjacent to the territory of Philip, whom Josephus describes as "a person of moderation and quietness" in addition to being a fair judge (Ant. 18.106–7). This contrasts with what we know of Antipas, whose reckless divorce of his first wife endangered his people and resulted in the Baptist's beheading (Mark 6; and Ant. 18.116–19), and whose misguided ambition and poorly timed self-promotion ultimately led to his banishment (Ant. 18.252; War 2.183).[85] In addition to Capernaum's closeness to Philip's territory, the Sea of Galilee provided immediate refuge and a host of landings outside Antipas's territory.

The extent to which Capernaum's location on the periphery of Antipas's power was factored into Jesus' ministry there depends largely on one's view of his message and ministry. It is quite likely that Jesus' programmatic itinerancy intentionally put him on the road, as a statement against either localizing the Kingdom of God or having the disciples serve as brokers for his ministry.[86] But this does not negate a secondary motive of Jesus, namely taking advantage of Capernaum's location on the periphery and on the lake to win the cat-and-mouse game with Antipas (Luke 13:31–33), a point that remains speculative.[87]

## Was Capernaum a Polis?

A further contribution that the archaeological reconstruction of Capernaum's character and size has to make to the study of the Gospels is the use of the term polis. Capernaum's modest population of between 600 and 1,500, the absence of public structures, and the lack of evidence for social elites dampens attempts to portray Jesus' base of operations as a thriving Greco-Roman metropolis and calls into question the Gospels' use of the

---

85. See the valuable prosopographical study by Hoehner, who tends to lay much blame at the feet of Herodias, as did Josephus, Herod Antipas, 264–65.

86. Crossan, The Historical Jesus, 225–353; and Gerd Theissen, "Wanderradikalismus. Literatursoziologische Aspekte der Überlieferung von Worten Jesu im Urchristentum," ZTK 70 (1973) 245–71.

87. I agree with both Theissen and Crossan that Jesus' itinerancy was theologically programmatic, as a means to avoid setting up brokerage. However, the fact that it might also have had a secondary purpose cannot be excluded. Hoehner has noted how Mark portrays Jesus' intention to withdraw and be alone with his disciples as soon as the crowds come, which might have the secondary purpose of avoiding Antipas after crowds drew attention to him, Herod Antipas, 201–2.

term polis for the site. Capernaum was simply not in the same league as Caesarea Maritima, Caesarea Philippi, Jerusalem, the cities of the Decapolis, or the Galilean cities of Sepphoris and Tiberias.

Admittedly, interest in population size is a comparatively recent development, and the ancients did not use this criterion to determine a settlement's status. Features other than population size defined a polis, or a city: most significantly, public structures that indicated a certain lifestyle and governance among the wealthier citizens. The Greek geographer Pausanius stripped the title polis from a village in central Greece because it had "no government buildings, no theatre, no agora, no water conducted to a fountain," it was a place "where the people live in hovels like mountain cabins on the edge of a ravine" (10.4.1). Moses Finley has aptly noted that this aesthetic-architectural definition was shorthand for a political and social definition: a genuine "city" was both a political and cultural center, where the elites could live a civilized life, "*urbanitas* in Roman parlance," in which they dominated socio-economic and political life.[88] Size was less relevant, as many genuine cities were no bigger than villages in population or area. The economy of the site did merit consideration, insofar as it afforded the material goods indispensable for civilized amenities for the wealthy elites.

Thus, the crucial criterion was that *poleis* ". . . tended to invest a large part of their income in their public buildings, so that these, rather than economic function, tended to become the criterion of a polis."[89] While Antipas's building programs at Sepphoris and Tiberias would have earned their recognition as *poleis*, Capernaum had nothing comparable and would not have been considered a polis by the Mediterranean literati. It lacked the features of civilized life: there was no wall, no aqueduct, no theater, no colonnaded thoroughfares, no administrative complex, no temples. It may, however, have had a synagogue, which in a Jewish context functioned not only as a religious temple, but also as a community building. Surely Pausanius would have denied it the title of polis.

Yet, Matthew (Matt 9:1, 11:20), Mark (Mark 1:33), and Luke (Luke 4:31) call Capernaum a polis. The Gospels' proclivity for the term is well known.[90] Matthew calls even Nazareth a polis (Matt 2:23); and so does Luke (Luke 1:26, 2:4,39, 4:29), who credits Nain (Luke 7:11,12) and Bethsaida (Luke 9:10) with the same status. John refers to Bethsaida in Galilee, Sychar in Samaria, and Ephraim in Judea as *poleis* (John 1:44, 4:5, and 11:54). The evangelists are more generous than Pausanius and other Graeco-Roman authors in their uses of the term. This generosity may be attributed in part

---

88. Moses Finley, *The Ancient Economy* (Berkeley: University of California Press, 1973) 124; I have used his translation of Pausanius.

89. Pounds, "The Urbanization of the Classical World," 135.

90. *TDNT* 6:529–30.

to ignorance of Palestinian geography, in part to lack of concern for precise definitions, and in part to theological motives; Luke, for example, is concerned to show that "this was not done in a corner" (Acts 26:26).

In the case of Capernaum, it is significant that the two earliest Christian sources that mention Capernaum, the sayings source Q and the putative signs source embedded in John, do not call it a polis. Q mentions Capernaum twice, in locating Jesus' healing of the centurion's son there and in the condemnation by Jesus (Q 7:1, 11:15). Q does not in any way describe the site, nor designate it as a polis or village.[91] The signs source also ignores its status; it is simply "Capernaum" (John 2:12, 4:46, 6:17, 24). The scribes behind these two sources, who perhaps had personal familiarity with Capernaum and its environs, never elevated its status to that of a polis.

Mark introduces for the first time polis as a designation for Capernaum. After narrating Jesus' healing on the Sabbath in its synagogue and his healing of Simon's mother-in-law, Mark says that, "the entire polis was gathered together at the door" to be healed (Mark 1:33). Mark obviously is not interested in the integrity of the term polis—how small must it be if the polis could all fit "at the door"? Mark does not use this term in its proper technical sense, as does Pausanius, but rather as part of his dichotomy between inhabited and uninhabited places, a theme carried throughout the first part of his Gospel. After noting that the polis was at the door, the next morning Jesus withdraws to a "lonely place" (Mark 1:35); after this healing, Jesus "could no longer openly enter a polis, but was out in the country" (Mark 1:45). This city-country dichotomy is repeated in the story of the Gerasene demoniac (Mark 5:14), and in the feeding of the five thousand (Mark 6:32–33).

Neither Matthew nor Luke was attuned to Mark's subtle use of polis as a contrast to uninhabited places when they redacted these Markan verses. Each was chronologically farther removed from the events described, and they were also geographically farther away, so that as far as they knew, Capernaum was a polis. Their most important source, Mark, had said so (Mark 1:33). Mark also informed Matthew and Luke that Capernaum had a fishing "industry" (Mark 1:16), a tollhouse (Mark 2:13–14), and at least one public building, the synagogue (Mark 1:21). The sayings source Q passed on to Matthew and Luke that Capernaum was large enough to station a centurion, which they might have thought implied a Roman and even a cohort of legionaries, the kind of force stationed in major cities (Q 7:1–10).

---

91. The woes in Q on the three Galilean cities (10:13–15) are preceded by the mission speech (10:2–12), which mentions going to cities (*poleis*), villages, and houses. But one should not assume that Q therefore thought of Capernaum as a polis.

It is no wonder that Luke matter-of-factly calls Capernaum "a polis of Galilee" (Luke 4:31). Luke even embellishes the centurion story with the civic ideal of euergistic sponsorship of buildings; the Centurion is said to have had the synagogue built for the Jews of Capernaum (Luke 7:5). Matthew likewise unwittingly calls Capernaum Jesus' "own polis" (9:1) and, along with Chorazin and Bethsaida, the *poleis* where Jesus did most of his miracles (11:20).

But a Markan inference that Capernaum was a polis, and the later explicit label by Matthew and Luke, should in no way count as evidence that Capernaum was a polis in any technical sense. Its public building program was meager at best. Its population of 600–1,500 was, relative to the surrounding Galilean cities, modest. As a political entity on the Galilean scene, it was unimportant and peripheral. It was, in short, the perfect place for Jesus' ministry.

## PART THREE

CHAPTER 6

# The Sayings Source Q in Galilee*

The provenance of the sayings source Q is fundamental to its understanding, its nature, and its place in Christian origins. The geographical locale of Q and the community behind it, however, is a matter of some debate. Scholars have variously placed it, some generically in Syria or Palestine, others in a more specific region like the Decapolis or Galilee, and a few very specifically in the cities of Tiberias and Sepphoris or the villages on the northern shore of the Sea of Galilee.[1] By geographically locating the text of Q, an interpretive die is cut whereby its sayings are understood, whether against a particular religious-cultural background, or within a specific socio-economic

---

\* This chapter represents a substantial elaboration and revision "The Social Map of Q," in *Conflict and Invention: Literary, Rhetorical, and Social Studies on the Sayings Gospel Q* (ed. John Kloppenborg; Philadelphia: Trinity Press International, 1995) 17–36.

1. Transjordan or the Decapolis has been suggested by among others, Sigfried Schulz, *Q. Die Spruchquelle der Evangelisten* (Zürich: Theologisher Verlag, 1972) 481. A Palestine-centered perspective in Q has been carefully articulated by Gerd Theissen, *The Gospels in Context: Social and Political History in the Synoptic Tradition* (Minneapolis: Fortress, 1991) 221–34. John Kloppenborg has suggested urban areas in Galilee or perhaps the Decapolis, "Literary Convention, Self-Evidence and the Social History of the Q People," in *Early Christianity, Q, and Jesus* (eds. John Kloppenborg and Leif Vaage; *Semeia* 55; Atlanta: Scholars Press, 1992) 96. Tiberias has been proposed by Wolfgang Schenk, "Die Verwünschung der Küstenorte Q 10,13–15: Zur Funktion der Konkreten Ortsangaben und zur Lokalisierung von Q," in *The Synoptic Gospels: Source Criticism and the New Literary Criticism* (ed. Camille Focant; BETL 110; Leuven: Leuven University Press, 1993) 477–90. The villages on the northern shore of the Sea of Galilee have been proposed by Ivan Haevner, *Q: The Sayings of Jesus* (Wilmington, Delaware: Michael Glazier, 1987) 42–45; and Dale Allison, *The Jesus Tradition in Q* (Harrisburg, Pennsylvania: Trinity Press International, 1997) 53.

setting. Having sketched the archaeology of Galilee in the previous chapters, the question of Q's fit within this Galilee remains to be examined, for, although Jesus' ministry can with considerable certainty be located there, the locale of the earliest collection of his teachings remains open.

The present study will attempt to locate Q and the Q community geographically in Galilee, in spite of the tentative and problematic nature of the enterprise. The provenance of New Testament texts is usually determined based on external evidence, using either later traditions or geographical patterns in the manuscript distribution. Thus, the dispute over the Gospel of Mark's locale has centered around the tradition of Petrine sponsorship in Rome, or the location of the Johannine literature has centered around the identification of John the Elder and his sphere of influence.[2] Internal evidence, or clues within the text itself, enters the discussion only at a secondary phase and in a supporting role. In the case of Q, however, where there is no external evidence, we are left with only the document itself, or more accurately, a reconstruction based on Matthew and Luke.[3] Given the lack of external evidence for the location of Q, placing Q and the Q community in Galilee based on internal evidence is somewhat provisional, though its place names, spatial imagery, and themes fit the social and cultural setting of Galilee quite well.

## Q's Narrative World, Social Map, and Real World

Too often geographical references in early Christian texts are studied simply through a cartographic comparison, and biblical authors are evaluated on whether they provide accurate geographical descriptions.[4] This strict empirical

---

2. On the Petrine tradition and authorship of Mark, see Kurt Niederwimmer, "Johannes Markus und die Frage nach dem Verfasser des zweiten Evangeliums," *ZNW* 58 (1967) 172–88; Martin Hengel, *Die Evangelienüberschriften* (Heidelberg: Carl Winter, Universitätsverlag, 1984) 14–15; and Dieter Lührmann, *Das Markusevangelium* (Handbuch zum Neuen Testament 3; Tübingen: J. C. B. Mohr [Paul Siebeck], 1987) 3–7. On the geographical location (and authorial identification) of the Johannine literature, see Martin Hengel, *The Johannine Question* (Philadelphia: Trinity Press International, 1989).

3. Papias's testimony to the *logia* used by Matthew is not external evidence relating to Q's location, see Dieter Lührmann, "Q: Sayings of Jesus or Logia?" in *The Gospel Behind the Gospels: Current Studies on Q* (ed. Ronald Piper; Leiden: Brill, 1995) 97–116; and James M. Robinson, "The *Incipit* of the Sayings Gospel Q," *RHPR* 75 (1995) 9–33.

4. Many simply study the historical geography of each place mentioned in the New Testament; see Gustaf Dalman, *Orte und Wege Jesu* (3rd ed.; Gütersloh: Bertelsmann, 1924). Chester C. McCown condemns Luke for his "geographical ineptitude" in "Gospel Geography: Fiction, Fact, and Truth," *JBL* 60 (1941) 15; see also "The Geography of Luke's Central Section," *JBL* 57 (1938) 51–66.

approach neglects the intricate blending between the literary and symbolic worlds and adds little to an understanding of the community's perspective on the world. On the other hand, by focusing only on the literary phenomena and the textual world, the text is severed from its particular historical context.[5] In using only the text of Q to locate the Q community, distinctions between the "textual world," "symbolic world," and "concrete world" must be kept in mind. The internal evidence for locating Q—the place names, spatial references, or themes—is encountered at the level of the textual world, that is to say, they are literary phenomena embedded in a text. The place names and spatial references in Q do not all correlate directly on the surface with actual geographical places visited by the Q community.

The places and the spatial images in the textual world of Q are born out of the symbolic world of the community behind Q, that is to say, are reflective of their geographical perspective on the world. Their spatial imagination, or social map, influences the manner in which this or that place is depicted in the text of Q. Geographers stress the social activity at work in the perception of places where people live or wish to live, and a social map is a community's shared symbolic system of spatial and social orientation.[6] Groups endow places with social meaning, so that places are not merely points at which two coordinates intersect; they are centers of meaning and characters in a community's mythic or symbolic world. For example, in the

---

5. The early redaction critical work of Karl Ludwig Schmidt focused on the use of place names as a literary phenomenon, *Der Rahmen des Geschichte Jesu* (Berlin: Trowitsch & Sohn, 1919) 259–269. Recent studies on the Lukan Travel Narrative have tended to avoid socio-historical questions, see David Moessner, *The Lord of the Banquet: The Literary and Theological Significance of the Lukan Travel Narrative* (Minneapolis: Fortress Press, 1989) 21–44; similarly in Mark, see Elizabeth Struthers Malbon, *Narrative Space and Mythic Meaning in Mark* (San Francisco: Harper & Row, 1986); and David Rhoads and Donald Michie, *Mark as Story* (Philadelphia: Fortress Press, 1982) 140–142. Mark, as a literary narrative, is more difficult to locate, since a single author has forged a narrative world in which the story takes place. Distinguishing those elements of the story's setting that are shaped by the plot from those elements that unconsciously emerge in the narrative from the author's mental map is a precarious venture.

6. David Stea and Roger M. Downs, "Cognitive Maps and Spatial Behavior," in *Image and Environment* (eds. D. Stea and R. M. Downs; Chicago: Aldine, 1973) 9; and Robert Lynch, "Some References to Orientation," in *Image and Environment*, 303. For a convenient summary of the state of the discipline, see Roger Downs and James Meyer, "Geography of the Mind: An Exploration of Perceptual Geography," *American Behavioral Scientist* 22 (September/October 1978) 59–77. See also C. C. Trowbridge, "On fundamental methods of orientation and imaginary maps," *Science* 38 (1913): 888–897; *Geographies of the Mind* (eds. David Lowenthal and Martyn Bowden; New York: Oxford University Press, 1976); Peter Gould and Richard White, *Mental Maps* (Baltimore: Penguin Books, 1974); and Robert Lynch, *The Image of the City* (Cambridge, Mass.: MIT Press, 1960). Jonathan Z. Smith has borrowed heavily from modern geographical theorists to stress the important category of "place" in religious thought, ritual, and myth, *To Take Place: Toward Theory in*

lament of Q 13:34–35, Jerusalem is not merely the capital of Judea, nor a city along the Kidron Valley, nor the intersection of the 31°E latitude and 35°N longitude, but a character personified in the Q community's social map. Various meanings are attributable to Jerusalem: it could be the city of David or of Jezebel, the stronghold that thwarted Sargon, or the unrepentant city crushed by Nebuchadnez'zar. Each group selects from the medley of meanings its own mental pastiche of Jerusalem; Hasmonean aristocrats do not share that of recently circumcised Idumeans, and neither shares that of the Galileans. Social maps are based in large part on their geographical locale, or home of the group, around which other places are oriented. Groups naturally describe the surrounding landscape and more remote places in relation to and under the influence of their home, which is the primary shaper of their perspective.

To locate the Q community, then, their social map must be reconstructed from the evidence at the textual level of Q. This social map contains the clues to their home in the concrete world, which shaped their spatial and geographical perspective in particular ways, and which also underlies important themes in their worldview.

## Locating Q in Previous Scholarship

Scholars working on Q have not always distinguished between the textual world in Q, the social map of the Q community, and the concrete world behind it when attempting to place it geographically. In selecting items from the text, different kinds of internal evidence have been accentuated to locate the Q community. The kinds of evidence and methods can be divided into three broad categories: 1) Q's conglomeration of place names and spatial references; 2) Q's particular themes or theological trends and their apparent connections to other early Christian literature; and 3) the social location appropriate to Q's genre and language.

The first approach to locating Q examines some of the place names, spatial references, and local conditions that would be derivative from a particular place. This approach holds some promise because, in general, such imagery is not part of the theological intent of the sayings or consciously shaped symbolic world of Q, but unconsciously made its way into the text of Q as a reflection of the community's social map. Most places mentioned, spatial allusions, and climatic conditions are not in themselves the content of the teaching, but appear reflexively and unintentionally as illustrations to score a theological point or foster parenesis, and hence provide a window into the social map from which the text was written. This approach, albeit in a more

---

*Ritual* (Chicago: University of Chicago Press, 1987); *Map is Not Territory: Studies in the History of Religions* (Leiden: E. J. Brill, 1978); and "The City as Place," in *Civitas* (ed. P. Hawkins; Atlanta: Scholars Press, 1983) 25–26.

or less anecdotal fashion, can be seen in Adolf von Harnack's work, who noted the ubiquitous agricultural images and metaphors in Q that he deemed appropriate to a home in Galilee.[7] Such an analysis, however, is limited by the extent to which the particularities of the ancient world are known, and the use of an overly simplistic template in which Galilee is rural, agricultural, and Jewish, while non-Palestinian sites are urban, Gentile, and Hellenistic; neither helps locate Q with any certainty, nor aids in appreciating the particular use of agricultural imagery and ties it to a specific regional setting.[8]

More recently, John Kloppenborg has undertaken a systematic analysis of the spatial imagery at the beginning of Q and noted its implications for the location of Q.[9] He addressed how the technical phrase ἡ περίχωρος τοῦ Ἰορδάνου ("the region of the Jordan") in Q 3:3 set the tone of a "story world" that hearkened back to the story of Lot and Sodom (repeated in Q 17:28–30) and looms throughout the document.[10] More generally, Q contrasts inhabited places with wilderness as the realm for divine disclosure. In moving from this literary setting to its generative social setting, he concluded that Q's attitude toward urban places was "quite compatible with the perspective of villagers in agrarian societies."[11] Without carrying the analysis of spatial imagery through the rest of Q, Kloppenborg rightfully stressed the interface between the real world of the redactors behind Q, their imaginative world, and the literary world in the text of Q.

The second approach to locating Q, which has dominated the discussion, is to speculate on the appropriate setting for the themes or theological tendencies

---

7. Adolf von Harnack tended to treat Q as a cipher for Jesus, so that his argument for a Galilean Q was at the same time an argument for the authenticity of Q's sayings, *The Sayings of Jesus: The Second Source of St. Matthew and St. Luke* (New Testament Studies 3; London: Williams & Norgate, 1907) 121; similarly also John M. C. Crum, *The Original Jerusalem Gospel: Being Essays on the Document Q* (New York: Macmillan, 1927) 49–63.

8. In a like manner, Schulz falsely assumed that the agricultural practices described in Q 13:19 were inappropriate to Palestine, since the Mishnah forbids the planting of mustard seeds in gardens (*m. Kil.* 3:2), *Q. Die Spruchquelle der Evangelisten*, 299. Schulz, however, completely misses the point; mustard was a weed, and the Mishnah's prohibition against its planting indicates that out-of-control mustard growth was a problem in Palestine, see Mikagu Sato, *Q und Prophetie. Studien zur Gattungs-und Traditionsgeschichte der Quelle Q* (WUNT, ser. 2, vol 29; Tübingen: J. C. B. Mohr [Paul Siebeck] 1988) 46; and John Dominic Crossan, *The Historical Jesus: The Life of a Mediterranean Jewish Peasant* (San Francisco: HarperSanFrancisco, 1991) 276–79.

9. John Kloppenborg, "City and Wasteland: Narrative World and the Beginning of the Sayings Gospel (Q)," in *How Gospels Begin* (*Semeia* 52; ed. Dennis Smith; Atlanta: Scholars Press, 1991) 145–160.

10. This is the LXX translation for *kikkar hayyarden* in Gen 13 and 19, and elsewhere, which refers to the area of Sodom and Gomorrah to the north and the east of the Dead Sea, Kloppenborg, "City and Wasteland," 150.

11. Kloppenborg, "City and Wasteland," 155.

in Q. The issue of the gentile mission has repeatedly been addressed ever since Dieter Lührmann's careful analysis of Q traced a polemic against "this generation" (=Israel) and an openness to gentiles as important themes in the redaction of Q.[12] The prominence of these themes has led some to assert that Q had abandoned the mission to Israel and that the gentile mission was in full swing, so that a provenience in Syria (Antioch?) seemed quite likely.[13] Others, however, have noted that these themes in Q do not encourage a mission to Gentiles, and that the use of Gentiles as positive examples represents an attempt to shame Jews into repentance, and not to bring Gentiles into the community.[14] In this case, a Palestinian provenance or a "Jewish-Christian milieu" is more appropriate.[15] The problem with this method, aside from the disputes over Q's theology, is the lack of precision with regard to the concrete world of antiquity and the questionable usefulness of the heuristic division between Palestinian Jewish Christianity and Hellenistic Gentile Christianity.[16]

Rather than focusing on a single theme and more attuned to social-historical details, Gerd Theissen examined several pervasive themes in Q and identified other groups with whom the Q community was in contact. Underlying the almost ambivalent role of Gentiles, the prominence of "Israel," and the conflict with the Pharisees, a "Palestinian-centered perspective" can be detected, present in other pericopes as well. For all its merit, Theissen's vague localization does not live up to the recognition of regional diversity within Palestine: the Golan, Upper Galilee, Lower Galilee, Samaria, Judea, and the coastal strip. Each has significantly different local histories, vastly different interactions with Gentiles, and varying degrees of Pharisaic

---

12. Dieter Lührmann, *Die Redaktion der Logienquelle* (WMANT 33; Neukirchen-Vluyn: Neukirchener Verlag, 1969).

13. See, e.g., Helmut Koester, who takes the mention of Tyre and Sidon in Q 10:13–15 as indicative of a gentile mission in these two cities, "The Sayings of Q and Their Image of Jesus," in *Sayings of Jesus: Canonical and Non-Canonical. Essays in Honor of Tjitze Baarda* (eds. William Petersen et al.; Leiden: Brill, 1997) 154 [137–54].

14. Paul Meyer, "The Gentile Mission in Q," *JBL* 89 (1970) 405–17; Uwe Wenger, *Der Hauptmann von Kafarnaum* (WUNT ser. 2, vol. 14; Tübingen: J. C. B. Mohr [Paul Siebeck], 1985) 296–334; and Christopher M. Tuckett, *Q and the History of Early Christianity: Studies on Q* (Edinburgh: T. & T. Clark, 1996) 393–404.

15. Athanasius Polag, *Die Christologie der Logienquelle* (WMANT 45; Neukirchen-Vluyn: Neukirchener Verlag, 1977) 30; Dieter Zeller, "Redaktionsprozesse und wechselnder 'Sitz im Leben' beim Q-Material," in *Logia: Les Paroles de Jesus—The Sayings of Jésus: Mémorial Joseph Coppens* (ed. Joel Delobel; BETL 59: Leuven: Peeters, 1982) 408–9 [395–409]; and Allison, *The Jesus Tradition in Q*, 53.

16. An alternative but even less convincing description of Galilee as highly Hellenized and syncretistic, and how Q's themes would fit in this setting, can be found in Burton Mack, "The Kingdom That Didn't Come," *SBLSP 1988* (ed. David Lull; Atlanta: Scholars Press, 1988) 608–635, and *The Lost Gospel: The Book of Q and Christian Origins* (San Francisco: HarperSanFrancisco, 1993) 51–68; similarly some proponents of a Cynic Jesus, Leif Vaage, *Galilean Upstarts: Jesus' First Followers According to Q* (Valley Forge, Pennsylvania: Trinity Press International, 1994) 10–15.

influence. To delimit a Palestinian provenance, therefore, makes an important contribution insofar as it narrows the boundaries of Q's locale, but it adds little to our understanding of the Q community's particular context. Theissen's study is a poignant reminder that no single theme in the Q community's symbolic world can be decisive in locating Q; instead, the various groups with which the Q community's symbolic world interacted and the constellation of themes in it must fit into a particular geographical setting.

Another approach, which raises often-neglected issues, inquires about the likely location in the concrete world of scribes responsible for articulating a document with Q's genre and language. Again, diverse opinions exist. On the one hand, Richard Horsley has described the content of Q as an attempt to revitalize Galilean village communities in opposition to Judean-sponsored Pharisaic control. This opposition is seen in the covenantal nature of the sermon (Q 6:20–49) and in the prophetic critique along the lines of the Northern Israelite prophets (e.g., Q 7:24–25; 13:28–29; 13:34–35; and 22:28–30), so that the symbolic universe of the Q community fits that of Galilean village culture.[17] In contrast, without postulating that Q was in any way a legal or regulatory text in its genre, Ronald Piper has noted the presence of legal language and patterns in several of Q's sayings clusters.[18] In spite of their familiarity with the local contractual or legal system, Piper notes how Q as a whole seems to reject it in favor of the providence of God and the hospitality of others.[19] Some of the people behind Q, at least at the level of its composition, were therefore scribes or administrators (Piper suggests in Galilee) who were familiar with local legal matters and who knew Greek. More broadly, Kloppenborg has contended that the sapiential elements in Q and particularly the counter-cultural ethos of blocks of Q, referring specifically to the formative stage, what he calls Q1, arose as part of social experimentation and dialogue among numerous scribes, so that the likeliest locale for Q would be in an urban sector, likely in the cities of Tiberias or Sepphoris, or in larger towns like Capernaum and Bethsaida, where a sufficiently dense scribal sector existed. Kloppenborg points to the important criteria in the concrete world, such as scribal and literacy levels as key considerations, and grapples with the serious question about a document written in Greek in Galilee.[20]

---

17. "Social Conflict in the Synoptic Sayings Source Q," in *Conflict and Invention*, 37–52. Horsley's idiosyncratic view of Galileans as Israelites, as opposed to Jews from Judea, underlies much of his thought, see *Galilee: History, Politics, People* (Valley Forge, Pennsylvania: Trinity Press International, 1995) and *Archaeology, History, and Society in Galilee: The Social Context of Jesus and the Rabbis* (Valley Forge, Pennsylvania: Trinity Press International, 1996).

18. Ronald Piper, "The Language of Violence and the Aphoristic Sayings in Q," in *Conflict and Invention*, 53–72.

19. Piper, "The Language of Violence," 65–66; Similarly William Arnal, "Gendered Couplets in Q and Legal Formulations: From Rhetoric to Social History," *JBL* 116 (1997) 75–94.

20. John Kloppenborg, "Literary Convention, Self-Evidence and the Social History of the Q People," 145–160. On the question of literacy levels and Q, see R.

This study intends to combine aspects of each approach in order to show that Q and the Q community can be located in Galilee, more specifically in the larger villages or towns on the northern shore of the Sea of Galilee. Three levels converge at each phase of the study. An analysis of the textual world of Q will be used to understand the social map of the Q community, from which Galilee as the concrete world behind Q can be deduced with reasonable certainty. In short, there are no compelling reasons to move Q outside Galilee; in fact, a better understanding of Galilee makes it a more certain fit for the Q community's locale. This study relies on a description of Galilee, which will be shown to be the concrete world of the Q community, generated from the archaeological record.

Although important features of an archaeologically sensitive portrayal of Galilee will be discussed at appropriate subsequent points, a brief sketch of several key points is in order at present. First, with regard to ethnicity, the archaeology of settlement patterns indicates that Jews from Judea settled Galilee under Hasmonean rule in the first century B.C.E. Galileans were thus descendants of Judeans and in an area on the periphery of the Temple complex, and at the same time surrounded by Gentiles, notably Syro-Phoenicians to the north and west, and the Decapolis to the east and south. The Galilean material culture was relatively homogenous with that of Judea with regard to ethnicity. Numerous identity markers, such as stone vessels, stepped pools, burial practices, and avoidance of pork, distinguished, on the one hand, Galilean Jews from their gentile neighbors, and, on the other hand, showed a close resemblance to characteristics of Jerusalem's material culture.

Second, with regard to socio-economic structures, the archaeological record shows a significant shift in demographics, as Galilee was urbanized under Antipas's rule at the turn of the common era. By creating model Jewish *poleis* at Sepphoris and Tiberias, population growth was fueled in Galilee, and much of it concentrated in these two cities, which focused Galilee's agricultural demands on feeding their inhabitants and in supplying the ruling elites with the income from the land to sustain the urban building projects. Noticeably absent in these cities are indications of larger gentile populations or even pagan architectural features that would have overtly offended Jewish sensibilities. However, while the style might have placated the local population by avoiding statues and iconography, pagan temples or

Conrad Douglas, "Once Again, 'Love Your Enemies': Rhetorical and Social Scientific Considerations of a Familiar Passage," in *Conflict and Invention*, 12. For an entirely Greek-speaking milieu, see Zeller, "Redaktionsprozesse und wechselnder 'Sitz im Leben' beim Q-Material," 409; and Koester, "The Sayings Gospel Q," 154. Horsley, however, seems not to worry about a document promoting renewal at the Galilean village written in Greek, especially when elsewhere he states that nothing more than "pidgin Greek" would have been spoken in Galilean villages, *Archaeology, History, and Society in Galilee*, 171, esp. note 45.

public baths, the economic structures introduced by the need for higher rates of return and taxes burdened the villagers and rural inhabitants with increased demand for taxes in kind. This sustained the ruling and social elites' need to live in more luxurious Greco-Roman style and consume, albeit in modest amounts, imported goods. At the same time, the peasantry was pushed out of a mode of self-sufficiency in their agricultural practices to cash crops, and some were even driven off the land altogether. Marked social inequities were increasingly accentuated and visible in Galilean culture, between the urban elites and the rural land-holders and between the land-holding and the landless peasants.[21]

The social map of the Q community closely fits this description of Galilee, and there are no convincing reasons for locating Q outside of this context.[22] The place names in Q converge on the central location of Capernaum on the northwest shore of the Sea of Galilee; and the particular use of Tyre, Sidon, and Jerusalem in Q cohere with a Galilean perspective. More generally, the spatial imagery and topographical references in Q, especially the urban-rural imagery, react against some of the aspects of social life brought about by Herod Antipas's urbanization projects. Recurring themes in Q, such as disparagement over civilized life in contrast to nature and a negative view of wealth, and distrust in the system of justice, likewise resonate with this Galilean setting. The setting for conflict with opponents in Q is the household and the agora, and primarily against the Pharisees, and not around either the Temple or priests, appropriate in a Jerusalem setting; nor on either elements of pagan public life appropriate to the gentile cities. Finally, there is sufficient evidence for a community interested in writing down in Greek and passing on the teachings of Jesus in Galilee. The Q community can be placed with reasonable certainty in Galilee, in a social setting among the larger villages such as Capernaum, but with first-hand awareness even of the urban centers of Sepphoris and Tiberias.

## Basic Assumptions on the Nature of Q and Its Community

Prior to delving into the geographical locale of Q, some of the basic assumptions concerning the nature of Q and its community need to be stated. The first assumption about the nature of Q is that it was a literary document written in Greek.[23] Although the early sayings may well have been first articulated

---

21. A situation which certainly accelerated social banditry, though perhaps not to the degree suggested by Richard Horsley, *Jesus and the Spiral of Violence: Popular Jewish Resistance in Roman Palestine* (San Francisco: Harper and Row, 1987).

22. Polag, *Die Christologie der Logienquelle*, 31.

23. John Kloppenborg, *The Formation of Q: Trajectories of Ancient Wisdom Collections* (Philadelphia: Fortress, 1987) 41–88.

in Semitic, attempts to uncover a written Aramaic *Vorlage* behind Q have failed.[24] Q, therefore, must be located in an area where at least some level of Greek literacy existed.[25]

The second presupposition, arising from the nature of the teachings themselves, is that Q held a canonical status in a community. Q defines both ethical and theological boundaries to distinguish its group from the larger society, i.e., "this generation" (Q 7:31; 11:29; 11:31–32; and 11:51), as well as from other groups within their society, notably the Pharisees (with vehemence, Q 11:39–52) and Gentiles (somewhat derogatorily, Q 6:32–33 and 12:30).[26] Much of the material in Q addresses group concerns and needs. Interpersonal and even hierarchical relations are prominent: judging other members is condemned (Q 6:36–38); pupils are warned about blind guides and teachers (Q 6:39–40); hypocritical brothers are chastised (Q 6:41–42); communal prayer is assumed (Q 11:2–4, note especially τὸν ἄρτον ἡμῶν, "*our* bread"); the humble will be exalted (Q 14:11); scandalous behavior is prohibited for the sake of the weaker members (Q 17:1–2); and the forgiveness of brothers is expected (Q 17:3–4). Although on the surface Jesus instructs the itinerant radicals in the mission speech (Q 10:2–12), in its Q context the instructions are to the community concerning the treatment and criteria with which to evaluate the itinerants, as well as to encourage their support.[27] There is, therefore, no less reason to speak of a community behind Q than, say, of the Pauline communities or the Matthean Church.

A further assumption concerning the nature of Q is that the community collected and preserved traditional material and adapted it to their situation, whether by juxtaposing sayings, modifying them, or adding new ones. Q is a collection of both earlier and later material, however complex a process one might envision.[28] Obviously, the traditional material can be placed in a Galilean context, deriving from the historical Jesus, but whether the redactional elements and later sayings stem from a Galilean context is less certain. Sigfried Schulz divided Q into an earlier prophetic-enthusiastic set of sayings

24. Heinz Gunther, "The Sayings Gospel Q and the Quest for Aramaic Sources: Rethinking Christian Origins," in *Early Christianity, Q, and Jesus,* 41–76.

25. A point stressed by Koester in challenging the assumption that Q was redacted in Galilee, "The Sayings of Q," 138–39.

26. Catchpole, *The Question of Q,* 38; and Allison, *The Jesus Tradition in Q,* 53.

27. Zeller, "Redaktionsprozesse und wechselnder 'Sitz im Leben,'" 404; Mack, "The Kingdom that Didn't Come," 623; and Risto Uro, *Sheep Among the Wolves* (Helsinki: Suomailainen Tiedeakatemaia, 1987) 242. Similarly Allison, *The Jesus Tradition in Q,* 1–36.

28. The seminal work on a single redaction in Q was by Lührmann, *Die Redaktion der Logienquelle.* Subsequent studies have argued for multiple redactions, so Jacobsen, "The Literary Unity of Q;" and Sato, *Q und Prophetie.* Clusters of sayings sapiential in orientation and with compositional coherence have been

at home in a Palestinian setting, and a later set of sayings with sapiential tendencies that coped with the delay of the parousia at home in a gentile and Hellenistic setting.[29] He accounted for differences in theological tendencies and literary forms with a shift in the geographical setting, so that tradition history is equated with geography. The scheme, however, relies on the same old overly simplistic picture of Jewish Palestine versus the wider Hellenistic world, as well as presupposing that the delay of the parousia is the key criterion for assessing early Christian theology.[30] For different reasons, Paul Hoffmann supposed that the redaction of Q was also completed outside of Palestine. Because Q's redaction was marked by opposition to the nationalistic zealot war party in Palestine (e.g., Q 6:27–36; 10:4), it should be placed outside Palestine.[31] Hoffmann's studies are marked by a keen interest in the social setting and background to Q's theology, but in locating Q outside Palestine, he relies primarily on a single theme in Q, pacifism and an anti-war stance, and neglects an important element in the Galilean political scene during the war. If there were any place for pacifistic Jews, it was in Galilee, at Sepphoris, whose pro-Roman and pacifistic stance led to the epitaph *Eirenopolis*, city of peace, on its coins.[32] Members of the pacifist Jewish sect behind the Q document would certainly not flee to the Decapolis, gentile cities on the coast, or Syria, when the Jewish communities already there were persecuted, and even the pro-Roman Jews who fought alongside the Greeks at Scythopolis were slaughtered (*War* 2.467). While Schulz and Hoffmann rightly draw attention to the redactional elements in locating Q, they also illustrate that a crucial *desideratum* is an awareness and understanding of the concrete world in

---

described by Dieter Zeller, *Die weisheitlichen Mahnsprüche bei den Synoptikern* (FB 17; Würzburg: Echter, 1977); and Ronald Piper, *Wisdom in the Q Tradition: The Aphoristic Teaching of Jesus* (SNTSMS 61; Cambridge: Cambridge University Press, 1989). Kloppenborg proposed two distinct blocks of material, Q1 (sapiential) and Q2 (apocalyptic), *The Formation of Q*. The basic observations regarding the architecture of Q and the redactional tendencies are not in dispute, but rather the stratigraphy, sequence, and emphasis of these elements, see Kloppenborg, "The Sayings Gospel Q," 11–12.

29. Schulz, Q. *Die Spruchquelle der Evangelisten.*

30. Analogously, Heinz Schürmann attributed elaborations in the Son of Man sayings in Q to a shift from Palestine to Hellenistic soil, "Beobachtungen zum Menschensohn-Titel in der Logienquelle," in *Jesus und der Menschensohn. Für Anton Vögtle* (eds. Rudolf Pesch et al., Freiburg: Herder & Herder, 1975) 144–47 [124–47].

31. Paul Hoffmann, "The Redaction of Q and the Son of Man: A Preliminary Sketch," in *The Gospel Behind the Gospels: Current Studies on Q* (ed. Ronald Piper; Leiden: Brill, 1995) 196–98; based on Odil Hannes Steck's earlier suggestion that Palestinian Jewish Christians were not involved in the revolt, *Das gewaltsame Geschick der Propheten* (WMANT 23; Neukirchen-Vluyn: Neukirchener, 1967) 310.

32. Yaakov Meshorer, "Sepphoris and Rome," in *Greek Numismatics and Archaeology: Essays in Honor of Margaret Thompson* (Wettern, Belgium: Cultura Press, 1979) 159–71; and Colin M. Kraay, "Jewish Friends and Allies of Rome," *American Numismatic Society Museum Notes* 25 (1980) 53–57.

Galilee. A misunderstanding of Galilee's nature and character should not lead one to move Q out of Galilee.

The final assumption has to do with the genre of Q, which is important insofar as it sheds light on how the place names and spatial images were shaped into the textual world of Q and has implications for the social location of the scribes responsible for writing down Q. Whether one is inclined to follow James M. Robinson's suggestion and envision Q along the trajectory of ΛΟΓΟΙ ΣΟΦΩΝ or, like Mikagu Sato, see it as a collection of prophetic oracles, Q was a collection as opposed to a narrative or other genre with a plot or settings. Even though Q's architecture shows some patterns through catch-word connections, thematic groupings, and elaborated themes, the whole reveals no sustained sequential coherence. True, the opening temptation authenticates Jesus and perhaps sets a mood by placing it in the wilderness (Q 3:3), but there is no narrative world sustained throughout the document. Put simply, Q lacks a literary design with a concomitant narrative world. The place names and spatial references are not strategically placed to alter the mood as one reads through Q, nor do they move the plot along, nor do they in general create an imaginary setting as is the case in Mark. Since it is a collection, the textual world of Q, therefore, closely reflects the Q community's social map.

An examination of the spatial references in Q's sparse narrative sections that introduce the sayings reveals its lack of a coherent authorial or editorial design. John the Baptist appears *ex nihilo*, as it were, surrounded by "all the region of the Jordan" in Q 3:3.[33] After the Baptist material, Q 4:1 opens the next scene with Jesus being led up into "the wilderness."[34] This is the only proper spatial connection between pericopes in all of Q indicating movement from one place to another, since the wilderness is, in terms of altitude, "up" (ἀνά) from the Jordan rift valley. But even this transition is accidental, since the verb ἀνάγω ("to go up") in connection with the wilderness or interior of a country is a common Greek idiom. Based on the Greek spatial imagination that the coastal strip of the Mediterranean littoral constituted

---

33. The ἐν τῇ ἐρήμῳ in Luke 3:2 and Matt 3:1 comes from Mark 1:4. But the πασα ἡ περίχωρος τοῦ Ιορδάνου / πασᾶν τὴν περίχωρον τοῦ Ἰορδάνου likely derives from Q, though the syntax is uncertain, as Kloppenborg has convincingly argued, "City and Wasteland," 149f, see also Chester C. McCown, "The Scene of John's Ministry and its Relation to the Purpose and Outcome of his Mission," *JBL* 59 (1940) 113–131.

34. Hoffmann and Robinson of the International Q Project correctly reconstruct Q 4:1 with the Matthean verb (ἀνήχθη) and preposition (εἰς). The verb has its only occurrence here in Matthew, and Luke is responsible for shaping the introduction to depict Jesus in the wilderness, where he is guided by the Spirit *Q 4:1–13, 16 The Temptation of Jesus, Nazara* (Documenta Q; ed. Christopher Heil; Leuven: Peeters, 1996).

the civilized world, in the Greek language movement to the interior—seen as "wilderness"—implied "going up."[35] After opening in the desert, there is a double change of scene in the temptation story: Jesus is transported into Jerusalem (Q 4:9),[36] and then to a place from which he can see all the kingdoms of the world.[37] The only other spatial reference in a narrative section occurs in Q 7:1 to introduce the story of the Centurion: "He entered Capernaum." The oddly spelled Nazareth (Ναζαρά) in both Luke 4:16 and Matt 4:13 is perhaps a vestige of a short narrative transition in Q but the uncertainty of its syntax highlights the lack of any coordinated spatial movement by the framers of Q.[38] There is no sense of movement in terms of a narrative plot in Q: John simply appears preaching in the regions of the Jordan; Jesus is authenticated in his temptation in the wilderness, then delivers the sermon, then enters Capernaum, then a series of sayings clusters or speeches appears.

Since the few narrative sections of Q are obviously the work of the Q community and cannot be placed on the historical Jesus' lips, they present by inference the unreflective spatial imagination of the Q community, in which an act of Jesus can only be located in one place, Capernaum of the Galilee. The other places where Jesus appears are outside of Galilee: the wilderness, the mountain, and Jerusalem, but these are places to which he is brought. The Holy Spirit leads Jesus to the wilderness, and the devil brings him to Jerusalem and atop the mountain.[39] Based on the genre of Q as a collection, the textual world closely reflects the social map of the Q community.

## Place Names in the Sayings

As often noted with regard to Q's place names, the region around Capernaum on the northern shore of the Sea of Galilee suggests itself as the

---

35. See for example, Herodotus and Xenophon's descriptions of travels from the coast of Asia Minor into the interior (*An.* 2.6.1). ἀναγεῖν also has the basic meaning "to embark on a journey," specifically of seafaring journeys (so Luke 8:22, and frequently in Acts).

36. Luke's Ἱερουσαλήμ is the preferred reading (so the reconstructions by Harnack, Luz, Polag, Schenk, and Zeller), as opposed to Matthew's τὴν ἁγίαν πόλιν.

37. Gundry demonstrates how the ὄρος ὑψηλὸν λίαν is very likely Matthew's attempt to style Jesus along Mosaic lines—the vocabulary is also distinctly Matthean, *Matthew*, 57.

38. In a reconstruction of Q 4:16 presented to the International Q Project at New Orleans, November 1990, Robinson suggests that Ναζαρά probably should be included in Q. See also James M. Robinson, "The Sayings Gospel Q," in *The Four Gospels, vol. 1 Festschrift Neirynck*, (eds. Frans Van Segbroeck et al.; University Press, 1992) 361–388.

39. Q's slim narrative elements show no interest in an itinerant or mobile Jesus—indeed, the narrative sections of Q alone give the impression of a sedentary Jesus: the few verbs of movement after Jesus enters Capernaum have John sending

provenance of the Q community.[40] It is not only the mention of Capernaum, Chorazin, and Bethsaida in Q 10:13–15, but their centrality in light of Q's other place names that suggests them as a locale for the Q community. The nine different places named in Q form a set of three concentric circles converging on Capernaum (Q 10:15). Within a short radius from Capernaum are Chorazin and Bethsaida (Q 10:13). The second of the concentric circles is formed by the twin cities of Tyre and Sidon to the north (Q 10:13–14) and Jerusalem to the south (Q 13:34). The final concentric circle forms the mythical boundaries of the Q community's social map made up of the epic cities of Sodom to the extreme south (Q 10:12) and Nineveh to the extreme north (Q 11:32).

Located on the northern end of the Sea of Galilee, Capernaum, Chorazin, and Bethsaida, a large town, small village, and small city, respectively, are the targets of Q's invective in Q 10:13–15. These three places are not only geographically at the center of the place names in Q, the vehemence of their condemnation points to their centrality and distinguishes them from the other six places in Q.[41] Their anonymity in antiquity contrasts with Sodom and Nineveh, Tyre and Sidon, and Jerusalem and Israel, each of which boasts a literary pedigree in the Hebrew Bible, ancient Near Eastern texts, and Greco-Roman literature. Chorazin, Bethsaida, and Capernaum lack such repute.

Chorazin is never mentioned by Josephus and appears only a few times in rabbinic texts. Dating to the third or fourth century C.E., *t. Mak.* 3:8, identifies it in a list of medium-sized villages. Archaeological excavations confirm the village's modest stature, and at its maximum growth in the Late Roman Period it was less than 10 hectares in size. What survived from this period are ruins of a few fieldstone basalt and mud built domestic complexes centered around an open market area and a later synagogue that was destroyed in the fourth century.[42] The Early Roman strata (50 B.C.E.–135 C.E.) are virtually nonexistent, testifying to the site's more modest and poor status in earlier times.

Capernaum is not mentioned in any literature prior to Q. In the later literature, it appears primarily in Christian texts relating it to Jesus' ministry, or in rabbinic texts identifying it as a home to *minim*, or heretics. Josephus does mention it, but only incidentally as the place to which he was taken

---

to Jesus his disciples (Q 7:19), John's disciples departing from Jesus (Q 7:24), and a questioner coming to Jesus (Q 9:57), each more indicative of Jesus' status than any narrative movement.

40. Haevner, *Q: The Sayings of Jesus*, 42–45; Sato, *Q und Prophetie*, 46; and Allison, *The Jesus Tradition in Q*, 53.

41. ". . . wegen der Unheilsankündigung (Lk 10,14 par) gewinnt hier das οὐαι viel deutlicher den Charakter der Ansage des Unheils (Merkmal 3.) als bei Lk 11,39–52 par," Sato, *Q und Prophetie*, 198.

42. Zeev Yeivin, "Chorazin," *NEAEHL* 1:301–4.

after falling off his horse (*Life* 403) and where a stream is located (*War* 3.519), but otherwise describes nothing of its role in the war, presumably because its larger neighbors, Tarichaeae/Magdala and Bethsaida, overshadowed it. Capernaum was a village of around 10 hectares and with a population of between 600 and 1,200 in the first century. The domestic architecture points to a modest existence: homes were constructed of basalt fieldstones with simple wooden door frames and thatch roofs. Inside, nothing of note was found other than agricultural implements and locally made coarse-ware cooking pots. There was no public architecture to speak of in the first century, as the synagogue and church at the site date to the Byzantine Period.

Bethsaida, on the other hand, appears more frequently in the literature, primarily associated with Herod Philip, who refounded and renamed it Julias in order to honor his Roman patron (*Ant.* 18.28). The archaeological excavations to date have revealed that the city was much more modest in stature and wealth than any of the other Herodian cities, including Philip's own Caesarea at the springs of the Jordan River. Bethsaida was mostly basalt, apparently with more hewn surfaces than at either Capernaum or Chorazin, but no marble sheeting has been found, nor columns, nor much evidence for fresco or mosaic. It was certainly Philip's "second city," and apparently was little more than a village on the upswing with the slightest Roman architectural veneer.

While anonymous to the wider Mediterranean and Near Eastern worlds, Capernaum, Chorazin, and Bethsaida were, judging by the acerbic tone of Q 10:13–15's woe oracle, of great prominence to the Q community.[43] The three sites' significance to the Q community is underscored in the past contrary-to-fact conditional phrase: "Because if the miracles done in you had been done in Tyre and Sidon, they would have repented long ago, sitting in sackcloth and ashes" (Q 10:13). The miracles alleged to have occurred in Chorazin and Bethsaida happened in the distant past, so that the community had been marginalized there for a while, or in their perspective had to put up with these villages' obstinacy for some time. Capernaum is singled out for special condemnation, perhaps because it was the site most closely tied to Jesus' ministry, or more likely because it remained an important center of Jesus' followers and the Q community.[44]

---

43. Bultmann notes that ". . . we have here a community formulation, since the sayings look back on Jesus' activity as something already completed, and presuppose the failure of the Christian preaching in Capernaum," *The History of the Synoptic Tradition*, 112 There are both redaction-critical and tradition historical grounds for considering Q 10:13–15 as late, see Sato, *Q und Prophetie*, 199f, 132; Lührmann, *Die Redaktion der Logienquelle*, 62–63; and Uro, *Sheep among the Wolves*, 110–116.

44. Capernaum is generally in the Gospels treated as the center of Jesus' ministry, see pp. 139–40. The Gospel traditions record no miracles in Chorazin, which only occurs here in Q 10:13. Bethsaida is also said to be the hometown of Philip,

Parenthetically, the command "to shake off the dust from your feet as you leave that city" (Q 10:11) should not be construed as evidence for the Q community's abandonment of or eviction from Capernaum, Chorazin, and Bethsaida. The composition of the mission speech links this early instruction to itinerants by redactionally adding the condemnation of the three cities (Q 10:13–15). This early kernel (Q 10:2–12) and the woes against the Galilean cities (Q 10:13–15) represent two distinct concerns: earlier instructions concerning itinerants and a later communal rationalization of rejection. One should not infer that the advice to itinerants would have been literally followed at a later date by the whole community. This is especially unlikely since the earliest archaeological evidence for Jesus' followers comes from Capernaum in the early second century, at the so-called House of Saint Peter. It seems probable that a community of Jesus' followers lived in Capernaum from the time of his ministry through the second century C.E., a generation or two after Q, and that it represented in part the community behind the document Q.

The next concentric circle of place names is formed by the Syro-Phoenician cities of Tyre and Sidon on the coast to the north and Jerusalem to the south.[45] The choice to juxtapose Tyre and Sidon with Bethsaida and Chorazin in Q 10:13–14 is designed to shame the Jewish villages.[46] Tyre and Sidon were scorned by the Israelite prophets (e.g., Is 23; Jer 25:22; Ez 26–29; Joel 3:4; Amos 1:9–10; Zech 9:2–3), but not as frequently as Egypt, Assyria, or Babylon. Yet, to Galileans, these cities were not merely relics in their epic imagination; they were still real cities in close proximity to Lower Galilee.

The cities of Tyre and Sidon were two of the wealthiest and most important ports on the Levantine coast. Archaeological evidence, especially recent studies on pottery and clay sources, have shown that Syro-Phoenician settlements

---

Andrew, and Peter (John 1:44, 12:21), and is where Jesus is said to have healed those in need of cures (Luke 9:10–12). He also is said to have traveled there (Mark 6:45), and even to have healed a man outside of the city (Mark 8:22–23).

45. Tyre (40 miles) is roughly half the distance (80 miles) that Jerusalem is from Capernaum. Even Sidon (50 miles) is closer to Capernaum than Jerusalem. Commentators do not mention the cities' proximity to Galilee, but cite exclusively the Hebrew Bible as determinative of Q's source, see Lührmann, *Die Redaktion der Logienquelle*, 63–63; Sato, *Q und Prophetie*, 199; and Uro, *Sheep Among the Wolves*, 163–164.

46. The distinction of Gentiles as "other" is apparent in several Q texts: the explicit reference to τα εθνη in Q 12:30; the contrast of Israel with the centurion in Q 7:1–10; and Q 13:28–30 are prominent examples, see Jacobson, "The Literary Unity of Q," 365–389. At times in Q Gentiles, those outside, are portrayed more favorably than Israel–those on the inside: In Q 11:31 the Queen of the South is favorably depicted since she came from the corners of the earth. In Q 13:29, people are described as coming from the east and west, the north and south to the eschatological banquet, while Q's intended audience will be locked out.

emanated from the cities of Tyre and Sidon and extended considerable distances inland. Along the Upper Galilean border, a series of villages, notably Kedesh, were part of the Tyrian-controlled Syro-Phoenician hinterland, and ceramic evidence has brought to light the existence of communities of Syro-Phoenicians all the way into the Huleh Valley and even into northern Golan, whose cultural and political orientation was Syro-Phoenician and toward the coast.[47] Furthermore, the majority of coins used in Galilee during the first century C.E. bore the Tyrian imprint; these coins were a daily reminder of Tyre's economic influence to Galilean commerce.[48] From Josephus and the New Testament we know that Tyre's wealth and economic stature cast a shadow over Galilee: imperial decrees warned Tyre against encroaching too far into Jewish lands in Galilee (e.g., *Ant.* 14.190–216), and on at least one occasion, in 43 B.C.E., Tyre seized considerable Galilean territory from the Jews under the tyrant Marion (*War* 1.238–39). Tyre was dependent on and hungry for the produce of Galilee (Acts 12:20), a point that the Galileans certainly resented whenever the ruling elite sold their produce to the highest bidder.[49]

Tyre and Sidon were thus not an arbitrary selection from the Hebrew prophets.[50] They were the closest gentile cities to Galilee that were part of their past epic traditions, and that were still part of their present social and economic situation, and as best we can tell, resented for economic and cultural reasons. In short, if Tyre and Sidon, seen as greedy and belligerent by Galileans, would have repented, how bad must these three villages have been?

The other place on Q's mid-ranged radius from Capernaum is Jerusalem,

---

47. Andrea Berlin, "From Monarchy to Markets: The Phoenicians in Hellenistic Palestine," *BASOR* 306 (1997) 75–88.

48. The interaction between Upper Galilee and Tyre were noted by Eric Meyers, "The Cultural Setting of Galilee: The Case of Regionalism and Early Judaism," *ANRW* 2.19.1 (1979) 700; and "Galilean Regionalism: A Reappraisal," in *Approaches to Ancient Judaism. Volume 5* (ed. William Green; Atlanta: Scholars Press, 1985) 123. On the numismatic evidence, see Richard Hanson, *Tyrian Influence in the Upper Galilee: Meiron Excavation Project 2* (Cambridge, Massachusetts: ASOR 1980). The presence of Tyrian coinage is in fact widespread across the entire Galilee, see Dan Barag, "Tyrian Currency in Galilee," *INJ* 6–7 (1982–83) 13; and the exemplary hoard from Migdal, Yaakov Meshorer, "The Hoard of Coins at Migdal," *'Atiqot* 11 (1976) 54–71.

49. Theissen, *The Gospels in Context*, 60–80.

50. Contra Sato, who describes the criterion of selection as "die Heiden vergangener Zeit (Tyrus, Sidon, Königin von Süden, Niniviten) . . .," *Q und Prophetie*, 199 note 283. Sato's limitation of restricting Q to a diachronic study linking it with the Hebrew Bible is apparent. Koester has suggested that the presence of Tyre and Sidon as a contrast implies that Q's provenance might be on the Southern Syrian coast, *The Sayings of Q*, 139–40, 154. While Koester is certainly right that the sayings of Jesus made their way rather early across a wide geographical area, there is no compelling evidence to locate it in Tyre or Sidon. If the saying presupposes knowledge of missionary activity in Tyre and Sidon, why could not Galilean followers of Jesus have known of this mission?

which occurs in only one saying, the double vocative of Q 13:34's lament.[51] Its tone and perspective reveal a certain distance from the city of Jerusalem. This distance has been noted in cosmic terms of the "supra-historical entity" of the addresser,[52] or described in temporal terms of the rejection of Jesus' message and messengers as a remote *fait accompli*.[53] But this distance perceived by commentators can also be explained in spatial terms in that the Q community viewed Jerusalem as remote on its social map. There is no illusion of Jerusalem holding a central place on the social map of the framers of Q, though the claim to centrality is obviously well known. Jerusalem is now, and has been, a pretentious city.[54] The oracle presents Jerusalem as a distant, spiritually barren city, and challenges Jerusalem's claim, implicitly mentioned in 35a, that it houses the divine presence and is the focal point of sacred geography. Instead, the Q community's social map envisions Jerusalem as forsaken and deserted.[55]

Q's relative disinterest in Jerusalem, in contrast to the synoptics and John, bears stressing. It is explicitly mentioned only twice: in the temptation (Q 4:9) and here in the lament (Q 13:34).[56] Q presents no detailed arguments over the place of the Temple, nor how priests should reform the sacrificial system centered on the Temple; there is little awareness of the inner workings of the Temple cult nor is there interest in it, apparently it is an abstraction on their social map.[57] Q simply points to the irony that Jerusalem's rejection of the prophets, up to and including Jesus, renders its

---

51. The rut of previous scholarship on the lament runs deep; for a discussion of the relevant issues and bibliography, see Steck, *Das Gewaltsame Geschick*, 40–58.

52. So Bultmann, *The History of the Synoptic Tradition*, 114.

53. So Sato *Q und Prophetie*, 159–60.

54. Steck has outlined the features and development of the Deuteronomistic view of history within texts of the second temple period, and has shown that the theme serves either to rationalize a recent catastrophe (such as 722, 586, or 167 B.C.E.) or to use a past catastrophe to inspire a repentant attitude in the present, *Das Gewaltsame Geschick*. But in Q 13:34–35 the theme of the rejected prophets is used simply to condemn Jerusalem.

55. This is of particular importance since Q envisions this desertion prior to the destruction of the Temple. The ερημος of Matthew may well be Q's reading, in light of the contrast set up between the wilderness and the city suggested by Kloppenborg, "City and Wasteland." The quotation "εὐλογημένος ὁ ἐρχόμενος ἐν ὀνόματι κυρίου" (LXX Ps 117:26), which had been resignified as an acclamation of the priests to the pilgrims at the Feast of Booths (*m. Sukk* 3.9), was added to mock the Jerusalemite religious activities: until Jesus and his message are recognized, the priests' performances will ring hollow.

56. Implicitly Jerusalem is also in mind in Q 11:51's description of bloodshed in the temple, but Jerusalem is hardly the "focus of unbelief and non-acceptance," so Kloppenborg, "City and Wasteland," 154.

57. In contrast to the literature from Qumran, such as the Temple Scroll, or Paul or the *Didache*.

claims to religious centrality a farce. But Jerusalem is not singled out as the Q community's primary antagonist, which is more broadly described as "this generation," and which can be found anywhere within Galilee.[58]

The final concentric circle, at the furthest radius from Capernaum, consists of Sodom to the far south and Nineveh to the far north. Both cities are on the periphery of Q's social map where reality blurs with fantasy. The city of Sodom, if it ever existed, was long gone by the time of the Q community. The city of Nineveh, though it still existed, was no longer of any social, political, or economic relevance to Galileans. These two places are invoked because of their mythical character; they are places unseen by the Q community, and hence can serve flat symbolic roles on their social map: Nineveh is the wicked gentile city that repented (Jonah 3), and Sodom is the inhospitable city that was destroyed (Gen. 19). That the Assyrians, who obliterated Galilee in 732 B.C.E., would now be compared favorably with this unrepentant generation, is highly ironic.

The use of distant ethnic groups to shame one's own group is a common *topos* in literature of the Greco-Roman period. Many geographical writers in antiquity envisioned an "inverse ethnocentric" scheme, in which peoples were more virtuous in proportion to their distance from the author's place of writing, with the author's audience the target of moral shame.[59] In Q their extreme distance from the community's locale gives the Ninevite and Sodomite, not the Ethiopian or Hyperborean as in Strabo, license to mock the people in the interior, in this case Israel. The two-fold "something greater . . . is here" (καὶ ἰδοὺ πλεῖον . . . ὧδε) in Q 11:31–32 places the focal point of Q's imaginative world on something greater than Solomon or Jonah, namely Jesus. Jonah's Galilean connections, whose tomb was venerated at Gath-Hepher only 3 km northeast of Nazareth, point to a Galilean-centered perspective.[60] The juxtaposition of Jesus and Jonah and his ties to Assyria are therefore particularly appropriate in a Galilean context.

Both mythical places are used to shame "this generation," identified elsewhere in Q as Israel (Q 7:9 and 22:30).[61] The Galileans were Jews and the geographical connotation of "Judean" (Ἰουδαῖοι) is appropriate for

---

58. Disagreeing with those who argue that the Pharisees performed the role of retainers for both the Temple and Herodian ruling apparatus, Anthony Saldarini, *Pharisees, Scribes and Sadducees: A Sociological Approach* (Wilmington, Delaware: Michael Glazier, 1988) 277–97; and Horsley, *Archaeology, History, and Society in Galilee.*

59. James Romm, *The Edges of the Earth in Ancient Thought* (Princeton: Princeton University Press, 1992), 47.

60. Theissen, *The Gospels in Context,* 43–46.

61. "This generation" occurs in Q 7:31, 11:29, 11:31, 11:32, and 11:51. There are no redactional clues to suggest that Q 22:28–30 is late since it coheres well thematically with the previous two sections, Lührmann, *Die Redaktion der Logienquelle,* 75. Though it does not seem to be redactionally connected with them, I presume, on tradition-historical grounds, that it is later.

Galileans given their historical roots in Judea. But it is notable that the term Ἰουδαῖοι never appears in Q, where instead "Israel" is cited. Without in any way implying that Galileans were not Jews, it is conspicuous that this term with southern connotations was avoided, and that the old term used also for the descendants of Abraham and later the Northern Kingdom was preferred.

An overview of the place names in Q highlights the centrality of Galilee. At the extremities lie the mythical cities of Sodom and Nineveh, the former to the far south, the latter to the far east; closer to the center lie the twin cities of Tyre and Sidon to the north and Jerusalem in the south; finally, centered around the hub of Capernaum lie the sites of Bethsaida and Chorazin. Not only do the geometry of the place names point to a Galilean setting, but so, too, do their particular uses and perspectives. The relative lateness of each of the sayings in which place names occur demonstrates the community's involvement in the selection of place names and in the shaping of the sayings themselves. Because the place names all belong to a later stage of Q's development, they are indicative of the Q community's social map, and, as was the case with Q's narrative material, not just reminiscences of Jesus' activities.

## Q's Spatial Imagery in a Galilean Context

Turning from the place names to the more general spatial imagery in Q, Galilee continues to suggest itself as the location from which it arose. The amalgamation of images and metaphors from agricultural, rural, natural, and urban life also makes sense in a first-century Galilean setting. Agricultural metaphors pervade Q's sayings from beginning to end. At the outset, John the Baptist scorches his audience with the plea to "bear fruit worthy of repentance," "for the ax is at the root" (Q/Luke 3:8–9), and the coming one with his winnowing fork will clear the threshing floor, put the grain in the silo, but burn the chaff (Q 3:17). Jesus also employs agricultural imagery in Q: the standard measure, customary in produce markets of agrarian economies (μέτρον, Q 6:38); healthy trees bearing good fruit (figs and grapes), rotten trees bearing bad fruit (Q 6:43–44); and the plowing of fields (Q 9:62). The mission speech begins by comparing Jesus' followers to workers at harvest time: "The harvest is large, but the workers are few . . ." (Q 10:2). Other allusions to agriculture dot the sayings of Jesus: grain baskets for storing grain (μόδιος, Q 11:33); spices easily grown on small plots of land (Q 11:42);[62] field hay used for cheap fuel (Q 12:28); grain of mustard

---

62. The μόδιος was also a common dry unit of measure, and not only a device for storage (see Plutarch, *Demitrius* XXXIII). Ulrich Luz has refuted Joachim Jeremias' claim, based on a cursory reading of Strack-Billerbeck's citations, that the μόδιος was a common device used to put out lamps, *Abba* (Göttingen:

seeds and small plots or gardens (Q 13:19, 17:6); cultivated fields (Q 14:18); the salting of dunghills (Q 14:35); millstones (Q 17:2); a sycamine tree (Q 17:6);[63] and the milling of grain together (Q 17:35).

With this high density of agricultural images, it is no wonder that Q, the Q community, not to mention Jesus himself, has frequently been located in an entirely rural environment, and that Galilee has been suggested as such. But agriculture was the basis of the entire Roman economy, and the primary industry of even the largest provincial cities. As Galilee was urbanized, more extensive and more efficient agricultural practices were developed that brought benefits to the elite but put pressure on the peasantry.[64] Douglas Edwards is surely correct when he writes of the importance of agriculture to the ancient economy in general that "agricultural images in the New Testament, therefore, may neither prove nor disprove a rural provenance."[65] Rather than simply tallying the agricultural images, their relation to other spatial imagery and themes, and impact of the recent building of Sepphoris and Tiberias on Q's spatial imagery needs examination.[66]

A portion of the agricultural images in Q are associated with activities that take place or items that exist in an exclusively rural area: cutting down trees (Q 3:8–9), winnowing and burning of chaff (Q 3:17), field hay (Q 12:28), fields (Q 9: 62 (?), 14:18), salting dunghills (Q 14:35), and sycamine trees (Q 17:6). But such activities or items could be done in or in proximity to Galilee's two major cities, Sepphoris or Tiberias, or the major villages of Galilee, such as Capernaum. Furthermore, numerous agricultural items cited in Q can be associated with the larger villages and cities themselves. Granaries are mentioned in Q 3:17 and Q 12:24; sizable storage chambers

---

Vandenhoeck & Ruprecht, 1966) 102. The μόδιος was, rather, a ubiquitous item in agrarian settings chosen to highlight the absurdity of the illustration, *Das Evangelium nach Matthäus (1–7)* (Zürich: Beninger, 1985) 221, esp. note 12.

63. συκαμίνος is preferred to Matthew's ὄρος. The usual Greek orthography for sycamine tree is συκομορος, which may explain the Matthean ὄρος. The tree was common to the coastal plain and lower regions of the Levant and Egypt. There was even a port off Carmel called *Sykamina* (Josephus, *Ant.* 188).

64. See especially Douglas Oakman, *Jesus and the Economic Questions of His Day* (Studies in the Bible and Early Christianity 8; Lewiston, New York: Edwin Mellen, 1986); and David Fiensy, *The Social History of Palestine in the Herodian Period. The Land is Mine* (Studies in the Bible and Early Christianity 20; Lewiston: Edwin Mellen, 1991).

65. Douglas Edwards, "First Century Urban/Rural Relations in Lower Galilee," in *SBLSP* 1988 (ed. David Lull; Atlanta: Scholars Press, 1988) 170.

66. Jonathan L. Reed, *Places in Early Christianity: Galilee, Archaeology, Urbanization, and Q* (Ph.D. diss., The Claremont Graduate School, 1994), 47–94; see also Douglas Edwards, "The Socio-Economic and Cultural Ethos of the Lower Galilee in the First Century: Implications for the Nascent Jesus Movement," in *The Galilee in Late Antiquity* (ed. Lee Levine; New York: The Jewish Theological Seminary of America, 1992), 65–66.

have been excavated in Sepphoris, and Tiberias also would have contained storage facilities for grain, and Josephus mentions imperial granaries else-where (*Life* 71, 118f). The standard measure mentioned in Q 6:38 and Q 11:33 was at home in an urban market setting, where grain or other produce was bought, sold, distributed, and taxed. Sepphoris and Tiberias were the major markets in Galilee, where the *agoranomoi* regulated weights and measures for the entire region.[67] Various spices and seeds are mentioned in Q 11:42, Q 13:18, and Q 17:6; seeds were commonly on sale at markets, and spices could easily be grown in small gardens or pots in the city. Milling grain with millstones is mentioned in Q 17:2 and Q 17:35. Millstones are ubiquitous in the Galilee; excavations at sites of all sizes, Capernaum, as well as Sepphoris, have uncovered millstones.

There is even a series of clues in the agricultural images that betrays a more urban perspective on agrarian practices. The phrasing of the mission speech: ". . . beg the lord of the harvest to send out (ἐκβάλῃ, Q 10:2) workers into his harvest," recalls the practice of the urban poor, who went out into the fields as day laborers in exchange for food during the harvest season.[68] While small farmers or peasants in hamlets would envision workers being brought out to the harvest, the phrase in Q betrays the perspective of those within a city or large village, who envision the harvest as a place to which one is "cast out."

An urban or non-peasant perspective underlies the use of the impersonal passive to describe some agricultural practices in Q. Relatively rare in Greek, the impersonal passive occurs twice in Q:[69] for the picking of fruit in Q 6:44, ". . . they do not gather figs from thorns . . ."; and for the salting of soil and dunghills in Q 14:35, ". . . if salt becomes insipid, . . . they throw it away."[70] The use of the impersonal passive describing these two agricultural practices is striking. The saying about figs and thorns—"they do not gather" (Q 6:44)— is surrounded by passages addressing the audience with the second person:

---

67. Yaakov Meshorer, "The Lead Weight," *BA* 49 (1986), 16–17; and Shagra Qedar, "Two Lead Weights of Herod Antipas and Agrippa II and the Early History of Tiberias," *INJ* 9 (1986–87) 29–30.

68. See Peter Garnsey, *Famine and Food Supply in the Graeco-Roman World* (Cambridge: Cambridge University Press, 1988) 44–45; Ramsey MacMullen, *Roman Social Relations* (New Haven: Yale University Press, 1974) 42, esp. note 44.

69. James H. Moulton, *A Grammar of the N. T. Greek, Vol. I, Prolegomena*, 3rd ed. (Edinburgh: T & T Clark, 1980) 58f; and Archibald T. Robertson, *A Grammar of the Greek New Testament in Light of Historical Research* (Nashville: Broadman, 1934) 820.

70. The Lukan reading κοπρίαν is preferred (so also the International Q project *JBL* 110 [1991] 498), although the point could easily be made with the Matthean reading as well. Dung heaps (κοπρία) were commonly located on farms in hamlets and rural villages of Palestine where livestock were kept, and salt was commonly used to check the fermentation of the dung heap, Eugene P. Deatrick, "Salt, Soil, Savior," *BA* XXV (May 1962): 41–47.

"Why do you see the speck that is in your brother's eye . . ." (Q 6:41–42) precedes it, and it is followed by "Why do you call me 'Lord, Lord'," (Q 6:46). The saying on savorless salt using the impersonal passive "they throw it out" is preceded by a saying on the conditions of discipleship, "Whoever finds his life" (Q 17:33), and is followed by a parable which is personalized with a second person rhetorical question.[71] Q tends to personalize its parables or sayings with the second person form or address, and uses the impersonal passive only for agrarian practices of the countryside, activities that "they" do. Thus, this set of images indicates that, although the sayings show a familiarity with agricultural practices, as one would expect in an agrarian society, some indicate a scribal perspective that seems at home in the larger villages or cities of Galilee.

The blend of specifically urban images or metaphors in Q also fits neatly in Galilee. The very word city, πόλις, occurs at least three times in Q, when the mission speech assumes that the followers of Jesus will go to cities (Q 10:8–11), and where the Q community expects to encounter resistance. Also mentioned are royal palaces (Q 7:25); market places (Q 7:32, 11:43); plazas (Q 10:10, 13:26, 14:21);[72] a collection of rooftops (Q 12:3); judges and prisons (Q 12:57–59); a city gate (πύλη, Q 13:24);[73] city banquets (Q 14:16–24);[74] and banks or moneychangers (τράπεζα, Q 19:23).[75]

Two specifically urban institutions are portrayed as the forum for the Q community's encounter with opposition in Q: the markets and courts.[76] Q 7:31–35 links the opposition to both Jesus and John to the market place or agora. This generation, considered the opponent by the Q community, is compared to children seated in the agora, playing the flute and singing dirges, with which both John the Baptist and Jesus are out of step (Q 7:32, note that according to Josephus, John was liked by the people, but not Herod and Herodians). The imagery in this passage points to the scene one would expect at the vibrant agora of Sepphoris or Tiberias, or possibly the larger villages like Magdala and Capernaum. It is a place where children sit and play, hire their musical services for parties or dirges, where ascetics, gluttons,

---

71. τί ὑμῖν δοκεῖ . . . Matt 18:12 or Luke's "Which one of you" (τίς ἄνθρωπος εχ υμων, Luke 15:4).

72. πλατεια or διεξόδος; 10:10 and 13:26 are in Luke only, but in 14:21, Matthew has διεξοδους, the place where the streets exit outside the city, see BAGD, 194 for examples.

73. Matthew only, Luke has θύρα.

74. It is clear from the parable in both Matthew and Luke that the banquet is given in a city, since the servants are asked later to invite those outside the city.

75. Matthew has τραπεζίτοι, bankers, Luke has τράπεζα.

76. On the urban imagery in Q 7:31–35 and the connection between the agora and the court in Greco-Roman cities, see the insightful article by Wendy Cotter, "The Parable of the Children in the Market-Place, Q (Lk) 7:31–35: An Examination of the Parable's Image and Significance," Novum Testamentum 29 (1987) 289–304.

drunks, tax collectors, and sinners pass through.[77] It is also, however, a place where the Q community is in conflict, and there is no need to look beyond Galilee for these particular urban images.

The social map of the Q community views another urban institution, the judicial system, with reservation. Although justice could be meted out on a local level in rural areas, the judicial concerns in Q reflect more formal issues to be resolved at a higher level, such as the courts of Sepphoris and Tiberias: suits, litigation, judges, prisons, magistrates, and rulers. Ronald Piper has pointed out the concern to avoid litigation present in Q 6:27–36, and a cluster of sayings in Q 12 reinforces the vulnerability felt by the Q group toward the courts. The question of how to deal with judicial institutions is acute in Q, and Q's answer, couched in "the language of legal and contractual procedures, seems to be 'Avoid the courts at all costs.'"[78]

This advice is explicit in Q 12:57–59, which concludes a cluster of sayings showing the judicial vulnerability perceived by the Q community: Settle quickly with a plaintiff, or he will hand you over to the judge, the judge to the bailiff, and the bailiff will throw you in prison. The view of justice is somber: "You will not get out of there until you have paid your last penny" (Q 12:59). Q 12:4–7 encourages followers of Jesus not to fear those able to kill the body but not the soul, a theme carried over in the exhortation to fearless confession (Q 12:8–9) and in the warning against blasphemy of the spirit (Q 12:10). Members of the Q community are furthermore encouraged not to worry when they are brought before rulers and magistrates (Q 12:11–12),[79] which demonstrates that the courts were not viewed from a distance; they were part of the real world of the Q community. This advice is particularly appropriate in Galilee under Antipas's reign. While Josephus lauds Philip as "a person of moderation and quietness" in addition to being a fair judge (*Ant.* 18.106–7), Antipas is caricatured as a more harsh and ambitious ruler.

Beyond these two urban features, the market and the courts, a general dissatisfaction with urbanization in general can be seen in the recurring theme in Q of "going out" as the first step to belief.[80] John's message of repen-

---

77. On descriptions of children, musicians, and street performers in cities' agoras, see William Harris, *Ancient Literacy* (Cambridge: Harvard University Press, 1989) 226; Andrew D. Booth, "Aspects of the Circulator by Persius and Horace," *Greece and Rome* 26 (1980) 166–169; and Alexander Scobie, *Aspects of the Ancient Romance and Its Heritage* (Meisenheim: Hahn, 1969) 27–29.

78. Piper, "The Language of Violence," 53–60.

79. Matthew has conflated Q and Mark here, so that since he has already mentioned the "governors and kings" in Matt 10:17, he deletes the "rulers and authorities" here.

80. A theme first articulated for Q by Kloppenborg, "City and Wasteland," 154: "One must 'go out' to see John and to hear his warnings; and the cities are not where Q expects to find a favorable hearing for the messages of John or Jesus."

tance is first encountered in the wilderness region of the Jordan (Q 3:2), and those coming out to hear him are said to have fled to him (Q 3:7). The same idea is repeated in Q 7:24–26 with the repeated rhetorical question "What did you go out to see?" John is found outside the cities in the wilderness, and he is explicitly contrasted with the urban elites, who were luxuriously clothed and living in palaces. Since the "shaken reed," refers to one of Herod Antipas's early numismatic emblems, then he is the one luxuriously dressed, and the city under attack is Tiberias, his new capital.[81] Salvation outside the city is also a theme in the banquet parable (Q 14:16–24), when the servant is told to go outside the city to invite guests after the wealthy urbanites rebuff the invitation.[82]

The particular amalgamation of urban imagery in Q provides considerable information about the Q community's social map and perception of cities. None of the amenities that urban life offered, such as the baths or the theater, appear in Q. Although Q betrays an awareness of the city, the Q community does not seem to have scaled the social hierarchy of the city very high. Rather, the blend of images portray a familiarity with those features of and places in the city open to the lower classes in the city and to peasants coming from outside the city: gates, plazas, streets, the agora, banks, and in the worst case, courts and prisons.[83] The blend appears particularly appropriate in a Jewish urban setting as opposed to a predominately gentile city, since issues such as nudity and public bathing, iconography and statues, temples and sacrificial meat, or eating with Gentiles are completely absent. At the same time, imagery appropriate for Jerusalem, such as the Temple, pilgrim concerns, and contact with priests, is entirely absent, so that familiarity with Galilean cities seems most likely.

The perception of the market place and courts, indeed the city as a whole, was filled with tension. Q also presents an anxious image of the civilized order as a whole: One can fall from the height of temples (Q 4:9), houses can be swept away by torrential floods if not built properly (Q 6:48), roofs are not worthy to cover Jesus (Q 7:6), divided houses collapse (Q 11:17), houses can be plundered if not guarded (Q 11:21–22), demons call their

---

81. Theissen, *The Gospels in Context*, 26–42; first published as "Das 'schwankende Rohr' (Mt 11,7) und die Gründungsmünzen von Tiberias," *ZDPV* 101 (1985) 43–55.

82. The identification of the city with Jerusalem in Matthew's version is his allegory. In Q there was no such Jew-gentile theme, only a story about a banquet being opened up to outsiders, specifically those outside the city, who, from the parable's social criticism, are seen as inferior by society.

83. Such banquets are criticized as a place where the social elite collect, and do not seem to be part of the Q community's social setting (Q 11:43, Q 14:16–24), see here Amy-Jill Levine, "Second Temple Judaism, Jesus, and Women: Yeast of Eden," *Biblical Interpretation* 2 (1994) 8–33.

abodes "houses" (Q 11:24), murderers build tombs (Q 11:48), the inner temple is filled with blood (Q 11:51), and homes are particularly vulnerable to crime at night (Q 11:39–40).

The need to flee the city and apprehension of civilized life is complemented on Q's social map by an appreciation of nature as the arena for divine disclosure.[84] In addition to the tension associated with the city and urban features, Q tends to ascribe to the civilized order danger, chaos, and an absence of the divine. Yet floral, faunal, and symbols of nature are often used to illustrate Q's message. Q tends to ascribe to these aspects of the natural order a sense of comfort, serenity, and divine revelation.

Images from nature are frequently embraced to express Q's vision. Nature is preferred as a simple, serene, and orderly arena: God can raise up children to Abraham from rocks (Q 3:8); trees are praised for their honesty, you can tell them by their fruit (Q 6:44); Jesus even surpasses foxes and birds in their need for a dwelling place (Q 9:58); the simplicity and natural beauty of ravens, lilies, and grass are a model for self-sufficiency (Q 12:22–32); meteorological phenomena can be plainly read (Q 12:54–56); and the biological growth of plants is compared to the kingdom of God (Q 13:18–19); in fact, the uncultivated wild mustard seed is portrayed as threatening cultivated and ordered agriculture.

Many of Q's passages bear a striking resemblance to the bucolic aspects of many Roman authors, who, as Rome grew in the late republic and Augustan era, began to praise the virtues of rural life and the countryside.[85] As Rome expanded and as Augustus erected more facades and constructed more buildings, numerous authors in Rome struck a chorus on the moral superiority of the rural life, with its nearness to nature.[86] Their turn to nature must be understood in terms of their frustrations with city life in Rome.

While no genealogical relationship between such Roman texts and Q is possible, the bucolic Roman poets and authors, by analogy, illuminate a not uncommon social phenomenon apparent in Q as a reaction to urbanization in Galilee, on an admittedly minuscule scale. Like these bucolic Roman poets and authors, Q observes the city or even civilized society from a tense and anxious perspective. It is a dangerous place where hostilities are encountered. This perspective fits the cultural developments of Galilee in the first century C.E., when Galilee was urbanized with the building of Sepphoris and Tiberias in its midst, which led to social distress and tensions.

---

84. On this, see Crum, *The Original Jerusalem Gospel*, 49–63; and Kloppenborg, "City and Wasteland," 154.

85. For a list of the appropriate passages, see John Stambaugh, *The Ancient Roman City* (Baltimore: The Johns Hopkins University Press, 1988), 45–47, 61–66.

86. See especially Varro's *On Agriculture*, Lucretius' *De Rerum Natura*, and Vergil's *Eclogues* and *Georgics*.

## Themes and Theology in Q

We return to briefly examine the major theological themes in Q to see if they, too, like the place names and spatial imagery, fit into a Galilean context. The very description of the new community envisioned by Jesus as the Kingdom of God contrasts with Roman sponsored Herodian rule in Galilee. Jerusalem seems distant, and the conflicts in Q are not centered around the Temple or Temple issues, but take place primarily in a household and family setting, or in public in the agora. The agora is also the locale where the Q community caricatures Pharisaic behavior (Q 11:43). The Pharisees are caricatured as eager to climb the social hierarchy at banquets, synagogues, and in the agora as well. They "love . . . greetings in the marketplace" (Q 11:43). In Q, the conflict between the Pharisees and the Q community does not have its primary locus in the synagogue, which is only mentioned here. Rather the conflict between the Pharisees and the Q community seems to be located in an urban setting, at banquets and in the market place, and focuses on social status. In several of the woes, banquet and market imagery reappear in the criticism of the Pharisees: in the preparation of cups and dishes prior to eating (Q 11:39–41), in the loading up of goods or merchandise (Q 11:46), and in the setting aside of purchased spices (Q 11:42). The agora in Q is a place of tension and opposition, implying that in the everyday life of the Q community, the agora was frequented.

The conflict in Q is part of an inner Jewish dialogue, in which the positive use of Gentiles is designed really to elicit a response from other Jews. Issues that would have arisen had Gentiles been a presence within the community, or even frequent inside the social-setting aspects of life are absent; no concerns over food restrictions or problems relating to pagan temples as in Paul can be found in the sayings source. The setting of Q is entirely Jewish as one would expect in Galilee.

To summarize: An analysis of the place names in Q strongly suggests the importance of Capernaum to the Q community. The remaining place names, especially Chorazin and Bethsaida; the negative comparison with Tyre; and a suspicious view of Jerusalem—all confirm a Galilean perspective. The particular amalgamation of agricultural and urban imagery, especially the positive examples of nature, make good sense, in the recently urbanized Galilee. Although I would not go so far as to locate the entire Q community in the cities of Sepphoris and Tiberias, themselves based on the spatial imagery, contact with these cities—illustrated primarily in the market and judicial imagery—on the part of the Q community is certain. While perhaps more at home in larger Galilean villages such as Capernaum, or other sites on the north shore of the lake, the Q community, through their frequent visits, looked at the major cities of the Galilee with some apprehension.

# CHAPTER 7

# The Sign of Jonah:
# Q 11:29-32 in its Galilean Setting*

Exegetes have often pondered the referent in the Sign of Jonah pericope (Q 11:29–32), disputed the authenticity of the son of man title, and outlined the literary relationship between the synoptic passages of Matt 12:38–42, 16:1–4, Mark 8:11–12, and Luke 11:29–32.[1] Since lengthy bibliographies have been generated on this passage, one hesitates to add another entry, but the neglect of Galilee as the setting for this saying in the secondary literature leads to its reconsideration here.

The purpose of this essay is to contribute to the discussion of the Sign of Jonah (Q 11:29–32) by raising the specifically Galilean connections of Jonah, and to sketch the other epic references in the Sayings Gospel Q in light of a Galilean background. The specific local conditions in which the saying originated and their implications for understanding the passage are the focus of this study; that is to say, we will look at the Galilean *Lokalkolorit* of the comparison between Jonah and Jesus.[2] This might not unlock the mystery of the Sign of Jonah's referent, but nevertheless can contribute to our understanding of the passage and its place in Q.

---

* This is a slightly revised version of a study first published as "The Sign of Jonah and Other Epic Traditions in Q," in *Rethinking Christian Origins: Festschrift for Burton Mack* (eds. Elizabeth Castelli and Hal Taussig; Philadelphia: Trinity Press International, 1996) 130–143.

1. For a complete survey of history of criticism, see Anton Vögtle, "Der Spruch vom Jonaszeichen," *Synoptische Studien: Alfred Wikenhauser zum siebzigsten Geburtstag* (München: Karl Zink, 1953) 230–277, and Richard A. Edwards, *The Sign of Jonah in the Theology of the Evangelists and Q* (SBT 2/18; London: SCM, 1971) 1–24.

2. Adopting the term and methods of Gerd Theissen, *The Gospels in Context: Social and Political History in the Synoptic Tradition* (Minneapolis: Fortress, 1991) 43–45.

The term *epic* refers to the way in which the Q community imagines a set of stories or symbols with respect to the past, as well as the community's imagination of how these stories and symbols relate to its present. The category epic shifts the focus from a textual examination of the Hebrew Scriptures to the selection of figures, events, and places found both within, alongside, and outside the Hebrew Scriptures.[3] By looking at the Sign of Jonah pericope under the rubric of epic, issues of community formation receive primary attention as the reason for the inclusion of Jonah and other epic figures by the compilers of Q is under investigation.[4]

Methodologically, this approach evades some of the thornier form-critical and redaction-critical concerns that have dominated recent debate on Q.[5] Although it was, of course, the application of redaction-critical observations that solidified the notion of a distinct and coherent theology for Q, instead of a description as a paraenetic supplement to the kerygma, the present concern is not with redactional layering within Q.[6] The linkage of redactional fissures or seams with genre or form-critical analyses (i.e., sapiential and apocalyptic) can be equated with social-history only at great risk.[7] Therefore, this study takes a compositional approach and considers Q in its final shape instead of attempting to examine the redactional elements of the sign of Jonah and other epic references in an effort to identify substrata of

3. The use of the term epic is indebted to the seminal work of Burton Mack, *Wisdom and the Hebrew Epic: Ben Sirach's Hymn of Praise to the Fathers* (Chicago: University of Chicago, 1985); see also Milton Moreland, "Jerusalem Imagined: Rethinking Earliest Christian Claims to the Hebrew Epic" (Ph.D. diss., Claremont Graduate University, Claremont, California, 1999).

4. The influence of Paul Hoffmann should be noted, whose work on Q has examined how traditions are adapted by the community to their particular situation (though he accentuates the geographical dimension to a lesser degree), see *Studien zur Theologie der Logienquelle* (NTAbh NF 8; Münster: Aschendorf, 1972); and the essays in *Tradition und Situation. Studien zur Jesusüberlieferung in der Logienquelle und den synoptischen Evangelien* (NTAbh NF 28; Münster: Aschendorf, 1995).

5. For the key issues, see John Kloppenborg's introduction to *The Shape of Q: Signal Essays on the Sayings Gospel* (ed. John Kloppenborg; Minneapolis: Fortress, 1994) 1–21.

6. First argued based on a distinct son of man christology by Heinz E. Tödt, *Der Menschensohn in der synoptischen Überlieferung* (Gütersloh: Gerd Mohn, 1959); and later convincingly demonstrated on redaction-critical grounds by Dieter Lührmann, *Die Redaktion der Logienquelle* (WMANT 33; Neukirchen-Vluyn: Neukirchner Verlag, 1969).

7. John Kloppenborg analyzed several (likely written) sapiential blocks to which several apocalyptic blocks were added, *The Formation of Q: Trajectories in Ancient Wisdom Collections* (Philadelphia: Fortress, 1987) 244–45; significantly, he stressed that "tradition history is not convertible with literary history," and assumed that independent earlier sayings might have been secondarily added to later materials. Burton Mack converted Kloppenborg's literary-critical observations into social history, i.e., the early Jesus movement was initially sapiential and later apocalyptic, *The Lost Gospel: The Book of Q and Christian Origins* (San Francisco: HarperSanFrancisco, 1993).

the Q community's history.[8] Unlike a diachronic analysis of the development from the historical Jesus through Q and into Matthew or Luke, the use of Jonah and other epic traditions will be examined in its synchronic context in Q. That is to say, the focus is on how divergent traditions are combined into a distinct and coherent whole in Q's final stage, and what the recurrent themes tell us about the community and the scribes who shaped it. Therefore, even though components of the Jonah saying might be traditional or even authentic, its final form in Q, along with other epic references in Q, will be examined with the Q community's compositional activities in mind, both choices of traditional material and redaction, in order to understand how they adapted the tradition to their situation.[9]

Their specific geographical locale was an important component of their situation. The Q community's distinct locality of Galilee, wherein the Sign of Jonah was adopted, is the interpretive question with which we seek to unlock their epic imagination. Locating a text in time and space as a prerequisite for exegesis lies at the very heart of the traditional historical-critical method. However, in light of the rich diversity within early Judaism now recognized by scholars of Christian origins, coupled with the importance of geographical regionalism as a factor in cultural developments, the spatial categories call for a more narrow definition. Instead of envisioning a very broad dichotomy between Palestinian Jewish communities and Hellenistic Gentile Christianity, smaller regions and their peculiarities need to be taken seriously. And unlike earlier attempts at localizing early Christian theological emphases, the Jerusalem pillars as opposed to the Antioch Hellenizers, efforts need to focus on the more general religious flavor and folklore of Galilee. Certainly Jewish groups and communities created or shaded their own particular reading of the Israelite epic in the context of their specific geographical locale. Attention to this geographical locale is important, as are the implications of its recent settlement by Hasmoneans in the first century B.C.E., its proximity to gentile cities and territories, and its distance from Jerusalem.

By focusing on the place in which the saying originated, the selection of Jonah—a Galilean prophet—as an analogy to Jesus, the strong indigenous

---

8. I do not assume that substantial portions of *Sondergut* belonged to Q, even conceding some of Heinz Schürmann's reminiscences and Petros Vassiliadis's criteria for including *Sondergut*, see Heinz Schürmann, "Sprachliche Reminiszenzen an abgeänderte oder ausgelassene Bestandteile der Redequelle im Lukas- und Mattäusevangelium," *Traditionsgeschichtliche Untersuchungen* (Düsseldorf: Patmos, 1968) 111–125; and Petros Vassiliadis, "The Nature and Extent of the Q Document," *NovT* 20 (1978) 49–73.

9. Theissen, *The Gospels in Context*, 205. There is a tendency to stress the secondary, redactional material at the expense of the formative materials that the redactors incorporated, see Sato, who describes entire blocks of materials as unmotivated or late additions to Q (e.g., 11:2–4, 9–13; 12:2–12, 22–31, 33–34), "The Shape of the Q Source," in *The Shape of Q*, 170–73.

tone of the passage becomes apparent. The linkage of Jesus to this local hero resonates with the portrayal throughout Q of the prophet as an ideal type or role model, a choice that implicitly provided a means to criticize the Jerusalem-based religious leadership and that specifically offered an avenue for the gentile mission.

## A Synoptic Comparison of the Sign of Jonah

The Sign of Jonah passage in Q, in which Jesus responds to a request for a sign, is preserved with a remarkably high degree of verbal agreement between Matt 12:38–42 and Luke 11:16, 29–32, and does not pose any serious problems in reconstructing its original form in Q. A similar response to a request for a sign appears in Mark 8:11–12, which helps assess the traditional nature of the request[10]:

| Matt 12:38–42 | Mark 8:11–12 | Luke 11:16, 29–32 |
|---|---|---|
| 38. Then some of the scribes and Pharisees responded: "Teacher, we wish to see a sign from you." 39. But responding he said to them: "An evil and adulterous generation seeks after a sign, and a sign will not be given to it except the sign of Jonah the prophet. 40. For just as Jonah was in the belly of the whale three days and three nights, so the son of man will be in the heart of the earth three days and three nights. 41. The Ninevites will stand up at the judgment with this generation and will condemn it, because they repented at the preaching of Jonah, and behold, something greater than Jonah is here! 42. The Queen of the South will rise up at the judgment with this generation and will condemn it, because she came from the ends of the earth to listen to the wisdom of Solomon, and behold, something greater than Solomon is here!" | 11. And the Pharisees came out and began to argue with him, seeking from him a sign from heaven, testing him. 12. And groaning to himself he said: "Why does this generation seek a sign? Truly I say to you, no sign will be given to this generation." | 16. But others, testing him, began to seek a sign from heaven from him. 29. As the crowds were crowding around he began to say: "This generation is an evil generation; it seeks a sign, and no sign will be given to it except the sign of Jonah. 30. For just as Jonah was a sign to the Ninevites, so will be the son of man to this generation. 31. The Queen of the South will rise up at the judgment with the men of this generation and will condemn them, because she came from the ends of the earth to listen to the wisdom of Solomon, and behold, something greater than Solomon is here! 32. The Ninevites will stand up at the judgment with this generation and will condemn it, because they repented at the preaching of Jonah, and behold, something greater than Jonah is here!" |

10. For a reconstruction of the Q reading, see Jon M. Asgeirsson and James M. Robinson, "The International Q Project Work Sessions 12–14 July, 22 November 1991," *JBL* 111 (1992) 500–508; pertinent arguments are found in Schulz, *Q. Die Spruchquelle der Evangelisten*, 250–57.

A synoptic comparison of the passages exposes Matthew's editorial activity in 12:40, where the first evangelist adds a quote from the Septuagint reading of Jonah 2:1, "in the belly of the whale three days and three nights."[11] This addition allegorically interprets the meaning of the sign as Jesus' own prediction of his resurrection and exhibits Matthew's tendency found elsewhere to introduce passages from the Hebrew Scriptures as messianic prophecies. This interpolation typifies Matthew's use of the Hebrew Scriptures as the key interpretive locus: according to Matthew this text must be searched carefully, since interpretive treasures therein are found even in short phrases.[12]

Matthew's scriptural addition does not, however, mark a radical deflection in the tradition's trajectory. Even at the level of Q's redaction or before, the scriptures were reflexively taken as recourse to interpret the sign of Jonah. Without referring to or citing a specific passage, verse, or phrase, the style of the Septuagint was nevertheless mimicked in Q's version of the Sign of Jonah at an initial stage. Darryl Schmidt has noted how the son of man saying in Q 11:30 parallels what he calls the "prophetic correlative" form of the LXX, in which the *protasis* (with a verb in the past or present tense) is joined to the *apodosis* (with a verb in the future tense) by "just as . . . so. . . ."[13] This form, modeled on a pattern frequent in the Septuagint, is prominent in Q (11:30, 17:24, 17:26, 17:28,30), and was also adopted by the scribes at Qumran to mimic a biblical style.[14] That the prophetic correlative in Q 11:30 is a later addition to Q 11:29 is also confirmed by Heinz Schürmann's observation that all of the son of man sayings in Q are to be found in a "Kommentarwort," that is to say they either interpret or explain sayings to which they are attached.[15] Thus, the son of man comparison in 11:30 is a later addition elaborating and commenting on 11:29.

---

11. Vögtle, "Der Spruch vom Jonaszeichen," 253–263, Georg Strecker, *Der Weg der Gerechtigkeit. Untersuchungen zur Theologie des Matthäus* (FRLANT 82, 3rd ed.; Göttingen: Vanderhoeck & Ruprecht, 1971) 103–104; and Edwards, *The Sign of Jonah*, 96–100. Krister Stendahl has suggested, based on the lack of this citation in Justin Martyr's *Dialogue with Trypho* 107.1, that this interpolation might have been added to Matthew's text at an even later period, *The School of St. Matthew—and its Use of the Old Testament* (ASNU 20; Lund: Gleerup, 1954) 132.

12. On Matthew's scribal use of the Hebrew Scriptures and as a source for messianic prophecies, see Ulrich Luz, *Das Evangelium Nach Matthäus (Mt 1–7)* (Zürich: Benzinger, 1985) 60–61, 131–141.

13. Darryl Schmidt lists 18 examples of this form from the prophetic books of the Hebrew Bible, and adds two similar forms in the Pentateuch, "The LXX Gattung 'Prophetic Correlative,'" *JBL* 96 (1977) 517–22.

14. Kloppenborg adds to this list two examples of this from Qumran: 1Q27 i.6 and 4QpsDanᵃ [=4Q 246] ii.1–2, *The Formation of Q*, 130 note 127. Edwards had earlier assumed that this "eschatological correlative" was a unique construction of the Q community, *The Sign of Jonah*, 47–58.

15. Heinz Schürmann, "Beobachtungen zum Menschensohn-Titel in der Redequelle," *Jesus und der Menschensohn: Für Anton Vögtle* (Freiburg: Herder & Herder, 1975) 124–147 (see Q 6:22–23; 7:33–34; 9:57–58; 11:30; 12:8–9, 10, 40;

There are other redactional clues indicating that Q 11:30 is a later addition to Q 11:29. Anton Vögtle has pointed out how 11:31–32 links through catchword connections with 11:29—only if 11:30 is present—with the words "Jonah," "Ninevites," and "this generation."[16] Indeed there is virtual unanimity among those working on redaction in Q that the double analogy (11:31–32) was added to 11:29 after the creation of 11:30 as a redactional clasp.[17] In dispute is whether the double analogy with Jonah and Solomon was an early independent (authentic?) saying that was attached, or a later elaboration created after the addition of 11:30.[18] A strong case can be made that the double analogy to Jonah and Solomon is early. The trajectory of the tradition began with the mention of the epic hero Jonah, to which was added in a scribal manner the Septuagint-like prophetic correlative; then at a later stage Matthew's allegorical midrash was added. Thus, the trajectory takes on an increasingly scribal and scriptural direction. If 31–32 is the latest element, however, it would reverse the trend, since the comparison to Jonah and Solomon alludes to contemporary haggadah, and not aspects of the stories found in the Hebrew Scriptures. Neither Jonah's preaching of repentance to the Ninevites nor their response is a focal point of the book of Jonah, yet it was in early Jewish discussions as well as here. The Queen of the South's visit to Solomon is only anecdotal to Solomon's wisdom in the Hebrew Scriptures, but the legendary visit became the basis of lively popular speculation in later periods.[19] It is therefore quite likely that two early, independent traditions were joined by 11:30: the refusal to give a sign except the sign of Jonah (11:29) and the analogy to Jonah and Solomon (31–32). Q 11:30 was created to connect the two, a redactional activity that goes along with the Q community's increased scribal direction, which comes to full bloom in Matthew's addition of 12:40. Accompanying this trend were redactions whose themes accentuated the conflict with "this

---

17:24, 26–27, 28–30). A detailed discussion of redactional reasons for seeing Q 11:30 as a later addition to Q 11:29, see Kloppenborg, *The Formation of Q*, 128–134.

16. Vögtle, "Der Spruch vom Jonaszeichen," 248–253; and Theissen, *The Gospels in Context*, 44.

17. So Lührmann, *Die Redaktion der Logienquelle*, 41–42; Hoffmann, *Studien zur Theologie der Logienquelle*, 181; Mikagu Sato, *Q und Prophetie* (WUNT ser. 2, vol. 29; Tübingen: J. C. B. Mohr [Paul Siebeck], 1988) 278–287; Arland Jacobson, "The Literary Unity of Q," *JBL* 101 (1982) 382; and Kloppenborg, *The Formation of Q*, 128–129, 134.

18. Rudolf Bultmann, *The History of the Synoptic Tradition* (revised edition; New York: Harper & Row, 1968) 113; and Hoffmann, *Studien zur Theologie der Logienquelle*, 157, 181. Martin Dibelius described the shorter Markan version as a *chreia, Die Formgeschichte des Evangeliums* (4th ed.; Tübingen: J. C. B. Mohr [Paul Siebeck], 1961) 159.

19. Louis Ginzberg, *The Legends of the Jews IV* (Philadelphia: The Jewish Publication Society of America, 1913) 142–149, 250–253 and notes in volume VI.

generation," introduced Gentiles in a favorable light to shame Israel, and appealed to epic traditions. [20]

At the core of this passage, however, is the well-attested request for a sign, to which the exception clause "except the sign of Jonah" originally belonged. While the exception clause does not appear in Mark, there is good reason to suppose that he knew the exception clause but omitted it; Mark shapes his plot through Jesus' controversy with the leaders, which is moved along by the question of Jesus' identity, an identity that Mark never has Jesus reveal in public. Several scholars including Kloppenborg have argued convincingly that here Mark ". . . abbreviated an originally longer tradition concerning the Sign of Jonah, leaving only the flat refusal of a sign. It is also conceivable that Mark . . . omitted it either because of his aversion to public disclosures, or because he found the phrase unintelligible."[21]

The tradition-historical situation can be summarized as follows: 1) the original stage consisted of the request for a sign and Jesus' refusal to give a sign "except the sign of Jonah" (11:29); 2) the explanatory son of man correlative was then added (11:30); 3) this enabled the originally distinct double comparison with Jonah and Solomon to be appended (31–32); and 4) the scriptural allegory of the resurrection was interpolated by Matthew (Matt 12:40).

The route taken in the bulk of secondary literature, which admittedly began early in the trajectory with the addition of the prophetic correlative (Q 11:30) and the Matthean scriptural allegory (Matt 12:40), is to focus on the referent of the sign of Jonah, usually in light of the Hebrew Scriptures. The phrase appears nowhere in Jewish literature or the Hebrew Scriptures, including the book of Jonah. Nevertheless, some have argued that originally the sign referred to Jonah 2 and his miraculous deliverance from the great fish (so already Matthew). More commonly, however, the sign is thought to refer simply to the preaching of Jonah in 3:4–8.[22] The route of looking for the referent in the Hebrew scriptures will be bypassed, and instead of

---

20. Lührmann, *Die Redaktion der Logienquelle;* and Jacobson, "The Literary Unity of Q."

21. Kloppenborg, *The Formation of Q*, 129; Burton Mack has also noted how the Markan plot necessitated this change, "Q and the Gospel of Mark: Revising Christian Origins," in Early Christianity, Q and Jesus, ed. John Kloppenborg and Leif Vaage; Semeia 55 (1991) 30. See also, John Dominic Crossan, *The Historical Jesus: The Life of a Mediterranean Jewish Peasant* (San Francisco: HarperSanFrancisco, 1991) 252; Harry Fleddermann, *Mark and Q: A Study of the Overlap Texts* (BETL 72; Leuven: University Press, 1995) 126–34; James Swetnam, "No Sign of Jonah," *Bib* 66 (1985) 126–30; and "Some Signs of Jonah," *Bib* 68 (1987) 74–79.

22. In various ways, Thomas W. Manson, *The Sayings of Jesus* (London: SCM Press, 1949) 89; Otto Glombitza, "Das Zeichen des Jona (Zum Verständnis von Matth. XII.38–42)," *NTS* 8 (1961–2) 365; and Edwards, *The Sign of Jonah*, 95.

searching for interpretive keys in texts to understand the sign of Jonah, the selection and use of Jonah as an epic figure, especially in the context of other epic references in Q against their Galilean setting, will be pursued.

## Jonah in Galilee

One of the most neglected aspects of the study of the pericope is that Jonah was not only a northern prophet who went to Nineveh, but also a Galilean prophet, and that there were local traditions that attest to his significance in the Galilee.[23] The importance of the Galilean connection is obvious for the saying if it is authentic, since Jesus' activity is surely to be placed in the Galilee, but the saying's presence in Q and traces of redactional activity point to its significance in the group behind the document, a point of special importance given the likelihood that Q was compiled and composed in Galilee.

The book of Jonah provides little biographical information about Jonah, other than that he was the son of Amittai (1:1), and only cursory geographical information, other than that he went to the port of Joppa and embarked for Tarshish instead of following God's call to Nineveh (1:3). In its description of Jeroboam II's reign over the Northern Kingdom (786–746 B.C.E.), however, 2 Kings 14:25 tells that the prophet Jonah, also here called the son of Amittai, came from Gath-Hepher.[24] According to the territorial allotment account in Joshua 19:13, Gath-Hepher was a site located within the boundaries of the tribe of Zebulun in Lower Galilee.[25] Nowhere else in the Hebrew Scriptures is the site of Gath-Hepher mentioned, nor do we hear of Jonah elsewhere. A rabbinic discussion of the *amoraic* period combines the two passages that mention Gath-Hepher, identifying not only the specific location of Gath-Hepher, but more importantly attesting to awareness of local traditions associating Jonah with the site. *Genesis Rabbah, parashah* 98:11 reads: "[One Sabbath] R. Levi entered and lectured: Jonah [the prophet] was

---

23. The neglect of Jonah's Galilean connection can be illustrated in the fact that it is not mentioned in any of the above-cited works. The connection between Jesus' comparison with Jonah and their respective Galilean origins was noted by Gustaf Dalman, but the romantic and latent anti-Semitic tone of his description no doubt contributed to more recent scholars' neglect of his point, *Orte und Wege Jesu* (3rd ed.; Gütersloh: Bertelsmann, 1924) 118. Even Theissen, who provides an excellent discussion of this passage in terms of local Palestinian perspectives, does not discuss the Galilean traditions of Jonah, *The Gospels in Context*, 43–45.

24. Γεθχοβερ in the LXX (with variant readings Γεθαχοερ, Γεθαχ(χ)οφερ, and Γαιθοφρα); the variant readings underscore that in the centuries up to the third century, likely transliterating the Hebrew into Greek, and were not thinking of a specific town that was well known.

25. Γεθθα in LXX A, Γεβερε in LXX B.

descended from Zebulun, as it is written, And the third lot came up for the children of Zebulun . . . and from thence it passed along eastward to Gath-Hepher (Josh. 19:10–13); while it is also written, According to the word of the Lord, the God of Israel, which He spoke by the hand of his servant Jonah the son of Amittai, the prophet, who was of Gath-Hepher (II Kings 14:25). (Gath-Hepher is Gobebatha of Sepphoris)."[26] Gath-Hepher, now in late antiquity called Gobebatha, is obviously a small village under the jurisdiction of the city of Sepphoris. A passage telling of the death of the legendary Judah Ha-nasi states that upon hearing of the rabbi's death, the rending of garments in Sepphoris was so violent that its sound reached Gobebatha three miles away.[27]

Whether Jonah was actually from a Gath-Hepher in Galilee, and that this site was the Gobebatha near Sepphoris is not an important question; in fact, based on this rabbinic citation alone one would be inclined to think that it was simply a midrashic catchword connection of the two scriptures with Gath-Hepher. However, not only did Rabbi Levi connect Jonah with the contemporaneous Galilean village, the Christian author Jerome also testifies to the connection between Jonah with Gath-Hepher in Galilee. In the preface to his commentary on the book of Jonah, he states his awareness of a tradition locating the tomb of Jonah in Gath-Hepher, "two miles on the road from Sepphoris, today called Diocaesarea, towards Tiberias," the same location found in the rabbinic sources.[28] Jerome prefers this spot for the prophet's tomb to another, more recent and Christian location, at a "Geth" by Diospolis or Lydda along the southern coast of Palestine, since the latter "Geth" does not include the distinctive "Hepher" as does the former. Jerome tends to juxtapose earlier Jewish traditions with later Christian ones, siding usually, in an inoffensive way to his readers, with the latter.[29] This is apparently the case

---

26. *Midrash Rabbah, Genesis II*, translated by H. Freedman (London: Soncino, 1939) 959. Later portions of this passage attest to a concerted interest to retain Jonah's connection to the inland areas thought of as Zebulun; Rabbi Yohanan corrects his pupil Rabbi Levi by noting that Jonah was in fact from Asher (based on the popular legend that Jonah was the son of the widow raised by Elijah, 1 Kings 17:9), to which Rabbi Levi tenaciously responds "in truth his father was from Zebulun while his mother was from Asher, for the verse AND HIS FLANK [i.e. his mother] SHALL BE UPON ZIDON means, the thigh whence he was sprung was from Zidon [i.e. in Asher]."

27. *Eccl. Rab.* 7:12 par *y. Ketub.* 12.35a, *y. Kil.* 5.32b. For a discussion of the rabbinic literature, see Adolf Neubauer, *La Géographie du Talmud* (reprint from the 1868 original; Hidesheim: Georg Olms, 1967) 200–201; and Dalman, *Orte und Wege Jesu*, 117–118.

28. *Comm. in Jonam, Prologus, PL* 25, 1119. Although Jerome does not specifically state that he learned of the location from Jewish traditions, in the preceding and following paragraphs he notes information borrowed from "the Hebrews" that he accepts as true, and one is to assume that his source for the tomb is also Jewish.

29. Joachim Jeremias, *Heiligengräber in Jesu Umwelt* (Göttingen: Vanderhoeck & Ruprecht, 1958) 24 note 2.

here, since there is no other Christian text indicating an awareness of a Galilean tomb of Jonah. Later Christian traditions, such as can be found on the sixth-century C.E. Madaba map and in later Christian pilgrim itineraries, associate Jonah with the shrine near Lydda on the southern coast.[30] In contrast, the Jewish pilgrim itineraries are full of references to the tomb of Jonah located just outside of Sepphoris on the way to Tiberias; the earliest, Benjamin of Tudela, dates to around 1170, and a Moslem pilgrim reported a visit to Jonah's tomb on a hill south of Cana in the Galilee in 1047, again placing it just outside of Sepphoris on the way to Tiberias.[31] Significantly, none of the Jewish reports show an awareness of a Christian location, so that one cannot infer that the site at Gath-Hepher was created in competition with the later Christian site.

The descriptions of the location of the site by the pilgrims, Jerome, and the rabbinic literature all coincide with the modern village of el-Meshhed (Hebrew *Mishhad*), where to this day its Palestinian inhabitants show visitors the tomb of *nebi junis*, Jonah the prophet. The modern village of el-Meshhed, which is certainly the site of the tomb described by the pilgrims and Jerome, lies three miles from Sepphoris, just to the west of the modern road linking Kefr Kana with Nazareth.

Although no excavations have been conducted in the village, a summit on the southern outskirts of el-Meshhed, called Tell el-Zurrua'a in Arabic, was examined by William F. Albright in 1929, who reported finding there Early Iron I and II sherds (from "Jonah's age").[32] Numerous factors weigh against the authenticity of the tomb of Jonah. For one, Zvi Gal, as part of his survey of the Galilee in the early eighties, conducted an examination of Tell el-Zurrua'a/Gath-Hepher, and made an extensive collection of surface pottery in the plowed fields around the village. The sherds reveal occupation of the site during the Early, Middle, and Late Bronze Ages, during Iron Age I and II, and during the Persian and Roman-Byzantine Periods.[33] Most significant is the complete lack of Iron III (731–500 B.C.E.) sherds, which indicates that the site was abandoned after the Assyrian campaigns of Tiglath-pileser III. This is not surprising, given that the entire Galilee was depopulated by the Assyrians and uninhabited during the seventh century B.C.E.. The possibility, then, of Jonah, who was associated with Jeroboam II's rule between

30. On the various traditional places for Jonah's tomb, see Félix-Marie Abel, "Le culte de Jonas en Palestine," *JPOS* 2 (1922) 175–183. See also Jeremias, *Heiligengräber in Jesu Umwelt*, 24–28.

31. The relevant references in the pilgrim itineraries are listed in Abel, "Le culte de Jonas en Palestine" 176; and Jeremias, *Heiligengräber in Jesu Umwelt*, 27.

32. "New Israelite and Pre-Israelite Sites: The Spring Trip of 1929," *BASOR* 35 (1929) 8; in terms of his chronology, sherds from "the time of Jonah" would have been from the tenth through eight century B.C.E.

33. Zvi Gal, *Lower Galilee during the Iron Age* (Winona Lake: Eisenbrauns, 1992) 18.

786 and 746 B.C.E., having a memorial tomb survive through the Assyrian Period is minimal. Moreover, the fact that very few Persian Period sherds were found around Tell el-Zurrua'a, and none from the Early and Late Hellenistic Periods, suggests that Gath-Hepher was not resettled until the first century B.C.E., which is when many Galilean sites were founded under Hasmonean rule.

Significantly, of all sherds found by Zvi Gal, most dated to the Roman-Byzantine Period, which confirms that the site was inhabited at and before the time Jerome wrote his commentary and when the rabbis discussed Gath-Hepher's connection to Jonah. It was located at a place that would have made it well known locally during the Roman Period: just up the hill off the main Roman road along the Beth Netofah Valley that connected the Sea of Galilee regions with the port at Acco-Ptolemais. This road also connected Sepphoris and Tiberias, which was frequently traveled by the rabbis according to the Talmud.[34] A spring at Gath-Hepher was one of the sources for the massive aqueduct and water system of Sepphoris, linking Gath-Hepher visually with the city of Sepphoris.

That faint traces of local traditions survive associating Jonah the prophet with Gath-Hepher is remarkable. Many commentators have noted the

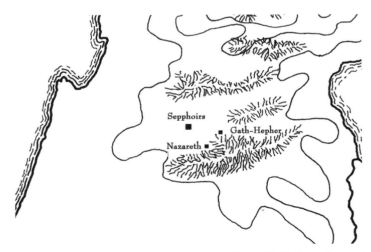

*Figure 7.1 Gath-Hepher in Galilee*

34. On the description of relations between Sepphoris and Tiberias, including travel between the two by rabbis, see Stuart S. Miller, "Intercity Relations in Roman Palestine: The Case of Sepphoris and Tiberias," *AJSR* 12 (1987) 1–24. Evidence for rebuilding exists for the Hadrianic period, see Michael Avi-Yonah, "The Development of the Roman Road System in Palestine," *IEJ* 1 (1950–51) 59.

appropriate first-century Judean background to the woe against the Jewish leaders for building the prophets' tombs without honoring their message (Q 11:47–48). Especially around Jerusalem, tombs commemorated kings, priests, and prophets, and under Hasmonean and even Herodian rule, priestly families and royal dynasties actively carried on their memories.[35] At Gath-Hepher, however, a small rural site in Galilee, there are memories of Jonah at a much more modest shrine, all the more remarkable since his work among the Ninevites could have made his prophetic career somewhat questionable. It seems probable that upon the resettlement of Gath-Hepher at the beginning of the Early Roman Period, its Jewish inhabitants revived the tradition linking Jonah's hometown with theirs as recorded in 2 Kings 14:25, and at some point began to nurture traditions of his burial there. It is likely that Jonah was venerated around Gath-Hepher and in Lower Galilean villages as a local hero. In fact, the use of Jonah in Q 11:29-32, originating either with Jesus in the Galilee or with his early followers in the Galilee, can be cited as evidence for this local tradition in the first century—the twice-repeated "here" underscores the geographical connections of the passage. If the geographical connections between Jonah, Jesus, Q, and the Galilee are taken into consideration, then one aspect of the Q community's epic imagination, its identification with prophetic figures, is illuminated.

The comparison of Jesus with a Galilean prophet here raises the question of other ideal types from the epic past in Q. Elsewhere in its selection and presentation of epic figures, the Q community seems to have consciously avoided appeal to the king as a type and the priest as a type, indeed each is implicitly criticized elsewhere. In the passage on the eschatological ingathering (Q 13:28–30), the trio of patriarchs Abraham, Isaac, and Jacob will sit at the table in the eschatological banquet, but no mention is made of kings or priests.[36] The patriarchs and the patriarchal age also are referred to in John's preaching in Q 3:8 (Abraham) and in the description of the coming son of man in Q 17:26–27 (Noah). The patriarchs antedate the priesthood and the monarchy, as well as their centralization in Jerusalem, and represent

---

35. Jeremias, *Heiligengräber in Jesu Umwelt*, 42–101. The author concurs with Jeremias that Q 11:47 has those prophets in mind who were martyred by their own kin, i.e., Isaiah and Zacharia (Q 11:51 alone makes this much clear), whose tombs were located in Jerusalem on the Ophel and Kidron Valley, respectively, Jeremias, *Heiligengräber in Jesu Umwelt*, 61–72. Q 11:47 is therefore not a critique of the memory of Jonah in Galilee.

36. In fact, if the Matthean reading in 8:12 "but the sons of the kingdom" were in Q, the rhetoric against royal figures is even more pronounced, and if the Lukan reading in 13:28, "And all the prophets" were in Q, the prophetic identification of the Q community would also be more prominent. Both readings were rejected by the International Q project, see James M. Robinson, "The International Q Project Work Session 16 November 1990," *JBL* 110 (1991) 497.

a time when God is seen to have acted in history on the basis of human relations and not privileged geographical locales. David, the Davidic covenant, and the Davidic lineage rooted in Jerusalem, on the other hand, are not mentioned in Q. Solomon is mentioned twice, but his wealth, which was at his disposal because of his social position as king, serves as a negative example in Q 12:27. The other mention of Solomon is, of course, part of the double analogy in the sign of Jonah passage (Q 11:31). However, Solomon is not revered here because of his social position as king, but because of his wisdom, to which the Queen of the South was also drawn. Present or earthly royalty is implicitly criticized in Q 22:30, where Jesus' followers are promised that they will assume a royal position on thrones in Jesus' kingdom. The Q community's vision of the kingdom of God, an implicit critique of royal rule by humans over humans, explains why royal figures are not singled out as heroes for the Q community.[37]

Like the primary royal figure David, the primary priestly figure, Moses, as well as the Mosaic covenant and the Mosaic laws, are nowhere appealed to in Q. The sacrificial system is simply ignored in Q. The law in general, including the Decalogue, is ignored as well. Indeed, in terms of Q's temporal views, law has given way to the kingdom of God (Q 16:16).[38] Furthermore, the series of woes in Q 11:39–52 directly attacks the one social group that typified concern for legal issues, the Pharisees and lawyers.[39] And the locus of priestly activities, the temple, is explicitly denounced in the lament in Q 13:35: "behold your house stands deserted."

From a spatial perspective, both the priest and the king as types had become localized in Jerusalem. The Davidic king ruled or would return to rule in Jerusalem, and the priests officiated in the Temple in Jerusalem. The prophet, however, as an ideal type, was not localized. The prophets traditionally served as a moral and social critic of kings and priests in particular, and at times even their centralization in Jerusalem (e.g., Micah 3:9–12; Jeremiah 26). For this reason the prophet as a model was the natural choice for a religious community in a Galilean setting. Galileans were further removed from the officially sanctioned religious center at Jerusalem, which made pilgrimage more difficult and perhaps also more special, yet at the

---

37. See the helpful comments in Mack, *The Lost Gospel*, 125–127.

38. The meaning of Q 16:17, in light of the rest of Q's avoidance of law as a determining factor in community life, might well be seen in a sarcastic tone ridiculing excessive attachment to the law, or as a later intrusion to render Q more nomocentric, see John Kloppenborg, "*Nomos* and *Ethos* in Q," *Gospel Origins and Christian Beginnings* (eds. James Goehring, et al.; Sonoma: Polebridge Press, 1990) 43–46.

39. Although it must be pointed out that the Pharisaic interpretation is what is being attacked, and not the law as such (Q 11:42, 46). The priest Zechariah is also mentioned in Q 11:51, but he, along with Abel, serves simply to mark a time period, and is implied or compared in this passage to a prophet, not a priest.

same time looked down upon by the Judeans. The prophet as a type did not need to succumb to the ruling apparatus in Jerusalem, and even provided a traditional avenue for criticizing the Jerusalem religious and political structures in a way that justified rejection.

This helps explain the ease with which the Deuteronomistic theme of the persecuted prophets was incorporated into Q. The theme appears in the lament over Jerusalem (Q 13:34–35), in the woes against the Pharisees and lawyers (Q 11:49–51), and in the beatitudes (Q 6:22–23). In Q 6:22–23 the members of the Q community are, in the conclusion to the persecution beatitude, compared to the prophets of old. The use of the theme is striking: typically in the Deuteronomistic historical view blessings are described for those who obey in a casuistic "if . . . then" proposition—here the blessings are placed in the consecutive "since . . . then" form, showing that the community had adopted for itself the role of prophets.

As part of their role as prophets, criticism of the Jerusalem establishment came naturally, even though criticism of Jerusalem does not seem to be the primary concern of the Q community.[40] At various points in Q, invectives are hurled against Jerusalem and those seen to represent Jerusalem. The woes against the Pharisees and lawyers (Q 11:39–52) can be seen as the rejection of any encroachment into Galilee from Jerusalem. The lament (Q 13:34–35) mocks Jerusalem's claim to house the divine and portrays Jerusalem as a distant, spiritually barren city.

And Jerusalem might even be in view in the sign of Jonah. In the late first-century *Vitae Prophetarum*, a tradition that used Jonah to shame Jerusalem can be found. A story is told of the Northern prophet Jonah having sojourned in the regions of Tyre (10:2) with his mother, who was the widow raised by Elijah, another prophet active in the North.[41] In the region of Tyre, which borders the Galilee, he spoke an oracle against Jerusalem predicting its imminent fall (10:10–11).[42] In a Proem to *Lamentations Rabbah*,

---

40. John Kloppenborg has elsewhere described Jerusalem as "the focus of unbelief and non-acceptance," "City and Wasteland: Narrative World and the Beginning of the Sayings Gospel (Q)," *Semeia* 52 (1991) 154.

41. If Luke 9:61–62 were in Q, then the would-be followers of Jesus would have to be even more fanatical than Elisha who is alluded to, and they would not even be allowed to bury their father, see Q, Vassiliadis, "Nature and Extent," 70.

42. Charles C. Torrey translates 10:2 as "Tyre" based on the likely Hebrew original, *The Lives of the Prophets. Greek Text and Translation* (Philadelphia: Society of Biblical Literature, 1946) 41. Götz Schmitt originally suggested the sign was directed against Jerusalem based on the *Vitae Prophetarum*, "Das Zeichen des Jonas," *ZNW* 69 (1978) 123–129. Although direct dependence on the *Vitae* is unlikely, since its date might be shortly after the first Jewish War, it is likely that the *Vitae* itself incorporated earlier traditions here, traditions that also later appear in *Lam. Rab.* Proem 31. It is noteworthy that the *Vitae Prophetarum* describes Elijah as coming from the region of the Arabs, that is to say the Decapolis controlled by the Nabateans, in light of the Gospels connecting Jesus' ministry in bordering this area as well.

Jonah's successful mission in the Assyrian capital and the repentance of the Ninevites is contrasted with Jerusalem's continued obduracy as an oppressive city. The second-century C.E. Rabbi Simeon b. Yohai, whose own burial site is said to be in the Upper Galilee at Meron, rebuked Jerusalem: "Ought she not have learnt from the city of Jonah, i.e. Nineveh? One prophet I sent to Nineveh and she turned in penitence; but to Israel in Jerusalem I sent many prophets . . . Yet she hearkened not."[43]

The connection between Q's portrayal of Jesus and the prophet Jonah thus overlap at another point, namely their openness to Gentiles, admittedly a somewhat belated development for the latter, according to the book of Jonah. Regardless of what the sign of Jonah might be, Q 11:29–32 clearly is designed to shame Israel, this generation, with the positive response of both the Ninevites and the Queen of the South. That Gentiles recognized what is here, their repentance and quest for wisdom respectively, is contrasted with this generation's obstinacy. In Q's perspective, the gentile centurion is beyond anyone's faith in all Israel (Q 7:1–10), the gentile cities of Tyre and Sidon would have reacted more favorably than the Galilean villages (Q 10:11–13), and people from the ends of the earth will replace the supposed heirs at the in-gathering (Q 13:28–29). In short, there are tantalizing hints that in Galilee the comparison with Jonah included both a component of openness to Gentiles and a critical edge toward Jerusalem, both important themes in Q's theology.

One must assume that Galileans were attuned to such local traditions surrounding Jonah, and that the sign of Jonah not only referred to the preaching of Jonah but contained a barb aimed at Jerusalem and its representatives, a barb that the representatives perhaps did not get, that Mark did not pick up and hence deleted, and that Matthew turned into a proof text for the resurrection. However, at a very early stage in the tradition, pre-Markan and while still in the Galilee, Jesus is compared to the prophet Jonah. This comparison itself implicitly contained a criticism of Jerusalem and those seeking a sign, and could later explicitly be developed into predictions of Jerusalem's destruction.

---

43. *Lam. Rab.* Proem 31, H. Harry Freedman and Maurice Simon, *Midrash Rabbah. Lamentations* (London: Soncino, 1939) 57–58.

CHAPTER 8

# Archaeology and the Galilean Jesus

The foregoing studies stress the importance of archaeology for historical
Jesus research and the study of the Jesus traditions. New Testament scholarship's shift from a preoccupation with the text and its exegesis, and onto the
social history of the early Christian communities, amplifies the importance
of archaeology, since the recovered material culture enables a more precise
reconstruction of their contexts. Current historical Jesus research no longer
restricts itself to examining textual stratigraphy, with the goal of determining
the authentic sayings of Jesus, but now takes greater account of plausible
explanations of the life and teachings of Jesus within his concrete Galilean
context. The study of early Christianity is thus a two-pronged enterprise. On
the one hand, the task still requires digging down through Gospel stratigraphy to establish the trajectories along which early Christian traditions moved.
On the other hand, the task of reconstructing the context involves digging
down through the archaeological stratigraphy of Galilean sites to recreate the
environment in which Jesus and his followers are comprehensible.

Historical Jesus research entails an interchange between both sides, those
analyzing the textual layers and their origins, and those reconstructing the
context from which they emerged, with the goal of establishing a plausible
fit. Although the current proliferation of historical Jesus research revolves to
a large extent around an analysis of early Christian texts, the scope of inquiry
has widened to embrace various disciplines that shed light on religion and
life in antiquity, including an examination of Galilee as the specific locale of
Jesus' life and teachings. New Testament scholars are therefore in dialogue
with specialists working on texts outside the Christian canon, such as the
rabbinic texts, Josephus, or the Dead Sea Scrolls, and are more aware of fields

of inquiry like the social sciences, ancient economy, or cross-cultural anthropology. The essays collected here make a plea for giving archaeology a more prominent voice in this debate, and accentuate the implications for historical Jesus research of the archaeological excavations in Galilee and volumes of artifacts from the Galilean material culture. The essays synthesize and reassess the archaeological data relating to first-century Galilee, thus providing a basis upon which the early Christian traditions themselves can be reassessed.

Both the individual chapters and the collection as a whole concentrate on the archaeology of first-century Galilee, and raise the implications for the historical Jesus only tangentially. In this way, the archaeological record sets the agenda, rather than asking of it narrowly conceived questions derived from Gospel studies. Part one set the stage by providing broad characterizations of first-century Galilee. Chapter one showed how Galilee's settlement history and material culture confirm its inhabitants' Jewish ethnicity and religion, and their close ties to Judea. Chapter two then noted how Herod Antipas's urbanization of Galilee early in the first century, by building Sepphoris and Tiberias, realigned Galilee's demographics, agricultural production, and land-holding patterns. At the same time, urbanization amplified social stratification in Galilee, both with respect to urban versus rural sites, and more generally between the lower classes and the elites. These general observations were borne out in Part two, where examinations of the city of Sepphoris and the village of Capernaum provided more detailed archaeological descriptions of two sites in Jesus' Galilean context. That Jesus was more closely tied to the latter, a modest Jewish village on the fringe of Herod Antipas's territory, rather than the former, a wealthier, somewhat Hellenized yet still Jewish city, and the seat of political power, is illustrative of Jesus' socio-economic class and original audience. Part three turned attention more explicitly to Gospel texts, specifically the Sayings Gospel Q, albeit with the archaeology of Galilee in the background. By locating the Sayings Gospel Q in Galilee, a significant continuity between the contexts of Jesus and the early Jesus traditions was established. Thus, the socio-economic and religious context for Jesus' teaching and for the essential message preserved in the early Gospel layers is the same, a point that helps bridge the gap between Jesus and the Jesus traditions. The prophetic critique drawn from the Jewish tradition, and the call to counter-cultural community in response to Antipas's urbanization, fit the specific Galilean setting of the first half of the first century, a context onto which the archaeological record sheds considerable light.

## The Value of Archaeology

In general, archaeology deserves a more prominent place in New Testament studies, and in particular, the archaeology of Galilee in historical Jesus research, because of its independence from the early Christian texts. This independence is twofold. First, archaeology is one of the few fields of inquiry in the study of antiquity that actively acquires new data. With rare exceptions, notably the discovery of the Dead Sea Scrolls or Nag Hammadi Library well over a generation ago, scholars working on Jesus and Galilee with literary evidence simply introduce new methods or innovative theories to analyze these texts. The collage of citations is re-shuffled or re-mixed, emphasizing some passages over others, while reinterpreting a few, perhaps in dialogue with other disciplines. Archaeologists, however, while similarly subject to methodological and theoretical developments, also uncover evidence on a continual basis. This new evidence is initially interpreted on a provisional basis, and then more systematically in light of the patterns in previously discovered materials. Since various excavations are always uncovering new evidence, the archaeological description of Galilee is continually being reassessed. Archaeology creates its own body of knowledge, which is growing and dynamic, and which exists independently of developments in literary studies. Scholars of early Christianity must, therefore, continually reassess their picture of Galilee in dialogue with archaeologists, and develop their reconstructions of the historical Jesus and their studies on the early Christian traditions with an awareness of the archaeological record.

Archaeology is also independent from texts in terms of the kind of evidence it uncovers for Jesus' Galilean context. The literary evidence that comments on first-century Galilee is problematic, either due to its biased perspective, distant geographical locale, or late date. The Gospels' comments on Galilee themselves are shrouded in Christology and were likely composed outside Galilee; the rabbinic citations focus on the ideal life and are either late or embedded in complex later layers; and Josephus is Judean, pro-Roman, and self-centered. Each of these texts was written by social elites and males, as all texts from antiquity were when literacy rates were extremely low. Unlike the literary corpus, the archaeological evidence is much more democratic in that it examines the stuff of everyday life left behind by all social strata. Ironically, the eyewitnesses who wrote in antiquity ignored the visual and commonplace aspects of everyday life; nevertheless, they assumed this knowledge on the part of their readers. Apart from the archaeological record, the authors and their audiences' visible and tangible world could hardly be reconstructed. Only archaeology can describe these aspects of the past that are unarticulated in the texts, but which underlie their interpretation.

Returning to the analogy of the crossword puzzle, where the across clues from texts fill in the rows and the down clues from archaeology fill in the columns, archaeology provides an independent set of clues to the puzzle of first-century Galilee. It is certainly appropriate, as has often been done, to use the archaeological data selectively to fill in lacunae in the rows where answers to the textual queries are uncertain. Thus, to examine archaeological remains in order to determine whether or not the term "synagogue" in the first century referred to a gathering or architectural structure is certainly a suitable use of archaeology. And using historical geography to locate particular sites mentioned in the New Testament can likewise be a worthy enterprise. In the same way, it is appropriate to use archaeological evidence to check the coherence of textual interpretations, such as whether the inscriptions found in Galilee point to an Aramaic- or Greek-speaking or bilingual population. The approach throughout this book, however, was not to allow the Gospels or textual studies to dictate the questions asked of the archaeological record. Instead, it reassessed as a whole the archaeological evidence for first-century Galilee, and used the material culture as the primary means to recreate the environment of Jesus and his first followers. In the process, some questions, such as the language(s) of Jesus or the shape of synagogues during his ministry were not addressed because of the paucity of first-century evidence, while other questions, such as the location of the crucifixion or the place of Jesus' burial, were avoided because they shed no light on his Galilean context.

In the studies collected here, the crossword puzzle of Galilee was almost exclusively reconstructed from archaeologically generated clues. In the process, other disciplines, such as sociology, cross-cultural anthropology, and theories of religion, as well as detailed exegesis of texts like Josephus and particularly the rabbinic literature, were slighted. However, if interdisciplinary collaboration holds any promise, it is not by diluting each of the disciplines into a mixture, but rather by seriously engaging each field. These studies intend to engage the archaeology of Galilee seriously in hopes of bridging the gap between literary studies of the Gospels and the study of the material culture. The syntheses of the archaeological evidence provide a corrective to some portrayals of the Galilean context while at the same time raising important issues for historical Jesus research. Four themes emerged from these studies that merit restatement and summary: (1) that Galilee was a definable region; (2) that it was Jewish; (3) that it underwent considerable socio-economic change under Herod Antipas's urbanization projects; and (4) that Jesus' message of the Kingdom of God responded to these changes by reinterpreting elements of the Jewish heritage.

## Galilee and Regionalism

The study of Galilean archaeology makes a significant contribution to the notion that Galilee was a definable region, shedding light on the meaning of the phrase "Jesus the Galilean." The archaeological record confirms the delineation of Galilee as a distinct region with its own material culture. While the early work of Eric Meyers correctly stressed regional variations within Galilee, a point that can now be further nuanced in light of more recent excavations, the fact that Galilee as a whole—Upper Galilee, Lower Galilee, and even portions of the Golan—was homogenous against its neighbors must be stressed. Galilee's material culture contrasts with those of the surrounding regions, accentuating its distinct character. The pottery assemblages, domestic architectural styles, burial practices, and profiles of imported wares of the Syro-phoenicians along the coast and in the Huleh Valley, the Itureans to the north around Mount Hermon, the inhabitants of the Decapolis to the east and south, and the Samaritans to the south stand in stark contrast to those of Galilee. The general lack of imported items from the broader Mediterranean world, especially when compared to the cities of the coast and the Decapolis in the Late Hellenistic and Early Roman Periods, implies that Galilee was not as well integrated into the international economy and its major trade networks. Describing Galilee as isolated is too strong, but characterizing it as provincial and with a limited regional economy is apt. It was, archaeologically speaking, a definable region, distinct from its immediate neighbors, but with close parallels to the material culture of Judea.

This observation from the archaeological materials coincides with the descriptions in the New Testament and contemporaneous literature, where Galilee and the Galileans are treated as a definable land and distinct people. Thus the character of Galilee and of their inhabitants should not be blurred into a pan-Palestinian Judaism. Even though Galilee was effectively integrated or incorporated into the Hasmonean Kingdom and under Herodian rule, and it and Judea shared many ties, Galilee had its own unique history and socio-economic, religious, and cultural developments. Historical Jesus research must focus on an interpretation of Jesus within this Galilean environment, and go about reconstructing that environment from the archaeology of Galilee as critically and as informed as it goes about examining the literature.

That Jesus' ministry is almost entirely in Galilee and that he and his named disciples were all Galileans is of utmost significance. Notice therefore must be taken when the Gospels portray Jesus as flirting along border regions, whether in making his apparent home base Capernaum on the periphery of Galilee, or in his frequent incursions into the regions, though never a city, of the Decapolis east of Galilee or Caesarea Philippi north of Galilee. These "crossings over" in the Gospels refer at a literal level to the lake, but reflect also the crossing over of a cultural barrier.

## Jesus in the Jewish Galilee

Over against its immediate neighbors, Galilee's material culture was clearly distinct, yet its closest parallel was that of Judea. Of particular importance to historical Jesus research is the observation that Galilee's essentially Jewish character was shared with Judea. Therefore, speaking of the Galilean Jesus is in no way intended as a contrast to the Jewish Jesus, but simply specifies or qualifies Jesus as a Galilean Jew. The Jewish ethnicity and religion of Galilee has been demonstrated from two vantage points—its settlement patterns and the presence of Jewish ethnicity markers there.

Until the time of the Maccabean expansion in the late second century B.C.E., Galilee was thinly populated. The Maccabean expansion can be traced in the archaeological record as emanating from Judea northward, at the time when Galilee was re-populated. The initial settlement of most of Roman-Byzantine sites in Galilee in the Late Hellenistic and Early Roman Periods coincides with the expansion of Hasmonean rule there. That these new inhabitants and their descendants were Jewish settlers or colonizers is clear from their material culture, which shares many features of the Judean material culture in the same period, notably stone vessels, *miqwaoth* or ritual baths, burial in *kokhim* shafts with ossuaries, and a diet absent of pork.

These general observations are apparent in the sites most closely associated with Jesus. Nazareth, his hometown, and Capernaum, his base of operations, are in this regard quite similar to Judea in their material culture, though in the latter *miqwaoth* are absent, likely due to its proximity with the lake and low socio-economic status. Significantly, the sites in Galilee that were most exposed to Hellenistic and Roman influences, the cities of Sepphoris and Tiberias, were just as thoroughly Jewish as far as the archaeological patterns of domestic space are concerned. At Sepphoris, which has been extensively excavated, stone vessels are ubiquitous in each domestic unit, *miqwaoth* are likewise present in each house, and pork is absent until the Byzantine Period. As Antipas's urban capital, Sepphoris was more Hellenized, likely more Greek-speaking, and more adaptive of the Greco-Roman architectural veneer, but none of this implies a non-Jewish character. In fact, there is a notable lack of evidence for significant numbers of Gentiles at these two sites, whether Romans, Greeks, or Syro-Phoenicians. Such did eventually make their mark there, clearly visible in the excavations at Sepphoris, but at a much later period. At the time of Jesus, there is little evidence for non-Jews, nor even for substantial trade and travel outside the region of Galilee, especially when compared to the evidence at urban sites along the coast or in the Decapolis.

While Sepphoris and Tiberias were Jewish cities that had been more Hellenized than the rest of Galilee, Jesus' activities in and around the more humble Jewish village of Capernaum ironically put him in closer proximity to Gentiles and pagan cities. Still clearly within a Jewish orbit among the Jewish villages on the northwestern shore of the Sea of Galilee, and with the same in portions of the Golan, the Gospels portray Jesus' ministry as taking place on the geographical and cultural fringe. There, he was surrounded by Greeks and other Gentiles living in the Decapolis, as well as by Syro-phoenicians in the

Huleh Valley and toward Caesarea Philippi. This setting fits rather well one of the key themes of the early Christian tradition, by using Gentiles as positive models to shame a Jewish audience into accepting the community's message. However, while the situation reflected in the early Gospel traditions anticipates the possibility of a gentile mission, this had not yet been carried out. The crucial problems associated therewith, such as diet and circumcision, issues that permeate the Pauline corpus and Acts in which the inclusion of Jews and Gentiles into a single community was at issue, are never addressed in the early traditions.

In this context it should be stressed that lacking a substantial component of gentile inhabitants, having only two Jewish cities in their infancy of Hellenization, and lacking much evidence for interregional trade, notions of Cynic itinerants influencing Jesus or his first followers make little sense. Though the scholarly comparison of Jesus' teaching with that of Cynicism merits attention as an analogy, any genealogical relationship between Jesus and Cynics is highly unlikely.

While the material culture shared a Jewish character with Judea, the basic attitudes of the Galileans and their differences with Judean Jews are not readily resolved from the archaeological record. One suspects, of course, that since much of the overlap in material culture, especially the implements relating to ritual purity, had some connection with the Temple and priests, that the Temple took an important symbolic role in the minds of the Galileans. The extent of pilgrimage to Jerusalem, and what element of nostalgia or sincere devotion to the Temple Galileans held in general, is elusive in the archaeological record. What is clear, however, is that with Jesus' trip to Jerusalem, he and his Galilean followers crossed a different kind of barrier, from the geographical margins of Judaism in Galilee to its center, the Temple in Jerusalem. That he reacted to the Temple cult and priestly hierarchy with a sense of alienation and protest is clear; the extent to which this represented the popular Galilean attitude is not.

## Jesus in Antipas's Urbanized Galilee

Another significant contribution of Galilean archaeology is its ability to detect the magnitude of socio-economic change in Galilee wrought by Herod Antipas's urbanization projects at Sepphoris and Tiberias. While Herod the Great's immense construction projects were known across the Mediterranean, the efforts consuming most of his energies and resources concentrated around Jerusalem and Caesarea, whereas Galilee was by and large ignored. Under his son Antipas, however, cities were constructed in Galilee and the area was urbanized in the era for the first time. The archaeological finds at Sepphoris and Tiberias reveal what kind of influence these cities had on Galilee, one that in the first century was not primarily cultural or religious, as only selective features of the Hellenistic polis or Roman urban parlance were introduced without offending Jewish sensibilities. Instead, their impact was first and foremost demographic and economic; they concentrated a considerable portion of the Galilean population at these two sites, housed Galilee's socio-economic elite, and focused agricultural production onto themselves.

This process accentuated and also accelerated social stratification in Galilee. Many of the houses at the urban sites of Sepphoris and Tiberias were built in styles that visually set them apart from village or rural houses in Galilee. Although mostly built in courtyard style, the houses of the urban elites adopted materials from the broader Mediterranean style. Inside, they had plastered and, at times, mosaic floors, and frescoed walls. Their sturdy walls were built with well-fitting hewn stones, stuccoed and whitewashed, covered with roof tiles, all in colors that were conspicuous. Such techniques and materials were infrequent in the villages of Galilee, where all but a few houses had walls made of unhewn stones, packed with mud, that were covered with thatched roofs. This pronounced social stratification was also visible in the kinds of materials found inside houses, with the wealthy able to afford some small imported items like lamps or items of personal adornment, as well as their local imitations. Notable also is the social stratification in artifacts that were essentially religious in nature, such as the style and type of burial in ossuaries, the size and shape of stone vessels, or the presence of private *miqwaoth* in private houses. Each of these forms also could serve as a status symbol. Ritual bathing by the majority of the population seems to have been done in the lake or streams or in the Jordan, in public sites such as synagogues, or in industrial sites such as olive presses, but the wealthier could perform in their own homes in *miqwaoth* in private houses.

Such status differentiation not only bespeaks increased production and wealth, but also indicates that the resources and wealth were being managed and redistributed in different ways. The strain on the agricultural production benefited the wealthy urban dwellers and some rural elites. But it was borne on the backs of the peasants, whose poverty in absolute terms is difficult to gauge, but whose poverty relative to the elites was apparent to all in antiquity and to archaeologists today.

This picture of Galilee fits the world portrayed in the sayings tradition, where concern for sustenance, poverty, and landlessness are dominant. Though the cities are not in any systematic way targeted for criticism, the wealthy are deemed arrogant or idolatrous, and wealth in general scorned as transitory and ephemeral. Related to these themes are the many sayings apparently deriding the family. In Antipas's new urbanized economy, the family or clan provided less of a safety net in case of crop failure or ill health. As the exchange of goods became increasingly asymmetrical between landowners and peasants, reciprocity at the local level and among the extended family no longer offered adequate protection for many Galileans. The call to exchange healing for food, and the plea for hospitality toward itinerant members of the movement, appears as a substitute or replacement of the protection of the family ties.

## The Kingdom of God in Galilee

The archaeological record helps one imagine Jesus' message of the Kingdom of God and his first followers' attitudes in Galilee by reconstructing the milieu in which they lived. Antipas's building of Sepphoris and Tiberias and the accentuation of social stratification and asymmetrical exchange created considerable stress on the population. It is not surprising that Jesus' proclamation of the Kingdom of God alluded to and directly addressed some of these concerns created by Antipas's kingdom building. True wealth's elusiveness and the false security of earthly possessions undermine the new Galilean economy, and much of Jesus' message resonates with prophetic critique of the Hebrew Bible. Given Galilee's essentially Jewish character, it is not surprising that Jesus' vision of the Kingdom drew on this aspect of the Jewish heritage. Similar to portions of the prophets, security was not to be found in the acquisition of objects or human-made structures, but in the divine and the new community's shared vision. Reliance on siblings, parents, or the extended family, including the entire kin of Abraham, was no longer adequate. Like the ancient Hebrew prophets, the new vision necessitated a radical response to the divine, which eventually led to a critique of most contemporary religious expressions within Judaism, even of the priestly apparatus and the Temple in Jerusalem. That this critique was "in-house" and represented some attempt at reform or revival, resulting from a sense of alienation or resentment rather than hostility or opposition, is clear from the Jewish character of Galilee. This critique, aimed at the end of Jesus' ministry towards a religious expression housed in a massive and expensive architectural structure, seems natural from a Galilean Jew, whose own region had most recently been subject to construction projects and their consequences.

# Bibliography

Abel, Félix-Marie. "Le culte de Jonas en Palestine." *JPOS* 2 (1922): 175–183.

———. "La liste géographique du papyrus 71 du Zénon." *RB* 32 (1923): 409–15.

———. "Le nom de Capharnaum." *JPOS* 8 (1928): 24–34.

———. *Géographie de la Palestine I: Géographie physique et historique.* 2nd ed. Paris: Librairie Lecoffre, 1938.

Adam, A. K. M. "According to whose Law?: Aristobolus, Galilee and the *nomoi ton Ioudaion.*" *JSP* 14 (1996): 15–21.

Adams, Robert McC. *Heartland of Cities: Surveys of Ancient Settlement and Land Use on the Central Floodplain of the Euphrates.* Chicago: The University of Chicago Press, 1981.

Adan-Bayewitz, David. "Kfar Hananya." *ESI* 7–8 (1988–89): 108.

———. *Common Pottery in Roman Galilee: A Study of Local Trade.* Ramat-Gan, Israel: Bar-Ilan University Press, 1993.

Adan-Bayewitz, David and Isadore Perlman. "The Local Trade of Sepphoris in the Roman Period." *IEJ* 40 (1990): 153–172.

———. "The Pottery." In *The Excavations of an Ancient Boat in the Sea of Galilee*, by Shelly Wachsmann, pp. 89–96. '*Atiqot* 19 [English Series]. Jerusalem: Israel Antiquities Authority, 1990.

Adan-Bayewitz, David et al. "Yodefat 1992." *IEJ* 45 (1995): 191–97.

Adan-Bayewitz, David and Mordechai Aviam, "Iotapata, Josephus, and the Siege of 67: Preliminary Report on the 1992–94 Seasons," *JRS* 10 (1997) 131–165.

Aharoni, Yohanan. "Survey in Galilee: Israelite Settlements and Their Pottery." *EI* 4 (1956): 56–64 [Hebrew].

Albright, William F. "New Israelite and Pre-Israelite Sites: The Spring Trip of 1929." *BASOR* 35 (1929): 7–12.

———. "Review of Waterman's Preliminary Report on the 1931 Excavations." *Classical Weekly* 21 (1938): 148.

Alcock, Susan. *Graecia Capta: The Landscape of Roman Greece.* Cambridge: Cambridge University Press, 1993.

Allision, Dale. *The Jesus Tradition in Q.* Harrisburg, Pennsylvania: Trinity Press International, 1997.

Alon, D. "Horvat Salit (Kh. Salantah)." *ESI* 5 (1986): 94–96.

Alt, Albrecht. *Kleine Schriften zur Geschichte des Volkes Israel,* 3 vols. München: C. H. Beck'sche, 1953–9.

————. "Zur Geschichte der Grenze zwischen Judäa und Samaria." In *Kleine Schriften zur Geschichte des Volkes Israel,* vol. 2, pp. 346–362. München: C. H. Beck'sche, 1959. Originally published in *Palästinajahrbuch* 31 (1935): 94–111.

————. "Galiläische Probleme." In *Kleine Schriften zur Geschichte des Volkes Israel,* vol. 2, pp. 346–362. München: C. H. Beck'sche, 1959. Originally published in *Palästinajahrbuch* 33 (1937): 52–88; 34 (1938): 80–93; 35 (1939): 62–82; and 36 (1940): 78–92.

————. "Die Stätten des Wirkens Jesu in Galiläa territorialgeschichtlich betrachtet." In *Kleine Schriften zur Geschichte des Volkes Israels,* vol. 2, pp. 441–47. München: C. H. Beck'sche, 1959. Originally published in *Beiträge zur biblischen Landes- und Altertumskunde* 68 (1949): 51–72.

Amiran, Ruth and Immanuel Dunayevski. "The Assyrian Open Court Building and its Palestinian Derivates." *BASOR* 149 (1958): 25–32.

Applebaum, Shimon. "Economic Life in Palestine." In *The Jewish People of the First Century II,* edited by Shemuel Safrai and Menachem Stern, 631–700. Compendia Rerum Iudaicarum ad Novum Testamentum. Amsterdam: Van Gorcum, 1976.

————. "Judaea as a Roman Province: The Countryside as a Political and Economic Factor." *ANRW* II.8, edited by Wolfgang Haase and Hildegard Temporini, pp. 355–96. Berlin: Walter de Gruyter, 1977.

————. "The Roman Villa in Judaea: A Problem." In *Judaea in Hellenistic and Roman Times: Historical and Archaeological Essays,* 124–131. Leiden: E. J. Brill, 1989.

————. "Romanization and Indigenism in Judaea." In *Judaea in Hellenistic and Roman Times: Historical and Archaeological Essays,* 155–65. Leiden: E. J. Brill, 1989.

Arav, Rami and Richard Freund. *Bethsaida: A City by the Northern Shore of the Sea of Galilee.* Bethsaida Excavations Project I. Kirkesville, Missouri: Thomas Jefferson University Press, 1995.

Arav, Rami and John J. Rousseau. "The Bethsaïda Excavations: Historical and Archaeological Approaches." In *The Future of Christianity: Essays in Honor of Helmut Koester,* edited by B. Pearson et al., pp. 77–106. Minneapolis: Fortress Press, 1991.

————. *Jesus and His World: An Archaeological and Cultural Dictionary.* Minneapolis: Fortress Press, 1995.

Ariel, Donald. "A Survey of Coin Finds in Jerusalem (Until the End of the Byzantine Period)." *LA* 32 (1982): 273–326.

Arnal, William. "Gendered Couplets in Q and Legal Formulations: From Rhetoric to Social History." *JBL* 116 (1997): 75–94.

Arnold, Dean. *Ceramic Theory and Cultural Process.* Cambridge: Cambridge University Press, 1985.

Asgeirsson, Jon M. and James M. Robinson. "The International Q Project Work Sessions 12–14 July, 22 November 1991." *JBL* 111 (1992): 500–508.

Avigad, Nahman. *Discovering Jerusalem.* Nashville, Tennessee: Nelson, 1980.

Avi-Yonah, Michael. "The Foundation of Tiberias." *IEJ* 1 (1950): 160–69.

————. "The Development of the Roman Road System in Palestine." *IEJ* 1 (1950-51): 54–60.

————. "The Caesarea Inscription of the Twenty-four Priestly Courses." In *The Teachers' Yoke: Studies in Memory of Henry Trantham,* edited by E. Jerry Vardaman et al., pp. 46–57. Waco: Baylor University Press, 1964.

———. "Historical Geography of Palestine." In *The Jewish People in the First Century: Historical Geography, Political History, Social, Cultural and Religious Life and Institutions*, vol. 1, edited by Shemuel Safrai and Menahem Stern, 78–116. Amsterdam: Van Gorcum, 1974.

———. *Gazetteer of Roman Palestine*. Qedem 5. Jerusalem: Hebrew University, 1976.

———. *The Holy Land from the Persian to the Arab Conquest: A Historical Geography*. Grand Rapids, Michigan: Baker Books, 1977.

Bagatti, Bellarmino. *Excavations in Nazareth. Volume I: From the Beginning till the XII Century*. Jerusalem: Franciscan Printing Press, 1969.

———. "Capharnaum." *MB* 27 (1983): 8–16.

Barag, Dan. "Tyrian Currency in Galilee," *INJ* 67 (1982–3) 7–13.

Barghouti, A. N. "Urbanization of Palestine and Jordan in Hellenistic and Roman Times." In *Studies in the History and Archaeology of Jordan II*, edited by Adnan Hadidi, pp. 209–227. Amman: Department of Antiquities, 1985.

Bar-Kochva, Bezalel. "Manpower, Economics, and Internal Strife in the Hasmonean State." In *Armées et fiscalité dans le monde antique*, pp. 167–194. Paris: Editions du centre national de la recherche scientifique, 1977.

Bassler, Jouette. "The Galileans: A Neglected Factor in Johannine Community Research." *CBQ* 43 (1981): 243–57.

Batey, Richard. "Is this not the Carpenter." *NTS* 30 (1984): 249–258.

———. "Jesus and the Theater." *NTS* 30 (1984): 563–574.

———. "Subsurface Interface Radar at Sepphoris, 1985." *Journal of Field Archaeology* 14 (1987): 1–8.

———. *Jesus and the Forgotten City*. Grand Rapids, Michigan: Baker, 1991.

Bauer, Walter. "Jesus der Galiläer." In *Aufsätze und Kleine Schriften*, edited by G. Strecker, pp. 91–108. Tübingen: J. C. B. Mohr [Paul Siebeck], 1964. Originally published in *Festgabe für Adolf Jülicher zum 70. Geburtstag, 26 Januar 1927*, edited by Rudolf Bultmann et al.; Tübingen: J. C. B. Mohr (Paul Siebeck), 1927, pp. 16–34.

Baumgarten, Joseph M. "The Pharisaic-Sadducean Controversies about Purity and the Qumran Texts." *JJS* 31 (1980): 157–70.

———. "The Purification Rituals in DJD 7." In *The Dead Sea Scrolls: Forty Years of Research*, edited by Devorah Dimant and Uriel Rappaport, pp. 199–209. Leiden/Jerusalem: E. J. Brill/Magnes/Yad Izhak Ben-Zvi, 1992.

Beacham, Richard C. *The Roman Theater and Its Audience*. Cambridge: Harvard University Press, 1992.

Beck, Rroger. "Cautes and Cautophates: Some Astronomical Considerations" *Journal of Mithraic Studies* 2 (1977): 1–17.

Beitzel, Barry J. "The Via Maris in Literary and Cartographic Sources." *BA* 54 (1991): 64–75.

Ben-David, Ayre. *Talumdische Ökonomie*, vol. 1. Hildesheim: Georg Olms, 1978.

Berlin, Andrea. "Between Large Forces: Palestine in the Hellenistic Period." *BA* 60 (1997): 2–51.

———. "From Monarchy to Markets: The Phoenicians in Hellenistic Palestine." *BASOR* 306 (1997): 75–88.

Berman, A. "Kfr Kanna." *ESI* 7–8 (1988–89): 107–108.

Betz, Hans-Dieter. "Wellhausen's Dictum 'Jesus was not a Christian, but a Jew' in Light of Present Scholarship." *Studia Theologica* 45 (1991): 83–100.

———. "Jesus and the Cynics: Survey and Analysis of a Hypothesis." *JR* 74 (1994): 453–475.

Bietenhard, H. "Die syrische Dekapolis von Pompeius bis Traian." *ANRW* II.8, edited by Wolfgang Haase and Hildegard Temporini, pp. 220–261. Berlin: Walter de Gruyter, 1977.

Bishop, Eric. "Jesus and Capernaum." *CBQ* 14 (1953): 427–37.

Blenkinsopp, Joseph. "The Literary Evidence." In *Excavations at Capernaum*, vol. 1, edited by Vasilios Tzaferis, pp. 201–211. Winona Lake, Indiana: Eisenbrauns, 1989.

Boatwright, Mary T. "Theaters in the Roman Empire." *BA* 53 (1990): 184–192

Bolyki, Janos. *Jesu Tischgemeinschaften.* WUNT, ser. 2, vol. 96. Tübingen: J. C. B. Mohr [Paul Siebeck], 1998.

Booth, Andrew D. "Aspects of the Circulator by Persius and Horace." *Greece and Rome* 26 (1980): 166–169.

Borg, Marcus. *Jesus: A New Vision.* San Francisco: HarperSanFrancisco, 1991.

Bornkamm, Günther. *Jesus von Nazareth.* Stuttgart: Kohlhammer, 1956.

Bösen, Wilibald. *Galiläa als Lebensraum und Wirkungsfeld Jesu.* Freiburg: Herder, 1985.

Bowerstock, Glen W. *Roman Arabia.* Cambridge: Harvard University Press, 1983.

——. "The Hellenism of Zenobia." In *Greek Connections*, edited by J. T. A. Koumoulides, pp. 19–27. Notre Dame: University of Notre Dame Press, 1987.

——. *Hellenism in Late Antiquity.* Ann Arbor: University of Michigan Press, 1990.

Bowsher, Julian M. C. "Architecture and Religion in the Decapolis: A Numismatic Survey." *PEQ* 119 (1987): 62–69.

Brandon, S. F. G. *The Fall of Jerusalem and the Christian Church.* 2nd ed. London: SCPK, 1957.

——. *Jesus and the Zealots.* Manchester: University Press, 1967.

Broshi, Magen. "The Standards of Street Widths in the Roman Byzantine Period." *IEJ* 27 (1977): 232–35.

——. "The Population of Western Palestine in the Roman-Byzantine Period." *BASOR* 236 (1980): 1–10.

——. "Agriculture and Economy in Roman Palestine: Seven Notes on the Babatha Archive." *IEJ* 42 (1992): 230–240.

Broshi, Magen and Ram Gophna. "The Settlements and Populations of Palestine During the Early Bronze Age II–III." *BASOR* 253 (1984): 41–53.

Büchler, Adolf. *The Political and Social Leaders of the Jewish Community of Sepphoris in the Second and Third Centuries.* London: Oxford University Press, 1909.

——. *'Am Ha-'Arez Ha-Galili*, translated by I. Eldad. Jerusalem: Mosad ha-Rav Kuk, 1964.

Bultmann, Rudolf. *Die Geschichte der synoptischen Tradition.* 2nd ed. FRLANT 29. Göttingen: Vandenhock & Ruprecht, 1931.

——. *Theologie des Neuen Testaments.* Tübingen: J. C. B. Mohr [Paul Siebeck], 1948–53).

——. *The History of the Synoptic Tradition.* Rev. ed. New York: Harper & Row, 1968.

——. *The Gospel of John.* Philadelphia: Westminster, 1971.

Burford, Alison. "Heavy Transport in Classical Antiquity." *Economic History Review* 13 (1960–61): 1–18.

Busse, Ulrich. *Das Nazareth-Manifest Jesu. Eine Einführung in das lukanische Jesusbild nach Lk 4,16–30.* Stuttgarter Bibelstudien 91. Stuttgart: Verlag Katholisches Bibelwerk, 1978.

Butler, Howard Crosby. *Ancient Architecture in Syria, Division II, Section A: Southern Syria.* Publications to the Princeton University Archaeological Expeditions to Syria. Leiden: E. J. Brill, 1907.

Byatt, Anthony. "Josephus and Population Numbers in First Century Palestine." *PEQ* 105 (1973): 51–60.

Cahill, Jane C. "The Chalk Assemblages of the Persian/Hellenistic and Early Roman Periods." In *Excavations at the City of David 1978–1985 Directed by Yigal Shiloh III: Stratigraphical, Environmental, and Other Reports*, edited by Alon de Groot and Donald T. Ariel, pp. 190–274. Qedem 33. Jerusalem: Hebrew University Press, 1992.

Carney, Thomas F. *The Shape of the Past. Models in Antiquity.* Lawrence: Coronado Press, 1975.

Carruth, Shawn. "Persuasion in Q: A Rhetorical Critical Study of Q 6:20–49." Ph.D. diss., The Claremont Graduate School, 1992.

Carruth, Shawn and James M. Robinson. *Q 4:1–13, 16 The Temptation of Jesus, Nazara*, edited by Christoph Heil. In *Documenta Q: Reconstructions of Q Through Two Centuries of Gospel Research Excerpted, Sorted and Evaluated.* Leuven: Peeters, 1996.

Case, Shirley-Jackson. "Jesus and Sepphoris." *JBL* 45 (1926): 14–22.

Charlesworth, James. *Jesus Within Judaism: New Light from Exciting Archaeological Excavations.* New York: Doubleday, 1988.

Charlesworth, James and Walter Weaver, eds. *What Has Archaeology to Do With Faith?* Valley Forge, Pennsylvania: Trinity Press International, 1992.

Chiat, Marilyn. "First-Century Synagogue Architecture: Methodological Problems." In *Ancient Synagogues: The State of Research*, edited by Joseph Gutman, pp. 50–58. Brown Judaic Studies 22. Chico, California: Scholars Press, 1981.

———. *Handbook of Synagogue Architecture.* Brown Judaic Studies 29. Chico, California: Scholars Press, 1982.

Chilton, Bruce. *Targumic Approaches to the Gospels: Essays in the Mutual Definition of Judaism and Christianity.* Lanham, Maryland: University Press of America, 1986.

Clamer, Christa. "'Ain ez-Zara Excavations 1986." *Annual of the Department of Antiquities of Jordan* 33 (1989): 217–25.

Clarke, David. *Analytical Archaeology.* 2nd and rev. ed. London: Methuen, 1978.

Cohen, R. "Ethnicity: Problem and Focus in Anthropology." *Annual Review of Anthropology* 7 (1978) 379–403.

Cohen, Shaye J. D. *Josephus in Galilee and Rome: His* Vita *and Development as a Historian.* Columbia Studies in the Classical Tradition 8. Leiden: E. J. Brill, 1979.

———. "A Virgin Defiled: Some Rabbinic and Christian Views on the Origins of Heresy." *USQR* 36 (1980): 1–11.

———. "Crossing the Boundary and Becoming a Jew." *HTR* 82 (1989): 13–33.

———. "Religion, Ethnicity, and Hellenism in the Emergence of Jewish Identity in Maccabean Palestine." In *Religion and Religious Practice in the Seleucid Kingdom*, edited by Per Bilde et al., pp. 204–223. Aarhus: Aarhus University Press, 1990.

———. "The Place of the Rabbi in Jewish Society of the Second Century." In *The Galilee in Late Antiquity*, edited by Lee Levine, 157–73. New York: Jewish Theological Seminary of America, 1992.

Conzelmann, Hans. *Die Mitte der Zeit. Studien zur Theologie Lukas.* 5th ed. BHT 17. Tübingen: J. C. B. Mohr [Paul Siebeck], 1964.

Conder, Claude R. and Horatio H. Kitchener. *The Survey of Western Palestine II: Samaria.* London: Palestine Exploration Fund, 1882.

Corbier, Mireille. "City, Territory, Taxation." In *City and Country in the Ancient World*, edited by John Rich and Andrew Wallace-Hadrill, pp. 211–39. Leichester-Nottingham Studies in Ancient Society 2. New York: Routledge, 1991.

226 Archaeology and the Galilean Jesus

Corbo, Virgilio. "Aspetti Urbanistici di Cafarnao." *LA* 21 (1971): 263–85.
————. "Scavi archeologici a Magdala (1971–1973)." *LA* 24 (1974): 5–37.
————. *Cafarnao 1: Gli edifici della città.* Studium Biblicum Franciscanum 19.
Jerusalem: Franciscan Printing Press, 1975.
————. "La città romana di Magdala, Rapporto preliminare dopo la quara cam-
pagna del 1975." *Studia Hierosolymitana* 1 (1976): 355–78.
————. "Piazza e villa urbana a Magdala." *LA* 28 (1978): 232–40.
Cotter, Wendy. "The Parable of the Children in the Market-Place, Q (Lk) 7:31–35:
An Examination of the Parable's Image and Significance." *Novum
Testamentum* 29 (1987): 289–304.
————. "Prestige, Protection and Promise: A Proposal for the Apologetics of Q2."
In *The Gospel Behind the Gospels*, edited by Ronald Piper, pp. 117–138. Leiden:
E. J. Brill, 1995.
Cross, Frank M. "Alphabets and Pots: Reflections on Typological Method in the
Dating of Human Artifacts." *MAARAV* 3 (1982): 121–36.
Crossan, John Dominic. *The Historical Jesus: The Life of a Mediterranean Jewish
Peasant.* San Francisco: Harper San Francisco, 1991.
————. *The Birth of Christianity: Discovering What Happened in the Years Immediately
After the Execution of Jesus.* San Francisco: HarperSanFrancisco, 1998.
Crum, John M. C. *The Original Jerusalem Gospel: Being Essays on the Document Q.*
New York: Macmillan, 1927.
Culham, Phyllis and Lowell Edmunds. *Classics: A Discipline and Profession in Crisis.*
Lanham, Maryland: University Press of America, 1989.
Dalman, Gustaf. *Orte und Wege Jesu.* 3rd ed. Gütersloh: Bertelsmann, 1924.
————. *Arbeit und Sitte in Palästina.* Gütersloh: Bertelsmann, 1928–42.
Dar, Shimon. "The History of the Hermon Settlements." *PEQ* 120 (1988): 26–44.
————. *Settlements and Cult Sites on Mount Hermon, Israel: Ituraean Culture in
the Hellenistic and Roman Periods.* BARIS 89. London: BAR, 1993.
Dar, Shimon and Nikos Kokkinos. "The Greek Inscriptions from Senaim on Mount
Hermon." *PEQ* 124 (1992): 9–25.
Deatrick, Eugene P. "Salt, Soil, Savior." *BA* 25 (May 1962): 41–47.
Deines, Roland. *Jüdische Steingefäße und pharisäische Frömmigkeit. Ein archäolo-
gisch-historischer Beitrag zum Verständnis von Joh 2,6 und der jüdischen
Reinheitshalacha zur Zeit Jesu.* WUNT, ser. 2, vol. 52. Tübingen: J. C. B. Mohr
[Paul Siebeck], 1993.
DeVaux, Roland. "On Right and Wrong Uses of Archaeology." In *Near Eastern
Archaeology in the Twentieth Century: Festschrift for Nelson Glueck*, edited by
James Sanders, pp. 30–79. New York: Doubleday, 1970.
Dever, William. "Syro-Palestinian and Biblical Archaeology." In *The Hebrew Bible
and Its Modern Interpreters*, edited by Douglas Knight and Gene Tucker, pp.
31–74. Philadelphia: Fortress, 1985.
————. "The Impact of the New Archaeology." In *Benchmarks in Time and Culture.
An Introduction to Palestinian Archaeology. Dedicated to Joseph A. Callaway*,
edited by Joel Drinkard et al., pp. 337–352. Atlanta: Scholars Press, 1988.
Dibelius, Martin. *Die Formgeschichte des Evangeliums.* 4th ed. Tübingen: J. C. B.
Mohr [Paul Siebeck], 1961.
Dothan, Moshe. *Hammath Tiberias: Early Synagogues and the Hellenistic and Roman
Remains.* Jerusalem: Israel Exploration Society, 1983.
————. "Research on Ancient Synagogues in the Land of Israel." In *Recent
Archaeology in the Land of Israel*, edited by Benjamin Mazar and Hershel
Shanks, pp. 89–96. Jerusalem: Israel Exploration Society, 1984.

Douglas, R. Conrad. "Once Again, 'Love Your Enemies': Rhetorical and Social Scientific Considerations of a Familiar Passage." In *Conflict and Invention: Literary, Rhetorical, and Social Studies on the Sayings Gospel Q*, edited by John Kloppenborg, pp. 116–31. Valley Forge, Pennsylvania: Trinity Press International, 1995.

Downing, F. Gerarld. "The Social Contexts of Jesus the Teacher: Construction or Reconstruction." *NTS* 33 (1987): 439–51.

————. *Christ and the Cynics: Jesus and Other Radical Preachers in First-Century Tradition*. JSOT Manuals 4. Sheffield: Sheffield Academic Press, 1988.

Downs, Roger and James Meyer. "Geography of the Mind: An Exploration of Perceptual Geography." *American Behavioral Scientist* 22 (Sept./Oct. 1978): 59–77.

Drinkard, Joel et al., eds. *Benchmarks in Time and Culture. An Introduction to Palestinian Archaeology. Dedicated to Joseph A. Callaway*. Atlanta: Scholars Press, 1988.

Duncan-Jones, Richard P. "City Population in Roman Africa." *JRS* 53 (1963): 85–90.

————. "Human Numbers in Towns and Town-Organizations of the Roman Empire: The Evidence of Gifts." *Historia* 13 (1964): 199–208.

————. *The Economy of the Roman Empire*. 2nd ed. Cambridge: Cambridge University Press, 1982.

Edwards, Douglas. "First Century Urban/Rural Relations in Lower Galilee: Exploring the Archaeological and Literary Evidence." In *SBLSP* 1988, edited by David Lull, pp. 169–182. Atlanta: Scholars Press, 1988.

————. "The Socio-Economic and Cultural Ethos of Lower Galilee in the First Century: Implications for the Nascent Jesus Movement." In *Studies on the Galilee in Late Antiquity*, edited by Lee Levine, pp. 53–73. New York: Jewish Theological Seminary, 1992.

Edwards, Douglas and C. Thomas McCollough, eds. *Archaeology and the Galilee: Texts and Contexts in the Graeco-Roman and Byzantine Periods*. South Florida Studies in the History of Judaism 143. Atlanta: Scholars Press, 1997.

Edwards, Richard. A. *The Sign of Jonah in the Theology of the Evangelists and Q*. SBT, ser. 2, vol. 18. London: SCM Press, 1971.

Elgavish, Joseph. *Archaeological Excavations at Shiqmona. Report Number 2. The Level of the Hellenistic Period—Stratum H*. Haifa: Museum of Art, 1974.

Engels, Donald. *Roman Corinth: An Alternative Model for the Classical City*. Chicago: The University of Chicago, 1990.

Escheman, Hans. *Die städtebauliche Entwicklung des antiken Pompeji*. Römische Abteilungen, siebzehntes Ergänzungsheft. Heidelberg: F. H. Kerle, 1970.

Esler, Philip. *Community and Gospel in Luke-Acts: The Social and Political Motivations of Lucan Theology*. SNTSMS 59. Cambridge: Cambridge University Press, 1987.

Evans, John K. "Wheat production and its social consequences in the Roman World." *CQ* 31 (1981): 428–42.

Fiensy, David. *The Social History of Palestine in the Herodian Period. The Land is Mine*. Studies in the Bible and Early Christianity 20. Lewiston: Edwin Mellen, 1991.

Finegan, Jack. *The Archaeology of the New Testament: The Life of Jesus and the Beginning of the Early Church*. Rev. ed. Princeton: Princeton University Press, 1992.

Finley, Moses. *The Ancient Economy*. Berkeley: The University of California Press, 1973.

————. "The Ancient City: From Fustel de Coulanges to Max Weber and Beyond." *Comparative Studies in Society and History* 19 (1977): 305–32.

————. *Ancient History: Evidence and Models*. London: Chatto & Windus, 1985.

Fisher, Moshe. "Figured Capitals in Roman Palestine. Marble Imports and Local Stones: Some Aspects of 'Imperial' and 'Provincial' Art." In *Archäologischer Anzeiger 1991*, pp. 119–44. Deutsches archäologisches Institut. Berlin: Walter de Greuyter, 1991.

Flesher, Paul. "Palestinian Synagogues before 70 C.E.: A Review of the Evidence." In *Approaches to Ancient Judaism*, vol. 6, edited by Jacob Neusner and Ernest Frerichs, pp. 75–80. Atlanta: Scholars Press, 1989.

Foerster, Gideon. "Notes on Recent Excavations at Capernaum." *IEJ* 21 (1971): 207–11.

————. "Excavations at Ancient Meiron." *IEJ* 37 (1987): 262–69.

Foerster, Gideon and Yoram Tsafrir. "Bet Shean Project, " in *ESI* 1987/1988 vol. 6. Jerusalem: The Israel Antiquities Authority, 1988, pp. 10–43.

Frankel, Rafael. "Har Mispe Yamim 1988–9." *ESI* 9 (1989–90): 100–102.

Fredrickson, Paula. *Jesus of Nazareth, King of the Jews: a Jewish Life and the Emergence of Christianity*. New York: Knopf, 1999.

Frevel, Christian. "Dies ist der Ort, von dem geschrieben steht . . ." *BN* 47 (1989): 35–89.

Freyne, Seán. *Galilee from Alexander the Great to Hadrain 323 B.C.E.. to 125 C.E.: A Study of Second Temple Judaism*. Wilmington, Delaware: Michael Glazier, 1980.

————. "Galilee-Jerusalem Relations according to Josephus' Life." *NTS* 33 (1987): 600–609.

————. *Galilee, Jesus, and the Gospels: Literary Approaches and Historical Investigations*. Philadelphia: Fortress, 1988.

————. "Bandits in Galilee: A Contribution to the Study of Social Conditions in First-Century Palestine." In *The Social World of Formative Christianity and Judaism*, edited by Jacob Neusner et al., pp. 50–68. Philadelphia: Fortress, 1988.

————. "The Geography, Politics, and Economics of Galilee and the Quest for the Historical Jesus." In *Studying the Historical Jesus: Evaluations of the State of Current Research*, edited by Bruce Chilton and Craig Evans, pp. 75–121. NTTS 19. Leiden: E. J. Brill, 1994.

————. "Jesus and the Urban Culture of Galilee." In *Texts and Contexts: Biblical Texts and Their Textual and Situational Contexts*, edited by Tord Fornberg and David Hellholm, pp. 596–622. Oslo: Scandinavian University Press, 1995.

Fritsch, Charles and Immanuel Ben-Dor. "The Link Marine Expedition to Israel, 1960." *BA* 24 (1961): 57–58.

Fritz, Volkmar. "Die Paläste während der assyrischen, babylonischen und persischern Vorherrschaft in Palästina." *Mitteilungen der Deutschen Orientalische Gesellschaft* 111 (1979): 63–74.

————. *Kinneret, Ergebnisse der Ausgrabungen auf dem Tell el-'Oreme am See Gennesaret 1982–1985*. Wiesbaden: Otto Harrassowitz, 1990.

Funk, Robert. *Honest to Jesus: Jesus for a New Millennium*. San Francisco: HarperSanFrancisco, 1996.

Gal, Zvi. "The Lower Galilee in the Iron Age II: Analysis of Survey Material and its Historical Interpretation." *Tel Aviv* 15–16 (1988–1989): 56–64.

————. "A Stone-Vessel Manufacturing Site in the Lower Galilee." *'Atiqot* 20 (1991): 25*-26*, English summary 179–180.

————. *The Lower Galilee during the Iron Age*. ASOR Dissertation Series 8. Winona Lake, Indiana, 1992.

Garnsey, Peter. *Famine and Food Supply in the Graeco-Roman World*. Cambridge: Cambridge University Press, 1988.

Garnsey, Peter. and Richard Saller. *The Roman Empire: Economy, Society and Culture*. Berkeley: University of California Press, 1987.

Gatti, Clementina. "A Proposito di una Rilettura dell'Epigrafe di Ponzio Pilato." *Aveum* 55 (1981): 13–21.

Gawlikowski, Michal. "A Residential Area by the South Decumanus." In *Jerash Archaeological Project 1981–1983*, edited by Fawzi Zayadine, pp. 107–36. Amman: Department of Antiquities, 1986.

Gersht, Rivka. "The Tyche of Caesarea Maritima." *PEQ* 116 (1984): 110–114.

———. "The Reader of the Scroll From Caesarea Maritima." *Tel Aviv* 13 (1986): 67–70.

———. "Dionysiac Sarcophagi from Caesarea Maritima." *IEJ* 41 (1991): 145–156.

Ginzburg, Carlo. "Spie. Radici di un paradigma indiziario." In *Crisi della ragione*, edited by Aldo Gargani, pp. 56–106. Torino: Guilio Einaudi, 1979.

Ginzberg, Louis. *The Legends of the Jews*. 7 vols. Philadelphia: The Jewish Publication Society of America, 1913.

Gitin, Seymour. "Tel Miqne-Ekron: A Type Site for the Inner Coastal Plain in the Iron II Period." In *Recent Excavations in Israel: Studies in Iron Age Archaeology*, edited by Seymour Gittin and William Dever, pp. 59–79. AASOR 49. Winona Lake, Indiana: Eisenbrauns, 1989.

Glombitza, Otto. "Das Zeichen des Jona (Zum Verständnis von Matth. XII.38–42)." *NTS* 8 (1961–2): 359–66.

Golomb, B. and Y. Kedar. "Ancient Agriculture in the Galilee Mountains." *IEJ* 21 (1971): 136–140.

Goodenough, Erwin R. *Jewish Symbols in the Greco-Roman Period*. 13 vols. New York: Pantheon Books, 1953–68.

Goodman, Martin. "The First Jewish Revolt: Social Conflict and the Problem of Debt." *JJS* 33 (1982): 417–427.

———. *State and Society in Roman Galilee, A.D. 132–212*. Totowa, New Jersey: Rowman & Allanheld, 1983.

Gottdiener, Mark and Alexandros Lagopoulos, eds. *The City and the Sign: An Introduction to Urban Semiotics*. New York: Columbia University Press, 1986.

Gould, Peter and Richard White. *Mental Maps*. Baltimore: Penguin Books, 1974.

Grabar, O. et al. "Sondages à Khirbet el-Minyeh." *IEJ* 10 (1960): 226–43.

Graf, David. "The Nabataeans and the Decapolis." In *The Defence of the Roman and Byzantine East*, edited by Philip Freeman and David Kennedy, pp. 785–796. British Institute of Archaeology at Ankara Monograph 8. Oxford: BAR, 1986.

Grant, Michael. *Cities of Vesuvius: Pompeii and Herculaneum*. New York: Penguin, 1971.

Greene, Kevin. *The Archaeology of the Roman Economy*. Berkeley: University of California Press, 1986.

Greenhut, Zvi. "Two Burial Caves of the Second Temple Period in Rehavia, Jerusalem." *'Atiqot* 29 (1996): 41*–46*, English summary 109.

Groh, Dennis. "The Clash Between Literary and Archaeological Models of Provincial Palestine." In *Archaeology and the Galilee: Texts and Contexts in the Graeco-Roman and Byzantine Periods*, edited by Douglas Edwards and C. Thomas McCollough, pp. 31–33. South Florida Studies in the History of Judaism 143; Atlanta: Scholars Press, 1997.

Grundmann, Walter. *Jesus der Galiläer und das Judentum*. Leipzig: Wigand, 1940.

Gundry, Robert. *Matthew: A Commentary on His Literary and Theological Art*. Grand Rapids: Eerdmans, 1982.

Gunneweg, Jan and Isadore Pearlman. "Hellenistic Braziers From Israel: Results of Pottery Analysis." *IEJ* 34 (1984): 232–238.

Gunther, Heinz. "The Sayings Gospel Q and the Quest for Aramaic Sources: Rethinking Christian Origins." In *Early Christianity, Q, and Jesus*, edited by John Kloppenborg and Leif Vaage, pp. 41–76. Semeia 55. Atlanta: Scholars Press, 1992.

Gutman, Joseph ed. *Ancient Synagogues: The State of Research*. Brown Judaic Studies 22. Chico, California: Scholars Press, 1981.

Gutman, S. and D. Wagner. "Gamla—1984/1985/1986." *ESI* 5 (1986): 38–41.

Hachlili, Rachel. *Ancient Jewish Art and Archaeology in the Land of Israel*. Lieden: E. J. Brill, 1988.

Hachlili, Rachel and Ann Killebrew. "Jewish Funerary Customs during the Second Temple Period, in the Light of the Excavations at the Jericho Necropolis." *PEQ* 115 (1983): 115–26.

Haevner, Ivan. *Q: The Sayings of Jesus*. Wilmington, Delaware: Michael Glazier, 1987.

Hamel, Gildas. *Poverty and Charity in Roman Palestine, First Three Centuries C.E.* Near Eastern Studies 23. Berkeley: University of California, 1990.

Hanson, Richard. *Tyrian Influence in the Upper Galilee: Meiron Excavation Project 2.* Cambridge, Massachusetts: ASOR, 1980.

Hanson, K. C. and Douglas Oakman. *Palestine in the Time of Jesus: Social Structures and Social Conflicts*. Minneapolis: Fortress, 1998.

Harnack, Adolf von. *Sprüche und Reden Jesu. Beiträge zur Einleitung in das Neue Testament II*. Leipzig: J. C. Hinrichs, 1907.

———. *The Sayings of Jesus: The Second Source of St. Matthew and St. Luke*. New Testament Studies 3. London: Williams & Norgate, 1907.

Harper, G. "A Study in the Commercial Relations between Egypt and Syria in the Third Century before Christ." *AJP* 49 (1928): 1–35.

Harrington, Hannah. *The Impurity Systems of Qumran and the Rabbis*. SBLDS 143. Atlanta: Scholars Press, 1993.

Harris, William. *Ancient Literacy*. Cambridge: Harvard University Press, 1989.

Hartel, M. "'Khirbet Zemel' 1985–6." *IEJ* 37 (1987): 270–2.

———. *Northern Golan Heights. The Archaeological Survey as a Source of Regional History*. Qatzrin: Israel Department of Antiquities and Museums, 1989.

Hartin, Patrick. *James and the Q Sayings of Jesus*. JSNTSS 47. Sheffield: Sheffield Academic Press, 1991.

Harvey, Paul. "Calculo de la poblacion de la antigua Roma: Datos, modelos y metodos." *Semana de Estudios Romanos*. Vol. 7, pp. 175–88. Instituto de Historia, Universidad Catolica de Valparaiso, 1991.

Hassan, Fekri. *Demographic Archaeology*. New York: Academic Press, 1981.

Haywood, Richard. M. "Roman Africa." In *An Economic Survey of Ancient Rome IV*, edited by Tenny Frank, pp. 1–119. Baltimore: The Johns Hopkins Press, 1938.

Hengel, Martin. "*Proseuche* und *Synagoge*: Jüdische Gemeinde, Gotteshaus, und Gottesdienst in der Diaspora und in Palaestina." In *Tradition und Glaube: das frühe Christentum in seiner Umwelt. Festgabe für Karl Georg Kuhn zum 65 Geburtstag*, edited by Gret Jeremias, Heinz-Wolfgang Kuhn, and Harmut Stegemann, pp. 157–84. Göttingen: Vanderhoeck and Ruprecht, 1971.

———. *Judaism and Hellenism: Studies in Their Encounter in Palestine during the Early Hellenistic Period*, 2 vols. Philadelphia: Fortress, 1974.

———. *Die Evangelienüberschriften*. Heidelberg: Carl Winter, Universitätsverlag, 1984.

———. *The 'Hellenization' of Judaea in the First Century after Christ*. Philadelphia: Trinity Press International, 1989.

————. *The Johannine Question.* Philadelphia: Trinity Press International, 1989.

Hengel, Martin and Roland Deines. "E. P. Sanders' 'Common Judaism,' Jesus, and the Pharisees." *JThS* NS 46 (1995): 1–70

————. "E. P. Sanders' 'Common Judaism,' Jesus und die Pharisäer." In *Judaica et Hellenistica. Kleine Schriften,* vol. 1, pp. 392–479. Tübingen: J. C. B. Mohr [Paul Siebeck], 1996.

Herbert, Sharon. *Tel Anafa I. Final Report on Ten Years of Excavation at a Hellenistic and Roman Settlement in Northern Israel.* JRA Supplemental Series 10.1. Ann Arbor, Michigan: Kelsey Museum of Archaeology, 1994.

Hermansen, Gustav. *Ostia: Aspects of Roman City Life.* Edmonton: The University of Alberta Press, 1981.

Herr, Larry. "The Iron Age II Period: Emerging Nations." *BA* 60 (1997): 114–83.

Hershkovitz, Malka. "Miniature Ointment Vases." *IEJ* 36 (1986): 50–51.

Hesse, Brian and Paula Wapnish. "Can Pig Remains Be Used for Ethnic Diagnosis in the Ancient Near East?" In *The Archaeology of Israel. Constructing the Past, Interpreting the Present,* edited by Neil Silberman and David Small, pp. 238–270. Sheffield: Sheffield Academic Press, 1997.

Hill, George F. "Some Palestinian Cults in the Graeco-Roman Age." In *Proceedings of the British Academy* 5 (1911–12): 411–27.

Hirschfeld, Nicolle. "The Ship of Saint Paul." *BA* 53 (1990): 25–30.

Hirshfeld, Yizhar. "Tiberias: Preview of Coming Attractions." *BAR* 17.2 (March/April 1991): 44–51.

————. "The 'Anchor Church' at the Summit of Mount Berenice near Tiberias." *Qadmoniot* 26 (1993): 120–27 [Hebrew].

————. *The Palestinian Dwelling in the Roman-Byzantine Period.* Jerusalem: Franciscan Printing, 1995.

Hirshfeld, Yizhar and Rivka Birger-Calderon. "Early Roman and Byzantine Estates Near Caesarea." *IEJ* 41 (1991): 81–111.

Hoehner, Harold. *Herod Antipas.* Cambridge: Cambridge University Press, 1972.

Hoenig, Sidney. "The Ancient City-Square: Forerunner of the Synagogue." *ANRW* 2.19.1. Edited by Wolfgang Haase and Hildegard Temporini, pp. 448–476. Berlin: Walter de Gruyter, 1979.

Hoffmann, Paul. "Die Versuchungsgeschichte in der Logienquelle." *BZ* NF 13 (1969): 207–23.

————. *Studien zur Theologie der Logienquelle.* NTAbh NF 8. Münster: Aschendorf, 1972.

————. "The Redaction of Q and the Son of Man: A Preliminary Sketch." In *The Gospel Behind the Gospels: Current Studies on Q,* edited by Ronald Piper, pp. 159–98. Leiden: E. J. Brill, 1995.

————. *Tradition und Situation. Studien zur Jesusüberlieferung in der Logienquelle und den synoptischen Evangelien.* NTAbh NF 28. Münster: Aschendorf, 1995.

Holum, Kenneth. *King Herod's Dream: Caesarea by the Sea.* New York: Norton, 1988.

Holzmann, Heinrich Julius. *Die Synoptischen Evangelien: Ihr Ursprung und geschichtlicher Charakter.* Leipzig: Wilhelm Engelmann, 1863.

Hopkins, Ian. "The City Region in Roman Palestine." *PEQ* 112 (1980): 19–32.

Hopkins, Keith. "Economic Growth in Towns in Classical Antiquity." In *Towns in Societies: Essays in Economic History and Historical Sociology,* edited by Philip Abrams and E. A. Wigley, pp. 35–77. Cambridge: University Press, 1978.

————. "Taxes and Trade in the Roman Empire." *JRS* 70 (1980): 101–25.

Horsley, Richard. "Ancient Jewish Banditry and the Revolt against Rome, A.D. 66–70." *CBQ* 43 (1981): 409–432.

————. *Jesus and the Spiral of Violence: Popular Jewish Resistance in Roman Palestine*. San Francisco: Harper & Row, 1987.

————. "Bandits, Messiahs, and Longshoremen: Popular Unrest in Galilee around the Time of Jesus." In *SBLSP 1988*, edited by David Lull, pp. 183–199. Atlanta: Scholars Press, 1988.

————. *Galilee: History, Politics, People*. Valley Forge, Pennsylvania: Trinity Press International, 1995.

————. "Social Conflict in the Synoptic Sayings Source Q." In *Conflict and Invention: Literary, Rhetorical, and Social Studies on the Sayings Gospel Q*, edited by John Kloppenborg, pp. 37–52. Valley Forge, Pennsylvania: Trinity Press International, 1995.

————. "Archaeology and the Villages of Upper Galilee: A Dialogue with Archaeologists." *BASOR* 297 (1995): 5–16, 27–8.

————. *Archaeology, History, and Society in Galilee: The Social Context of Jesus and the Rabbis*. Valley Forge, Pennsylvania: Trinity Press International, 1996.

Horsley, Richard and John S. Hanson. *Bandits, Prophets, and Messiahs: Popular Movements at the Time of Jesus*. New York: Winston (A Seabury Book), 1985.

Houston Smith, R. "The Southern Levant in the Hellenistic Period." *Levant* 22 (1990): 123–130.

Hume, David. "Essay XI: Of the Populousness of Ancient Nations." In *Essays, Moral, Political, and Literary*, edited by Eugene Miller. Indianapolis: LibertyClassics, 1985.

Ilan, Z. "Horvat Arbel." *ESI* 7–8 (1988–89): 8–9.

Jacobsen, Arland. "The Literary Unity of Q." *JBL* 101 (1982): 365–89.

————. "Wisdom Christology in Q." Ph.D. diss., The Claremont Graduate School, Claremont, California, 1978.

————. "Divided Families and Christian Origins." In *The Gospel Behind the Gospels: Current Studies on Q*, edited by Ronald Piper, pp. 361–80. Leiden: E. J. Brill, 1995.

Jeremias, Joachim. *Heiligengräber in Jesu Umwelt*. Göttingen: Vanderhoeck & Ruprecht, 1958.

————. *Abba*. Göttingen: Vandenhoeck & Ruprecht, 1966.

————. *Jerusalem zur Zeit Jesu. Eine kulturgeschichtliche Untersuchung zur neutestamentlichen Zeitgeschichte*. 3rd ed. Göttingen: Vandenhoeck & Ruprecht, 1969.

Jones, Arnold H. M. "The Urbanization of Palestine." *JRS* 21 (1931): 78–85.

————. *The Roman Economy*, edited by P. A. Brunt. Totowa, New Jersey: Rowman & Littlefield, 1974.

Jongman, Willem. *The Economy and Society of Pompeii*. Amsterdam: J. C. Gieben, 1988.

Käseman, Ernst. "Das Problem des historischen Jesu." *ZTK* 51 (1954): 125–53.

Kasher, Aryen. *Jews, Idumaeans, and Ancient Arabs: Relations of the Jews in Eretz-Israel with the Nations of the Frontier and the Desert during the Hellenistic and Roman Era (332 B.C.E.–70 C.E.)*. TSAJ 19. Tübingen: J. C. B. Mohr [Paul Siebeck], 1988.

Kautsky, John. *The Politics of Aristocratic Empires*. Chapel Hill, North Carolina: University of North Carolina Press, 1982.

Kee, Howard Clark. "The Transformation of the Synagogue after 70 C.E.: Its Import for Early Christianity." *NTS* 36 (1990): 1–24.

————. "Early Christianity in the Galilee: Reassessing the Evidence from the Gospels." In *The Galilee in Late Antiquity*, edited by Lee Levine, pp. 3–22. New York: The Jewish Theological Seminary of America, 1992.

Kennedy, Hugh. "From Polis to Madina: Urban Change in Late Antique and Early Islamic Syria." *Past and Present* 106–109 (1985): 3–27.

Kessler, Rainer. "Frühkapitalismus, Rentenkapitalismus, Tributarismus, antike Klassengesllschaft. Theorien zur Gesellschaft des alten Israels." *ET* 54 (1994): 413–427.

Kittel, Gerhard and Gerhard Friedrich, eds. *Theologisches Wörterbuch zum Neuen Testament.* Stuttgart: W. Kohlhammer, 1933–79.

Klein, Samuel. *Galilaea vor der Makkabäerzeit.* Palästina-Studien 4. Berlin: Menorah, 1928.

Kloner, Amos. "A Tomb with Inscribed Ossuaries in East Talpiyot, Jerusalem." *'Atiqot* 29 (1996): 15–22.

Kloppenborg, John. "The Formation of Q and Antique Instructional Genres." *JBL* 105 (1986): 452–54.

————. *The Formation of Q: Trajectories in Ancient Wisdom Collections.* Studies in Antiquity and Christianity Philadelphia: Fortress Press, 1987. Second edition, Harrisburg, Pennsylvania: Trinity Press International, 2000.

————. *Q Parallels: Synopsis, Critical Notes, & Concordance.* Sonoma: Polebridge Press, 1988.

————. "City and Wasteland: Narrative World and the Beginning of the Sayings Gospel (Q)." In *How Gospels Begin*, edited by Dennis Smith, pp. 145–160. Semeia 52. Atlanta: Scholars Press, 1990.

————. "*Nomos* and *Ethos* in Q." In *Gospel Origins and Christian Beginnings,* edited by James Goehring, Charles Hedrick, and Jack T. Sanders, pp. 35–48. Sonoma: Polebridge Press, 1990.

————. "The Sayings Gospel Q: Recent Opinion on the People Behind the Document." *CRBS* 1 (1993): 9–34.

————, ed. *The Shape of Q: Signal Essays on the Sayings Gospel.* Minneapolis: Fortress, 1994.

————. "Literary Convention, Self-Evidence and the Social History of the Q People." In *Early Christianity, Q and Jesus,* edited by John Kloppenborg and Leif Vaage, pp. 145–160. Semeia 55. Atlanta: Scholars Press, 1991.

————. "The Sayings Gospel Q: Literary and Stratigraphic Problems." *Symbols and Strata: Essays on the Sayings Gospel Q.* Suomen Eksegettisen Seuran Julkaisuja 65. Helsinki/Göttingen: Finnish Exegetical Society/Vanderhoeck & Ruprecht, 1996.

Koester, Helmut. "The Sayings of Q and Their Image of Jesus." In *Sayings of Jesus: Canonical and Non-Canonical. Essays in Honor of Tjitze Baarda,* edited by William Petersen et al., pp. 137–54. Leiden: E. J. Brill, 1997.

Kohl, Heinrich and Carl Watzinger. *Die antiken Synagogen in Galilaea.* Leipzig: Hinrichs, 1916.

Kolendo, Jerzy. "La répartition des places aux spectacles et le stratification sociale dans l'empire romain." *Ktema* 6 (1981): 300–10.

Kondoleon, Christine. *Domestic and Divine: Roman Mosaics in the House of Dionysos.* Ithaca: Cornell University Press, 1994.

Kopp, Clemens. "Beiträge zur Geschichte Nazareths." *JPOS* 18 (1938): 191–228.

————. *Die Heiligen Stätten der Evangelien.* Regensburg: Friedrich Pustet, 1959.

Koucky, F. L. "The Regional Environment." In *The Roman Frontier in Central Jordan I,* edited by Thomas Parker, pp. 11–40. BARIS 340[i]. London: BAR, 1987.

Kraay, Colin M. "Jewish Friends and Allies of Rome." *American Numismatic Society Museum Notes* 25 (1980): 53–57.

Kraabel, A. Thomas. "The Roman Diaspora: Six Questionable Assumptions." *JJS* 33 (1982): 445–64.

Kraemer, Ross. "On the Meaning of the Term 'Jew' in Greco-Roman Inscriptions." *HTR* 82 (1989): 35–53.

Krauss, Samuel. *Griechische und Lateinische Lehnwörter im Talmud, Midrasch, und Targum.* 2 vols. Berlin: S. Calvary, 1898–9.

————. *Talumudische Archäologie,* 3 vols. Leipzig: G. Fock, 1910–12.

Kreissig, Heinz. "Die Landwirtschaftliche Situation in Palästina vor dem judäischen Krieg." *Acta Antiqua* 17 (1969): 223–54.

Kroll, Gerhart. *Auf den Spuren Jesu.* Leipzig: St. Benno, 1980.

Kuhnen, Hans-Peter. *NordwestPalästina in hellenistisch-römischer Zeit. Bauten und Gräber im Karmelgebiet.* Quellen und Forschungen zur prähistorischen und provincialrömischen Archäologie. Weinheim: VCH Acta Humaniora, 1987.

Landau, Yohanan H. "A Greek Inscription Found Near Hefzibah." *IEJ* 16 (1966): 54–70.

Landau, Yohanan H. "The Site of Tiberias." In *Eretz Kinnaroth.* Jerusalem: Jewish Palestine Exploration Society, 1950 [Hebrew].

Landes, George M. "Jonah in Luke: The Hebrew Bible Background to the Interpretation of the 'Sign of Jonah' Pericope in Luke 11:29–32." In *A Gift of God in Due Season. Essays on Scripture and Community in Honor of James A. Sanders,* edited by Richard Weiss and David Carr, pp. 133–63. JSOTSS 225. Sheffield: Sheffield Academic Press, 1996.

Lang, Friedrich. "'Über Sidon mitten ins Gebiet der Dekapolis.' Geographie und Theologie in Markus 7,31." *ZDPV* 94 (1978): 145–60.

Laughlin, John. "Capernaum: From Jesus' Time and After." *BAR* 19.5 (Sept./Oct. 1993): 54–61.

————. "The Identification of the Site." In *Excavations at Capernaum,* vol. 1, edited by Vasilios Tzaferis, pp. 191–99. Winona Lake, Indiana: Eisenbrauns, 1989.

Lenski, Gerhard. *Power and Privilege: A Theory of Social Stratification.* New York: McGraw-Hill, 1966.

Levine, Amy-Jill. "Second Temple Judaism, Jesus, and Women: Yeast of Eden." *Biblical Interpretation* 2 (1994): 8–33.

Levine, Lee. "The Hasmonean Conquest of Strato's Tower." *IEJ* 24 (1974): 62–69.

————. *The Rabbinic Class of Roman Palestine in Late Antiquity.* New York: Jewish Theological Seminary of America, 1989.

————, ed. *The Galilee in Late Antiquity.* New York: Jewish Theological Seminary of America, 1992.

Lifshitz, Baruch. "Die Entdeckung einer alten Synagoge bei Tiberias." *ZDPV* 78 (1962): 180–84.

Livio, Jean-Bernard. "Nazareth: les fouilles chez les religieuses de Nazareth." *MB* 16 (1967): 26–34.

Loffreda, Stanislo. *A Visit to Capernaum.* Jerusalem: Franciscan Press, 1972.

————. "The late Chronology of the Synagogue of Capernaum." *IEJ* 23 (1973): 37–42.

————. *Cafarnao II: La ceramica.* Studium Biblicum Franciscanum 19. Jerusalem: Franciscan Printing Press, 1974.

Loftus, Francis. "A Note on συνταγμα των Γαλιλαιων B.J. iv 558." *JQR* 65 (1974): 182–83.

————. "The Anti-Roman Revolts of the Jews and the Galileans." *JQR* 68 (1977): 78–98.

Lohmeyer, Ernst. *Galiläa und Jerusalem.* FRLANT 34. Göttingen: Vanderhoeck & Ruprecht, 1936.

Longstaff, Thomas. "Nazareth and Sepphoris: Insights into Christian Origins." *Anglican Theological Review, Supplementary Series* 11 (1990): 8–15.

Lowenthal, David and Martyn Bowden, eds. *Geographies of the Mind.* New York: Oxford University Press, 1976.

Lüdemann, Gerd. "The Successors of Pre-70 Jerusalem Christianity: A Critical Evaluation of the Pella-Tradition." In *Jewish and Christian Self-Definition,* vol. 1, edited by E. P. Sanders, pp. 161–73. Philadelphia: Fortress, 1989.

Lührmann, Dieter. *Die Redaktion der Logienquelle.* WMANT 33. Neukirchen-Vluyn: Neukirchner, 1969.

———. *Das Markusevangelium.* Handbuch zum Neuen Testament 3. Tübingen: J. C. B. Mohr [Paul Siebeck], 1987.

———. "Q: Sayings of Jesus or Logia?" In *The Gospel Behind the Gospels: Current Studies on Q,* edited by Ronald Piper, 97–116. Leiden: E. J. Brill, 1995.

Luz, Ulrich. *Das Evangelium Nach Matthäus (Mt 1–7).* Zürich: Benzinger, 1985.

———. *Das Evangelium Nach Matthäus (Mt 8–17).* Zürich: Benzinger, 1990.

Lynch, Kevin. *The Image of the City.* Cambridge, Massachusets: MIT Press, 1960.

Mack, Burton. *Wisdom and the Hebrew Epic: Ben Sirach's Hymn of Praise to the Fathers.* Chicago: University of Chicago, 1985.

———. *A Myth of Innocence.* Philadelphia: Fortress Press, 1988.

———. "The Kingdom that Didn't Come." In *SBLSP 1988,* edited by David Lull, pp. 608–635. Atlanta: Scholars Press, 1988.

———. "Q and the Gospel of Mark: Revising Christian Origins." In *Early Christianity, Q, and Jesus,* edited by John Kloppenborg and Leif Vaage, pp. 15–39. Semeia 55. Atlanta: Scholars Press, 1991.

———. *The Lost Gospel: The Book of Q and Christian Origins.* San Francisco: HarperSanFrancisco, 1993.

MacMullen, Ramsey. "Market-Days in the Roman Empire." *Phoenix* 24 (1970): 333–41.

———. *Roman Social Relations: 50 B.C. to A.D. 284.* New Haven: Yale University Press, 1974.

Magen, Yizhak. *The Stone Vessel Industry in Jerusalem in the Days of the Second Temple.* Tel Aviv: Society for the Protection of Nature, 1988 [Hebrew].

———. "The Ritual Baths (*Miqva'ot*) at Qedumim and the Observance of Ritual Purity Among the Samaritans." In *Early Christianity in Context: Monuments and Documents,* edited by Frédéric Manns and Eugenio Alliata, pp. 181–192. Jerusalem: Franciscan Printing Press, 1993.

———. "Jerusalem as a Center of the Stone Vessel Industry during the Second Temple Period." In *Ancient Jerusalem Revealed,* edited by Hillel Geva, pp. 244–256. Jerusalem: Israel Exploration Society, 1994.

———. *"Purity Broke out in Israel:" Stone Vessels in the Late Second Temple Period.* The Reuben and Edith Hecht Museum, Catalogue No. 9. Haifa: University of Haifa, 1994.

Mahnke, Hermann. *Die Vesuchungsgeschichte im Rahmen der synoptischen Evangelien.* BBET 9. Frankfurt: Lang, 1978.

Malbon, Elizabeth Struthers. *Narrative Space and Mythic Meaning in Mark.* San Francisco: Harper & Row, 1986.

———. "Galilee and Jerusalem: History and Literature in Markan Interpretation." *CBQ* 44 (1982): 242–55.

Malina, Bruce. *The New Testament World: Insights from Cultural Anthropology.* Atlanta: John Knox, 1981.

————. *Christian Origins and Cultural Anthropology*. Atlanta: John Knox, 1986.
————. *The New Testament World: Insights from Cultural Anthropology*. Rev. ed. Louisville: Westminster John Knox, 1993.
Malina, Bruce and Richard Rohrbaugh. *Social Science Commentary on the Gospels*. Minneapolis: Fortress, 1992.
Manns, Frédéric. *Essais sur le judéo-christianisme*. Jerusalem: Franciscan Printing, 1977.
Manson, Thomas. W. *The Sayings of Jesus*. London: SCM Press, 1949.
Marxsen, Willi. *Der Evangelist Markus. Studien zur Redaktionsgeschichte des Evangeliums*. FRLANT 49. Göttingen: Vanderhoeck & Ruprecht, 1956.
Mazar, Benjamin. *Beth She'arim. Report on the Excavations during 1936–1940 I–III*. 2nd ed. Jerusalem: Israel Exploration Authority, 1957 [Hebrew with English summary].
Mazar, Benjamin and Immanuel Dunayevsky. "En-Gedi: Fourth and Fifth Seasons of Excavations. Preliminary Report." *IEJ* 17 (1967): 142–3.
Mazar, Benjamin and Hershel Shanks, eds. *Recent Archaeology in the Land of Israel*. Jerusalem: Israel Exploration Society, 1984.
McCane, Byron. "Let the Dead Bury Their Own Dead: Secondary Burial and Mt. 8:21–22." *HTR* 83 (1990): 31–43.
McCown, Chester C. "Luke's Translation of Semitic into Hellenistic Custom." *JBL* 58 (1939): 213–36.
————. "The Scene of John's Ministry and its Relation to the Purpose and Outcome of his Mission." *JBL* 59 (1940): 113–131.
————. "Gospel Geography: Fiction, Fact, and Truth." *JBL* 60 (1941): 1–25.
————. *The Ladder of Progress in Palestine: A Story of Archaeological Adventure*. New York: Harper & Brothers, 1943.
————. "The Density of Population in Ancient Palestine." *JBL* 66 (1947): 425–436.
McNicoll, Anthony, Robert H. Smith, and Basil Hennessy. *Pella in Jordan I*. Canberra: Meditarch, 1982.
McRay, John. *Archaeology and the New Testament*. Grand Rapids, Michigan: Baker Book House, 1991.
Meadors, Edward. *Jesus the Messianic Herald of Salvation*. WUNT ser. 2, vol. 72. Tübingen: J. C. B. Mohr [Paul Siebeck], 1995.
Meeks, Wayne. *The First Urban Christians: The Social World of the Apostle Paul*. New Haven: Yale University Press, 1983.
Meier, John P. *A Marginal Jew: Rethinking the Historical Jesus I*. New York: Doubleday, 1991.
Meiggs, Russel. *Roman Ostia*. 2nd ed. Oxford: Clarendon, 1973.
Meshorer, Yaakov. "The Hoard of Coins at Migdal." *'Atiqot* 11 (1976): 54–71.
————. "Jewish Symbols on Roman Coins Struck in Eretz Israel." *Israel Museum News* 14 (1978): 60–63.
————. "Sepphoris and Rome." In *Greek Numismatics and Archaeology: Essays in Honor of Margaret Thompson*, edited by Otto Morkholm and Nancy M. Waggoner, pp. 159–71. Wettern, Belgium: Cultura Press, 1979.
————. *Ancient Jewish Coinage*. Dix Hills, New York: Amphora Books, 1982.
————. *City-coins of Eretz-Israel and the Decapolis in the Roman Period*. Jerusalem: The Israel Museum, 1985.
————. "Preliminary Report: The Lead Weight." *BA* 49 (1986): 16–17.
Meyer, Paul. "The Gentile Mission in Q." *JBL* 89 (1970): 405–17.
Meyers, Carol. "Sepphoris and Lower Galilee: Earliest Times through the Persian Period." In *Sepphoris in Galilee*, edited by Rebecca Nagy, pp. 15–19. Winona Lake, Indiana: Eisenbrauns, 1996.

Meyers, Eric. "Galilean Regionalism as a Factor in Historical Reconstruction." *BASOR* 220/221 (1975–76): 93–101.

———. "The Cultural Setting of Galilee: The Case of Regionalism and Early Judaism." *ANRW* 2.19.1, edited by Wolfgang Haase and Hildegard Temporini, pp. 686–702. Berlin: Walter de Gruyter, 1977.

———. "Galilean Regionalism: A Reappraisal." In *Approaches to Ancient Judaism*, vol. 5, edited by William Scott, pp. 115–31. Atlanta: Scholars Press, 1985.

———. "Identifying Religious and Ethnic Groups through Archaeology." In *Biblical Archaeology Today, Proceedings of the Second International Congress on Biblical Archaeology, 1990*, edited by Avraham Biran and Joseph Aviram, pp. 738–45. Jerusalem: Israel Exploration Society, 1990.

———. "The Challenge of Hellenism for Early Judaism and Christianity." *BA* 55 (1992): 84–91

———. "Roman Sepphoris in the Light of New Archaeological Evidence and Research." In *The Galilee in Late Antiquity*, edited by Lee Levine, pp. 321–38. New York: Jewish Theological Seminary, 1992.

———. "An Archaeological Response to a New Testament Scholar." *BASOR* 297 (1995): 17–26.

———. "Jesus und seine galiläische Lebenswelt." *Zeitschrift für Neues Testament* 1 (1998): 27–39.

———. "Sepphoris on the Eve of the Great Revolt (67–68 C.E.): Archaeology and Josephus." In *Galilee Through the Centuries*, edited by Eric Meyers, 109–122. Winona Lake, Indiana: Eisenbrauns, 1999.

———, ed. *Galilee Through the Centuries*. Duke Judaic Studies Series 1. Winona Lake, Indiana: Eisenbrauns, 1999.

Meyers, Eric, Ehud Netzer, and Carol Meyers. "Artistry in Stone: The Mosaics of Ancient Sepphoris." *BA* 50 (1987): 223–31.

———. "A Mansion in the Sepphoris Acropolis and Its Splendid Mosaic." *Qadmoniot* 21 (1988): 87–92 [Hebrew].

———. *Sepphoris*. Winona Lake: Eisenbrauns, 1992.

Meyers, Eric and James F. Strange. *Archaeology, the Rabbis and Early Christianity.* Nashville: Abingdon, 1983.

Meyers, Eric et al. "The Meiron Excavation Project: Archaeological Survey in Galilee and Golan, 1976." *BASOR* 230 (1978): 1–24.

———. *Ancient Synagogue Excavations at Khirbet Shema, Upper Galilee, Israel 1970–1972.* AASOR 42. Durham, North Carolina: ASOR, 1976.

———. *Excavations at Ancient Meiron, Upper Galilee, Israel 1971–72, 1974-75, 1977.* Cambridge, Massachusetts: American Schools of Oriental Research, 1981.

———. "Preliminary Report on the 1980 Excavations at en-Nabratein, Israel." *BASOR* 244 (1981): 1–26.

———. "Second Preliminary Report on the 1980 Excavations at en-Nabratein, Israel." *BASOR* 246 (1982): 35–54.

———. *Excavations at the Ancient Synagogue of Gush Halav. Meiron Excavation Project Volume V.* Winona Lake, Indiana: Eisenbrauns, 1990.

*Midrash Rabbah. Genesis II*, translated by H. Harry Freedman, London: Soncino, 1939.

*Midrash Rabbah. Lamentations*, translated by H. Harry Freedman and Maurice Simon. London: Soncino, 1939.

Millar, Fergus. *The Roman Near East 31 B.C.–A.D. 337.* Cambridge: Cambridge University Press, 1993.

Miller, Stuart S. *Studies in the History and Traditions of Sepphoris.* Leiden: E. J. Brill, 1984.

———. "Intercity Relations in Roman Palestine: The Case of Sepphoris and Tiberias." *AJSR* 12 (1987): 1–24.

———. "Sepphoris, the Well Remembered City." *BA* 55 (1992): 74–83.

———. "The *Minim* of Sepphoris Reconsidered." *HTR* 86 (1993): 377–402.

———. "Further Thoughts on the *Minim* of Sepphoris." In *Proceedings of the Eleventh World Congress of Jewish Studies B.1.* Pp. 1–8. Jerusalem: World Union of Jewish Studies, 1994.

Millet, Merril. "Roman Towns and their Territories: An Archaeological Perspective." In *City and Country in the Ancient World*, edited by John Rich and Andrew Wallace-Hadrill, pp. 169–189. Leichester-Nottingham Studies in Ancient Society 2. New York: Routledge, 1991.

Mitius, Otto. *Jonas auf den Denkmälern des christilichen Altertums.* Archäologische Studien zum Christilichen Altertum und Mittelalter 4. Tübingen: J. C. B. Mohr [Paul Siebeck], 1897.

Moessner, David. *The Lord of the Banquet: The Literary and Theological Significance of the Lukan Travel Narrative.* Minneapolis: Fortress Press, 1989.

Moreland, Milton. "Imagining Epic Imaginations." Paper presented to The Claremont Graduate School's New Testament Seminar. March 23, 1993.

———. "Jerusalem Imagined: Rethinking Earliest Christian Claims to the Hebrew Epic." Ph.D. diss., Claremont Graduate University, Claremont, California, 1999.

Moulton, James H. *A Grammar of the N. T. Greek, Vol. I, Prolegomena.* 3rd ed. Edinburgh: T & T Clark, 1980.

Moyers, James C. and Victor H. Matthews. "The Use and Abuse of Archaeology in Current Bible Handbooks." *BA* 48 (1985): 149–159.

Na'aman, Nadav. "The Brook of Egypt and Assyrian Policy on the Border of Egypt." *Tel Aviv* 6 (1979): 68-90.

———. "Population Changes in Palestine following Assyrian Deportations." *Tel Aviv* 20 (1993): 104–24.

Nagy, Rebecca et al. *Sepphoris in Galilee: Crosscurrents of Culture.* Raleigh, North Carolina: North Carolina Museum of Art, 1996.

Najjar, N. "Kafr Reina." *ESI* 18 (1988): 28 [English], 41 [Hebrew].

Narkiss, Mordecai. "The Snuff-Shovel as a Jewish Symbol." *JPOS* 15 (1935): 14–28

Naroll, Raoul. "Floor Area and Settlement Population." *American Antiquity* 27 (1962): 587–89.

Netzer, Ehud. "Herod's Building Projects: State Necessity of Personal Need." In *Biblical Archaeology Today, 1990, Proceedings of the Second International Congress on Biblical Archaeology*, edited by Avraham Birhan and Joseph Aviram, pp. 48–61. Jerusalem: Israel Exploration Society, 1993.

Neubauer, Adolf. *La Géographie du Talmud.* Reprint of 1868 original. Hidesheim: Georg Olms, 1967.

Neusner, Jacob. *Rabbinic Traditions about the Pharisees Before 70*, 3 vols. Leiden: E. J. Brill, 1971.

Niederwimmer, Kurt. "Johannes Markus und die Frage nach dem Verfasser des zweiten Evangeliums." *ZNW* 58 (1967): 172–88.

North, Robert G. "Discoveries at Capernaum." *Bib* 58 (1977): 425–26.

Nun, Mendel. *Sea of Galilee: Newly Discovered Harbours From New Testament Days.* Rev. ed. Ein Gev: Kinnereth Sailing, 1989.

Oakman, Douglas. *Jesus and the Economic Questions of His Day.* Studies in the Bible and Early Christianity 8. Lewiston, New York: Edwin Mellen, 1986.

Oded, Bustenay. *Mass Deportation in the Neo-Assyrian Empire.* Wiesbaden: Reichert, 1979.

———. "The Inscriptions of Tiglath-pileser III: Review Article." *IEJ* 47 (1997): 104–108.

Oehler, Wilhelm. "Die Ortschaften und Grenzen Galiläas nach Josephus." *ZDPV* 28 (1905): 1–26, 49–74.

Oppenheimer, Aharon. *The 'Am Ha-Aretz: A Study in the Social History of the Jewish People in the Hellenistic-Roman Period.* Leiden: E. J. Brill, 1977.

Oren, Eliezer. "Ethnicity and Regional Archaeology: The Western Negev under Assyrian Rule." In *Biblical Archaeology Today, 1990, Proceedings of the Second International Congress on Biblical Archaeology,* edited by Avraham Birhan and Joseph Aviram, pp. 102–105. Jerusalem: Israel Exploration Society, 1993.

Orfali, Gaudenzio. *Capharnaum et ses ruines d'après les fouilles accomplies à Tell-Houm par la Custodie Franciscaine de Terre Sainte, 1905–1921.* Paris: A. Picard, 1922.

Overman, J. Andrew. "Who Were the First Urban Christians? Urbanization in Galilee in the First Century." In *SBLSP 1988,* edited by David Lull, pp. 160–168. Atlanta: Scholars Press, 1988.

———. *Matthew's Gospel and Formative Judaism: The Social World of the Matthean Community.* Minneapolis: Fortress, 1990.

———. "Recent Advances in the Archaeology of the Galilee in the Roman Period." *CRBS* 1 (1993): 35–57.

Packer, James E. *The Insulae of Imperial Ostia.* Memoirs of the American Academy in Rome 31. Rome: American Academy in Rome, 1971.

Patterson, John. "Settlement, City and Elite in Samnium and Lycia." In *City and Country in the Ancient World,* edited by John Rich and Andrew Wallace-Hadrill, pp.147–168. Leichester-Nottingham Studies in Ancient Society 2. New York: Routledge, 1991.

Peacock, D. P. S. *Pottery in the Roman World: An Ethnoarchaeological Approach.* London: Longman, 1982.

Pearl, Zeev and Mordechai Margaritz. "The Marble Source of the Tel Naharon-Scythopolis Heads." *'Atiqot* 20 (1991): 46–47.

Piper, Ronald. *Wisdom in the Q Tradition: The Aphoristic Teaching of Jesus.* SNTSMS 61. Cambridge: Cambridge University Press, 1989.

———, ed. *The Gospel Behind the Gospels: Current Studies on Q.* Leiden: E. J. Brill, 1995.

———. "The Language of Violence and the Aphoristic Sayings in Q." In *Conflict and Invention: Literary, Rhetorical, and Social Studies on the Sayings Gospel Q,* edited by John Kloppenborg, pp. 53–72. Valley Forge, Pennsylvania: Trinity Press International, 1995.

Polag, Athanasius. *Die Christologie der Logienquelle.* WMANT 45. Neukirchen-Vluyn: Neukirchener, 1977.

Pounds, Norman. "The Urbanization of the Classical World." *Annals of the Association of American Geographers* 59 (1969): 135–157.

Pritz, Ray. *Nazarene Jewish Christianity: From the End of the New Testament Period Until Its Disappearance in the Fourth Century.* Leiden: E. J. Brill, 1988.

Pucci, Giuseppe. "Pottery and Trade in the Roman Empire." In *Trade in the Ancient Economy,* edited by Peter Garnsey, Keith Hopkins, and C. R. Whittaker, pp. 105–17. Berkeley: University of California Press, 1983.

Qedar, Shraga. "Two Lead Weights of Herod Antipas and Agrippa II and the Early History of Tiberias." *Israel Numismatic Journal* 9 (1986–87): 29–35.

Rahmani, L. Y. "Roman Miscellanea." *IEJ* 39 (1989): 66–75.

Ravani, B. and P. P. Kahane. "Rock-cut Tombs at Huqoq." *'Atiqot* 3 [English Series] (1961): 121–147.

Raynor, Joyce and Yaakov Meshorer. *The Coins of Ancient Meiron.* Winona Lake, Indiana: Eisenbrauns, 1988.

Read, David W. "Towards a formal theory of population size and area of habitation." *Current Anthropology* 19 (1978): 312–317.

Reed, Jonathan L. "The Population of Capernaum." *Occasional Papers of the Institute for Antiquity and Christianity 24.* Claremont, California, 1992.

———. "Population Numbers, Urbanization, and Economics: Galilean Archaeology and the Historical Jesus." In *SBLSP 1994,* edited by Eugene Lovering, pp. 203–219. Atlanta: Scholars Press, 1994.

———. "The Social Map of Q." *In Conflict and Invention: Literary, Rhetorical, and Social Studies on the Sayings Gospel Q,* edited by John Kloppenborg, pp. 17–36. Philadelphia: Trinity Press International, 1996.

———. "The Sign of Jonah (Q 11:29–31) and Other Epic References in Q." In *Reimagining Christian Origins: A Colloquium Honoring Burton L. Mack,* edited by Elizabeth Castelli and Hal Taussig, pp. 130–143. Valley Forge, Pennsylvania: Trinity Press International, 1996.

———. "Galileans, 'Israelite Village Communities,' and the Sayings Gospel Q," In *Galilee Through the Centuries,* edited by Eric Meyers, pp. 87–108. Winona Lake, Indiana: Eisenbrauns, 1999.

Reich, Ronny. "The Persian Building at Ayyelet ha-Shahar: The Assyrian Palace of Hazor?" *IEJ* 25 (1975): 233–37.

———. "Archaeological Evidence of the Jewish Population at Hasmonean Gezer." *IEJ* 31 (1981): 48–52.

———. "The Hot Bath-House (*balneum*), the *Miqweh,* and the Jewish Community in the Second Temple Period." *JJS* 39 (1988): 102–107.

———. "Miqvaot (Jewish Ritual Immersion Baths) in Eretz-Israel in the Second Temple Period and the Mishnah and Talmud Periods," Ph.D. dissertation, Hebrew University Jerusalem, 1990 [Hebrew with English summary].

———. "The Great Mikveh Debate." *BAR* 19 (1993): 52–53.

Renfrew, Colin. *The Emergence of Civilization.* London: Methuen, 1972.

———. *Towards an Archaeology of the Mind: An Inaugural Lecture Delivered before the University of Cambridge on 30 November 1982.* Cambridge: Cambridge University Press, 1982.

———. *Approaches to Social Archaeology.* Cambridge: Harvard University Press, 1984.

Rhoads, David and Donald Michie. *Mark as Story.* Philadelphia: Fortress Press, 1982.

Rich, John and Andrew Wallace-Hadrill, eds. *City and Country in the Ancient World.* Leichester-Nottingham Studies in Ancient Society 2. London: Routledge, 1991.

Richardson, Peter. *Herod the Great: King of the Jews and Friend of the Romans.* Columbia: University of South Carolina Press, 1996.

Robertson, Archibald T. *A Grammar of the Greek New Testament in Light of Historical Research.* Nashville: Broadman, 1934.

Robinson, Edward. *Later Biblical Researches in Palestine and in the Adjacent Regions: A Journal of the Travels in the Year 1852, Volume 3.* Boston: Crocker and Brewster, 1857.

———. *Biblical Researches in Palestine and in the Adjacent Regions: A Journal of Travels in the Year 1838, Volume 2.* Boston: Crocker and Brewster, 1868.

Robinson, James M. *A New Quest of the Historical Jesus and Other Essays.* Philadelphia: Fortress, 1983.

————. "The International Q Project Work Session 16 November 1990." *JBL* 110 (1991): 494–498.

————. "The Sayings Gospel Q." In *The Four Gospels, vol. 1 Festschrift Neirynck,* edited by Frans Van Segbroeck et al., pp. 361–388. Leuven: University Press, 1992.

————. "The *Incipit* of the Sayings Gospel Q." *RHPR* 75 (1995): 9–33.

————. "The Son of Man in the Sayings Gospel Q." In *Tradition und Translation. Zum Problem der interkulturellen Übersetzbarkeit religiöser Phänomene. Festschrift für Carsten Colpe zum 65. Geburtstag,* edited by Christoph Elsas, pp. 315–35. Berlin: Walter de Gruyter, 1994.

Robinson, James M. and Helmut Koester. *Trajectories Through Early Christianity.* Philadelphia: Fortress, 1971.

Rohrbaugh, Richard, ed. *The Social Sciences and New Testament Interpretation.* Peabody, Massachusetts: Hendrickson, 1996.

Romm, James. *The Edges of the Earth in Ancient Thought.* Princeton: Princeton University Press, 1992.

Rostovtzeff, Michael. *The Social and Economic History of the Roman Empire I–II.* 2nd rev. ed. by P. M. Fisher. Oxford: Clarendon, 1957.

Russel, James. "The Roman Bathhouse at Capernaum," paper delivered at the annual meeting of the American Schools of Oriental Research in Boston, November 1988.

Russell, Josiah. C. *Late Ancient and Medieval Population.* Transactions of the American Philosophical Society N.S. 48.3. Philadelphia: American Philosophical Society, 1958.

Rykwert, Josian. *The Idea of a Town: The Anthropology of Urban Form in Rome, Italy, and the Roman World.* London: Faber & Faber, 1976.

Safrai, Shemuel and Menahem Stern, eds. *The Jewish People of the First Century: Historical Geography, Political History, Social, Cultural and Religious Life and Institutions,* 2 vols. Compendia Rerum Iudaicarum ad Novum Testamentum. Amsterdam: Van Gorcum, 1976.

Safrai, Zeev. "The Roman Army in the Galilee." In *The Galilee in Late Antiquity,* edited by Lee Levine, pp. 103–114. New York: Jewish Theological Seminary, 1992.

————. *The Economy of Roman Palestine.* London and New York: Routledge, 1994.

Saldarini, Anthony. *Pharisees, Scribes and Sadducees: A Sociological Approach.* Wilmington, Delaware: Michael Glazier, 1988.

————. "The Gospel of Matthew and Jewish-Christian Conflict." In *The Galilee in Late Antiquity,* edited by Lee Levine, pp. 23–38. New York: Jewish Theological Seminary, 1992.

Saller, J. "Hellenistic to Arabic Remains at Nebo, Jordan." *LA* 17 (1967): 41–43.

Saller, Richard. Review of *Roman Corinth: An Alternative Model for the Classical City,* by Donald Engels. In *Classical Philology* 86 (1991): 351–358.

Sanders, E. P. *Judaism: Practice and Belief 63 B.C.E.–66 B.C.E.* Philadelphia: Trinity Press International, 1992.

————. *The Historical Figure of Jesus.* London: Penguin, 1993.

Sato, Mikagu. *Q und Prophetie: Studien zur Gattungs und Traditionsgeschichte der Quelle Q.* WUNT, ser. 2, vol. 29. Tübingen: J. C. B. Mohr [Paul Siebeck], 1988.

Schacht, R. "Estimating Past Population Trends." *Annual Review of Anthropology* 10 (1981): 124–131.

Schenk, Wolfgang. "Die Verwünschung der Küstenorte Q 10,13–15: Zur Funktion der Konkreten Ortsangaben und zur Lokalisierung von Q." In *The Synoptic Gospels: Source Criticism and the New Literary Criticism,* edited by Camille Focant, pp. 477–90. BETL 110. Leuven: Leuven University Press, 1993.

Schiffman, Lawrence. "Was there a Galilean Halakhah?" In *The Galilee in Late Antiquity*, edited by Lee Levine, pp. 143–156. New York: Jewish Theological Seminary, 1992.

Schiffman, Lawrence and Eric Meyers. Review of *Jesus and the Forgotten City*, by R. Batey. *BA* 55 (1992): 105–7.

Schmeller, Thomas. "Jesus im Umland Galilläas." *BZNF* 38 (1994): 44–65.

Schmidt, Darryl. "The LXX Gattung 'Prophetic Correlative.'" *JBL* 96 (1977): 517–22.

Schmidt, Karl Ludwig *Der Rahmen der Geschichte Jesu: Literarkritische Untersuchungen zur ältesten Jesus-Überlieferung.* Berlin: Trowitsch & Sohn, 1919.

Schmitt, Götz. "Das Zeichen des Jonas." *ZNW* 69 (1978): 123–129.

Schneider, A. M. "Hirbet El-Minje am See Genesareth." *Annales archéologiques de Syrie* 2 (1952): 23–45.

Schottroff, Luise and Wolfgang Stegemann. *Jesus and the Hope of the Poor.* Maryknoll, New York: Orbis, 1986.

Schottroff, Willi. "Die Ituräer." *ZDPV* 98 (1982): 125–47.

Schulz, Sigfried. *Q: Die Spruchquelle der Evangelistien.* Zürich: Theologischer Verlag, 1972.

Schumacher, Gottlieb. *The Jaulan: Surveyed for the German Society for the Exploration of the Holy Land.* London: R. Bentley, 1888.

Schürer, Emil. *The History of the Jewish People in the Time of Jesus Christ.* 3 vols. Revised, edited, and translated by Geza Vermes et al. Edinburgh: Clark, 1973–87.

Schürmann, Heinz. "Sprachliche Reminiszenzen an abgeänderte oder ausgelassene Bestandteile der Redequelle im Lukas- und Mattäusevangelium." In *Traditionsgeschichtliche Untersuchungen*, pp. 111–125. Düsseldorf: Patmos, 1968.

————. "Beobachtungen zum Menschensohn-Titel in der Redequelle." In *Jesus und der Menschensohn: Für Anton Vögtle*, edited by Rudolf Pesch et al., pp. 124–147. Freiburg: Herder & Herder, 1975.

Schwank, Benedict. "Das Theater von Sepphoris und die Jugendjahre Jesus." *Erbe und Auftrag* 52 (1976): 199–206.

————. "Die Neuen Ausgrabungen in Sepphoris." *BK* 42 (1987): 75–79.

Schwartz, Seth. "Israel and the Nations Roundabout: 1 Maccabees and the Hasmonean Expansion." *JJS* 41 (1991): 16–38.

Scobie, Alexander. *Aspects of the Ancient Romance and Its Heritage.* Meisenheim: Hahn, 1969.

Segal, Arthur. *Theaters in Roman Palestine and Provincial (ell) Arabia.* Mnemosyne, Bibliotheca Classica Batava Supplementum 120. Leiden: E. J. Brill, 1995.

Shennan, Stephen. *Archaeological Approaches to Cultural Identity.* London: Unwin Hyman, 1989.

Sherwin-White, Adrian N. *Roman Society and Roman Law in the New Testament.* Oxford: Oxford University Press, 1963.

Shiloh, Yigal. "The Population of Iron Age Palestine in the Light of a Sample Analysis of Urban Plans, Areas, and Population Density." *BASOR* 239 (1980): 25–35.

Siegelmann, Azriel. "The Identification of Gaba Hippeon." *PEQ* 116 (1984): 89–93.

Small, David. "Social Correlation to the Greek *Cavea* in the Roman Period." In *Roman Architecture in the Greek World*, edited by Sarah Macready and F. H. Thompson, pp. 85–93. London: Society of Antiquaries of London, 1987.

————, ed. *Methods in the Mediterranean: Historical and Archaeological Views on Texts and Archaeology.* Leiden: E. J. Brill, 1995.

Smith, Jonathan Z. *Map Is Not Territory: Studies in the History of Religions*. Leiden: E. J. Brill, 1978.

———. *Imagining Religion: From Babylon to Jonestown*. Chicago: University of Chicago Press, 1982.

———. "The City as Place." In *Civitas*, edited by P. Hawkins, pp. 25–38. Atlanta: Scholars Press, 1983.

———. *To Take Place: Toward Theory in Ritual*. Chicago: University of Chicago Press, 1987.

———. *Drudgery Divine*. Chicago: University of Chicago Press, 1990.

Smith, Morton. *Jesus the Magician*. New York: Harper & Row, 1978.

Smith Houston, Robert. "The Southern Levant in the Hellenistic Period." *Levant* 22 (1990): 123–130

Sperber, Daniel. "The Centurion as a Tax-Collector." *Latomus* 28 (1969): 186-88.

———. *The City in Roman Palestine*. Oxford: Oxford University Press, 1998.

Spijkerman, Angusto. *Cafarnao III: Catalogo della monete della città*. Studium Biblicum Franciscanum 19. Jerusalem: Franciscan Printing Press, 1975.

Stambaugh, John. *The Ancient Roman City*. Baltimore: The Johns Hopkins University Press, 1988.

Stauffer, Ethelbert. *Jesus: Gestalt und Geschichte*. München, Francke, 1957.

Stea, David and Roger M. Downs, eds. *Image and Environment*. Chicago: Aldine, 1973.

Steck, Odil Hannes. *Israel und das gewaltsame Geschick der Propheten*. Neukirchen-Vluyn: Neukirchner, 1967.

Stemberger, Günther. "Galilee—Land of Salvation?" In *The Gospel and the Land: Early Christian and Jewish Territorial Doctrine*, by W. D. Davies, pp. 409–438. Berkeley: University of California Press, 1974.

Stendahl, Krister. *The School of St. Matthew—and its Use of the Old Testament*. ASNU 20. Lund: Gleerup, 1954.

Stern, Ephraìm. *The Material Culture of the Land of the Bible in the Persian Period 538–332 B.C.* Warminster: Aris and Philips, 1982.

———. "Between Persia and Greece: Trade, Administration and Warfare in the Persian and Hellenistic Periods." In *The Archaeology of Society in the Holy Land*, edited by Thomas Levy, pp. 432–45. London: Leicester University Press, 1995.

Stern, Menahem. "The Reign of Herod." In *The World History of the Jewish People*, ser. 1, vol. 7, edited by Michael Avi-Yonah, pp. 75–132. Jerusalem: Massada, 1975.

———. "Economic Life in Palestine," in *The Jewish People in the First Century*, vol. 2, edited by Shemuel Safrai and Menahem Stern, pp. 631–700. Compendia Rerum Iudaicarum ad Novum Testamentum. Amsterdam: Van Gorcum, 1976.

Stevenson, M. "Sourdoughs and Cheeckakos: The Formation of Identity-Signaling Social Groups." *Journal of Anthropological Archaeology* 8 (1989): 270–312.

Strange, J. F. "The Capernaum and Herodium Publications." *BASOR* 226 (1977): 65–73.

———. "Has the House Where Jesus Stayed in Capernaum Been Found?" *BAR* 8 (1982): 26–39.

———. "Some Implications of Archaeology for New Testament Studies." In *What Has Archaeology to Do with Faith?*, edited by James Charlesworth and Walter Weaver, pp. 23–59. Valley Forge, Pennsylvania: Trinity Press International, 1992.

———. "Six Campaigns at Sepphoris: The University of South Florida Excavations, 1983–1989." In *The Galilee in Late Antiquity*, edited by Lee Levine, 339–355. New York: Jewish Theological Seminary, 1992.

————. "The Eastern Basilica Building." In *Sepphoris in Galilee: Crosscurrents of Culture*, edited by Rebecca Nagy et al., pp. 117–121. Raleigh, North Carolina: North Carolina Museum of Art, 1996.

————. "The Sayings of Jesus and Archaeology." In *Hillel and Jesus: Comparative Studies of Two Major Religious Leaders*, edited by James Charlesworth, pp. 291–305. Minneapolis: Fortress, 1998.

Strange, James F. and Hershel Shanks. "Synagogue Where Jesus Preached Found at Capernaum." *BAR* 9 (1983): 24–31.

Strange, James F. et al. "Excavations at Sepphoris. The Location and Identification of Shikhin, Part II." *IEJ* 45 (1995): 171–187.

Strecker, Georg. *Der Weg der Gerechtigkeit. Untersuchungen zur Theologie des Matthäus* 3rd ed. FRLANT 82. Göttingen: Vanderhoeck & Ruprecht, 1971.

Sukenik, Eleazar L. *Ancient Synagogues in Palestine and Greece*. London: The British Academy, 1934.

Sumner, William. "Estimating Population by Analogy: An Example." In *Ethnoarchaeology: Implications of Ethnography for Archaeology*, edited by Carol Kramer, pp. 164–74. New York: Columbia University Press, 1979.

Swetnam, James. "No Sign of Jonah." *Bib* 66 (1985): 126–30.

————. "Some Signs of Jonah." *Bib* 68 (1987): 74–79.

Syon, Danny. "Gamla: Portrait of a Rebellion." *BAR* 18.1 (Jan./Feb., 1992): 20–37.

Tadmor, Hayim. *The Inscriptions of Tiglath-Pileser III King of Assyria: Critical Edition, with Introductions, Translations, and Commentary*. Fontes ad res Judaicas spectantes. Jerusalem: Israel Academy of Sciences and Humanities, 1994.

Talgam, Rina and Zeev Weiss. "'The Life of Dionysos' in the Mosaic Floor of Sepphoris." *Qadmoniot* 21 (1988): 93–99 [Hebrew].

Taylor, Joan. *Christians and the Holy Places: The Myth of Jewish-Christian Origins*. Oxford: Clarendon Press, 1993.

Tcherikower, Victor. "Palestine under the Ptolemies (A Contribution to the Study of the Zenon Papyri)." *Mizraim* 4–5 (1937): 9–90.

Testa, Emmanuel. *Cafarnao IV: I graffiti della casa di S. Pietro*. Studium Biblicum Franciscanum 19. Jerusalem: Franciscan Printing Press, 1972.

Theissen, Gerd. "Wanderradikalismus. Literatursziologische Aspekte der Überlieferung von Worten Jesu im Urchristentum." *ZTK* 70 (1973): 245–71.

————. "Das 'schwankende Rohr' (Mt 11,7) und die Gründungsmünzen von Tiberias." *ZDPV* 101 (1985): 43–55.

————. *The Gospels in Context: Social and Political History in the Synoptic Tradition*. Minneapolis: Fortress Press, 1991.

————. *Social Reality and the Early Christians*. Minneapolis: Fortress, 1992.

Thomsen, Peter. "Die römischen Meilensteinen der Provinzen Syria, Arabia und Palaestina." *ZDPV* 40 (1917).

Tödt, Heinz E. *Der Menschensohn in der synoptischen Überlieferung*. Gütersloh: Gerd Mohn, 1959.

————. *The Son of Man in the Synoptic Tradition*. London: SCM Press, 1965.

Torrey, Charles C. *The Lives of the Prophets. Greek Text and Translation*. Philadelphia: Society of Biblical Literature, 1946.

Trowbridge, C. C. "On fundamental methods of orientation and imaginary maps." *Science* 38 (1913): 888–897.

Tsafrir, Yoram. "More Evidence for the Cult of Zeus Akraios at Beth-She'an." In *EI* 19, pp. 81* [English summary] 282–283 [Hebrew]. Jerusalem: Israel Exploration Society, 1987.

Tuan, Yi-Fu. "Literature and Geography: Implications for Geographical Research." In *Humanistic Geography*, edited by David Ley and Marwyn S. Samuels, pp. 194–206. Chicago: Maaroufa, 1978.

Tuckett, Christopher M. "A Cynic Q?" *Bib* 10 (1989): 349–376.

————. *Q and the History of Early Christianity: Studies on Q.* Edinburgh: T. & T. Clark, 1996.

Tzaferis, Vasilios, ed. *Excavations at Capernaum*, vol. 1. Winona Lake, Indiana: Eisenbrauns, 1989.

Tzuk, Ttsvika. "The Aqueducts of Sepphoris." In *Sepphoris in Galilee: Crosscurrents of Culture*, edited by Rebecca M. Nagy et al., pp. 45–49. Winona Lake, Indiana: Eisenbrauns, 1996.

Ulansey, David. *The Origins of the Mithraic Mysteries: Cosmology and Salvation in the Ancient World.* Oxford: Oxford University Press, 1989.

Uro, Risto. *Sheep Among the Wolves.* Helsinki: Suomailainen Tiedeakatemaia, 1987.

Vaage, Leif. *Galilean Upstarts: Jesus' First Followers according to Q.* Valley Forge, Pennsylvania: Trinity Press International, 1994.

Vale, Ruth. "Literary Sources in Archaeological Description: The Case of Galilee, Galilees and Galileans." *JSJ* 18 (1987): 209–226.

Vardaman, E. Jerry et al., eds. *The Teachers' Yoke: Studies in Memory of Henry Trantham.* Waco: Baylor University Press, 1964.

Vassiliadis, Petros. "The Nature and Extent of the Q Document." *NovT* 20 (1978): 49–73.

Vermes, Geza. *Jesus the Jew.* New York: Macmillan, 1973.

————. *The Religion of Jesus the Jew.* Minneapolis: Fortress, 1993.

Vitto, F. "Two Marble Heads of Goddesses from Tel Naharon-Scythopolis." *'Atiqot* 20 (1991): 33–45.

Vögtle, Anton. "Der Spruch vom Jonaszeichen." In *Synoptische Studien: Alfred Wikenhauser zum siebzigsten Geburtstag*, pp. 230–277. München: Karl Zink, 1953.

Wachsmann, Shelly. "The Galilee Boat: 2,000-Year-Old Hull Recovered Intact." *BAR* 14.5 (Sept./Oct. 1988): 18–33.

Wachsmann, Shelly et al., "The Excavations of an Ancient boat in the Sea of Galilee." *'Atiqot* [English Series] 19. Jerusalem: Israel Antiquities Authority, 1990.

Waldbaum, Jane C. "Greeks in the East or Greeks and the East? Problems in the Definition and Recognition of Presence." *BASOR* 305 (1997): 1–18.

Wallace-Hadrill, Andrew. *Houses and Society in Pompeii and Herculaneum.* Princeton: Princeton University Press, 1994.

Waterman, Leroy. *Preliminary Report of the University of Michigan Excavations at Sepphoris, Palestine, in 1931.* Ann Arbor, University of Michigan Press, 1937.

Webb, Robert L. *John the Baptizer and Prophet: A Socio-Historical Study. JSNTSupp* 62. Sheffield: Sheffield Academic Press, 1991.

Weber, Max. *The City*, translated and edited by Don Martindale and Gertrud Neuwirth. Glenco, Illinois: Free Press, 1958.

Weiss, Zeev. "Hellenistic and Roman Sepphoris: The Archaeological Evidence." In *Sepphoris in Galilee: Crosscurrents of Culture*, edited by Rebecca Nagy et al., pp. 29–37. Raleigh: North Carolina Museum of Art, 1996.

————. "The Mosaics of the Nile Festival Building." In *Sepphoris in Galilee: Crosscurrents of Culture*, edited by Rebecca Nagy et al., pp. 127–32. Raleigh: North Carolina Museum of Art, 1996.

————. "The Synagogue Mosaic." In *Sepphoris in Galilee: Crosscurrents of Culture*, edited by Rebecca Nagy et al., pp. 133–39. Raleigh: North Carolina Museum of Art, 1996.

Wenger, Uwe. *Der Hauptmann von Kafarnaum.* WUNT ser. 2, vol. 14. Tübingen: J. C. B. Mohr [Paul Siebeck], 1985.

White, L. Michael. *Building God's House in the Roman World: Social Aspects of Architectural Adaptation among Pagans, Jews, and Christians.* Baltimore: American Schools of Oriental Research, 1990.

Will, Ernest. "L'urbanisation de la Jordnie aux époques hellénistique et romaine: conditions géographiques et ethniques." In *Studies in the History and Archaeology of Jordan II,* edited by Adnan Hadidi, pp. 237–41. Amman: Department of Antquities, 1985.

Wilson, Charles. *The Recovery of Jerusalem: A Narrative of Exploration and Discovery in the City and the Holy Land.* London: R. Bentley, 1871.

Wilson, John and Vasilios Tzaferis. "Banias Dig Reveals King's Palace." *BAR* 24.1 (Jan–Feb 1998): 54–61.

Wolff, Samuel. "A Second Temple Period Tomb on the Shu'afat Ridge, North Jerusalem." *'Atiqot* 29 (1996): 23–28.

Wrede, William. *Das Messiasgeheimnis in den Evangelien.* Göttingen: Vandenhock & Ruprecht, 1901.

Wright, Benjamin. "Jewish Ritual Baths—Interpreting the Digs and the Texts: Some Issues in the Social History of Second Temple Judaism." In *The Archaeology of Israel. Constructing the Past, Interpreting the Present,* edited by Neil A. Silberman and David Small, pp. 190–214. JSOTSS 237. Sheffield: Sheffield Academic Press, 1997.

Wuellner, Wilhelm. *The Meaning of "Fisher of Men."* Philadelphia: Westminster, 1967.

Yavor, Z. "Nazareth." *ESI* 18 (1988): 32 [English], 48 [Hebrew].

Yeivin, Zeev. "Bet Shean Project." *Excavations and Surveys in Israel 1987/1988,* vol. 6, pp. 7–45. Jerusalem: The Israel Exploration, 1988.

Zanker, Paul. *The Power of Images in the Age of Augustus.* Ann Arbor: University of Michigan Press, 1990.

Zeller, Dieter. *Die weisheitlichen Mahnsprüche bei den Synoptikern.* FB 17. Würzburg: Echter, 1977.

―――. "Redaktionsprozesse und wechselnder 'Sitz im Leben' beim Q-Material." In *Logia: Les Paroles de Jésus—The Sayings of Jesus: Mémorial Joseph Coppens,* edited by Joel Delobel, 395–409. BETL 59. Leuven: Peeters, 1982.

Zeitlin, Solomon. "Who were the Galileans? New Light on Josephus' Activities in Galilee." *JQR* 64 (1974): 189–203.

Zori, Nehemia. "An Archaeological Survey in the Beth-Shean Valley." In *The Beth-Shean Valley: The Seventeenth Archaeological Convention,* pp. 135–198. Jerusalem: Israel Exploration Society 1962 [Hebrew].

―――. *The Land of Issachar: An Archaeological Survey.* Jerusalem: Israel Exploration Society 1977 [Hebrew].

―――. "A Contribution to the Problem of the Persian Period at Beth-Shean." *PEQ* 109 (1977): 103–105.

Zorn, Jeffrey. "Estimating the Population Size of Ancient Settlements: Methods, Problems, Solutions, and a Case Study." *BASOR* 295 (1994): 31–48.

# Index